PSYCHOANALYSIS
AND
SHAKESPEARE

Books by Norman N. Holland

THE FIRST MODERN COMEDIES

THE SHAKESPEAREAN IMAGINATION

PSYCHOANALYSIS AND SHAKESPEARE

Norman N. Holland

PSYCHOANALYSIS
AND
SHAKESPEARE

McGRAW-HILL BOOK COMPANY

New York   Toronto   London

To Jane

for starting this and much else

TO THE READER

This book tries to speak to three different groups: people interested in psychoanalysis; people interested in Shakespeare; people interested in humanistic thought in general. Because of this multiplicity, it may help you in approaching the book to think of it in two interlocked halves. Roughly one-half of the book consistently develops a consistent argument that you can—and should—read from beginning to end. As a way of establishing a context for the rest of the book, Chapters 1–5 state what the psychoanalytic theory of literature presently is, putting together in one place scattered remarks of Freud, Kris, and others. Then, the summaries at the ends of Chapters 6, 7, 8, and 9 state briefly how this theory has worked out with Shakespeare. Finally, Chapters 10 and 11 draw general conclusions, some about Shakespeare, but others about the way psychoanalysis adds to modern humanistic thought essential information without which we cannot understand our relation to Shakespeare or any other writer.

The other half of the book is somewhat encyclopedic. The larger parts of Chapters 6, 7, 8, and 9 (that is, all but their conclusions) survey, summarize, and evaluate piece by piece everything psychoanalysis has said about Shakespeare and his works, from the beginnings of psychoanalysis up to 1964. Rather than read this *Guide Michelin* continuously, you may prefer to consult it for particular plays, poems, or topics that interest you.

Because it has these multiple and ambitious aims, many people have contributed to this book in many different ways. Indeed, my indebtednesses double themselves, not only because this book walks in two fields, but also because it is one of William James' "twice born." I originally finished the book in the spring of 1960, basing it upon the kind of "reading knowledge" of psychoanalysis Chapter 1 so sharply criticizes. At that time, through the kindness and interest of Dr. Joseph Michaels, I had become a nonmedical student at the Boston Psychoanalytic Institute, and I embarked upon their training program. One result was that I totally rewrote this book, basing it upon a different and more valid knowledge of psychoanalysis. Among the many candidates and faculty members at the Institute who have helped me, I shall mention only one, Dr. Elizabeth Zetzel, to whom I am uniquely thankful.

In the other field, academic and literary, I am greatly indebted to my friends and colleagues who have read all or part of the manuscript at various stages in its double birth: C. L. Barber, Gordon Ross Smith, Simon O. Lesser, Irving Singer, Bruce Mazlish, Leonard F. Manheim, Steven Gilborn, and Max Bluestone. Each of you by your comments has left this book better than my efforts alone could have made it. I hope the result justifies your pains.

Both I and the book have profited, too, from the discussions made possible by the Group for Applied Psychoanalysis and the literature-and-psychology group of the Modern Language Association. M.I.T. and my department have been more than generous in providing typing, a term off for writing, support for summer research, but, perhaps most important, tolerance and trust. Four libraries have graciously helped: the M.I.T. library, the Library of Harvard College and of the Boston and New York Psychoanalytic Institutes. I am particularly indebted to Miss Katherine Murphy and Mrs. Irma Johnson of M.I.T.: Diana herself could have done no more than they in tracking down and spearing the elusive game here displayed.

On the publishing front, I am grateful to my agent and comrade in arms, Mr. Sterling Lord, for his keen efforts *pro bono libri.* Shorter versions of Chapters 5 and 10 appeared in *PMLA* and *The Hudson Review,* respectively, and I am indebted to Mr. John H. Fisher and Mr. Frederick Morgan, respectively, for permission to present those essays again here.

My final gratitudes are both personal and familial: to Dr. G. Henry Katz of Philadelphia who by precept and example opened up for me the possibilities of psychoanalysis; but most of all to the lady of the dedication.

To all of you who have helped in these many ways, let me simply say that I will have done well if I have managed to write a book that even imperfectly matches your own magnanimity.

NORMAN N. HOLLAND

Cambridge, Massachusetts
September, 1965

Contents

Part I

THE PSYCHOANALYTIC VIEW OF LITERATURE

Part II

THE PSYCHOANALYTIC VIEW
OF SHAKESPEARE

Part III

CONCLUSIONS: PSYCHOANALYSIS, SHAKESPEARE, AND THE CRITICAL MIND

10 CONCLUSIONS LOGICAL

11 CONCLUSIONS NOT SO LOGICAL

PSYCHOANALYSIS
AND
SHAKESPEARE

[*Part I*]

THE
PSYCHOANALYTIC
VIEW OF
LITERATURE

[1]

Groundwork

FOR the last sixty years or so a revolution has been going on in our understanding of literature. Quite simply, it has become possible in this century to answer with some certainty the traditional puzzles about literature: What is the nature of inspiration? The creative process? How do we respond to literature? How does form work in our response? Meaning? Identification? How does literature have a moral effect? Why do we like one work better than another? Why does Shakespeare seem to tower over all other writers? By no means have all of these questions been answered, but it has become possible to answer them, some with certainty, others simply with greater precision, but in every case the answers can make a stronger claim on our belief than mere tradition or opinion would, a claim, in fact, approaching that of science.

Freud's inconspicuous discovery of the unconscious mind at the end of the nineteenth century bids fair to be the defining event in the intellectual life of the twentieth. Already, psychoanalysis seems to have touched everyone from the carefree delinquent on the corner to the scholar in his study, even when most unwilling to be touched. Biography, history, literary criticism—whatever baleful light psychoanalytic theory sheds into the desert places of the human mind, it sheds on these and other disciplines as well—and not least, the study of Shakespeare.

In fact, one of the first literary gestures of psychoanalysis was to point out that Hamlet has an oedipus complex, and, in the course of time, his oedipus complex has become as common and irritating a feature of the popular image of Shakespeare as the controversy about authorship. In general, Shakespeare has been the favorite preserve of psychoanalytic literary criticism, yet, so far, Shakespeareans and psychoanalytic critics have had little to say to one another—and that often unfriendly. Both parties seem to agree, although for different reasons, with that friend of Buck Mulligan's who pronounced Shakespeare "the happy hunting ground of all minds that have lost their balance."

Nothing seems to provoke so angry a response from lovers of literature as the application of psychoanalysis to the world of letters. As one cannibal said to the other, "Did you ever eat a psychoanalyst?" "Eat one!" replied the other. "Did you ever try to *clean* one!" And, indeed, some of the more lurid insights of psychoanalysis must seem an index and obscure prologue to the history of lust and foul thoughts. Nevertheless, this book is written in hopes that where conflict was, there shall insight be—and perhaps even acceptance.

If such an acceptance is to happen, the literary man will have to meet the psychoanalytic one halfway, for nobody can "prove" the scientific validity of psychoanalysis (and therefore its relevance to literature) to an unwilling audience. As Freud wrote one of his first followers:

First they [the opponents of psychoanalysis] write as though we had never published a dream analysis, a case history or the interpretation of parapraxes; then if the evidence is forcibly brought to their notice, they say: "Yes, but that's no proof, that's arbitrary." Just try to produce a proof to someone who is set against it! There is nothing to be done with logic. . . .[1]

Nor will experiments do much more, Freud wrote an anthologist in 1930:

I would like to comply with your wish and make a contribution to your collection of solutions to scientific problems. But in trying to find some suitable examples I have encountered strange and almost insuperable obstacles as though certain procedures that can be expected from other fields of investigation could not be applied to my subject matter. Perhaps the reason for this is that within the methods of our work there is no place for the kind of experiment made by physicists and physiologists.[2]

One must take a different tack in understanding psychoanalysis. At best, argument or experiment might convince someone of the validity of psychoanalysis as an abstract theory or philosophical system, but that is not the important thing.

"The teachings of psychoanalysis," Freud wrote, "are based upon an incalculable number of observations and experiences and no one who has not repeated these observations upon himself or upon others is in a position to arrive at an independent judgment of it,"[3] and that *caveat,* it seems to me, should apply not only to rejection, but also acceptance. It does, however, make psychoanalysis sound like a cult to be believed or disbelieved, not by verification, but by indoctrination or initiation—and yet not so. Psychoanalysis is that science which tries to speak objectively about subjective states, specifically, subjective states resisted but arrived at in the psychoanalytic interview. "The only subject matter of psychoanalysis is the mental processes of human beings and it is only in human beings that it can be studied," [4] wrote Freud.

As with any science, one can only judge its theoretical constructs if one has some knowledge of the data those constructs and generalizations are designed to explain, in this instance, subjective states, particularly those we are most resistant to. To find the real validity of psychoanalysis, one must listen beneath the theoretical grace notes, recognizing that psychoanalysis is the systematizing of a very special kind of data obtained in a very special way. The unique, nonrepeatable, two-person intimacy of patient and analyst makes up both the data and the observational procedure of classical analysis. The patient brings to this "dyadic" relationship his free associations. The analyst provides, as they seem appropriate, his interpretations on the basis of prior experience generalized as theory. When his interpretations are sound, they will modify the free associations coming from the patient and they will either confirm or call for modification of theory. Thus, there is a feedback relationship between patient and analyst. In so far as the patient changes, one speaks of therapy. Conversely, in so far as interpretation does or does not confirm the analyst's experience, one speaks of theory, and that part of the patient's experience which becomes part of the analyst's thereby takes its place in sixty years of such data derived from hundreds of analysts and thousands of patients. In addition, of course, to this basic source of data, psychoanalytic theory has drawn from myth, folklore, anthropology, literature, and even experimental psychology.

From all this data Freud and the analysts after him have erected (not without a number of false starts and changes in direction) a hierarchy of propositions within the theory. We can distinguish five levels: the data of observation; individual interpretations to patients; clinical generalizations (for example, phenomena that recur with a certain age group, impact of a certain experience, and so on); clinical theory (dealing with such concepts as regression, return of the repressed, defense, and the like); and, finally, metapsychological generalizations, such as psychic energy, Eros, or the death instinct. These last, Freud noted, were "not the bottom but the top of the whole structure, and they can be replaced and discarded without damaging it." [5]

Most unfortunately, when psychoanalysis gets bandied about in intellectual circles, this sensible, scientific procedure is turned topsy-turvy to produce a *Vulgärfreudismus*. Instead of data generating theory, theory generates data. The intellectual Freudian typically begins with a "reading knowledge" of Freud (neglecting other

analysts, despite the great importance of ego psychology, largely
developed after Freud's death). He parades the most speculative and
tentative of Freud's abstractions from data (sometimes even after
they have been abandoned as valid constructs). Then, he treats them
as moral philosophy, aesthetics, theory of culture, philosophy of history, or what have you. The "death instinct," for example, seems to
have a magnetic attraction for this kind of treatment. It is usually
used as developed in *Beyond the Pleasure Principle* (1920) without
the important modifications Freud felt it necessary to make in 1932
(*New Introductory Lectures*, XXXII).[6] By 1932 Freud "places" the
death instinct as a construct to bring together certain clinical patterns,
particularly "moral masochism" and "the negative therapeutic reaction." Many analysts do not accept the construct of a death instinct at
all. Those who do, recognize it is a construct very far removed from
clinical data, perhaps directly manifest only in the need for rest. "The
instincts are mythical beings," wrote Freud, "superb in their indefiniteness," [7] but somehow in *Vulgärfreudismus* a "silent" instinct can
explain, say, the rise of capitalism.

Such pseudo-philosophical legerdemain, not unlike using Einstein
to prove moral relativity, greatly adds to the confusion about an already difficult subject. It serves as the latest way of avoiding the painful truths of psychoanalytic data by transforming them into innocu-
ous philosophy which can be accepted or rejected simply as an act of
taste. Thus, one has the peculiar spectacle of a most distinguished
literary critic using Freud to analyze Shakespeare's tragedies, Jung
for the romances, and Adler for the histories. It is as though he were
choosing psychologies like pickles in a barrel, according to whether
they are sweet or sour.

Acceptance without a sense of the data of psychoanalysis is no
acceptance at all. What is needed is an understanding in the pulse. As
one of Ernest Jones's patients, in a moment of sudden insight, ex-
claimed, "I knew that Freud's theories were true, but I did not know
they were *so* true!" Freud is quite correct to insist that either acceptance or rejection must be based on an experience of the data of
psychoanalysis—one must either analyze or be analyzed. Unfortunately, not many of us are in a position to do either. The next best
thing is to read, not Freud's theoretical papers, but the voluminous
literature of case histories, both by Freud and by others. A few hours
spent with the tragedies and satyr plays that make up psychoanalytic
practice will do more than anything else except personal experience
to give a feeling for psychoanalytic concepts in action and thus to
avoid the empty use of psychoanalysis as a theory cut off from data.
Such a feeling is particularly necessary for using psychoanalysis to
look at literature.

The psychoanalytic view of anything, I suppose, begins with Freud, but rarely ends there. For Freud, "Some rationalistic, or perhaps analytic, turn of mind in me," he wrote, "rebels against being moved by a thing without knowing why I am thus affected and what it is that affects me." [8] It is not surprising, then, that he was led down the corridors of literary criticism. It is important to remember, however, that his critical excursions into literature and the arts were sidelines to his psychoanalytic explorations, that he used the analysis of literature mostly to strengthen the clinical data he had already gotten for his psychoanalytic hypotheses. For that reason he did not work up a theory of literature as such, and his literary insights remain scattered among his nonliterary writings. People, as a result, have often misunderstood or underrated his contributions, even though many of them coincide with ideas of long and distinguished lineage in literary theory. (For example, Freud's psychological insights do not overthrow the traditional view of catharsis but rather deepen and enrich it by giving it a scientific underpinning.)

Freud's literary remarks are scattered, and therefore finding in them a coherent theory of literature calls for assembling a series of scattered quotations. The late Ernst Kris, himself the most brilliant of psychoanalytic literary theorists after Freud, has criticized this "quotation method" as creating a "static system," as not showing "the gradual unfolding of Freud's ideas." [9] Were we concerned primarily with the growth of psychoanalytic theory, Kris's objection would bite. It would indeed be foolish to discuss any aspect of psychoanalytic theory on the basis of scattered quotations taken without regard for date and such major changes in theory as Freud's shift in 1926 from a "toxicological" to a signal theory of anxiety, the development after 1920 of the structural constructs of superego, ego, and id, or the five stages in the theory of instincts. But we are concerned, not with psychoanalytic theory, but with literature. Looked at from that limited point of view, Freud's ideas about literature simply do not change very much because they are like his ideas about dreams, so close to the raw data of psychoanalysis. The general theory of psychoanalysis changes and unfolds around a relatively unchanging approach to literature (as we shall see). While different periods in the development of psychoanalysis create different lights and stresses within that established approach, Freud's basic idea of art remains the same.

For Freud, art is "an activity intended to allay ungratified wishes —in the first place in the creative artist himself and subsequently in his audience or spectators." [10] Freud thus stands with those who (like, say, John Dewey) see the audience's experience of art as the re-creation of the artist's activity. Essentially, what Freud adds is, first, that art for both artist and audience gratifies wishes, and, second, that the wishes gratified are those (both unconscious and preconscious) discovered by psychoanalysis.

Broadly speaking, we can distinguish three attitudes toward the work of literature as such. To the classical or neoclassical critic, both writer and reader were to refer the text to nature: "Art imitates nature" or art is a "just representation of general nature" (Johnson). The Romantics and pre-Romantics, influenced by Cartesian skepticism and the psychologies that arose from the British empirical philosophies, tended to translate the objective truth of classical "nature" into a fluctuating, subjective "experience": "imagination" and "originality" became the plus words. In its extreme form, say, in a writer like Poe, this Romantic conception renders art mere self-expression, and "the good critic is he who narrates the adventures of his soul among masterpieces" (Anatole France). The modern or formalist or "New" critic emerges as a reaction against this impressionism, but he is still within the Romantic tradition. The text in literature becomes an end in itself, removed from "nature" and author alike.

Freud, in effect, draws on all three of these traditions in the three key essays in which he deals with the three separate stages in the artistic process and in which his "theory of literature" most clearly emerges. Freud is primarily a Romantic in his description of poetic creation as a sophisticated kind of daydreaming in "Creative Writers and Day-Dreaming" (1908). He seems almost a "New Critic" when he considers the work of art in isolation ("The Moses of Michelangelo" [1914]). Finally, he becomes Aristotelian when he describes the cathartic effect of literature in "Psychopathic Characters on the Stage," not published until 1942, but written in 1905 or 1906. All three of these essays he wrote before the major changes in psychoanalytic theory of the twenties and thirties, which would have produced shifts in emphasis and terminology but would not alter this basic literary frame of reference. Within it, Freud's remarks, scattered through all his work, elaborate a detailed and comprehensive view of the artistic process.

His approach falls quite naturally into three parts as it applies, first, to the artist, second, to the work of art itself, third, to the audience. It is in these three segments that we will consider Freud's "theory of literature" in order to place the psychoanalytic study of Shakespeare in its proper context. More generally (or at least more ambitiously), in order to see in the conclusions to this book the directions it can and should take, we need first to see what the psychoanalytic theory and practice of literary criticism presently is.

[2]

Freud on the Artist

WHEN he speaks of the artist, Freud is very much in the Romantic tradition, seeing art as self-expression. The artist, in effect, fantasies. As Freud says, "Mental work is linked to some current impression, some provoking occasion in the present which has been able to arouse one of the subject's major wishes. From there it harks back to a memory of an earlier experience (usually an infantile one) in which this wish was fulfilled; and it now creates a situation relating to the future which represents a fulfillment of the wish." [1] This, however, is only ordinary mental work or fantasying. If we add in the special attributes of the writer, the fact that *poeta nascitur non fit,* or his use of artistic techniques, we can state Freud's notion of artistic creation as a kind of equation: the finished work of art is a function of four "variables": (1) the artist's natural endowment *qua* artist; (2) as an individual, his innate drives and infantile wishes, which live yet in his unconscious, both those particular to him and those he shares with all men; (3) the writer's immediate experiences and impressions; (4) his artistic techniques for reworking his personal experience.[2]

Freud had a good deal to say about the first of these four "variables," the artistic constitution—although much of what he said consisted of saying he had nothing to say. Nevertheless, although psychoanalysis offers no final recipe for producing artistic talent eugenically, it does suggest some of the ingredients. First, Freud found in the childhood of the artist especially strong instinctual needs of the same amiably polymorphous or perverse type as in any ordinary person's childhood.[3] The unique factor for the artist would seem to be the sheer quantity of libido or energy; most artists, in other words, are lively, energetic people. Balanced against this larger-than-usual amount of drive are the normal processes of growing up: these impulses are either frustrated by reality,[4] or redirected through the artist's "extraordinary capacity for sublimating the primitive instincts" [5] or suppressed and reversed by reaction formation [6] or overcompensation. Of these three endowments, the artist or writer seems

9

to have a special ability to sublimate. According to Freud, he seems also to have "a certain degree of laxity in the repressions which are decisive for a conflict," that is, the neurotic conflict which the artistic sublimation has in whole or in part relieved.[7] It is this "laxity of repression" which gives the writer or artist the sensitivity to perceive the hidden impulses in the minds of others and the courage to let his own unconscious speak.[8]

As Lionel Trilling has pointed out in "Art and Neurosis," these remarks about the artist's special ability to sublimate and his flexibility of repression are the most striking of Freud's insights into art. They make art a thoroughly normal—even normal*izing*—activity. Repeatedly Freud said that art was an alternative to neurosis rather than an outgrowth of it. The "sickness" or "health" of a work of art stands collateral to, does not depend on, the sickness or health of the artist. Freud devoted an entire essay, "Creative Writers and Day-Dreaming," to the thesis that the prototype of literature is normal, ordinary child's play. In most people, the impulse to play grows up into the practice of daydreaming; the writer simply makes a career of it, and we bless him for doing so. Art and literature are parts in the whole continuum of activities which psychoanalysis identifies as wish fulfilling: dreams and daydreams; parapraxes, such as slips of the tongue or lapses of memory; various neurotic symptom formations; and sublimations such as occupations or hobbies. Thus, "Dreams *invented by writers* will often yield to analysis in the same way as *genuine* ones."[9]

In short, art and literature are perfectly normal—or at least as normal as anything else:

We no longer think that health and illness, normal and neurotic people, are to be sharply distinguished from each other. . . . Today we know that neurotic symptoms are structures which are substitutes for certain achievements of repression that we have to carry out in the course of our development from a child to a civilized human being. We know, too, that we all produce such substitutive structures, and that it is only their number, intensity, and distribution which justify us in using the practical concept of illness. . . .[10]

Freud found in general that the highest productions of culture assume forms similar to those of the various neuroses: imaginative art resembles hysteric fantasies; religious ceremonials and prohibitions look like the symptoms of obsessional neurotics; and "the delusions of paranoics have an unpalatable external similarity and internal kinship to the systems of our philosophers."[11] All human activities, in other words, stem from the mind, and the mind is a continuum; there is no sharp division between "higher" and "lower" activities or sick and healthy. "Why may not imagination trace the noble dust of Alexander, till he find it stopping a bunghole?"

One important conclusion from this view is that folk art, myths, *märchen,* or such ritual forms as early tragedy stem from the same root as personal artistic creations—the wishes are simply those of a whole people instead of an individual writer.[12] Not only is the artist no sicker than the "normal" person; he is perhaps less so; and also he is restored to his primal role as the mythmaker.

Happy as these consequences may be, they do not tell us about the artistic constitution. Freud mentions three factors: an unusual amount of drive; an extraordinary capacity for sublimation; and a special laxity of repression. These, however, only push the question back a step. That is, where did *they* come from? Freud repeatedly said he didn't know, and psychoanalysis did not provide an answer. For example, in 1910, after defining Leonardo's special tendency to repression and sublimation, he concluded:

Instincts and their transformations are at the limit of what is discernible by psychoanalysis. From that point it gives place to biological research. We are obliged to look for the source of the tendency to repression and the capacity for sublimation in the organic foundations of character on which the mental structure is only afterwards erected.[13]

But, in 1930, Freud wrote: "An artist's joy in creating, in giving his phantasies body, or a scientist's in solving problems or discovering truths, has a special quality which we shall certainly one day be able to characterize in metapsychological terms." [14] Whether or not he meant by this remark that he would be able to discover the source of the artist's special gifts is a good question.

As for the next two "variables" in the statement of the process of artistic creation, the infantile wishes and the adult experiences (which the artist's skills mold together into art), since these two factors must necessarily vary from one work of art to another, from one artist to another, Freud has little to say about them in general terms. We must get down to cases, or, at any rate, one case. The writer Freud analyzed with most care *qua* writer is Dostoevsky.[15]

Writing in 1927, Freud concluded that Dostoevsky had been born with an unusual intensity of emotional life, a predisposition to bisexuality, and an "unanalysable" artistic endowment. In infancy, Freud deduced, the novelist had had the oedipal impulses common to all men, to get rid of the father and possess the mother, but in Dostoevsky's case, he said, the matter was complicated by a tendency to bisexuality. Dostoevsky did not resolve his oedipus complex in the ordinary way; that is, he did not simply repress the wish to take his father's place because he feared his father's retaliation. Rather, because of his bisexual disposition, Dostoevsky must have partly wanted to put off the retaliation by identifying with the mother and becoming the passive object of his father's physical love. But to do so, the boy would have had to become a woman, be castrated, and so the fear of castration ruled that solution out, too. Then *two* factors were repressed: the oedipal wish to get rid of the father and have the mother; second, the wish to be a woman to the father. The end result of such a development is that the ego, the developing rational self, became passive with respect to the incorporated influence of his father, the conscience or superego; in other words, Dostoevsky would have a great need for punishment, a great need to suffer the pangs of guilt. Events in Dostoevsky's youth must have reinforced the infantile situation Freud infers from Dostoevsky's adult behavior. In particular, the violent temper of the senior Dostoevsky would have increased the boy's fears and his tendency to adopt a feminine, masochistic position with respect to his father. Thus, Freud is seeing Dostoevsky in terms of the defensive and structural considerations that assumed importance after 1926 (not simply in terms of unconscious impulses expressed).

Freud is quite willing to concede that his description is "unsavoury and incredible," but insists that general psychoanalytic experience "has put these relations . . . beyond the reach of doubt." Freud's evidence in the particular case of Dostoevsky comes from his biography, the patterns of his adult behavior, in particular, the novelist's defenses against the forbidden behavior. It is clear enough that Dostoevsky had an exaggerated sense of guilt. He was also given to exaggerated acts of kindness (attempts to act out a denial, Freud says, of aggressive impulses). The latent homosexuality turns up in the importance of male friendships to the writer and in his strangely forgiving attitude toward rivals in love (particularly his first wife's lover). Similarly, Freud argues, Dostoevsky's epilepsy should be understood as an identification with the dead father. In his early youth Dostoevsky suffered from a great fear of death and deathlike seizures. These, Freud says, constituted an identification with the father he wished dead; that is, "you wanted to kill your father and become him—now you are your dead father, and your father is killing *you!*" The deathlike seizures satisfied both repressed wishes, the wish to be the father, and the wish to be the passive object of his love. These seizures eventually became epilepsy, a development undoubtedly heightened by the fact that Dostoevsky's father was murdered when the writer was eighteen. Freud sees Dostoevsky's later political conservatism as another strategy to abase himself before the father, now the father in his role as ruler, the Czar. Similarly, Dostoevsky's wish to play the part of Christ means, unconsciously, a wish to be the father's victim and also to be the father. His compulsive gambling is onanistic: both an acting out of the impulse to "play" and a defense against it, busying the hands, the defense backed up by the terrible fear of the father.

In *The Brothers Karamazov,* under the religious, political, and intellectual concerns of the adult novelist, Freud finds the child-old problem, the central *motif* in Dostoevsky's emotional life which Freud inferred from the biographical data: a wish to kill the father and suffer for it. In the novel, the wish is projected away from the hero Dmitri onto another "son," Smerdyakov, although the real criminal reveals himself through the murderer's epilepsy: it is as though Dostoevsky "were seeking to confess that the epileptic, the neurotic, in himself was a parricide." Because the murder itself is projected onto another, the accompanying *motif* of sexual rivalry can be openly expressed (as in *Hamlet*). Details of the son's childhood crises with his father turn up elsewhere in the novel, for example, in the defense attorney's description of psychology as a double weapon—we would say "a knife that cuts both ways"; the Russian idiom is "a cudgel with two ends." The image is, as it were, bisexual and the intellectual content, Freud points out, is: it is not the actual guilt that counts but the feeling of guilt—exactly Dostoevsky's problem. Similarly, in the scene in which Father Zossima kneels to Dmitri, he, in effect, identifies Dmitri as the Redeemer, the man who takes on himself the guilt of others (particularly Dostoevsky).

Freud gave no more clues to what psychic matters the novel expressed than these, but his method of analysis is clear enough. From the adult experience and behavior of the writer he extrapolates to his infantile and hereditary situations, using whatever evidence he can get, trying to fit it all together into a coherent picture of effect and cause. The artist himself, or his biography, at least, appears as the first three variables in Freud's explanation of artistic creation: artistic constitution, infantile wishes, and the artist's experience. To get from these first three, biographical, variables to the work of art itself, Freud takes into account the fourth variable: artistic transformation or disguise.

Aristotle saw this fourth variable as central to the nature of art: How is it that artistic productions "do not spare the spectators (for instance, in tragedy) the most painful experiences and can yet be felt by them as highly enjoyable?" [16] Freud's first three variables do not sharply distinguish art from dream; what does? Artistic works, Freud concluded, differ "from the asocial, narcissistic products of dreaming in that they [are] calculated to arouse sympathetic interest in other people and [are] able to evoke and to satisfy the same unconscious wishful impulses in them, too. Besides this, they [make] use of the perceptual pleasure of formal beauty as what I have called an 'incentive bonus.' " [17] Freud describes this transformation of the daydream variously, sometimes as comprising two changes, sometimes, in his fuller remarks, as comprising three. First, the artist disguises and elaborates his fantasy, a special part of this disguise being the removal of its egotistic quality. Second, the artist molds his material so that it expresses the ideas of his fantasy and involves his audience in them. Third, he makes the work of art conform to the aesthetic "laws" of formal beauty.

Of these three transformations of daydream to art, Freud had much to say about the first and relatively little to say about the other two. Freud's interest centered on the artist's method of disguising the wish because that, he said, took place by the prelogical laws of unconscious thought, primary-process thinking. In other words, the artist's disguising of his wish fulfillment poses a psychological problem analogous to defensive mechanisms in general. The other two factors in transforming dream to art, the artist's involving his audience or obeying the canons of his art, these, Freud seems to have felt, do not truly fall within the province of psychology.

Freud gave two very full and elaborate descriptions of these prelogical, primary processes of disguise or defense, in Chapter 6 of *The Interpretation of Dreams* and with more immediate relevance to artistic problems, in *Jokes and Their Relation to the Unconscious*. It is, of course, from the study of defenses that psychoanalysis took its new direction after Freud changed his theory of anxiety and developed the structural hypothesis of id, ego, and superego in the early twenties. Nevertheless, in discussing works of art, he tended to use, not the elaborated defenses of Anna Freud's *The Ego and the Mechanisms of Defense* (1936), but rather his original formulation in *The Interpretation of Dreams* (1900) in terms of two kinds of *disguise:* condensation and displacement. By displacement, we transfer intense feelings from their real objects onto less revealing substitutes. In condensation, we form fresh unities out of elements our conscious and logical minds would keep separate. Together, these two mechanisms result in dreams being "overdetermined." That is, a single element in the dream as we remember it (the manifest dream) will express several elements in the latent thoughts giving rise to the dream. Conversely, a single latent thought will find expression in several elements of the manifest dream.

Thus, condensation plays a key role in the *language* of literature: most of Freud's examples of the process occur in *Jokes and Their*

Relation to the Unconscious—descriptions of particular lines in Shakespeare or Heine or Goethe. He does mention, too, in his analysis of Jensen's *Gradiva* the condensation involved in some of the hero's speeches which have double meanings.[18] Condensation, to the extent it is confined to language, corresponds roughly with what a literary critic would call "ambiguity," or, if the condensation is sharp and sudden, "wit." Condensation, however, is not limited to the language of literature. As in dreams, plot elements and characters usually express more than one element in the pattern of wishes and defenses giving rise to the finished work. For example, Old Karamazov is not only "the father," but also a sexual rival; still further, he is the living embodiment of a harsh, irrational source of guilt (the superego or, more properly, the author's feelings toward it), the guilt itself being represented in the novel as a money debt.

Condensation is basically a contracting, particularly suited to focusing intense feelings on a single image, person, phrase, or event. Displacement operates in the direction of expansion, and hence is perhaps easier to see in the development from impulse to work of art. In his analyses of particular works, Freud tends to speak almost entirely in terms of one or another kind of displacement, that is, *the transfer of attributes and emotions associated with one thing onto another.* He seems to distinguish (in his analyses of works of art) four major kinds of displacement, depending on the qualities stressed in the object *to* which the transfer is made.

If the important thing about the object displaced onto is that it is *outside* of, *separate from,* the object displaced from, Freud speaks of *projection.* Typically, an internal impulse becomes a perception of the external world. For example, in *Oedipus Rex,* the hero's (axiomatic) wish to kill his father and marry his mother becomes the prediction of an oracle. In *Hamlet,* the villain acts out the hero's oedipal wish. In *The Brothers Karamazov,* the villain, not the hero, carries out part of the hero's oedipal wish, namely, to kill his father.[19]

If the important attribute of the thing displaced onto is that it is the *opposite* of the thing displaced from, Freud speaks of *reversal* or *representation through the opposite.* For example, Freud describes the role of the chorus in Greek tragedy as a reversal. Originally, he argues (on the basis of Andrew Lang's and E. B. Tylor's now-obsolete comparative mythology), tragedy was the ritual re-enacting of a primal crime in which the horde of brothers slew the father. By reversal, "one might even say, as the product of a refined hypocrisy," the slain father becomes the suffering (and rebelling) hero; the horde of brothers becomes the chorus who advise against the crime.[20]

If the essential factor in the displacement is the breaking up of one thing into several, Freud speaks of *decomposition* or *splitting*. He mentions it in one of his earliest literary analyses, that of a story by C. F. Meyer in which the good and bad aspects of both mother and father are split off, displaced onto four figures, two for each parent.[21] The same thing takes place in E. T. A. Hoffmann's tale, "The Sand-Man": the father is split into a bad father who threatens to blind the hero and a good father who intercedes for him.[22] Again, in the early Greek tragedies: at first there was only the hero and the chorus. "Later, a second and third actor were added, to play as counterpart to the hero and as characters split off from him." [23] There are so many examples of splitting, I suppose, because nothing will quite so quickly elaborate a simple wish into an elaborate work of fiction as the doubling or splitting of characters.

The only form of artistic disguise (or defense) of which there are more examples analyzed in Freud's works is *symbolization,* which, for the purpose of this somewhat oversimple classification, we can consider a displacement from one thing to another based on a *physical or psychic similarity* between the two. Phallic symbols are fairly notorious, for example, Autolycus'

> Pins and poking-sticks of steel;
> What maids lack from head to heel,

but there really are other kinds, too; the examples Freud gives in his works are legion. In Jensen's *Gradiva,* for example, an archaeological past symbolizes one's own infancy.[24] Leonardo depicts his mother's supposedly ambivalent feelings toward him as an enigmatic smile.[25] In *Oedipus Rex* and in various spooky tales, blinding, particularly tearing out the eyeballs, symbolizes castration.[26]

Freud's neat little explication of the story of the Medusa's head will serve to suggest the ways symbols come together to serve multiple functions, that is, are "overdetermined." [27] The legend tells of a woman with snakes for hair, the sight of her face being so horrible that any man who looks upon her turns to stone; even when the head is cut off, it has this terrible power, as when it is worn on a shield. Obviously enough, the legend concerns sight, particularly horrifying sight, and things being cut off. Freud links the story to the child's horror, as he "sees" the facts which put an end to his earliest state of sexual naïveté. That is, at first the child (boy or girl) believes that all adults are physically masculine. At some point in development he will see an adult woman's genitals (usually his mother's), and the sight will terrify him. He interprets her lack of masculinity as a threat that his own could be taken away. Some people are castrated—I could be, too. The legend, Freud says, serves the wish to avoid this sight—or to master it. The taboo against looking suggests that the Medusa is taboo, thus a symbol for the mother.

The frightening event is handled by "displacement upward" (transferring emotionally charged events below the waist to relatively safer territory above the waist). The face serves, he says, as a symbol for the genitals, and the terror is displaced onto the snaky hair, which in turn symbolizes the body hair around the genitals, thought of as biting or stinging. On another level the snakes are a wish-fulfilling reversal. That is, they are phallic symbols, and the fact that there are so many of them says, in effect, "Not only is the woman (or mother) not without a phallus; she has lots of them." The Medusa's victims become as stiff as a stone. On one level this symbolic erection says in a mythic way, "See? I still have a phallus despite the terrifying fact that some people don't." On another level, becoming a stone symbolizes castration—"I become dead; I become the now-dead part of me which has been taken away."

Lurid as Freud's descriptions of unconscious contents are, once one begins to look, one can find similar contents in work of art after work of art. One finds, too, the same processes of defense or disguise—condensation, displacement, symbolization—all rendering the lurid wish palatable, eliminating its personal and egotistic quality.

As for the other two ways, besides disguise, for transforming daydream into art, Freud had little to say about them. The second, the artist's molding his material into an objective reality in which the audience becomes involved, also serves to remove some of the egotistic quality of the daydream by simply objectifying it—although at the same time sharply distinguishing it from "real" reality.[28] Yet he, the artist, and we, the audience, give to this fake all the emotional impact of actuality. The reason apparently is, Freud implies, that both he and we regress in art to that stage of magic or infantile thinking (the "omnipotence of thoughts") in which wishes, conscious or unconscious, control reality—we wish things into being; we wish the work of art, like the sleeping beauty, into life.[29] Furthermore, within this merely psychic reality, "the storyteller has a *peculiarly* directive power over us; by means of the moods he can put us into he is able to guide the current of our emotions, to dam it up in one direction and make it flow in another, and he often obtains a great variety of effects from the same material. All this is nothing new, and has doubtless long since been fully taken into account by students of aesthetics." [30]

This dry and wily reference to scholars takes us to the third factor in transforming daydream to art. With a truly Germanic faith in *wissenschaft,* Freud calls it "obeying the laws of beauty." [31] The writer "bribes us by the offer of a purely formal, that is, aesthetic pleasure in the presentation of his phantasies." This formal pleasure Freud terms an "incentive-bonus" or "fore-pleasure"; [32] he is using a theory of G. Th. Fechner's. Earlier, he had applied it to the formal appeal of wit which triggers the deeper unconscious release, and he had applied it, too, to sexual activity.[33] Yet he did not try to analyze the operation of any of these so hopefully regarded "laws."

Freud was always careful to spell out what he considered within psychoanalysis' province and what was not, sometimes running to extremes as in his blanket *caveat* at the beginning of the essay on Dostoevsky: "Unfortunately, before the problem of the creative artist, analysis must lay down its arms"—the rest of his thoughts on art hardly bear that one out. As we have seen, however, he more or less exempted two factors in artistic creation from psychoanalytic investigation: the artistic gift and artistic technique. What psychoanalysis could tell us, he said, was the way the author's personality determined the characteristics of a work of art, the factors that awakened his creative genius, the subject matter it was destined to choose.[34] In addition, psychoanalysis suggested the function of the various genres in the psychic economy of artist and audience (lyric poetry giving vent to intense feelings exhibitionistically; epic enabling us to feel the triumph of a great hero; tragedy letting us play the triumphing rebel and then—masochistically—triumph in defeat as well).[35]

Essentially, literature allows the ungifted reader to re-experience, re-enjoy the more gifted writer's act of creation; the writer's act of creation and the reader's of re-creation are parallel. Freud sees the process of artistic creation as involving four factors working together. The first, naturally enough, is the artist himself, his constitution and personality, in which four things are crucial: a strong libido; strong forces of repression (today we would say "defense"); an "extraordinary" capacity for sublimation; and an unusual "laxity" of repression. The second and third factors in artistic creation are the experiences of the artist (either infantile or contemporary with the work of art) and his infantile wishes which give experience an emotional force. Contemporary experiences, naturally, vary greatly from artist to artist. Infantile wishes (primal scene fantasies, castration fears, oedipal wishes, and the like) will vary, too, but not so greatly from individual to individual—indeed, their relative constancy makes art possible by enabling the artist's unconscious to speak the same language as his audience.

These first three factors in artistic creation set it in the continuum of man's wish-fulfilling activities, everything from neurotic symptoms to philosophies, but, in particular, artistic creation is like playing or daydreaming. It is the fourth factor, defensive disguise (in more aesthetic terms, form), that sets artistic creations off from the rest of our wish fulfillments. With his constitutional gifts, the writer transforms his experiences and his infantile wishes (which persist in his adult unconscious) into a fantasy which, in turn, he transforms into art by three more or less simultaneous processes. First, the artist, the shape-shifter, disguises the wish, hiding its egotistic character by such non-logical primary processes as condensation and displacement (projection, reversal, splitting, symbolization). Second, he embodies the wish in a sensuous form, a conventionally accepted reality that offers something with which the audience can identify or otherwise become involved. Third, the artist works out this sensuous, conventional representation according to the "laws of formal beauty."

Of these three processes of transformation Freud felt that psychoanalysis could deal with the artist's subject matter (i.e., his unconscious wishes) and with the genre he chose, that is, the first and second of the three. Sometimes, though, Freud spoke as though psychoanalysis could contribute to the understanding of the third as well, the "laws of formal beauty" (as in the conscious mechanisms of jokes). Similarly, Freud sometimes excluded the artistic gift from psychoanalytic investigation (particularly the capacity for sublimation); sometimes he did not.

For Freud, then, the one basic, unchanging, irreducible factor in art is the artist himself, his impulses and his disguises of or defenses against them. It is fitting that Freud's clearest expression of the point came in 1931 in two charming little notes to Yvette Guilbert and her husband, "Uncle Max." [36] The celebrated *diseuse* was about to write her life story, explaining the secret of her acting as the "transparency" of her own ego, her ability to obliterate her own personality and replace it with an imagined character. "I rather suspect," Freud gently suggested, "that an element of the opposite mechanism is indispensable . . . that one's own person is not obliterated but that parts of it—repressed desires and traits that haven't had a chance to develop—are employed to represent the chosen character and in this way find expression and give it the stamp of realistic truth." And he confirmed his explanation with an analysis of that "especially simple, transparent case," Charlie Chaplin, playing always the one part, a "weak, poor, helpless, clumsy boy," thus compensating for his own grim youth.

It would be possible, in an age reacting against Romanticism so sharply in so many ways as ours is, to look down on Freud's conception of the creative process as "mere" self-expression. Today, in literary history, we stress contemporary conventions, intellectual background, and social concerns as "influences"; in criticism, myths and archetypes funnel through a seemingly helpless poet, and the intricate interrelations of theme and image in the finished work are to be considered utterly separate from the artist's "intention." While these statements of the artist's passivity are all at least partly correct, they need to be balanced by the psychoanalytic view (demonstrably correct) in which art is, in the deepest sense, the artist's making. Freud's view of the creative process makes art both product and proof of the dignity of man.

[3]

Freud on the Work

FOR Freud, in discussing art and literature, the artist counted most. He had much less to say about the audience or about the work in isolation (as, say, a New Critic would consider it). Psychoanalysis, after all, deals with minds, and in art or literature the most obvious mind to look at is the artist's. Nevertheless, Freud showed on occasion a modern critic's formalist interest in the significance of textual details and at other times a quite classical interest in the work of art as a just representation of general nature and the poet as *vates* or seer. "Creative writers," he wrote, placing himself on the side of "the ancients,"

are valuable allies and their evidence is to be prized highly, for they are apt to know a whole host of things between heaven and earth of which our philosophy has not yet let us dream. In their knowledge of the mind they are far in advance of us everyday people, for they draw upon sources which we have not yet opened up for science.[1]

What prompted this remark was the fact that writers (in this case Wilhelm Jensen) attribute to dreams the same importance that psychoanalysts do.

Similarly, writers "for thousands of years" have depicted for us the reasons people fall in love with the people they do: "The writer can indeed draw on certain qualities which fit him to carry out such a task: above all, on a sensitivity that enables him to perceive the hidden impulses in the minds of other people, and the courage to let his own unconscious speak." [2] To analyze "Some Character-Types Met with in Psycho-Analytic Work," Freud turned not "to cases of clinical observation, but . . . to figures which great writers have created from the wealth of their knowledge of the mind," Richard III, Lady Macbeth, and Ibsen's Rebecca.[3] As these quotations should suggest, Freud even when he looks at the work of art by itself looks again for a mind, in this case, not the artist's, but the character's; one could instance almost indefinitely Freud's and later psychoanalytic critics' uses of literary characters to get at traits of human nature in general.

At the same time, however, Freud insists that these links between the artist's work and the classical critics' "nature" are weak links, not to be trusted. "One has scarcely the right to expect a poet to present us with clinically perfect examples of mental illness," he wrote to a correspondent.[4] What lessens "the evidential value" of the artist's insights are "the privileges of what is known as 'poetic license.'" "Writers," Freud not unreasonably notes, "are under the necessity to produce intellectual and aesthetic pleasure, as well as certain emotional effects. For this reason they cannot reproduce the stuff of reality unchanged, but must isolate portions of it, remove disturbing associations, tone down the whole, and fill in what is missing."[5] Even, or perhaps especially, in portraying character, the writer must distort. In reality, people show a complication of motives, overdetermination, a combination of mental activities, while the writer "simplifies and abstracts when he appears in the character of a psychologist."[6]

The Master seems to have come to a contradiction: on the one hand, the psychologist should rate the storytellers' testimony high; on the other, its "evidential value" is weak, particularly when the writer is playing the psychologist. The contradiction is, however, illusory. The writer's testimony is strong when it deals with his special competence, which, in a psychoanalytic sense, is his insight into and access to his unconscious mind, and, through it, the unconscious minds of others. His testimony is weak on particular details of objective, external reality, because art is a bridging of the contradiction between man's search for pleasure and his awareness of reality. "Art," in other words, "is a conventionally accepted reality in which, thanks to artistic illusion, symbols and substitutes are able to provoke real emotions. Thus art constitutes a region halfway between a reality which frustrates wishes and the wish-fulfilling world of the imagination—a region in which, as it were, primitive man's strivings for omnipotence are still in full force."[7] Nevertheless, they must not be given full rein. Freud admitted he was conservative in the matter of "poetic license" versus "historical reality."

Where there is an unbridgeable gap in history or biography a writer may step in and try to guess how things were. An uninhabited country he may well settle with the creatures of his imagination. Even if the happenings are known but are far removed and alien to common knowledge he can disregard them. . . . On the other hand he should respect reality where it is established and has become common property. Bernard Shaw, who makes his Caesar gape at a stony Sphinx as if he were a Cook's tourist, and forget to take leave of Cleopatra when he sails from Egypt, shows what a clown he is who puts jesting above everything else.[8]

In a curious way Freud's attitude seems somewhat like Aristotle's: the poet must "make like" the things of reality, not necessarily as they are, but either as they are or as they ought to be. He is going beyond his own Romantic tendency to treat the work of art solely as an expression of the artist's self; he is stressing, as a classical or neoclassical critic would, the importance of the dialogue between the work of art and the world.

Similarly, Freud stresses, as a modern critic would, the importance of examining the details of form and structure in the work rather than taking merely a general impression of it. With all the glee of a positivist beating a metaphysical carpet, he dismisses maunderings about beauty: "The science of aesthetics investigates the conditions under which things are felt as beautiful; but it has been unable to give any explanation of the nature and origin of beauty, and, as usually happens, lack of success is concealed beneath a flood of resounding and empty words." [9] And as for connoisseurs of art, "They are eloquent enough, it seems to me. But usually in the presence of a great work of art each says something different from the other; and none of them says anything that solves the problem for the unpretending admirer." [10]

This response of the solid scientist to the blue-and-white young men occurs in what is perhaps the most puzzling of Freud's essays, "The Moses of Michelangelo." One puzzling aspect is that it was first published anonymously. The editors of *Imago* prefaced the article with a note (apparently Freud's) to the effect that although the essay was not psychoanalytic, the author belonged to psychoanalytic circles (surely the understatement of the decade), and "his mode of thought has in point of fact a certain resemblance to the methodology of psychoanalysis." Coyness aside, Freud had written a purely aesthetic attempt to account for the posture of the statue—psychoanalysis is scarcely mentioned. His efforts, he says, "do not stop short at the general effect of the figure, but are based on separate features in it; these we usually fail to notice, being overcome by the total impression of the statue and as it were paralyzed by it."

His method, in other words, is not far removed from that approach represented in the fine arts by Wölfflin, Berenson, Bell, or Fry, and in literature by the Russian formalists or the American and English "New Critics." Freud went on to compare his efforts with those of an art connoisseur who, in questions of authenticity, insisted

that attention should be diverted from the general impression and main features of a picture, and [he laid] stress on the significance of minor details, of things like the drawing of the fingernails, of the lobe of an ear, of halos and such unconsidered trifles which the copyist neglects to imitate and yet which every artist executes in his own characteristic way. ... It seems to me that his method of inquiry is closely related to the technique of psychoanalysis. It, too, is accustomed to divine secret and concealed things from despised or unnoticed features, from the rubbish heap, as it were, of our observations.

Nevertheless, even if Freud's method of aesthetic analysis is sometimes like the modern critic's, he seems flagrantly guilty of what the modern critic would call the intentional fallacy or the intentional heresy (depending on whether the critic regards his efforts as science or religion). "In my opinion," Freud writes,

what grips us so powerfully can only be the artist's *intention*, in so far as he has succeeded in expressing it in his work and in getting us to understand it. I realize that this cannot be merely a matter of *intellectual* comprehension; what he aims at is to awaken in us the same emotional attitude, the same mental constellation as that which in him produced the impetus to create. But why should the artist's intention not be capable of being communicated and comprehended in *words*, like any other fact of mental life? Perhaps where great works of art are concerned this would never be possible without the application of psychoanalysis. The product itself after all must admit of such an analysis, if it really is an effective expression of the intentions and emotional activities of the artist. To discover his intention, though, I must first find out the meaning and content of what is represented in his work; I must, in other words, be able to *interpret* it. It is possible, therefore, that a work of art of this kind needs interpretation, and that, until I have accomplished that interpretation, I cannot come to know why I have been so powerfully affected. I even venture to hope that the effect of the work will undergo no diminution after we have succeeded in thus analyzing it.

There is some muddling in Freud's statement of emotional effect and intellectual content, but he seems to distinguish two approaches to a work of art. The first is what he calls "interpretation" (*Deutung*); it seems to be intellectual and it gets at "the meaning and content" (*den Sinn und Inhalt*). After interpretation comes "the application of psychoanalysis" which reveals the "emotional attitude," the "mental constellation" (*die Affektlage, die psychische Konstellation*). Together, emotional attitude and intellectual content seem to make up what he calls "intention" (*die Absicht*). The artist's mind speaks to his audience's, the conscious to the conscious, the unconscious to the unconscious.

For instance, Freud says the "intention" in Michelangelo's "Moses" is "to make the passage of a violent gust of passion visible in the signs left by it on the ensuing calm." Whether or not we agree with the *content* of his statement, in *form* it is the kind of thing a modern critic would say. Again, like a modern critic, Freud scrupulously avoids the "heresy of paraphrase," and indeed, he ultimately avoids the intentional fallacy. That is, he insists that intention (the configuration of the artist's mind, conscious and unconscious) is to be determined by examining in detail the work itself; the significance of the work is not to be determined (limited) by some necessarily speculative "intention" derived from outside the work.

He makes the same kind of answer to objections based on such a hypothetical "intention" as, say, Brooks and Wimsatt might make:

What if we have taken too serious and profound a view of details which were nothing to the artist, details which he had introduced quite arbitrarily or for some purely formal reasons with no hidden intention behind? What if we have shared the fate of so many interpreters who have thought they saw quite clearly things which the artist did not intend either consciously or unconsciously? I cannot tell. I cannot say whether it is reasonable to credit Michelangelo . . . with such an elementary want of precision, especially whether this can be assumed in regard to the striking and singular features of the statue under discussion.

Although in this essay, "The Moses of Michelangelo," Freud seems to endorse the modern critic's interest in textual minutiae, this is only a marginal essay, anonymous, unpsychological, atypical. Much the strongest strain in Freud's approach to a literary text is the Romantic one of the work of art as the expression of the artist. In all his formal literary studies, of *The Brothers Karamazov, Dichtung und Wahrheit,* Jensen's *Gradiva,* and assorted plays of Shakespeare, in all these other comments, the work itself behaves more or less like a telescreen out of science fiction. That is, it first appears as a murky surface, quite clearly there but not of primary interest; then, at a push of the psychoanalytic button, the work seems to vanish and before us stands the mind of the writer, the real aim of the inquiry. Freud was a psychologist, not a critic. When he looked at a work of art, he saw it oftener as a mental event than as an end in itself or as a just representation of general nature.

Nevertheless, where the Romantic critics worked from relatively primitive psychologies, the sophisticated psychology of psychoanalysis offers the modern critic a sophisticated Romanticism: the work of art expresses and stimulates both the conscious and the unconscious. Freud's real contribution to literary criticism of the work by itself is his insistence on "levels" in the work, or at least that different elements in the work stimulate different levels in the reader's and writer's mind. After Freud, a criticism that considers only one level is only half a criticism. Freud has made art an imitation of nature in a fuller sense than any classical critic. Art is, society and each of us is, an amphibian. The work of art lives half on the visible shore, half in a submnemonic sea.

[4]

Freud on the Response

IN GENERAL, Freud (and subsequent analysts) preferred to talk about writers rather than readers. As a result, a comprehensive psychoanalytic theory for the response to literature remains to be written. And yet, as we shall see in the conclusions to this book, the part of the literary process that psychoanalysis can and should tell us most about is, in fact, response.

A psychoanalyst, I suppose, feels surest when he is dealing with a real person's mind; perhaps that is why Freud is most ready to talk about the artist's mind when he talks about art. In the analysis of particular works he turns to the audience's mind only when there is no writer—as in myths and folk tales, for example, his analysis of "The Medusa's Head" or "The Theme of the Three Caskets." From these mythological subjects it is only a short step to his analyses of non-artistic reactions based on the combination of infantile wishes and current experience, "The Subtleties of a Faulty Action," "A Note on the Prehistory of the Psycho-Analytic Movement," or, for that matter, *The Interpretation of Dreams* or *The Psychopathology of Everyday Life*. Again, Freud's theory of art places it in a continuum of human activity and leads us back to his general theory of human behavior and personality.

Unfortunately, though, Freud did not develop a general theory of responses to literature to match his general theory of its creation. He did describe audience response in some detail for certain specific forms. In "The 'Uncanny' " (1919) he showed how horror stories work because the artist manipulates unconscious mechanisms in his reader. In "Psychopathic Characters on the Stage" (published posthumously but written late in 1905 or early in 1906), an essay which such post-Freudian dramatists as Arthur Miller and Tennessee Williams would do well to read, he discussed audience responses to tragedy. But these descriptions tend to be fragmentary. The art form Freud lavished attention on is the joke. He devoted an entire book, *Jokes and Their Relation to the Unconscious* (1905), and an important revising essay, "Humour" (1927), to our response to jokes. One could wish he had picked a more respectable form.

Nevertheless, the joke can serve as a model for longer and more aesthetic works of literature. Jokes, for example, have a "frame," as serious literature does, that marks them off from ordinary experience and leads us into an attitude of playful attention, a special combination of involvement and distancing, the aesthetic stance, just as the appearance of a poem on the page does. Jokes present us with the problem of form in an even more acute way than poetry does: no form, no joke, but clearly form alone is not what makes a joke funny. Jokes have content, that is, rational thought, social and moral purpose, but, clearly, editorial content is not what makes a joke funny, either. Rather, jokes get their response from some interaction of form and content every bit as subtle as a poem's. Jokes call for a particular emotional response, as more important literature does, and they succeed or fail—are "good" or "bad" jokes—according to whether they achieve that response.

In short, we can use his general psychology to extrapolate from the particular audience responses with which Freud dealt—to the joke in particular, but also to tragedy and the uncanny—to arrive at a coherent account of responses to literature in general. It is worth taking the time and space for such an extrapolation, not just as a context for psychoanalytic comments on Shakespeare, but as a starting point for a better understanding of our responses to literature in general. We shall work, as it were, from the outside in, from frame to form to content.

In a late writing [1] Freud discussed something related to the "frame" of art or literature: the defense mechanism of "isolation," that is, a marking off or separating of a particular experience from the stream of experiences. Obsessional neurotics often put a "quiet time" or other barrier around a significant act, the defense serving to interrupt disturbing associations to the act, notably aggressive and sexual impulses to "touch." Normal people, Freud pointed out, also use isolation to pay attention and to hold off distracting thoughts. The "frame" of a work of art (that is, entering a theater or concert hall, recognizing on the printed page, that "this is a poem" or "that is a joke") seems to me to serve the same purpose. Our attention is held, but our normal emotions are held off: we do not "touch" the actors, musicians, or paintings. We perceive them as a separate segment in the stream of our experiences.

Thus, isolation would seem to be the psychoanalytic term for aesthetic "distancing" (the term introduced by Bullough to describe the separation of the affective self from a work of art). Isolation helps us put aside our normal aggressive and sexual reactions in favor of some other response. And perhaps this emotive substitution is itself the elusive "aesthetic emotion" sought by philosophers in the past. Be that as it may, literature does its work within our ability to isolate it, to pay attention to it as literature separated from life.

We have already seen Freud's assertion that both the artist's act of creation and the finished work exist on two levels like a dream: there is a manifest form and a latent content. In the same way he divides the response to a work of literature into two phases. In the first, the reader is responding to what Freud calls variously the "perceptual pleasure of formal beauty," the "incentive-bonus," or the "fore-pleasure"—he is speaking, not of form as such, but of a *pleasure* in form which draws the audience in deeper. In the second phase the reader so drawn in responds to the text in terms of his own unconscious feelings, fantasies, and fears.

Of the first stage in reader response Freud had relatively little to say, preferring to leave the matter (somewhat optimistically) to professors of aesthetics. This is the fore-pleasure, the pleasure we take in such purely formal elements of technique as structure, rhyme, or, in Aristotelian terms, diction, song, spectacle, and the skillful presentation of plot, character, and thought. Freud discusses this fore-pleasure (in narrower terms) in connection with "innocent jokes," that is, jokes in which little or no unconscious content is involved.[2] Freud, by this point in the essay, has discussed twenty-three joke techniques—he now brings them into three large groups. (1) Those in which words substitute for things. He notes that children, schizophrenics, hysterics, and aphasics often lose this distinction. As normal adults we avoid such muddled thinking, and jokes of this type represent a relief from our adult inhibitions against childish thinking. (2) Jokes in which we rediscover something familiar. We expected to have to cope with something new—instead, we find something we already know and, as a result, we save effort. This technique, he notes, applies not only to jokes, but also to rhyme, alliteration, or refrains, and it accounts for the use of allusions, particularly topical allusions, in jokes. (3) Jokes based on pleasure in nonsense, that is, illogic, absurdity, faulty thinking, representation by the opposite, and, in general, displacement. Again, he points out, in normal adult life we are not supposed to jumble things up (displace them). Yet children who are just learning to talk take great pleasure in babbling, and so do adults under the influence of alcohol.

In short, all three of these kinds of techniques give us pleasure by economizing. They relieve us of psychic expenditures we ordinarily make. (1) and (3), replacing things by words and the use of absurdity, relieve us from psychic expenditures we are already making to keep ourselves on the straight-and-narrow path of reason. (2), the rediscovery of the familiar, saves us an expenditure in responding to something new.

This psychic economy, however—or psychic sloppiness—is not enough to make wit or art. Confronted with raw play alone, as with children's jabber, the talk of psychotics, or descriptions of unconscious fantasies like dreams, we draw away from them; we experience unpleasant feelings of defense. What turns play into art is the presence of logic, of meaning, of "sense in nonsense." We are all familiar with the way jokes use the cleverest operations of the mind to supplement the psychic short circuits that make the punch line. In other words, mental "play" becomes a true joke when the senseless combination of words or the absurd linking of thoughts makes sense after all. "The pleasure of wit arises from word play or the liberation of nonsense, and . . . the sense of wit is meant only to guard this pleasure against suppression through reason."

"Meaning" or "content," then, in jokes (and, by extension, in all art) is, with respect to form, a *defense rather than a source of pleasure in itself.* The real pleasure in artistic form comes from illogic and nonsense, which, in turn, represent "the economy of psychic expenditures or alleviation from the pressure of reason." Our sense of pleasure comes from releasing or economizing on energy normally used to keep ourselves logical; we experience a sudden sense of psychic energy to spare, a feeling of sudden psychic profit from cutting down expenses.

Similarly, Freud writes, "It is also generally acknowledged that rhymes, alliterations, refrains, and other forms of repeating similar verbal sounds which occur in verse, make use of the same source of pleasure—the rediscovery of something familiar." As in a child's babbling, the word becomes a thing in itself; there is an element of multiple use or condensation. But we would not enjoy this babbling if it did not offer a "sense in nonsense" by coming at logical points in the thought, either at measured intervals or on key words.

The "discovery of the familiar" plays another part in the forepleasure of art because of "the close connection between recognizing and remembering." That is, the *cognitio* or *anagnorisis,* our sense of the "rightness" of a denouement should also be considered a "discovery of the familiar." (Aristotle's example of events having the appearance of design comes to mind: Mitys' murderer, while watching at a public spectacle, was killed by a statue falling on him—Mitys' statue. The poetic justice has the same kind of multiple use or condensation as a simple rhyme or *le mot juste.*) One suspects that all works of art in which we are aware that things are less complicated, more structured and ordered than in real life, in other words, all works of art having an organic unity, give us pleasure through this sense of recognition or condensation which is akin to "the act of remembering [which] in itself is accompanied by a feeling of pleasure. . . ." If we give Freud's view its broadest statement (as some later theorists have done) we can say that we react to any work of art as though we were remembering it. Poetry, Keats said, and I think Freud would agree, "should strike the Reader as a wording of his own highest thoughts, and appear almost a Remembrance." That is, with both a memory and a work of art we have the same feeling that we are in control, can give or withdraw our attention as we wish; we have the same feeling that the details have a greater—and richer —coherence than ordinary events.

Freud thus sees form and content bound together in a complex interplay. Having accepted the "frame" or "isolation" of the poem, play, or whatever, we feel or guess that it "means something." Bribed by this promise of "sense in nonsense," we (preconsciously) relax our thinking inhibitions to take pleasure in the illogic or unrealism of formal order. That initial pleasure in form then serves as a trigger to unbalance other inhibitions, opening up still deeper sources of pleasure from our own unconscious wishes and impulses. The writer, in creating, disguised his raw fantasy by various defensive maneuvers —we, his audience, unmask his fantasy, at least preconsciously. Thus, for Freud, the "art in art" becomes the essential thing: without this conscious, intellectual organization and disguise we cannot get down to the even deeper sources of pleasure in the content of the work of art.

In short, the fore-pleasure in form bribes us into becoming still further involved. In part, we become involved by being in the mood, in the right state of mind for, say, a joke. In part, too, we sense a license, either from the artist (for example, the teller of the joke) or from other members of the audience—we feel we are entitled to "let go," to give ourselves over to the work of art.

The most important factor, however, for Freud (as for Aristotle) is identification.

If, as has been assumed since the time of Aristotle, the purpose of drama is to arouse "terror and pity" and so "to purge the emotions," we can describe that purpose in rather more detail by saying that it is a question of opening up sources of pleasure or enjoyment in our emotional life, just as, in the case of intellectual activity, joking or fun open up similar sources, many of which that activity had made inaccessible. . . . And the playwright and actor enable [the spectator] to do this by allowing him *to identify himself* with a hero.[3]

Drama serves the spectator as play serves the child. It enables him "to be a hero," "to stand in his own person at the hub of world affairs," "to feel and to act and to arrange things according to his desires." At the same time, because he acts the hero vicariously, and because he sees the situation is isolated, gamelike, he is freed from the pains, fears, and qualms he would suffer if he were really to do what the stage hero does. Most important in tragedy, he is freed of the fear of actual death. Thus, the essence of dramatic identification is that the spectator is simultaneously at one with and distanced from his protagonist on the stage,[4] or, for that matter, the protagonist of a book or poem. Drama, in other words, depends not just on "form," but on the whole atmosphere or context of being "in a theater."

The spectator at a drama, of course, presents the clearest instance of identification, but Freud insists that other forms of creative writing work by identification also. In the epic or the novel the spectator identifies with the hero; in a cheap novel he enters a world of good guys and bad guys, that is, people who help him or people who oppose him. In more sophisticated novels, the ego, the character with whom we identify, is likely to be split up among several characters. When we identify, we vicariously act through our internal conflicts projected into this community of interacting parts of a single personality.[5] In the case of lyric poetry, we identify with the poet, and in dance, with the dancer.[6] In the case of a ghost or horror story we feel fear only if we identify with the person in the story who fears; if we see the events from the point of view of the one creating the fear or if we know how the fear is being created and so feel superior, then there is no identification to produce in us a feeling of fear.[7] We have already seen how Freud's discussion of the "Moses" of Michelangelo proceeds on the assumption that the artist is trying to waken in us the same "mental constellation" as his own.[8] Even in the lowly joke there must be a sort of rudimentary identification: for the joke to come off, the hearer must have the same kind of inhibition as the teller. Only then does the joke release the energy tied up in the inhibition so that we laugh.[9]

In short, though Freud, I believe, never makes the blanket statement that all artistic effects depend on identification, when he talks about drama, epic, novel, dance, sculpture, the uncanny, wit, and the comic—in all of them he treats the effect as stemming from identification. Unfortunately, "identification" is a difficult concept in or out of art, and Freud's discussion of it in *Group Psychology and the Analysis of the Ego* does not shed much light on aesthetic issues. Freud's discussion of the creative process, however, does.

That is, our "identification" matches the artist's "soften[ing] the character of his egoistic daydreams." In general, we have been looking at Freud's theory of artistic response from the outside in, whereas we considered his theory of artistic creation from the inside out. But the two match.

At the outermost level the artist has presented his work to the public, not as his self, but as his creation, distanced from his self. We, his public, accept this "frame" or isolation by our aesthetic attitude. The artist has disguised his raw fantasy by giving it aesthetic form. We, bribed by the promise of meaning (and how angry we are when we don't get "meaning"!), take a slightly illicit pleasure in the illogic and unrealism of form. The artist disguises the egoistic character of his work; we, in unwrapping the form, accept that egoistic character by identifying with him (perhaps through his protagonists).

Identification, however, is only a means, not an end in itself. It is a gate, in effect, through which we let strong feelings emerge which would otherwise be inaccessible to us. At his innermost level the artist was gratifying his deepest wishes in fantasy; at our innermost level we do the same. In discussing these unconscious sources which art taps, Freud dealt in detail with (again) tragedy, the uncanny story, and the joke.

In the basic action of tragedy the hero rebels, is punished, and suffers. Because the tragedy tends to concentrate on the suffering, our pleasure, Freud says, is "due to masochistic satisfaction as well as to direct enjoyment of a character whose greatness is insisted upon in spite of everything." [10] This tragic suffering may come about because the hero opposes something divine or something social or someone of strong character or even where one impulse in the hero struggles against another. In every tragedy, however, whether it is religious, social, characterological, or psychological, the drama gains its effect by getting us to identify with the hero, to experience for ourselves his impulses to rebel against authority, to suffer, and masochistically to enjoy our suffering for that rebellion. Finally, with the tragic resolution, we re-repress the rebellious impulse. Thus, when in October, 1897, Freud hypothesized love of the mother and jealousy of the father as general phenomena of early childhood, he wrote:

If that is the case, the gripping power of *Oedipus Rex,* in spite of all the rational objections to the inexorable fate that the story presupposes, becomes intelligible. . . . Every member of the audience was once a budding Oedipus in phantasy, and this dream-fulfillment played out in reality causes everyone to recoil in horror, with the full measure of repression which separates his infantile from his present state.[11]

Later, Freud mentioned with approval Otto Rank's *Das Inzest-motiv in Dichtung und Sage* (1912), citing it for the proposition that the choice of subject matter "especially for dramatic works," comes mostly from the oedipus complex.[12]

In other words, if I may broaden Freud's remarks, literary works, be they fiction or drama, which concentrate on real interactions of love and hate between people (as opposed to, say, lyric poetry), such works draw on the audience's earliest childhood experience with other people, namely the family. When the tragic hero rebels against fate or society or God, these abstractions take on some of the quality of the father, the original against whom we all rebelled. Later analysts (particularly Ludwig Jekels) and nonanalysts (notably Northrop Frye) have suggested that dramatic comedy also has an oedipal root, although the "happy ending" foists the punishment and guilt off on the father-villain, whereas tragedy thrusts it on the son-hero.

In lyric poetry and the dance Freud seemed to consider the basic unconscious appeal to be exhibitionistic. We identify with the artist who is freely and publicly airing his feelings, and therefore we feel free to do the same.[13] Since the significance of watching theatrical performances in dreams generally means watching the parents in the act of love, presumably such genres as theater, dance, film, or television, in which watching plays an important part, gratify in part unconscious scoptophilic impulses.[14]

Freud's extensive analysis of wit showed that the "tendentious joke"—that is, the joke that gives us pleasure not only through the intellectual activity involved in joking but also through its content—such a joke, Freud said, allows the expression of unconscious impulses, either sexual or aggressive. In obscene jokes, where the sexual content is not unconscious, Freud found still another source of laughter—the releasing of exhibitionistic impulses.[15]

In his analysis of "The 'Uncanny,'" Freud concluded that we experience the feeling when some childish way of thinking which we have either repressed or outgrown turns up again either in reality or in a fiction in which the writer makes us feel the events are really happening. Thus, stories in which telepathic communication takes place, in which omens and presentments are valid, stories of the "evil eye" and the like, these all use the childish or primitive habit of mind called "omnipotence of thought," the feeling that thoughts are as good (or bad) as deeds, that we can wish things into reality. Stories of blinding or of severed hands and feet that take on lives of their own, these draw on both the omnipotence of thought and the fear of castration. Stories of inanimate objects coming to life or the dead returning impinge on the old feeling that "I can never die"—they simply carry out the idea that death does not exist. *Doppelgänger* stories of twins and doubles suggest the same idea (as does the Egyptian *ka*); they also hark back to a kind of thinking appropriate to the earliest stages of childhood when the child is just beginning to distinguish himself from the rest of reality. Stories in which things recur, a number keeps turning up, the hero keeps coming back to the same place no matter how hard he tries to go elsewhere, or in which we feel that all this has happened before, such stories carry into actuality the "repetition compulsion," the tendency that neurotics (and all of us) have to go through the same thing over and over again.[16]

Freud's point is that various kinds of literature, narrative, drama, poetry, jokes, the uncanny, achieve their effect by *bringing to consciousness unconscious or preconscious impulses, wishes, fantasies, or ways of thinking.* There are three things we should note. First, Freud has described a continuum, not an either-or, either conscious content or unconscious; rather, literature in his description seems to play up and down a psychic gamut. Second, literature achieves its basic effect by alleviating an existing psychic tension in the unconscious material. We experience pleasure from a feeling of psychic over-plus; we suddenly feel in possession of that energy we had been using up in inhibiting the unconscious or preconscious material in real life. Thus, pleasure in art depends on our ability to accept the "as if-ness" of the artistic situation. Third, in most cases (most jokes, most tragedies) we get a kind of actual pleasure from gratifying by identification or fantasy aggressive and sexual impulses that had been unconscious or preconscious.

So far we have been talking generally. To speak of specifics we would have to look at the events, language, and images of the particular work of literature in question. In doing so we would proceed by the same method as for the analysis of *The Brothers Karamazov* or the Medusa's head legend. We could, for example, analyze the joke at the opening of this section (p. 4).

Nothing seems to provoke so angry a response from lovers of literature as the application of psychoanalysis to the world of letters. As one cannibal said to the other, "Did you ever eat a psychoanalyst?" "Eat one!" replied the other, "Did you ever try to *clean* one!"

The almost formulaic clause, "As one [blank] said to the other," serves as the frame. It signals us that a joke is coming and isolates the joke from the discourse around it. We "set" ourselves for a special combination of tightening and relaxing our normal inhibitions.

This joke, like any other, promises a point or meaning, and this meaning is a point indeed—the joke needles psychoanalysts. This "sense in nonsense" enables us to take pleasure in what would otherwise be a quite pointless series of displacements. The first operative word in the joke, "cannibal," conjures up, not unnaturally, the notion of a savage who devours human flesh. For most of us such an act is surrounded by the strongest taboos, but it was not always thus. Psychoanalysis aside, common experience tells us that children bite, and the cry, "I'm gonna eat you up" is not unknown in nursery or playground. The word "cannibal" draws on whatever vestiges of this infantile oral sadism still reside within us; the word at the same time mobilizes a defense against any such impulse: "I don't want to eat anybody—*he* does."

The cannibal's casual question, "Did you ever eat a . . . ," continues to play on our unconscious impulse and continues our projection of it onto the cannibal. The word "psychoanalyst," which must come as somewhat of a shock, gives an object for the sadistic impulse, a quite appropriate one, for psychoanalytic experience demonstrates that the child's impulse to devour somebody usually is directed toward a parent: eating them up would not only get rid of someone who keeps saying no, it would also make a loved person forever part of the child. The admonishing, threatening figure of the analyst can evoke at least the hostile feelings toward a parent, which are projected onto the primitive (childish) figure of the cannibal. At this point the joke has generated in its hearer a tense balance between unconscious impulses (oral sadistic) and defenses (projection and symbolization). We feel this "damming up of psychic energy" (Freud's phrase) as intellectual puzzlement—How will the joke bring these disparate ideas of cannibal, psychoanalyst, and eating together?

The punch line triumphantly does bring them together in an idea almost poetic in the sharpness of its condensation, "A psychoanalyst would be dirty food for a cannibal." The open phrasing, "Did you ever try to *clean* one?" suggests that the cannibal did not, in fact, get around to eating a psychoanalyst—we perhaps breathe a sigh of relief: my impulse to devour a loved one's innards was not acted out. (The analyst, however, seems not particularly better off.) The joke conjures up (in my mind, anyway) an eviscerated chicken or cow or a particularly bony fish—and certain diagrams of Elizabethan disembowellings. One's hostile feelings get gratified, but with a certain safe distancing from the impulse actually mobilized.

At the same time the word "clean" brings to consciousness and acts out the precise nature of the feelings the joke drew on, hostility toward the analyst as parent. "He makes me feel dirty or guilty." And the punch line asserts, "He's the guilty-dirty one." The psychoanalyst is pre-eminently that kind of adult who makes my secret dirt show; the joke, however, grants me a reversal—it reveals his hidden dirt. At the same time the black figure of the cannibal (who seems "dirty") stands as yet another buffer in the chain of displacements between me and dirt. The dirt visible in the analyst's belly or the cannibal's mouth or skin replaces any secret dirt an analyst might have heard from my mouth. Also, mental dirt has become bodily dirt, as though one could "clean out" one's mind as easily as one's body, another wish fulfillment. And we can guess that the joke may also evoke the thought, "I would have been clean food" for those whose devouring impulse masks a still deeper wish, to be devoured.

Our approach being a scientific one, we could now even essay experiments to test the reading. Would the joke work with "lawyer"? Probably, but probably not with "engineer," except perhaps among a group of engineers. How would the joke go over with a group of psychoanalysts? (That was where I first heard it, and it went over very well—perhaps the unconscious feeling was, "We're dirty and we like it.") Suppose the second cannibal answered, "Yes, but he was sure hard to clean." And so on.

In short, although Freud has spoken only of certain special types, he has, between the lines, as it were, set out a general theory of literature in terms of form and content, impulse and defense. And with the theory goes a method of analyzing the audience reaction to a work of literature (if the humble joke be allowed to stand as the model for more complex types). First, one should consider the nature of the pleasure provided by the outstanding features of the genre: What unconscious impulses does this genre gratify? Jokes gratify sexual and aggressive impulses, while in tragedy, the answer would be masochistic impulses to suffer, oedipal feelings toward the father, and in so far as we think of the tragedy as a staged play, scoptophilic impulses. Second, we would consider form and ask what combination of sense and nonsense, what intellectual "play," loosens the psychic bonds, for example, the displacements and condensation in our joke. Third, we would go on to the unconscious significance of the broad patterns of action in the particular work in question, devouring the dirt in the joke, or the theme of parricide in *The Brothers Karamazov*. Finally, one would consider the individual details of the work, particular little events, specific images. What unconscious or preconscious things does a word like "clean" stir up? One could, I suppose, go even further and consider the separate reactions of individual spectators. That is, younger men presumably identify more easily with Hamlet than with King Lear. It is in such considerations that both the audience's and the artist's individualities will emerge. Usually, however, an analysis of the effect of literature, although it proceeds from the general to the particular, from outside to inside, would draw the line at the general unconscious effect on most of the audience or, more properly, what aspects of the work stimulate that effect.

The effect itself is the discharge of emotions, or, as Freud paraphrased Aristotle

The prime factor is unquestionably the process of getting rid of one's own emotions by "blowing off steam"; and the consequent enjoyment corresponds on the one hand to the relief produced by a thorough discharge and on the other hand, no doubt, to an accompanying sexual excitation; for the latter, as we may suppose, appears as a by-product whenever an affect is aroused, and gives people the sense, which they so much desire, of a raising of the potential of their psychical state.[17]

On the one hand, there is the satisfaction of the impulse; on the other, there is the feeling of psychic wealth from the release of energy used in maintaining psychic order, and this feeling of release, Freud says, has a sexual element.

There is no guarantee, however, that such a discharge will take place; in fact, certain conditions must be rather carefully observed for there to be an affective response. Having considered the process of that response and a method of analyzing it, completeness asks that we now consider these conditions for the response. Freud spells them out for the special situations of the joke, the uncanny, and tragedy.

For the joke he notes three conditions: first, since wit involves the release of energy used to inhibit a forbidden impulse, the joke will not raise a laugh unless the person to whom it is told, either has or can raise that inhibition. (In Huxley's *Brave New World* the citizens who have no sexual inhibitions cannot understand *Othello* or *Romeo and Juliet*.) Second, the energy must really be released; that is, it must be discharged (in laughter), not reassigned to another psychic task. (A worried man does not enjoy a play so much as a man who is easy, who can spare his psychic energy.) Third, to get the most out of the joke, the inhibition in the person to whom it is told must be heightened.

These conditions, although formulated for wit, obviously apply to other artistic processes as well. For example, the second, the demand that the energy released be put to no other psychic use, bears on a spectator's involvement with a drama; if he cannot get his mind on the play, he cannot enjoy it. Yet if he gets his mind too much on the play, if it gets too touchy for him (the man who knows his wife is deceiving him will probably not enjoy *Othello*), his reactions will be seriously distorted. Freud suggests the best procedure for getting the audience's mind on the joke is the use of form. Ambiguities, a riddling quality, a logical or syllogistic façade, all have the effect of focusing the hearer's attention on the joke but diverting his attention from the *process* of the joke. (Thus, we rarely know *when* we are laughing at a joke *why* we are laughing.) Form would play a similar role in any artistic work; in particular, the narrative device of the "frame" (now I am going to see a play) would both focus and divert attention. Similarly, for the third condition, the teller of the joke tries to build up suspense, creating a kind of psychic damming. So, too, any work of literature will try to build up suspense or re-create the inhibition which the resolution of the work will break down.

In jokes, Freud points out, there is a rudimentary process of identification involved. That is, the man who tells a joke does not laugh; only the man who hears it laughs—and then the teller can laugh as if by ricochet. That is, the teller seems to seek the release of his own inhibitions by seeing the hearer release his, just as artists in general receive satisfaction from seeing their audiences receive satisfaction.[18] If the hearer does not laugh, then the teller suffers a sharp feeling of embarrassment and failure as his inhibitions (or his superego) clamp down again; there are few things in the world that create as much nervousness as a joke that falls flat.

Another special case for which Freud spelled out the conditions for the satisfying emotional discharge was the uncanny story. There, he pointed out, we get the feeling of the uncanny only if we are made to feel that the buried modes of thought are really coming into existence. The writer can control our reactions by joking about the horrifying situation, by explaining it, or by using point of view to let us see it through the eyes of the horrifier rather than the horrified. Freud thus makes an important point about unconscious content, namely, that the emotional effect can be quite independent of unconscious content if the writer handles his material to make it so—or, as literary people have long said, form and content are inseparable.[19]

Considering tragedies based on neurotic conflicts in the hero, Freud analyzed the way *Hamlet* succeeds in its effect on the audience by contrasting *Hamlet* with an unsuccessful contemporary tragedy he had recently seen. His analysis led him to posit three preconditions necessary if the spectator was to identify with the hero and experience the same psychopathic conflict between a conscious impulse and an unconscious. First, he said, the hero must not be psychopathic at the outset; he must become psychopathic in the course of the action.

Otherwise, "we shall be inclined to send for the doctor ... and pro-
nounce the character inadmissible to the stage." Second, the repressed impulse must be one which all of us similarly repress (the
oedipus complex, for example), for it is this repression which is
loosened by the situation in the play, and without it the play will have
no effect. Freud, in other words, is prescribing here a criterion of universality. Third, "it appears as a necessary precondition of this form
of art that the impulse that is struggling into consciousness, however
clearly it is recognizable, is never given a definite name; so that in the
spectator, too, the process is carried through with his attention
averted, and he is in the grip of his emotions instead of taking stock
of what is happening." In our own day, now that such words as sibling rivalry or oedipus complex are part of any cocktail party's lingua
franca, the demand on a playwright like Tennessee Williams or
Arthur Miller is greater: not only must he not name the unconscious
impulse himself; he must not draw it so obviously that every member
of the audience who has had an introductory course in psychology
can name it.

These cautions about wit, tragedy, or the uncanny lead us to certain rules, the violation of which will spoil the effect of the work.
Thus, it is not true that psychoanalytic criticism, as people sometimes
say, does not concern itself with aesthetic value, that the psychoanalyst can point to no difference between *Hamlet, Helen Trent,* and
Hopalong Cassidy. On the contrary, Freud's essay, "Psychopathic
Characters on the Stage," deals directly with the question why *Hamlet* succeeds and Hermann Bahr's *Die Andere* fails. No criticism can
make judgments of aesthetic value rigorous (the naturalistic fallacy),
and it would be idle to pretend that psychoanalysis has laid this
philosophical side of the problem to rest. Nevertheless, psychoanalytic criticism sheds some new and important lights on questions
of value, and we can conclude "Freud on the Response" by bringing
together his remarks on some of the larger issues involved in audience reaction: the question of literary value; the moral and social
function of literature; the feeling of sadness beauty evokes.

In general, psychoanalytic psychology makes it possible to give
rigor to what Professor Monroe Beardsley classifies as "affective reasons" for aesthetic value judgments, for example, the statement that
"Titus Andronicus is good because I like it," or, more fully, "The
majority of sensitive persons, past, present, and future enjoy (did enjoy, will enjoy) it aesthetically, and *would* enjoy (or have enjoyed) it
aesthetically if they were (or had been) brought into repeated contact
with it." Professor Beardsley notes that such reasons for judgments

of aesthetic value present two difficulties: first, one cannot point to *what* in the work we like; second, one cannot distinguish the pleasure given by a work of art from that, say, of a well-mixed martini.[20]

Psychoanalytic criticism offers answers to both questions. The special quality of artistic pleasure lies in the transformation of unconscious impulses; it differs, therefore, from sensuous pleasure much the way any sublimation like a job or a hobby does. Art differs from jobs, hobbies, or what other intellectual pleasures reality offers, for art provides a steady flow of satisfying "shifts in cathexis," that is, shifts in what our mind is accenting, different identifications, a stress first on pleasure, then on morality, and so on. Art, in other words, is contrived and formed, unlike random reality or everyday experience. Second, psychoanalysis enables us to see in considerable detail exactly what it is we like in, say, that joke, or *Macbeth,* exactly what unconscious impulse is being transformed (that is, evoked and defended against, aroused and purged), how it is being transformed as the work progresses, even perhaps how it is being transformed in a single line or word.

Speaking about evaluation in general, Freud argued that "man's judgments of value follow directly his wishes for happiness—that, accordingly, they are an attempt to support his illusions with arguments." [21] Psychoanalysis, as the science of the "pleasure principle," can show how certain objective factors in the work of art are likely to satisfy a certain audience's unconscious needs (be they of id, ego, or superego). The psychoanalytic view of literature offers, in other words, canons which bridge affective and objective reasons for aesthetic value judgments. Psychoanalysis can show how "I like" criteria grow out of specific things in the work of art itself. Such canons, moreover, will be, not merely statements of value, but factual predictions based on psychological "laws" having a scientific claim on our belief. We have seen, for example, Freud's statement that a tragedy will fail of its effect (we will not feel it—like it—as a tragedy) if it names the unconscious impulse it liberates. A ghost story will not produce its uncanny effect unless the writer so handles his material as to make us feel that a childish process of thought is actually happening in reality. A joke will not make us laugh unless it evokes the inhibition it then breaks down, and so on. Such canons allow for the personal and cultural variability of "I like" judgments at the same time that they state general and universal laws about art which refer to objective factors in the work of art itself.

Professor Beardsley names three canons that a great many critics have settled on to back up value judgments: unity, complexity, and intensity. We have already seen the psychoanalytic justification for the first: unity gives us a sense of "the discovery of the familiar." All those loose ends, slightly disturbing and unsettling, fall into place.

Freud offers an affective justification for a second traditional canon of aesthetic value: complexity. In effect, Freud treats complexity as the work's creating a span of "higher" and "lower" satisfactions. For example, Freud notes about jokes:

> When we laugh at a refined obscene joke, we are laughing at the same thing that makes a peasant laugh at a coarse piece of smut. In both cases the pleasure springs from the same source. We, however, could never bring ourselves to laugh at the coarse smut; we should feel ashamed or it would seem to us disgusting. We can only laugh when a joke has come to our help.[22]

Curiously, the Renaissance critic, Castelvetro, anticipates Freud's remarks on the role of joking in obscenity:

> But it is to be noted that [indecencies] do not make us laugh when they are set openly before the eyes of the body or of the mind in the presence of others; rather they overcome us with shame. . . . Then the aforesaid things make us laugh when they are presented . . . under a veil, by means of which we are able to give the appearance of laughing not at the indecency but at something else.[23]

In effect, although he speaks of the process as though it were conscious, Castelvetro has hit upon Freud's point: that complexity in jokes serves a defensive, disguising function, easing our inhibitions. And not just in jokes.

In discussing the general relationship of creative writing to daydreaming, Freud distinguishes kitsch from better fiction (tactfully, he speaks of "the less pretentious writers of novels, romances, and short stories who nevertheless have the widest and most eager circle of readers of both sexes"); these, he says, are hero centered—we identify with a single figure who undergoes all the perils of Pauline (or Marina) and comes through invulnerable. More complex works —and, Freud seems to imply, "better"—split up the ego "into many part egos, and in consequence . . . personify the conflicting currents of . . . mental life in several heroes." [24] Thus, Freud seems to take complexity as itself a value in art.

As for Beardsley's third canon, intensity, that seems to correspond to Freud's general view of literature as satisfying (under the right conditions) unconscious desires or resolving unconscious tensions. Freud's theory of literature is essentially a pleasure theory, not a moralistic one. For Freud, the moral and social purpose of literature is to satisfy unconscious desires, although literature can have a "moral" in the crude sense: a literary work, he says, can inculcate "wise lessons." [25] Fundamentally, however, literature serves simply to give pleasure, the fore-pleasure of artistic form or the yet greater pleasure it triggers by the release of unconscious tension. These pleasures involve much more than a mere "happy ending" *à la* Hollywood. Art, particularly tragic art, turns the most painful experiences of life into enjoyment. Such painful experiences, however, can be turned into pleasure only if they are not real. This is not to say that literature cannot deal with reality and give insights, but only that art is illusion or symbolization; not action, but imitation of action.

The effect of art, its ability to be both moral and pleasurable, hinges on a fact that was one of the earliest psychoanalytic discoveries, "that there is no 'indication of reality' in the unconscious, so that it is impossible to distinguish between truth and emotionally-charged fiction." [26] And this fact remained a central insight: "The substitutive satisfactions, as offered by art, are illusions in contrast with reality," Freud wrote in 1930, "but they are none the less psychically effective, thanks to the role which phantasy has assumed in mental life." [27] Art, precisely because it is an illusion, can serve as the "mild narcotic," the substitute gratification for "the oldest and still most deeply felt cultural renunciations." Thus, literature serves a communal social and moral purpose; it eases the dissatisfaction felt by all the community at renouncing pleasures in the interests of society as a whole.

From a social point of view, then, the important satisfactions in literature are not of the ego's wish for mastery nor the moral demands of the superego, but rather of the dark impulses of the id, the wildest drives of our earliest childhood, whose dissatisfaction necessarily lingers on. In participating as a group in the substitute gratifications offered by art and literature, we gratify these impulses licitly, and we repeat their renunciation (as the work of art resolves itself); we identify with our cultural group and we recall the ideals of our particular culture.[28] In a very real sense, in our responses to literature, ontogeny repeats phylogeny; the individual reaction repeats the cultural subservience to reality.

In sum, although it comes in a fragmentary form as separate psychological problems touch on literature, Freud presents a quite coherent account of the response to literature from a psychoanalytic point of view. In all works of literature he found two levels, manifest and latent, a conscious content and an unconscious. To see both levels, he insisted, one must look closely at the text, as a modern critic would, in order to grasp the "mental constellation" of the whole. The reader confronted with the work experiences it on these two levels, just as the writer creating it was acting on two levels. First, there is the "fore-pleasure," the enjoyment of literature as form, as intellectual "play" (condensation and displacement and their resulting gambols in mental energy). Second, the reader identifies or otherwise becomes involved in the work of art, and, when he does, the work calls out certain of his unconscious impulses and he gratifies them vicariously and in fantasy. Some of these the genre itself satisfies; some are satisfied by broad patterns of action which evoke those unconscious impulses all the members of the writer's audience share; and, finally, some unconscious impulses satisfied by literature will be highly personal, and they account for our preferences.

In order for a writer's audience to experience the literary work in this dual, latent-manifest way, the writer must obey certain rules as he creates. These rules, then, act as canons for judging the value of works of art by showing relations between objective factors in the literary work and the subjective or affective reactions of its audience. Finally, in gratifying unconscious impulses in a world of strong imagination, literature and art perform social and moral functions; in them we re-enact the original capitulation to society we made when we grew up. And the work of art does the same, simply because the illusion must come to an end, the great globe itself dissolve and leave not a rack behind.

In a little paper called "On Transience" (1916)[29] Freud discusses this elegiac sense that beautiful things pass away, perhaps the most pervasive of all literary themes: *ubi sunt*, mutability, where are the snows of yesteryear? He recounts a conversation one summer in the Dolomites with two friends, one of them a poet, whose enjoyment of the beauty of the mountains was disturbed by the feeling that it would all fade away with the coming of winter. He was reacting in one of the typical ways of poets, and all of us, to this sense of mutability: a great feeling of sadness and a sense that impermanent things are valueless. The other typical reaction is to say that beautiful things cannot pass away; they are immortal. (I am reminded, naturally, of the *Sonnets* where these two reactions constantly interplay.) Freud, ever the apostle of rationality, reasoned with his two friends: "Since the value of all the beauty and perfection is determined only by its significance for our own emotional lives, it has no need to survive us and is therefore independent of absolute duration." But his argument was of no avail, whereupon he concluded that "some powerful factor was at work which was disturbing their judgment." He found his answer in the phenomenon of mourning, the conservatism of our love which will not leave the lost object. Both reactions are a foretaste of the defensive stratagems of mourning: one, a denial of the loss,

"These things will not fade away; they are immortal"; the other, an attempt to detach oneself from the lost object by devaluing it, saying, in effect, "It is not worthy of my love; I need not love it; I do not love it."

Freud pointed to the similarly painful renunciations caused by the great war. And yet, he concluded, "When once the mourning is over, it will be found that our high opinion of the riches of civilization has lost nothing from our discovery of their fragility. We shall build up again all that war has destroyed, and perhaps on firmer ground and more lastingly than before." It is a good remark with which to close this long summary of Freud's theory of art and literature, which should indeed build up "on firmer ground" our love of beauty.

[5]

And Beside Freud

THIS far we have been considering only Freud's views on art, which, indeed, have often been summarized before (though, if we wish to use psychoanalysis to study Shakespeare's works, it is a part we cannot be too perfect in).[1] Freud's account of the creative process appears at scattered points in his writings, in both the earliest and the latest development of these theories. But, like the theory of dreams, his theory of literature changed relatively little; his explanation of Hamlet's delay, for example, comes out much the same in 1897, 1928, or 1938. Other analysts have extended and worked out Freud's ideas, a few contemporaries of Freud's in the terms of the earliest versions of psychoanalysis, most second-generation analysts in terms of the later developments, the structural constructs of id, ego, and superego, and the discoveries and emphases of ego psychology, defenses, adaptive maneuvers, the notion of neutralized energy as well as libidinal and aggressive. Where Freud's remarks on art are brief and scattered, these other writers have tackled the various problems individually and in detail.

Strangely, the problem that seems to have nagged most at Freud, the writer's innate gifts, the artistic constitution, has received the least attention from other analytic writers on art.[2] Ernst Kris, however, has given a comprehensive account of artistic inspiration—the artist responds passively to the drives of the id, then actively masters and reproduces them at the ego level. Thus, the artist must be, not a helpless neurotic, but a man with an unusually strong ego (as, indeed, was implicit in Freud's view).

Many of the psychoanalytic writings after Freud on the theory of art have tried to find a sort of lowest common denominator which will define the literary impulse. A. A. Brill has suggested simply that poetry satisfies oral or sucking needs through the rhythmical expression of pleasurable sounds. Other writers, notably Ludwig Jekels and Hanns Sachs, have turned to the more mythic aspects of psychoanalysis and identified the creative impulse as Eros, the drive to unite oneself with reality, and the impulse toward form as Thanatos, the drive to destroy, the work of art representing a fusion of the two. Still others have treated literature as a defense on the part of the writer as well as a direct gratification. Edmund Bergler, for example, has treated writing as the writer's defense against very early childish wishes to become passive and suffer by being completely dependent on the mother; Hanns Sachs suggests that literary productions relieve the writer's feeling of guilt about his fantasies by embodying them (and himself) in what he hopes is a perfect form. Dr. Harry Lee has tried to explain the compulsive quality of literary production, the writer's feeling that he *must* create, as an attempt magically to undo aggressive impulses. Under the influence of Melanie Klein, a number of analysts in England have developed the "restitution" theory, the idea that the artist tries to rebuild in his works the loved ones he destroys in his fantasies.[3] There is little need, though, to choose among these theories, for any particular writer probably has a combination of such impulses and defenses. As so often in aesthetic theories, either-or must give way to both-and.

Other psychoanalytic writers have treated in a general, theoretical way the work of literature by itself (in so far as we can ever consider it apart from writer or reader). Ludwig Jekels and Edmund Bergler have suggested that artistic unity serves both artist and reader by balancing and resolving competing psychic tensions. Other writers have considered the problem of "pure form" as an attempt to distance the artist and his audience from raw reality. Plot splitting and doubling have been treated by both analytic and nonanalytic writers as attempts to isolate and project conflicting psychic impulses.[4] Particularly important to future psychoanalytic criticism is the recent work in England and by Lawrence S. Kubie in this country on symbolism and its relation to ego psychology and the preconscious. The theories evolved suggest that symbols play a very basic and generalized role in all our adaptations to reality; thus literature again, as with Freud, becomes central to human life.[5] Other writers have dealt with language (obviously a crucial factor in the future of any literary criticism), both generally but also with respect to particular kinds of language: ambiguity, obscene words, figures of speech (particularly useful in considering Shakespeare), clichés, and rhythm (with suggestions ranging from the ingenious notion that rhythm re-creates the jouncing of our prenatal state to the blunt behaviorist view that rhythm is "reinforcement").[6]

With respect to the problem of reader response, later analytic theorists have tended to start with the idea of identification. In this area of literary criticism (as in many others), Edward Bullough's study of psychic "distancing" in art has proved remarkably fruitful. Ernst Kris has gone on to suggest that unconscious impulses represent another kind of reality from which the artist establishes the reader's "distance" through form; thus he gives form a key role in enabling us to take pleasure in representations of the unpleasant, that is, to experience catharsis. Ludwig Jekels has studied pity and shown its relation to fear, and Dr. Daniel Schneider has expounded the dynamics of catharsis as a sequential process.[7] A speculation by the art critic Roger Fry (nonanalytic, even anti-analytic) leads to the idea that form in art represents an abstract recurring pattern of emotional life. His suggestion finds support in recent psychoanalytic studies of identification, particularly the apparent growth of identification from its most childish form, simply eating the object, to a much more sophisticated process of identifying with a pattern of satisfaction and nonsatisfaction.[8] "I know," T. S. Eliot wrote of his method of composition, "that a poem or a section of a poem tends to appear first in the shape of a rhythm before developing into words, and that this rhythm is capable of giving birth to the idea and the image."

Finally, very little psychoanalytic writing on art and literature, even that which looks primarily at the audience, attempts to set the work in relation to a historical audience, for psychoanalytic theory (up until quite recently) saw our earliest family relations as determining culture and therefore as prior to historical setting in determining our reaction to works of art. An exception to this general ahistoricity is Walter Abell's study of the changing conventions of a medieval monster image; his book itself is based on Ernst Kris's study of the growth of caricature as an art form. Also, Franz Alexander has studied modern art as the unconscious expression of a cultural *zeitgeist*. Possibly the psychoanalytically oriented anthropologists may open a way to look at a work of art as an expression both of an individual psyche and of the "psyche" of an entire culture (as the late Clyde Kluckhohn did for myth and ritual).[9]

Despite these lacunae, analysts other than Freud have elaborated a highly sophisticated—and scientific—theory of the creative process, one to which traditional or even "new" literary critics have paid entirely too little attention. Perhaps the best way to see the tenor of post-Freudian psychoanalytic literary theory is to consider *e pluribus unum* some of the ideas of the late Ernst Kris. An art historian turned psychoanalyst, Kris proved a brilliant theorist of psychoanalysis in general and the finest of psychoanalytic literary theorists after Freud. Some of his work on particulars I have already alluded to above; for general purposes, we can consider his broad essay "Approaches to Art" (1952).[10] In it Kris brought Freud's early discoveries about jokes and art into the framework of modern ego psychology, an approach opened up by Freud in the Dostoevsky essay but developed considerably further after his death.

By 1895 Freud had discovered the dynamic unconscious with its freight of drives and fantasies pushing for expression in dreams, neurotic symptoms, and works of art. In the early twenties certain clinical phenomena led Freud to posit a part of the unconscious that behaved more like a conscience or a parent than like a child wanting. This new element was the superego, which then required him to posit an ego from which it sprang and an id for the drives. What Freud had called "the Censor" in his early writings became the defenses operating in the unconscious part of the ego. What we think of as our conscious, intellecting selves was assigned by later ego psychology to a "conflict-free sphere of the ego" or the "autonomous ego." Needless to say (were it not for misunderstandings by critics of psychoanalysis), these terms, "id," "ego," and "superego," are not (probably) parts of the brain, but abstractions or constructs defined so as to bring clinical experience together in a meaningful way.

The result of this "structural hypothesis" has been a shift in point of view: the modern analyst sees psychic phenomena, not simply as expressions of the id and its biological roots, but from the point of view of the ego with its social and cultural tasks of adaptation, synthesis, and integration. Seen from the ego, a work of literature cannot be regarded simply as the expression of the writer's wish fulfillment; rather, it represents a complex synthesis of id strivings, ego defenses, and formal elements wrought by relatively autonomous ego activities.

As Kris puts it, early psychoanalysis stressed the generality of the basic drives, while "psychoanalytic ego psychology has sharpened our eyes for the specific within the general." One needs, therefore, to ask how the traditional themes (from the id) have varied in different cultural and socioeconomic conditions (expressed by the ego). For example, if we grant Freud's notion that Leonardo's painting of Christ with two mothers has its roots in infantile conflict, we should go further and say why Leonardo puts the three figures in a pyramidal form. Instead of accepting Freud's early division of form from content (but see above, p. 30), we should deal with their interaction.

To consider this interaction, Kris uses a case history of a girl's fantasy plus the equally pathological story of Baron Corvo to show how a work of art grows from an illicit and solitary fantasy through the ego activities of delay, translating the visual fantasy into words, and wooing the self-esteem of others as a way of warding off unconscious self-criticism (from the superego). The artist as artist has invited his audience to a "common experience in the mind" (as against a call to common action or a common spiritual experience—the artist as propagandist or priest).

Such a call does not succeed with everyone. When the aesthetic illusion ("situation," I suspect, might be a better word for what Kris is describing) breaks down or never takes hold, we realize that the aesthetic illusion ordinarily serves as a protection or defense. Aesthetic pleasure, then, is not simply the discharge of repressed emotions; the discharge must also come under the protection of the aesthetic illusion—we take pleasure, too, in our feeling of being in control. Response can be overcontrolled or distanced, too "thin," if there is no point in the work of art for identification and, through identification, energy discharge. On the other hand, control can fail, the illusion or situation break down, when not enough energy is neutralized by artistic convention. (Kris, here, is drawing on later developments in libido and instinct theory: that there are two basic drives, one to unite with and one to destroy the object, and two basic kinds of energy, libido and aggressive energy. The task of the ego is, in part, to neutralize these energies and so make them available for relatively conflict-free activities.)

The artist himself has a feeling of control, which makes art for him an almost magical activity. In magic, though, by a social agreement we and the artist hallucinate or project onto the object as if it is something else, the god or soul it represents. Art, however, presupposes the loss of this convention. Art must communicate in such a way that we recognize the object for itself. Thus, the artist passively takes in the reality he wishes to represent, then actively reproduces it, mastering it by ego and motor actions, which by a sort of feedback enable him to take more reality in, reproduce more, and so on.

The artist first receives passively (enabled to do so by his preconscious expectation that the audience will approve); then he actively creates the work of art as an extension of himself. His audience does the same. After recognizing the work of art, we receive it passively, then actively elaborate, "understand," and master it in a way parallel to the artist's. We should understand catharsis, then, as the work of art's opening the way for a neutralization of energy. And the shifts in distribution of psychic energy, the cathexes themselves, give pleasure as we move from recognition and passive stimulation to active ego control and mastery.

Among the questions Kris raises from this account are: What kinds of cathexes are involved in the different genres, the comic, for example, or the sublime? In connection with imagination and intuition, how can the ego give an id impulse not simply complete expression, no expression, or a compromise, but an expression which is overdetermined, and which, in art, gives us the feeling of a multiplicity of meanings? As for the artistic "gift," Kris notes, the original notion was of an endowment which the artist's environment either fostered or smothered. A more modern approach would ask the reversed and more sophisticated question: How did endowment change life experience? How did endowment manage to detach certain ego functions from conflict? Instead, then, of speaking of "flexibility of repression" and "sublimation" as Freud did, Kris wants to look at "neutralization" as creating conditions for the fusion of sexual and aggressive energies leading to mastery of the material. Conversely, how does the degree of pathology affect the success of an artist in his particular cultural environment? For example, the pathological artist seems to "go" in the Romantic era, but not in classical periods. How, then, is "style" an adaptive device? And what do we do with the post-Freudian artist who knows his unconscious in an intellectual, not a feeling, way?

Kris's essay, quite properly, asks almost as many questions as it answers, since he is not only using psychoanalysis to throw light on artistic problems but also our familiar reactions to art to illuminate psychological processes. Kris points particularly to "regression in the service of the ego," that is, the ability to loosen the psychic bonds and to become as a child again, not in a neurotic way, but in order to receive passively either external reality or reality from within so that the ego can then actively master it (as in jokes, art, dreams—and psychoanalytic therapy).

Kris's work is highly technical, written for the psychoanalytic sophisticate. A no less accurate book, but one much more accessible to the layman, is Professor Simon O. Lesser's *Fiction and the Unconscious* (1957).[11] A literary scholar with extensive psychoanalytic training, Professor Lesser writes in such familiar terms as form, language, point of view, and so on. He begins with the "narcotic" view of literature, the earliest psychoanalytic view that fictions give us gratifications life deprives us of, but goes on to show "fiction provides us with images of our emotional problems expressed in an idiom of characters and events." Thus, he moves from the original view that literature simply expresses an impulse to the more modern one, that literature expresses both an impulse and its adaptation.

In life, he notes, conflict is painful, yet in fiction it gives us pleasure—why? Because a successful fiction achieves a real balance between the claims of id, superego, and ego. Fiction at least expresses and often grants repudiated unconscious desires, albeit in a disguised form. The disguise itself is a concession in the direction of the superego, and a further superego satisfaction is the way fiction customarily metes out to its characters punishment and retribution for their forbidden drives. For the reader, his superego behaves like a forgiving parent after a confession (expression) of these forbidden impulses. In this sense a good fiction gives "punishment-with-love."

In fiction, form (Lesser defines it as "the whole group of devices used to structure and communicate expressive content") gives pleasure in itself, simply the pleasure of using all our minds. Form enables us to "spy on" the characters better, at the same time that it protects us in this slightly illicit acivity. Form also relieves guilt or anxiety by expressing particular defenses. In general, by keeping the unconscious materials of the story masked with order and control, form binds the unconscious material through the synthesizing and integrating functions of the ego—it gives us a sense of our own mastery and almost a child's pleasure in watching a parent (the author) doing a stunt.

The language of fiction is close to primary-process thinking: it tends to be pictorial, to tell its story in juxtaposed images. This kind of language is ideal, therefore, for putting our own problems into an external world, giving them order but at the same time preserving ambiguities. The swift movement of fiction (as against the real time our egos live in) involves less anxiety and, again, lets us "spy" better.

Fictions distance material by objectifying it. They also "bind" the material by tying it down to the story so that flights of fantasy do not go too far. At the same time, the story opens up fantasies; it busies our conscious egos, and the less conscious parts of ourselves are free to enjoy rapid, pre-verbal associations. We identify with and mentally act out the different competing elements in the story. We "analogize," that is, we invent quick little fantasies relating material to our own lives and thus we link ourselves further to the story's hero. Then, late in the story, if it has an unhappy ending, we, in effect, release ourselves and, distanced, watch the hero's punishment—our own egos reestablish control over our unconscious reactions. This is the meaning of "catharsis."

Control must take us back, too, to what is, after all, our real subject, Shakespeare, for whom this opening theoretical overview is only a context. This survey has, I hope, justified its length by putting aside the *Vulgärfreudismus* that so many literary people take for the psychoanalytic theory of literature; "the notion that psychoanalysis regards the artist as the prisoner of his emotions and the victim of his conflicts and that it reduces his art to 'nothing but' the automatic, helpless response to them"—so Professor Louis Fraiberg has phrased it in contrasting the older and newer psychoanalytic views.[12] The modern psychoanalytic critic does not simply pounce on an oedipus complex or a phallic symbol. Rather, modern psychoanalysis sees the creative process as, like everything else in life, a complex dialectic of impulse and defense. To some extent such an approach was implicit in all of Freud's work, even his very earliest comments on literature. It is, nevertheless, only with the emergence of ego psychology that the full usefulness of psychoanalysis to literature becomes clear.

Psychoanalysis offers a comprehensive view of the literary process as a whole and of each of its stages, writer, work, and reader, of many details such as the role of particular genres, and of such basic issues as the question of aesthetic value. Such a view of literature, moreover, has scientific backing, not perhaps the niceties a philosopher might demand, but the principles, after all, do stem from the experience of hundreds of working analysts and their patients. Further, the psychoanalytic view stands not far from the traditional views of, say, Aristotle or Keats or Castelvetro. Its notions of value, catharsis, the moral function of literature, the role of details in the work, the productive madness of the creative process, these are all highly traditional ideas. The psychoanalyst, after all, looks at the same nature that critics and artists have always viewed, and psychoanalytic criticism has no radical disagreements with traditional ideas about literature. Rather, her principles are, as good criticism has always been,

discovered, not devised,
Are Nature still, but Nature methodised.

Part II

THE
PSYCHOANALYTIC
VIEW OF
SHAKESPEARE

[6]

Freud on Shakespeare

We can start this survey of psychoanalytic views of Shakespeare on very solid ground by noting that Sigmund Freud was not a literary critic or scholar, but a psychologist. Freud's comments on Shakespeare are scattered through his works, not systematic, but incidental to his real study, the mind of man. Only five times did Freud set out to analyze systematically a work by Shakespeare. Mostly, the psychologist used the poet's insights as evidence for his own. To use Freud's remarks on Shakespeare for literary purposes we must turn them inside out, making his inductions deductive applications of general psychological principles to particular aspects of Shakespeare's plays and poems. When we do, we find his remarks are not without purely literary interest. Further, if we take all of Freud's remarks on Shakespeare, from his fairly extended analyses of *Hamlet, Macbeth,* and *King Lear* to his unglozed quotations, they establish him as a Shakespearean commentator of more than passing importance. Conversely, the student of psychoanalysis will find in these comments much that illumines the workings of Freud's own mind, particularly a curious ambivalence in his attitude toward Shakespeare, although Freud admired the poems and plays greatly.

Freud thought Shakespeare purely and simply "the greatest of poets," [1] and used him as a touchstone with which to test the status of other writers, Dostoevsky, for example,[2] although he thought the cultural level of Shakespeare's England, which he measured by its standards of cleanliness, low: "We read that there was a big dung-heap in front of his father's house in Stratford." [3] He felt, moreover, that Shakespeare's genius should not be placed above examination, that genius "should not be called upon as an explanation until every other solution has failed." [4] Freud's biographers tell us that he began reading Shakespeare at the age of eight and read him over and over again; he was always ready with a Shakespearean quotation. He admired particularly Shakespeare's power of expression (Freud himself was no mean stylist) and his insights into human nature. Dr. Jones says that Shakespeare was Freud's "favorite," [5] and Joan Rivière, in speaking of "his astonishing knowledge of literature," noted "his memory, especially for Shakespeare." [6] He knew English well (and French, Italian, and Spanish),[7] and most of his quotations from Shakespeare are in English rather than German; he urged his fiancée Martha, if she could not understand some of his quotations in English, to "consult none other than A. W. Schlegel's translation." [8]

Among his psychoanalytic friends, "Shakespeare," Hanns Sachs writes, "was the most frequent topic of our discussions when they turned to literature." Sachs also recalled Freud's showing him how Shakespeare could display or conceal his characters' motivations at will, throwing logic to the winds and courting contradictions if they suited the emotional situation.[9] The *Minutes* of the Vienna Society record Freud's saying that incest, as such, occurs comparatively rarely in Shakespeare's plays because "most of his plays are adaptations of old texts and that the texts are therefore not really his own." [10] Ludwig Binswanger remembered Freud's stating it was a well-known idea that Shakespeare's extensive use of disguise, one person masquerading as another, was a dramatic device corresponding to substitution of setting in dreams.[11]

In spite of his admiration of Shakespeare's works, Freud entertained doubts about their authorship, not unnaturally in a way, for Freud was often interested in people or things not being what they seemed to be, dreams of slips of the tongue, for example. He did, however, reject the Baconian hypothesis,[1] albeit on the doubtful grounds that, "in that event Bacon would then have been the most powerful brain the world has ever borne, and it seems to me that there is more need to share Shakespeare's achievement among several rivals than to burden another man with it." [2] For a time he flirted with the notion that Shakespeare's face seemed more Latin than English, "could therefore not be that of an Anglo-Saxon but must be French, and he suggested that the name was a corruption of Jacques Pierre." Freud later told Jones that he had gotten this idea from "Professor Gentilli of Nervi." [3] Even so, Freud greatly admired the English and rather disliked the French—changing Shakespeare's nationality meant no compliment to the poet.

Finally, however, Freud settled down with the notion that the plays were written by Edward de Vere, 17th Earl of Oxford. About 1923 he read J. Thomas Looney's *Shakespeare Identified* (London: C. Palmer, 1921) and in 1926 expressed his enthusiasm for the idea to Jones. A year later he reread the book, and in 1928 he asked Jones (whose essay on *Hamlet* had already established him as the Shakespearean in the circle) to investigate the psychoanalytic conclusions that would result from assigning the plays to Oxford. He was disappointed at Jones's skeptical reply.[4] In 1930 he wrote Theodore Reik, "I have been troubled by a change in me . . . I no longer believe in the man from Stratford." [5] and in that year he began to state his doubts about the authorship of Shakespeare's works publicly.

In a speech accepting the Goethe Prize he announced, "It is undeniably painful to all of us that even now we do not know who was the author of the Comedies, Tragedies, and Sonnets of Shakespeare; whether it was in fact the untutored son of the provincial citizen of Stratford, who attained a modest position as an actor in London, or whether it was, rather, the nobly-born and highly cultivated, passionately wayward, to some extent *déclassé* aristocrat Edward de Vere." [6] (Either way, his description is hardly flattering.) Also in 1930 Freud added a footnote to the new edition of *The Interpretation of Dreams* stating that he had "ceased to believe that the author of Shakespeare's works was the man from Stratford." [7]

In complimenting Dr. Richard Flatter on his translation of the *Sonnets,* he referred him to Gerald H. Rendall's *Shakespeare's Sonnets and Edward de Vere* (London: J. Murray, 1930) and said, "The sonnets become much more understandable" with the realization that the Earl of Oxford wrote them.[8] In another letter Freud related Lear's three daughters and the relative dates of their marriages to Oxford's three daughters and the dates of their marriages; he described *King Lear* as a play symbolically compensating for the fact that Oxford was a wretched father. If Oxford was Shakespeare, Freud said, he had suffered the miseries of Othello, too. Freud accepted the identification of Lord Derby, Oxford's first son-in-law, as Albany in *Lear* and Horatio in *Hamlet.* He went on to deduce from the discrepancy between the dates of publication and performance and the date of Oxford's death (1604) that "the poet did not finish one play after another," but worked on several at once, so that when he died he left several unfinished. These, Freud concluded, were finished by friends.[9]

In 1935, in an addition to his autobiography, Freud withdrew the observation (so useful to an oedipal reading of the play) that "Shakespeare wrote *Hamlet* very soon after his father's death," and announced, instead, that he was "almost convinced" that Oxford was the author, and for the first time mentioned Looney by name.[10] James Strachey, Freud's translator, pointed out that the connotation of the name had the unfortunate effect of strengthening the scholarly view that the Oxfordian hypothesis was crackbrained, but Freud inserted the name in the American edition anyway.[11] In 1938, on Freud's arrival in England, Looney wrote him a note of welcome;

Freud replied in a letter expressing admiration for Looney's "remarkable book, to which I owe my conviction about Shakespeare's identity, as far as my judgment in this matter goes." [12] Even in his last writings, Freud clung to the idea, relating Hamlet's oedipus complex to the fact that the Earl of Oxford's beloved father had died when the supposed playwright was still a boy, and his mother (whom he later repudiated) had quickly remarried. "The name *William Shakespeare* is very certainly a pseudonym, behind which a great mysterious stranger [*ein grosser Unbekannter*] is hidden." [13]

Freud's Oxfordian views on authorship have always presented a troublesome dram of eale to anyone trying to gain Freud a hearing in literary circles. Elsewhere * I have tried to pull the thorn by showing that Freud's doubts about authorship are part of a general pattern of ambivalence in his personality, of which he himself was well aware (although he did not alter his views because, I suppose, there are always enough Oxfordians around to keep one another convinced). Freud noted, for example, in his Goethe Prize essay the importance for all of us of affective relations with great men but noted, too, that such feelings—as toward a father—will be ambivalent: we will admire and emulate, but we will also resent. And Freud's phrasing in his last published words on authorship, *"ein grosser Unbekannter,"* suggest that his own feelings toward Shakespeare were not devoid of such filial ambivalence.

Ernest Jones interprets Freud's doubts about Shakespeare's identity, along with his interest in telepathy and the occult, as showing a wish that "a certain part of reality could be changed," presumably by just thinking it changed. I believe Jones's interpretation can be supplemented by recognizing that, for Freud, the artist was pre-eminently the man who wishes a changed reality into being through the "poetic license" that so concerned Freud in his writings on literature in general. We can see these feelings in a variety of Freud's writings about artists from his pre-psychoanalytic days to the very end. "Poets are irresponsible beings; they enjoy the privilege of poetic license." The artist "is actually a being of a special kind, exalted, autocratic, villainous, and at times rather incomprehensible." In his artistic fantasies "he actually becomes the hero, king, creator, favorite, he desired to be without pursuing [like the scientist] the circuitous path of creating real alterations in the outer world." He is the "great man," more powerfully endowed sexually, who "got there before the other," who "has the master key to open with ease all female hearts, whereas we stand helpless at the strange design of the lock," who, "with hardly an effort," gets at "the deepest truths, to which we others have

* "Freud and the Poet's Eye," *Literature and Psychology*, XI (1961), 36–45.

to force our way, ceaselessly groping amid torturing uncertainties."

Much as we may regret Freud's Oxfordian vagary, we need to recognize that it stems from an ambivalence we probably all feel to some degree toward Shakespeare; also, that this ambivalence was, for Freud, adaptive in an important way. Had he not seen the artist as a kind of totem whom he both resented and emulated, he might very well not have created psychoanalysis which bridges science and art.

Happily, Freud did not confine his remarks on Shakespeare to eccentric views on authorship, and when he talked about the plays he had better things to say. *Hamlet* was his favorite; he would, he said, include it and *Macbeth* in a list of "the ten most magnificent works of world literature." ¹ The ghost caught his attention in this play as the supernatural elements did in *Macbeth, Julius Caesar, The Tempest,* and *Midsummer Night's Dream.*² Although he was himself an uncompromising materialist, he respected (and, I think, envied) the poet's "right" to the unreal. "We adapt our judgement to the imaginary reality imposed on us by the writer, and regard souls, spirits and ghosts as though their existence had the same validity as our own has in material reality." ³

Freud's most famous statement about *Hamlet*, indeed, his most famous contribution to Shakespeare scholarship generally, was to point out Hamlet's oedipus complex. Perhaps, though, it is not so much that Freud brought the oedipus complex to *Hamlet* as that *Hamlet* brought the oedipus complex to Freud. In the very letter (dated 15 October 1897) in which Freud first said, "I have found love of the mother and jealousy of the father in my own case, too, and now believe it to be a general phenomenon of early childhood," he immediately went on to apply the concept to *Oedipus Rex* and *Hamlet*. It is almost as though the two plays guided him in his self-analysis. Indeed, as he wrote a month later, "I can only analyse myself with objectively acquired knowledge (as if I were a stranger); self-analysis is really impossible." He related his discovery to the *effect* of *Oedipus Rex:* "Every member of the audience was once a budding Oedipus in phantasy, and this dream fulfillment played out in reality causes everyone to recoil in horror, with the full measure of repression which separates his infantile from his present state." He treated *Hamlet* differently, however, referring the complex to Shakespeare's unconscious and showing that the character and hesitation of Hamlet are lifelike. He used the oedipus concept to explain Hamlet's hesitation (despite his readiness to act in the cases of Laertes, Rosenkrantz, and Guildenstern), his pangs of conscience (guilt), his coldness to Ophelia, his sexual distaste, and his final destruction.⁴

(In a curious Freudian slip, Freud had substituted Laertes' death for the impetuous killing of Polonius.)

After some hesitation [5] Freud first publicly stated his reading of *Hamlet* in *The Interpretation of Dreams* (1900). He said, first, that in *Oedipus Rex* the wish is acted out while in *Hamlet* it is repressed. This, he said, showed "the secular advance of repression in the emotional life of mankind." Second, he pointed out that Hamlet hesitates in avenging his father, although he can act resolutely in other things, because "Hamlet is able to do anything—except take vengeance on the man who did away with his father and took that father's place with his mother, the man who shows him the repressed wishes of his own childhood realized." Third, Freud argued that his reading of *Hamlet* explained Shakespeare's distaste for sexuality at this period (giving *Timon* as an example) and fitted in with Georg Brandes' statement that *Hamlet* was written after the death of Shakespeare's father and his son Hamnet. (As we have seen, Freud's Oxfordian fancies made him withdraw these two corroborations in 1930.) Freud related his oedipal or father-and-son reading of *Hamlet* to *Macbeth* ("written at approximately the same period"), which, he said, dealt with the theme of childlessness. "It can, of course," he concluded, "only be the poet's own mind which confronts us in Hamlet." [6]

In this first period of discovery Freud wrote a highly significant (and much-neglected) essay, "Psychopathic Characters on the Stage," which, as we have seen, amounts to a psychoanalytic reworking of the traditional idea of dramatic catharsis. He discussed the preconditions for the enjoyment of a psychopathic character on the stage, using Hamlet as the example of a successful characterization: (1) The character must not start out psychopathic, he said, but must become psychopathic in the course of the play. (2) The impulse the character represses must be one common to all of us, if we are to identify ourselves with him. (3) The impulse struggling into consciousness must never be named, so that the spectator is carried along unaware. This is the most important condition (and one almost invariably disregarded by post-Freudian dramatists); if it is not observed, the spectator's resistance is mobilized. "The conflict in *Hamlet*," he somewhat haughtily said, "is so effectively concealed that it was left to me to unearth it." [7]

At a 1907 meeting of the Vienna Society Freud used Hamlet to explain a patient, again asserting that Hamlet cannot carry out his vengeance because he sees his own image in his rival. [8] At a later meeting he stated again that the play was Shakespeare's reaction to the deaths of his father and his son, giving Brandes as his authority. [9]

In a seminar in 1910 a student labored the hypothesis that Hamlet's splitting of his attitude toward his father between Claudius and Polonius was like the splitting up of a personality in dreams. Freud dismissed the matter as a "well-established fact." [10]

After this first period of discovery Freud added little new to his oedipal explanation of *Hamlet,* although he repeated it often: in his American lectures,[11] in his analysis of Michelangelo's "Moses" [12] (where he did, however, make it clear that the oedipus complex explained the *effect* of *Hamlet,* as well as Hamlet's hesitation and Shakespeare's choice of subject), in the *Introductory Lectures,* [13] in his autobiography,[14] and in his analysis of *The Brothers Karamazov.*[15] A comparison of this 1928 version with his original formulation in 1897 shows—slightly—the intervening development in psychoanalysis. The early insight stresses the portrayal of a neurotic crisis: Hamlet's unconscious impulse acted out by another and his unconscious sense of guilt for it. Hence, Hamlet delays; he is sexually cold toward Ophelia—a displacement of his hostile wish from his father to her: "Why wouldst thou be a breeder of sinners?" "And," says Freud, "does he not finally succeed, in just the same remarkable way as my hysterics do, in bringing down his punishment on himself and suffering the same fate as his father, being poisoned by the same rival?" The 1928 version, however, accents the defenses against the impulse: it is projected onto Claudius, allowing the sexual rivalry then to emerge. The projection enables Hamlet to displace his guilt, transforming the guilt for the impulse to take his father's place into self-reproach for delay and into a sense of the rottenness of all men.

In a still later reference to his insight, Shakespeare's use of the oedipus complex in *Hamlet,* Freud said, was evidence for the general principle that poets are more sensitive to unconscious attitudes than most people.[16] In *An Outline of Psychoanalysis,* which he was working on up to his death, he rather wryly commented on his discovery about *Hamlet,* "The general lack of comprehension displayed by the literary world showed how ready is the mass of mankind to hold fast to its infantile repressions." [17]

One would expect a psychiatrist to be interested in the vexed question of Hamlet's madness. Freud, however, seems to have taken it for granted that Hamlet was not mad, and refers to Hamlet's madness only to suggest by analogy that the madness of dreams, like Hamlet's, is not without method.[18] Dreams, too, conceal the truth under "a cloak of wit and unintelligibility." They are "but mad north-north-west." [19]

Pretty clearly *Hamlet* seems to have been Freud's favorite play; at least he quoted from it more than from any other. For example, he used, "Thrift, Horatio, thrift [sic]" to epigrammatize the economy of wit; [20] "the funeral baked meats" furnished a metaphor for jokes where one element serves two purposes.[21] "There needs no ghost . . . come from the grave / To tell us this," said Freud, as he made an obvious point.[22] On the other hand, Theodore Reik recalls a lecture in which Freud urged his audience not to dismiss prematurely the distinctly unobvious point he was raising "from the tomb of the past, like the Ghost in *Hamlet*," but, rather, "As a stranger give it welcome." [23]

Freud's favorite quotation (from any source), says Dr. Jones, was:

> There are more things in heaven and earth, Horatio,
> Than are dreamt of in your philosophy.[24]

Apparently Freud used it frequently in conversation; in his writings, it turns up at least five times. In his analysis of wit, he quoted Lichtenberg's joke, "But there is also in philosophy much which is found neither in heaven nor on earth." [25] He quoted the couplet to say that storytellers, those "valuable allies" for the psychoanalyst, know much "that our academic wisdom does not even dream of." [26] He compared Hamlet's words to Leonardo's "*La natura è piena d'infinite ragioni che non furono mai in isperienza.*" [27] He used the quotation to state his own surprise at one difficult case; [28] he also used it to define occultism [29] (a subject in which he was much interested).

He used, though, many quotations from *Hamlet* besides I.v.166–167. False constructions in analysis he compared to Polonius' "bait of falsehood," [30] and from Jean Paul who, in turn, was quoting Polonius, he noted, "Brevity is the soul of wit." [31] Hamlet's love verses to Ophelia served to illustrate the idea that the obsessional neurotic's universal doubts are in reality a doubt of his own love,[32] and with "words, words, words," he dismissed a controversy.[33] He used "madness" with "method in't" to discuss delusions; [34] we have already seen him use this phrase and Hamlet's "mad north-north-west" in discussing the madness of dreams.[35] In one of his own dreams he came across "caviare to the general" as an association.[36] Freud twice commented on Hamlet's remark, "Use every man after his desert, and who should 'scape whipping?" The first time he said, "There can be no doubt that whoever holds and expresses such an opinion . . . that man is ill." [37] Yet twenty-one years later he himself wrote to Arnold Zweig to dissuade him from writing Freud's biography, "Wasn't Prince Hamlet right when he asked who would escape a whipping if he had his just deserts?" [38]

More pleasantly, he complained to Martha that a Jewish holiday

kept them from speaking because centuries ago Jerusalem was destroyed: "But what's Hecuba to me?" [39] In the "to be or not to be"
soliloquy Freud pointed to the oddity of having Hamlet wonder about
a life after death when he has just spoken to a ghost.[40] "That undis-
covered country, from whose bourn no traveller returns," served him
as a euphemism for death,[41] and "Thus conscience does make
cowards of us all," he used to illustrate the discontents and inhibitions civilization must impose on us.[42] He analyzed a joke about
Arthur Schnitzler based on holding "the mirror up to nature." [43]
Calling Hamlet "a world-famous neurotic," he quoted against over-
hasty analysts, "You would pluck out the heart of my mystery," [44]
and to show man's faith in the omnipotence of thoughts, he recalled
Claudius' "My words fly up." [45] Freud misquoted Hamlet's "the
readiness is all" as "to be in readiness"; his translators, however,
changed Freud's already English phrase to "ripeness," thus confusing
it with *King Lear,* V.ii.11.[46] Finally—all too finally—on fleeing
Vienna in 1938, he wrote leaving his brother the good cigars and,
evidently referring to his troubles with the Gestapo, said, "The rest
—you will know what I mean—is silence." [47]

Although Freud quoted (and misquoted) *Hamlet* far more than
any other of Shakespeare's plays, he did have interesting things to say
about the rest. In the *Henry IV* plays, the humorous effect of Falstaff
(like that of Don Quixote) illustrated his formula, "economized expenditure of affect" or feeling. That is, we expect to feel indignation
at the knight (the fat one) for his gluttony, cowardice, and dishon-
esty, but we don't because of his shape, the harmlessness of his activities, the comic lowness of those he deceives, and the fact that he
ultimately becomes a puppet in Hal's hands. We "turn all we econo-
mize in him in indignation into comic pleasure." Like many another
comic character, "Sir John's own humor really emanates from the
superiority of an ego which neither his physical nor his moral defects
can rob of its joviality and security." [1]

Freud quoted Falstaff's "if reasons were as plentiful as blackber-
ries," [2] not once, but twice,[3] and in his self-analysis the misquotation
of *I Henry IV,* V.i.127, as "thou owest Nature [it should be 'God']
a death" played an important part in one of his chains of association.[4] Ernest Jones explains the misquotation as derived from
Tristram Shandy, Book V, Ch. 3, although the phrase also occurs in
Wilhelm Meisters Lehrjahre, B. VI. Anyway, Freud did not change
it when he included the analysis in *The Interpretation of Dreams,*[5] or
when he repeated the phrase in his 1915 paper on war.[6] "Discharge
thyself of our company, Pistol" was an example of "the double mean-

ing of a name and of a thing denoted by it." [7] In analyzing one of his own dreams he noted, "Wherever there is rank and promotion the way lies open for wishes that call for suppression. Shakespeare's Prince Hal could not, even at his father's sick-bed, resist the temptation of trying on the crown." [8] The implication is that Hal's speech, which consciously deals with the cares of kingship, masks an unconscious wish for his father's death (as, indeed, Henry IV says).

Unlike most readers Freud did not neglect the *Henry VI* plays. He was familiar enough with them to find an association in analyzing one of his own dreams between the putting of a flower in his buttonhole with the scene in *I Henry VI* (II.iv), "which represented the beginning of the Wars of the *Red* and *White* Roses." [1]

Another play Freud knew well enough to dream about (although he discounted the supernatural elements)[1] was *Julius Caesar*. The part that seems to have affected him most was Brutus' speech justifying himself to the crowd in III.ii. In the antithetical structure of Brutus' sentences Freud found a pattern of ambivalence in his own emotional life: "I had been playing the part of Brutus in the dream." He had actually, as a child, played the part of Brutus in a duologue of Schiller's, although, Jones points out, he failed to mention its "pronouncedly parricidal content." In further analyzing this dream, Freud returned to the phrase, "As he was ambitious, I slew him," which he associated to Prince Hal's putting on the crown (see above).[2] This same speech with its juxtaposition of "as Caesar loved me" and "I slew him" served to describe a patient, "Rat Man's," repressed hatred for his father.[3] (Although Freud did not say so, this psychological reading could be said to throw some light on Brutus' repressed feelings, too.)

He used Antony's ironic "for Brutus was an honorable man" as an example of representing an idea through its opposite, as in wit and dreams; [4] another phrase from Antony's speech, "My heart is in the coffin here [*sic*]" served as a way to say his own real interest was not in medical practice, but in the study of neurosis.[5] Finally, he gave the murdering of Cinna for his name as an instance of the practice, common to magic, dreams, forgettings, and *lapsus linguae,* of using the name in lieu of the person.[6]

Although Freud found the opening love contest in *King Lear* "an improbable premiss," [1] he devoted a large part of his most polished literary essay, "The Theme of the Three Caskets" (1913), to elucidating it. Cordelia's behavior, he said, reminds one of other stories (for example, Cinderella, Psyche, or the choice of Paris) in which the third of three women surpasses the other two. Often this third woman is mute, and muteness in dreams or stories frequently symbolizes death. Freud therefore concluded that Cordelia, the third, the mute woman, as in the tradition of triple mother goddesses, stood for death. The fact that she is the most attractive and loving, he said, is a case of "replacement by the opposite" which often occurs in dreams and stories where the reality is too grim. Lear's initial rejection of Cordelia, then, signifies his resistance to death and his longing for the love of woman. His final entrance is also a reversal: Lear's carrying Cordelia symbolizes his own being carried away by the ultimate mother, Mother Earth. Only in these terms, said Freud, could the *effect* of the tragedy be accounted for.[2]

There are some personal sidelights to this essay. In 1883, long before his discovery of dream symbolism, he wrote Martha calling her Cordelia, apparently because she had a sore throat. Laughingly he recounted to her a conversation with Breuer in which he told Breuer that he called his sweetheart Cordelia, although in reality they could say anything to each other. Breuer replied that he, too, always called his wife Cordelia—because she was incapable of displaying affection, even to her own father.[3] At the time of writing the essay itself (a year before it was published), he dismissed it (to Ludwig Binswanger) as a "trifle," "pleasant to discuss . . . at length during a walk along the lake, but not important enough to write about."[4] A year later he commented to Ferenczi that a man's fate "assumes the form of one (or several) women," noted that he was particularly close to his daughter Anna, and hinted, "You will long ago have guessed the subjective condition for the 'Choice of the Three Caskets.' "[5]

As for Lear's madness, in response to a question by Dr. Richard Flatter, Freud replied that Lear's insane behavior did not "justify a diagnosis of hysteria" or "represent a consistent psychosis." The clinical inaccuracy, however, he dismissed as unimportant: "It should be enough if our instinctive reaction is nowhere upset."[6] As always, Freud was acutely aware of poetic license.

Lear's insanity, however, proved important in another context. In a letter to J. S. H. Bransom about his book, *The Tragedy of King Lear* (Oxford: B. Blackwell, 1934), Freud agreed that "the secret meaning of the tragedy" lay in Lear's "repressed incestuous claims on the daughter's love." The older married sisters have outgrown and repressed any sexual love for the father; Cordelia has not, nor can she bring herself to speak of this forbidden love. Lear's insanity in this context signifies "a forceful rejection of the content of the dream" (i.e., play) both by Lear and by Shakespeare, who, he noted, had added Lear's insanity to the sources. Lear's madness says, in effect, "Only a madman would have such desires." Freud found reinforcement of this aspect of the theme in Shakespeare's curious silence about the mother of the three girls. Freud went on to explain that his earlier discussion of *Lear* dealt with "the mythological content of the material." This new psychological angle, he said, put the earlier meaning in the background, although "I hope to show," he wrote, "that in Shakespeare's *Lear* the old meaning glimmers at times through the new one." [7]

He never did, but it is possible to see how they relate, anyway. Lear's desire for Cordelia (indeed, all his behavior in the love contest) is regressive and childish. His angry rejection of Cordelia, throwing her away to her suitor, repudiates his regressive desires, but it also repudiates her for not responding to them. Mythologically, as Freud's earlier essay showed, Lear is also childishly rejecting death. His final union with Cordelia ("Have I caught thee?") represents on the mythological level a mature acceptance of death; psychologically, it is a further regressive attempt to "have" his daughter. This ambivalence between child and wise old man is, as the Fool points out, Lear's folly throughout; it persists even to his final words, the mad insistence that Cordelia must be alive even as death is gathering them both in. This ambivalence, indeed, is not only the basis for the character of Lear (and his daughters); it is also a unifying theme of the play, the divorce of what is from what ought to be, the schism between earthly fact and heavenly value—as in the idealizing of the third, mute woman, Mother Earth, in the triad of the mother goddess.

Such a combination of the early essay and the later letter would make *Lear* the play that Freud most fully analyzed, although he quoted from it only once—in analyzing a joke about a fat lady, "Every fathom a queen." [8] *Love's Labour's Lost* was another play Freud quoted only once, for the proposition that,

> A jest's prosperity lies in the ear
> Of him that hears it, never in the tongue
> Of him that makes it,

a point that Freud's theory of wit explains.[1]

After *Hamlet*, *Macbeth* seems to have been the Shakespearean play that most interested Freud. In his first public statement of Hamlet's oedipus complex, he mentioned simply in passing that "*Macbeth* . . . is concerned with the subject of childlessness." [1] Freud himself did little more with the point, but other analysts, notably Ludwig Jekels, developed it, and showed how basic the ideas of parenthood, progeny, and procreation are in the play. At the Vienna Society Freud said the play gave proof of what a poet can do with a drama written for a special occasion,[2] and compared what he took to be the immediate stimulus behind *Macbeth,* the desire to pay tribute to

James I, to the "whole content of the drama," "its grandeur and its mystery." In the same way, he said, the immediate stimuli behind a dream give no insight into the whole content of the dream.[3]

Despite Freud's overweening respect for reality and despite the supernatural elements in *Macbeth*, Freud said he would include it in a list of "the ten most magnificent works of world literature." [4] *Macbeth's* unreality even prompted him to a defense of the poet's power to tamper with reality: "It is no valid criticism of Shakespeare that about the year 1000 Macbeth was a just and benevolent King of Scotland. On the other hand [the poet] should respect reality where it is established and has become common property." [5] Freud used the "hallucinations" of Macbeth and Richard III to illustrate Sir James Frazer's theories about ghosts.[6] These ghosts represent the poet's privilege; [7] although they are not frightening, we consider them as real within the play.[8]

The character of Lady Macbeth seems to have been the most interesting part of the play for Freud. In 1895 he described the case of a woman with "mysophobia," a fear of dirt, who would touch door handles only with her elbow and who washed her hands constantly. "It was the case of Lady Macbeth. The washing was symbolic, designed to replace by physical purity the moral purity which she regretted having lost." [9] A few months later the same case appeared in *Studies in Hysteria*, but was described by Freud's coauthor Breuer.[10] In 1907 the gentlemen of the Vienna Society were discussing a case of somnambulism and nocturnal delirium in which the patient would talk in her sleep but without betraying the secret at the root of her neurosis. Again, Lady Macbeth seemed apposite, and Freud suggested that talking in sleep never betrays the really important secret, only a substitute for it. Lady Macbeth, it is true, does betray the secret of the murder, but this, Freud argued, is her husband's secret, not hers, only connected to hers.[11] In an unpublished paper (described by Dr. Jones) he compared the Empress Charlotte to Lady Macbeth: "Charlotte's husband, Maximilian, had been completely impotent. . . . So she, like Lady Macbeth, had turned all her energies into ambitious plans." [12]

Finally, in 1916, relying on Ludwig Jekels' two essays on *Macbeth* (see his *Selected Papers* [New York: International Universities Press, 1952]) Freud gave a full analysis of the character.[13] What piqued Freud was the following problem: Since neurosis is caused by frustration, why does Lady Macbeth break down when she achieves success? All through the play it is she who is resolute; even in the sleepwalking scene she repeats the words she used to put heart into her husband. Yet remorse finally breaks her. Why?

In answer Freud first noted the importance of parents and children in *Macbeth*. The recent death of the childless Elizabeth provided the occasion for the play; the witches' prophecies gave the crown to Banquo's children; Macbeth's hope of children (Freud cites I.vii. 72–74) is defeated; and finally there is Macduff's shattering cry: "He has no children!" Macduff himself is a "sinister" exception to the laws of generation. Freud concluded,

It would be a perfect example of poetic justice . . . if Macbeth could not become a father because he had robbed children of their father and a father of his children, and if Lady Macbeth had suffered the unsexing she had demanded of the spirits of murder. I believe one could without more ado explain the illness of Lady Macbeth, the transformation of her callousness into penitence, as a reaction to her childlessness, by which she is convinced of her impotence against the decrees of nature, and at the same time admonished that she has only herself to blame if her crime has been barren of the better part of its desired results.

Similarly, the reaction to childlessness could also explain "the change in Macbeth to a sanguinary tyrant." Inexplicably, however, Freud assumes that the events of the play take place in *one week,* and he rejects this line of explanation.

Alternatively, Freud goes on to suggest another motive, a structural one (taken from Jekels), namely, that Macbeth and Lady Macbeth "are the divided images of a single prototype," and neither character makes psychological sense until recombined with the other; she finally fulfills the madness his pangs of conscience had anticipated earlier. "She is incarnate remorse after the deed, he incarnate defiance—together they exhaust the possibilities of reaction to the crime, like two disunited parts of the mind of a single individuality." Finally, Freud hinted (after discussing other things) that, since the sense of guilt seems to be derived from the oedipus complex, the reason the forces of conscience induce illness on attaining a forbidden end may well be simply the basic pattern taken over from the oedipus situation: we would break down were we ever to fulfill our oedipal wishes. Certainly, this explanation would have some bearing on Lady Macbeth's remorse for helping kill a man who resembled her father.

As with *Hamlet,* Freud used quotations from *Macbeth* to explain his own ideas and feelings, the prophetic character of childhood fantasies,[14] or (in a letter of 1878)[15] his feeling that the vision of his collected works startled his prescient mind as Macbeth was startled by seeing the line of English [*sic*] kings "stretch out to the crack of doom." In his paper trying to straighten out the priority of the cocaine discoveries [16] he repeated his statement, again using it to express his wealth of ideas. (No wonder in the Leonardo essay he

would say the creative man thought of his works as his children.)
Freud likewise drew on *Macbeth* to express his own hope that he
would die in harness.[17] He noted the symbolic significance of
Macduff's Caesarean birth: "Birth is both the first of all dangers to
life and the prototype of all the later ones that cause us to feel anxiety, and the experience of birth has probably left behind in us the
expression of affect which we call anxiety. Macduff of the Scottish
legend, who was not born of his mother but ripped from her womb,
was for that reason unacquainted with anxiety." [18]

We have already seen Freud's points about *Lear* which he made in
"The Theme of the Three Caskets." Oddly enough, the essay did not
say a great deal about *The Merchant of Venice.* Bassanio's speech
choosing the lead casket he found unconvincing enough to suggest
concealed motives. Following the Müller-like solar mythology of
Eduard Stucken, *Astralmythen* (Leipzig: E. Pfeiffer, 1896–1907),
he compared the Prince of Morocco and the gold casket to the sun,
the Prince of Aragon and the silver casket to the moon, Bassanio and
the leaden casket to the stars. Behind this astrological folklore, however, the three caskets are "symbols of the essential thing in woman,
and therefore of a woman herself." (He might also have mentioned
the three rings associated with Portia, Nerissa, and Jessica.) The
choice among three women relates in turn to Lear's choice among his
three daughters and other such choices among three women in
mythology. The third woman, being pale and silent or else most
lovely, represents—ultimately—Death (see above).[1] We can relate
Freud's idea to the play as a whole through the theme of venturing,
which links the romantic plot to the mercantile one. This third
woman, Death (lovely, rich, and merciful in a Christian view), stands
for the investor's return in the great venture of life itself.

Freud twice quoted with approval Otto Rank's description (in
Zentralblatt für Psychoanalyse, I, 109–110) of Portia's slip of the
tongue in the casket scene:

> One half of me is yours, the other half yours—
> Mine own, I would say—but if mine, then yours,
> And so all yours.

" 'The poet with exquisite fineness of feeling' " lets Portia's real
thought slip through. " 'It shows that the poets well understand the
mechanism and meaning of such slips and assume that the audience
will also understand them.' " [2]

In *A Midsummer Night's Dream,* although Freud regarded the
fairies as mere poetic fiction,[1] he found a larger significance in
Titania's actions. "In the neuroses belief is transposed: it is withheld

from the *repressed* material if it forces its way to reproduction [consciousness?] and—as a punishment, one might say—is transposed on to the *defensive* material. So Titania, who refused to love her rightful husband Oberon, was obliged instead to shower her love upon Bottom, the ass of her imagination." [2] (Such a reading would apply to the transpositions of the lovers, too, and to dreams, thus giving a richer significance to the play's title.) Theodore Reik recalls two other comments Freud made on *A Midsummer Night's Dream*. At a lecture in Vienna (unpublished) he suggested that the play was concerned with "the maliciousness of objects," a particular case of the magical, animistic thinking of children and primitives.[3] In a conversation with Reik in the thirties Freud said, "Look how impoverished the poet's imagination really is. Shakespeare, in *A Midsummer Night's Dream*, has a woman fall in love with a donkey. The audience wonders at that. And now, think of it, that a nation of sixty-five millions have. . . ." [4] Very early in his analytic thinking Freud found a true account of the creative imagination in Theseus' description of "the lunatic, the lover, and the poet." [5] Josef Breuer (probably at Freud's suggestion) applied the description of Peter Quince's play ("The best in this kind are but shadows") to physiological explanations of psychic processes.[6] Freud himself compared the lion that concealed Snug the joiner to lions in dreams which do not frighten the dreamer; such figures, he said, refer to superiors of whom one is not afraid.[7]

Much Ado About Nothing gave him just one quotation, Dogberry's advice to the watch to avoid thieves, which Freud applied to physicians who thought it dangerous to bring complexes to consciousness.[1] *Othello*, we have seen, served to confirm the Oxfordian hypothesis.[1] Also, in the Moor's outbursts over the lost handkerchief, Freud found an example of displacement,[2] and similarly, he quoted Desdemona's song, "I call'd my love false love," as an example of "projected jealousy." That is, the jealous one is often projecting his own impulses on his partner.[3] (Possibly the song serves by reflection, as it were, to illuminate part of Othello's motives.)

Freud made one curiously oblique reference to *Pericles*. In describing earliest childhood, he came up with the phrase, "O inch of nature!" (in English). A bit puzzled himself, he wrote to Theodore Reik asking if he could locate it. On Reik's (understandable) failure to do so, Freud urged him not to trouble himself further. "No one was able to locate it. Where I could have picked it up remains a mystery, for it is hardly likely to be of my own coining. Since, besides Shakespeare, I used to read only Milton and Byron, there is still the possibility that it might be found in Byron." (Evidently Freud is listing the English authors which were his favorites.) In the *Standard Edition,* Freud's editors did turn up the elusive quotation, not in *Pericles* itself, but in the novella based on the play, George Wilkins' "The Painfull Adventures of Pericles Prince of Tyre" (1608). The editors point out that Freud probably knew the phrase (addressed by Pericles to his infant daughter), not from stuffing his head with all such reading as was never read, but because the phrase appears in Georg Brandes' book. The incident suggests not only the workings of Freud's memory but also his extraordinary familiarity with this one critic.[1]

He caught a "Freudian slip" in *Richard II,* the Duke of York's addressing the Queen: "Come, sister—cousin I would say—pray pardon me." [1] York has just learned of his sister's death, and surely that must have something to do with his *lapsus linguae,* but Freud said simply that this was an example of a slip of the tongue used by a writer to reveal character and explained no further.

In discussing neurotics who consider themselves "exceptions" to the ordinary rules of life, Freud gave the example of Richard III's opening soliloquy. It seems to say that since Richard cannot prove a lover, he will play a villain. "So wanton a cause of action," Freud said, "could not but stifle any stirring of sympathy in the audience," and for the play to succeed "the writer must know how to furnish us with a secret background of sympathy for his hero." "The bitterness and minuteness with which Richard has depicted his deformity" have a hidden effect; they make us feel "that we ourselves could be like Richard." "Richard is an enormously magnified representation of something we can all discover in ourselves," namely, the tendency to reproach nature and destiny for our own lack of perfection and to "demand reparation for early wounds to our narcissism, our self-love," in short, the tendency to consider ourselves "exceptions." Shakespeare, however, has very subtly not revealed this aspect directly, and so he keeps us identified with his hero without our quite knowing why. Had he let us know Richard's appeal, Freud said, "our cool, untrammelled intelligence . . . would preclude any great degree of illusion." [1] Another aspect of the play, Richard's wooing of Anne beside the bier, touched on a topic of recurring interest to Freud—the poet's "right" to alter reality. The dramatist, he said, is free to shorten the natural timing of events to enhance dramatic effect so long as he only affronts probability; such a shortening is not justified "when it breaks the causal connection" (as in his supposition that the events of *Macbeth* took only a week).[2] The unreal ghosts in *Richard III* simply represented for Freud "a superstitious fear" of the slain.[3]

Romeo and Juliet served him with one quotation to describe the two political possibilities for Austria in 1934: "A plague on both your houses." [1] He illustrated the dominant influence on dreams of the wish to sleep with Juliet's "It is the nightingale and not the lark" —in dreams, only interpretations of somatic stimuli "are admitted which are consistent with the absolute censorship exercised by the wish to sleep." [2]

As we have seen, Freud felt that the *Sonnets* gave further proof that Shakespeare was the Earl of Oxford; [1] he did not say, though Shakespeareans often seem to think he did, that the *Sonnets* showed Shakespeare was a homosexual. Curiously, although he thought *The Tempest* autobiographical like the *Sonnets,* he never analyzed, he only quoted it. (The supernatural elements he took to be, again, poetic license.) [1] When he was shown a hostile book (Charles E. Maylan's *Freud's Tragischer Komplex* [Munich: Ernst Reinhardt, 1929]), which purported to give a psychoanalytic description of Freud's own personality, he simply repeated Caliban's "You taught me language; and my profit on't is, I know how to curse." [2] Ariel's song, "Full fathom five," with its notion of a sea change, he used to illustrate the substitutions which must have arisen for the real memory of killing "the primal father." [3]

Timon of Athens, he said, showed the same distaste for sexuality that *Hamlet* did and so proved it could only be "the poet's own mind which confronts us in Hamlet." [1] At the Vienna Society he said this period of embitterment (on the basis of the Brandes' dating) raised a suspicion of venereal infection.[2] A much more satisfying reference with which to conclude this long listing is his use of *Twelfth Night* in a letter to his future wife; he quoted Feste's "frolicsome lines":

> Journeys end in lovers meeting,
> Every wise man's son doth know.

> What is love? 'Tis not hereafter;
> Present mirth hath present laughter;
> What's to come is still unsure:
> In delay there lies no plenty;
> Then come kiss me, sweet and twenty,
> Youth's a stuff will not endure.[1]

And beyond that there are only trivia.[1]

Freud was indeed a lover of Shakespeare, an *amateur* in the finest sense. It is true that his views on authorship were at least eccentric if not downright hostile. It is true, too, that, quoting from memory rather than from a text, he often misquoted and that he was frequently mistaken about the facts of Shakespeare's life or of the plays;

he was far too ready to accept without questioning the vagaries of continental scholars such as Darmstetter or, in particular, Brandes. Nevertheless, a summary of Freud's remarks on Shakespeare shows two things. First, he had some extraordinary insights into Shakespeare's works; second, his treatment of Shakespeare—much greater in bulk than his comments on any other writer—established the basic methods of applying depth psychology to literature.

Freud's method was to take a pattern of mental life (which had been established scientifically) and hold it up, as it were, against the play to discover a congruous pattern. Merely establishing the congruity was not enough; Freud did not simply play (as some of his followers have) here-a-phallic-symbol-there-a-phallic-symbol. Rather, he went on to draw conclusions either about psychoanalysis or about the author, the play's effect, the probability of some or all of the plot, the structure, or the language. If about the author, Freud would point to two things: first, an infantile wish common to all men embodied in the play; then some event in the author's biography that would reactivate the wish at the time of writing the play (Hamlet's oedipal feelings at the time of John Shakespeare's death; the theme of childlessness in *Macbeth* and the English succession). If Freud's conclusion was about the play's effect on an audience, he would speak in terms of a common unconscious factor, explaining, for example, that a villain like Richard III appeals to us because he plays on our own wish to be an "exception."

Freud had relatively little to say about the play itself in isolation, except with respect to character. His comments on Shakespeare's language were almost entirely limited to showing that in wit and poetry, not logic but the prelogical primary process of unconscious thought operates. Freud remarked on structure only rarely and then in terms of the psychic mechanism of decomposition or splitting; that is, various attitudes toward the father are decomposed into the several father figures of *Hamlet;* Lady Macbeth and Macbeth are splits of a single protagonist.

Usually, if Freud was discussing the play itself, he would conclude that a certain character or event was lifelike or probable in psychoanalytic terms, that Hamlet's delay was natural under the circumstances, or that all of us make slips of the tongue as Portia does. On the other hand, he would sometimes (where an event was obviously unrealistic) find in it the truth of dreams, a psychological rather than a literal truth, the love contest in *Lear,* for example, the various ghosts, the choice among the three caskets, or Titania's showering her love on Bottom. Thus, in Freud's writings at the very beginning of psychoanalytic criticism we find the basic schism in method that has persisted ever since: psychoanalysis used on the one hand to justify the realism of the events; on the other, to find in unreal events a psychological truth.

This split, of course, is intrinsic in Shakespeare's half-medieval style, and it runs through the body of ordinary Shakespearean criticism as well as psychoanalytic studies. Yet this mingling of realism and fantasy clearly had a special relevance for Freud, bothered as he was by "poetic license." The writer possessed powers of insight and discovery that he himself wished for. At the same time the artist was a daydreaming child conjuring up a world of illusions and fantasies quite alien to the reality with which the hard-working scientist concerned himself. It can scarcely be an accident that this basic ambivalence in Freud's attitude toward the artist shows in his practical criticism of Shakespeare's works. Nor is it strange that later psychoanalytic critics should have come up against the same ambiguity, for psychoanalysis does, after all, bring together art and science, fantasy and reality.

Freud's remarks on Shakespeare also show a slight shift in his approach to literature as the concepts of psychoanalysis developed over the years. (The history of psychoanalytic concepts remains to be written; my dates, therefore, are quite approximate.) In the earliest period, from 1895 on, just as psychoanalysis in general was concerned with infantile sexuality as expressed in particular neurotic symptoms, Freud saw works of literature as essentially the working out of a neurosis (as, for example, in *Hamlet,* either the prince himself, or Shakespeare's writing the play). We can date a formal interest in myth and symbolism from about 1910 on, and the typical work of this period is "The Theme of the Three Caskets," which represents a second and somewhat contradictory approach to literature (contrast, for example, Freud's two approaches to *King Lear*). In 1908 Freud first approached the problem of character (in the sense of the enduring aspects of personality rather than neurotic crises); his first literary contribution in this field comes in the "Character-Types" essay of 1916 with its analyses of Lady Macbeth, Richard III, and Ibsen's Rebecca. This approach, like the earliest, is essentially realistic, while the intervening approach through symbol and myth is antirealistic, treating the work of art as a dream.

The papers on instincts and other metapsychological concerns that begin in 1914 have little bearing on practical criticism, but the shift in the theory of anxiety and the development of the structural hypothesis of id, ego, and superego in the early and middle twenties do suggest a synthesis of the three earlier approaches. Unfortunately, Freud's interest in studying particular works seems to have fallen off quite sharply in this period: only the essay on Dostoevsky (1928) with its passing remarks on *Hamlet* works out this later approach, which was thus left to Kris and others to develop.

As for Freud's particular insights, some of these are well known: Hamlet delays because reactivated oedipal wishes have precipitated a neurotic crisis; Lady Macbeth washes her hands in an attempt to wash off moral guilt; symbolically and mythologically the three caskets in the *Merchant of Venice* and the three daughters in *Lear* mean the three aspects of woman that represent man's fate. Others of Freud's insights are less well known than they should be: his explanation of the humorous appeal of Falstaff; the psychological approach to *King Lear;* the sense of the Macbeths as a split protagonist; his explanation of our empathy with the thoroughly unsympathetic Richard III. Readers of Shakespeare have already had to cope with a few Freudian readings; confronted with more, as in the chapters to follow, they may well cry, "Rest, rest, perturbed spirit." Freud, I am sure, would have replied, "There are more things in heaven and earth, Horatio . . ."

A Note on Scope

Après Freud, *le deluge*. The flood comes, of course, not just as writings on Shakespeare but not all phases of psychoanalysis. Nor did the flood come entirely after Freud. Long before his death in 1939 the volume of analytic writings had begun to bulk large on library shelves. In part this bulk stems from theoretical developments; in part, from differences in theoretical developments. These differences, important as they are to psychoanalytic theory, generally do not touch this present business of *Psychoanalysis and Shakespeare*. They do, however, give rise to certain troubles in the selection and ordering of material.

So far as selection is concerned, what writers come under the heading "psychoanalysis"? In the largest sense, almost any twentieth-century intellectual does, for he has been affected. In the narrowest sense, only psychoanalysts who are members of the International Psycho-Analytical Association do. Freud himself defined the badges of "psychoanalysis" differently at different times. In 1913, "Psychoanalysis stands or falls with the recognition of the sexual component instincts, of the erotogenic zones and of the extension thus made possible of the concept of a 'sexual function' in contrast to the narrower 'genital function'" (*SE*, XII, 323). In 1914, "The theory of repression is the cornerstone on which the whole structure of psychoanalysis rests" (XIV, 16), while in 1920 the recognition of the oedipus complex "has become the shibboleth that distinguishes the adherents of psychoanalysis from its opponents" (VII, 226n.). Finally, in 1923, he put them all together: "The assumption that there are unconscious mental processes, the recognition of the theory of resistance and repression, the appreciation of the importance of sexuality and of the oedipus complex—these constitute the principal subject matter of psychoanalysis and the foundations of its theory. No one who cannot accept them all should count himself a psychoanalyst" (XVIII, 247), or, I suppose, a writer of "psychoanalysis."

Writers who accept these assumptions constitute the hard core of the chapters that follow, and I can say with some confidence that I

76

have included *all* writers and writings on Shakespeare up to 1964 that meet these qualifications. Beyond this core matters get very fuzzy very quickly, however. In order to present a complete picture, I have included below writings by literary people who simply seem psycho-analytically inclined, and I have also included writings by followers of Jung, Adler, Rank, Stekel, Fromm, Sullivan, Horney, and so on, even behaviorist or experimental psychologists from academia, when they seem to deal with phenomena which an orthodox psychoanalyst would consider as "unconscious," or even, simply, when their contributions seem interesting or appropriate. My criteria, then, once we have passed the boundaries of true psychoanalysis, are sufficiently subjective so that I am unwilling to guarantee that the reader will find everyone included —or excluded—that he might wish.

Myth-and-ritual readings presented a special problem. Historically, I think, this approach to Shakespeare stems from a *mariage de convenance* of Jungian psychology to folkloric anthropology (for ex-ample, the Germanic successors to the brothers Grimm or such writers as Sir James Frazer or Gilbert Murray). Such readings are hardly "psychoanalytic," and I have excluded them except where they seemed to relate explicitly to a conception of "unconscious mental processes" even if the conception is one at which an orthodox psychoanalyst would wince. I have excluded approaches to Shake-speare through Elizabethan humours psychology and also, for the most part, through ordinary medical psychiatry (those writers in the tradition of Bucknill who classify the various insanities depicted in Shakespeare's plays).

As for the quality or value of these studies and remarks on Shakespeare, I find the percentage of "hits," real contributions, about the same as that of ordinary Shakespearean criticism, which, in my experience, has about the same batting average as a good major-league hitter. The psychoanalytic critic, however, when he strikes out seems to do a far more bizarre job of it than his literary counterpart —when psychoanalytic criticism is bad, it is horrid. Nevertheless, because my aim is to put *all* psychoanalytic criticism of Shakespeare on view, I have not excluded any item on the basis of quality alone. But since this is, or should be, a *bibliographie raisonnée*, I have taken the liberty of abbreviating my account of some of the odder items. As for my own position in all this, I am simply trying to make a lucid presentation of all psychoanalytic writings about Shakespeare. To that end I will sometimes suggest additional sources of support for a given view, but you should not assume I agree with any of these restatements and amplifications of others' positions unless I specifi-cally say so (with the vertical pronoun).

No less a problem than selecting materials was the matter of ordering them. The psychoanalytic critic on Shakespeare may draw three kinds of conclusion: first, something about Shakespeare the man, his biography; second, something about a psychoanalytic theory, usually of art; third, something about the work itself, a character or episode in it, or its effect on an audience. According to the psychoanalytic view of art, particularly the idea that in the work of art the unconscious of the artist speaks to the unconscious of his audience, all these three types of conclusion are intimately related, and a single psychoanalytic study will often draw all three kinds. To the reader of literature, however, there is quite a difference between them. Therefore, I have sorted out these various conclusions, and where a given study draws conclusions of different kinds I have mentioned it more than once. The three chapters of this section, then, correspond to those three kinds of conclusion the psychoanalytic critic draws from Shakespeare: Chapter 9, conclusions about the work itself; Chapter 8, conclusions about psychoanalytic theory; and, in the next chapter, conclusions about Shakespeare the man.

[7]

Psychoanalysis
and the Man

FREUD himself, we have seen, had relatively little to say about Shakespeare the man, except that he had great respect for Shakespeare's abilities as a writer and for his insights into human nature. Freud did suggest that the death of Shakespeare's father and son prompted *Hamlet* and a period of depression marked by sexual distaste as in *Timon* or Hamlet's harsh words to Ophelia. He found in *Macbeth* Shakespeare's supposed concern with childlessness. Mostly, alas, Freud in writing about the man Shakespeare simply insisted he wasn't Shakespeare; and Freud expressed a variety of doubts as to Shakespeare's identity, ranging from the common Oxfordian heresy to the extraordinary notion that Shakespeare was really a Frenchman named Jacques Pierre. As Jones points out in his biography, Shakespeare was not the only great man whose personality interested Freud; there were also Moses and Leonardo da Vinci, and for all three men Freud introduced questions of identity. Evidently, as Dr. Jones concludes, "something in Freud's mentality led him to take a special interest in people not being what they seemed to be." Whether because of a recognition that this was a mere idiosyncrasy of the master's or because of Dr. Jones's own resolutely Stratfordian orthodoxy, or out of a simple respect for evidence, later Freudians have been content to pass by in silence Freud's anti-Stratfordianism—with one exception.

Dr. A. Bronson Feldman has brought forth an extended analysis of the *Sonnets* to prove psychoanalytically they were written by the Earl of Oxford.[1] The only truly psychoanalytic aspect of this study, however, is Freud's letter to J. Thomas Looney, the original Oxfordian, which Feldman enthusiastically quotes. Feldman also has produced analyses of *Othello, Pericles,* and *The Comedy of Errors* to the same Oxfordian end (we shall consider them when we consider biographical readings of individual plays).

Much more interesting is Dr. Feldman's analysis of the psychology of bardolatry.[2] He notes two recurring themes: first, the use of religious imagery (Ben Jonson's loving the man "on this side Idolatry" would be an early example); second, a tendency to point to Shakespeare's financial success. He concludes that "the Stratfordian cult" persists because it gratifies unconscious wishes. That is, by accepting Shakespeare as the author of the plays, people work out through him such things as oedipal wishes for the mother (Mary Fitton, he says, was a surrogate for Shakespeare's mother; Shakespeare symbolically took possession of his mother by acquiring what Dr. Feldman takes to be the Arden coat of arms). Stratfordians also satisfy, he says, wishes for financial success; wishes to dishonor the parents (as Dr. Feldman says Shakespeare did); or wishes to attack the father (through Shakespeare's supposedly slaughtering beef). Most important, he says, Stratfordians symbolically kill their own fathers when they "kill" the true author, who is a father figure, and substitute the butcher's apprentice of Stratford (sic).

It would be interesting to see a similar analysis of anti-Stratfordian "cults"; but then perhaps there needs no analyst come from the couch to tell us the motives of those who wish to replace the bailiff's son with an earl. Professor Gordon Ross Smith has most eloquently pointed out that the evidence for Shakespeare's authorship is quite overwhelming and that no psychoanalytic conclusions based on internal evidence from the plays can shake this fact, well established by external evidence.[3] Luckily, most psychoanalytic writers have been content to accept the same documents the scholars do, and, having considered the lone Oxfordian, we are free to turn to Shakespeare himself—or his biography.

The analytic writer's use of biographical facts, though, differs rather markedly from the ordinary biographer's; indeed, it is likely to prove rather disconcerting to him. That is, the biographer is primarily interested in writing the poet's life history; for him, documentary evidence is the most reliable, internal evidence from the works the least reliable. To the psychoanalytic biographer, documentary evidence (while factually it may be the most reliable) is likely to be the least valuable psychologically.

Indeed, I know of only one psychoanalytic comment on Shakespeare which starts from an external biographical fact, a brief remark by Otto Rank at the Vienna Society in 1907 to the effect that many great poets start their careers with a kind of flight—in Shakespeare's life, his move from Stratford to London. Rank suggested that for most poets such a flight means an emancipation from the families of their childhood, from parents and siblings. Shakespeare, however, freed himself of wife and child, although Rank said they were displacements from the parents.[4]

Such external biographical facts, however, simply do not give much useful material from a psychological point of view. Documents from our own day, let alone Shakespeare's, are hardly likely to provide the kind of information the psychoanalytic biographer would wish about the infantile life of the poet, say, his feelings at the age of two toward his mother. On the other hand, the poet's choice of words and themes in his adult life, the internal evidence from his works, tells more than any document can about the infantile wishes still active in his unconscious, and one can infer the actual infantile situation. Thus, the typical psychoanalytic study of Shakespeare as a man will start from the works, either ignoring the documentary evidence or using it to confirm a family situation that agrees with the psychological pattern found from internal evidence. As the late Hanns Sachs said, the psychoanalytic biographer best utilizes external biographical data, "not by accepting them as the raw material for the work, but by using them to find and fixate the exact spot where the creative fantasy was stirred, the spot where it deviated from the reality and replaced it by a world of its own making."

At this point the Shakespearean scholar (even one who accepts the basic psychoanalytic proposition that infantile wishes still nag the adult) is likely to object. Internal evidence, he would point out, is necessarily mixed. Shakespeare could have put a given element in a play for any one of a number of reasons: because it was in his source for the play, because that was the way Elizabethans wrote plays, because someone in the King's Men wanted it that way, and so on. Reluctantly, the psychoanalytic critic (I suppose) would have to agree, although (it seems to me) he is entitled to two *caveats*.

The first is against either-or thinking. The whole point of the psychoanalytic view of art—and life—is that any given person must be seen, as it were, in terms of geological strata. Today's outcropping, be it choice of word or burst of rage, expresses a continuing growth of personality from deepest, earliest infancy to the present time. Recognizing in a literary work the infantile, unconscious strata in the author's mind does not exclude the importance of sources or conventions; rather, it puts them at their proper late and adult level.

Second, in the matter of sources, the mere fact that a given element in a play is in the source for the play does not rule it out of the author's mind. Where the writer invents the element outright or where he deliberately alters the source, we are close to his fantasy life. Where he takes over the element from a source unchanged, we are further away, but the element of choice is still there: he could have omitted it—and an author's omissions can be as revealing as his inclusions. In short, had Shakespeare wished to change his source he could have done so; were the source not congenial to his artistic invention, he would not have chosen it in the first place. Sources may qualify our reading of the man in his works; they do not rule out such reading.

In practice, Shakespeare's psychological biographers have been fairly careful in the matter of sources; virtually every psychological study of one of Shakespeare's plays that looks back through the works to the poet considers the role of the source. Psychoanalytic writers on Shakespeare have paid rather less attention to the formal exigencies of Shakespeare's stage and acting company or the tastes of his audience. Even here, though, the same considerations apply: we do things in life for many reasons at many levels; and surely Shakespeare was successful enough financially and popular enough as an author to vary convention or toss it aside where it suited him to do so. Shakespeare, Jonson, Dekker, Marlowe, Heywood, Beaumont and Fletcher—they were all writing for more or less the same stage and audience, yet their works are as different as, presumably, their personalities. Even conventions and sources do not rule out the theoretical possibility of looking back through the poet's works to his mind.

In practice Shakespeare's psychological biographers have faced just the opposite problem from his documentary biographers, a plethora of evidence rather than a paucity. There are three kinds of psychological study, each based on a different segment of the works. One group looks at Shakespeare's personality through extensive study of a single character or a single work. A second group looks at Shakespeare through over-all patterns of action in all his works or a group of them. A third group of writers, mostly nonpsychoanalytic, looks at images and metaphors rather than action or character. The permutations and combinations possible in all this are bewilderingly many, and, in hopes of keeping our course obvious, I offer at this point a chart in the form of an outline. We have already considered the lone Oxfordian and the one writer who begins with an external fact.

The remaining psychoanalytic biographers all work on the assumptions that Shakespeare was Shakespeare and that the proper place to begin the psychological study of the man is in his works, either in

I. Single works or characters:
  a. *The Sonnets* (notes 5–9)
  b. Attitudes toward the father as shown in
     i. *Hamlet* (10–18)
     ii. Others: *Caesar* (19), *Macbeth* (20–21)

THE SONNETS AND HOMOSEXUALITY

For those psychoanalytic critics who have turned to one or more isolated works for Shakespeare's psyche, the *Sonnets* have proved most popular because they are—or seem to be—openly auto-biographical. Many, many psychoanalytic writers mention them in passing to show that Shakespeare had a homosexual side; only one psychoanalytic writer has analyzed them in detail. Most simply note, as Otto Rank does, two factors in the sonnet "story": first, that woman is treated as "an evil, disturbing daemon"; second, that Shakespeare's glorification of the "friend" functions in his mind as a glorification of himself ("What is't but mine own when I praise thee?").[5] H. McC. Young has argued very strenuously *per contra* that the *Sonnets* themselves show that Shakespeare could not have been homosexual (in particular, Sonnets 20 and 151, relied on rather heavily by the pro-homosexualists).[6] A homosexual, he says, would not urge his love to marry, would find no appeal in a "woman's face," and the "one thing" with which "nature prick'd thee out for women's pleasure" would not be to his purpose nothing. But Young, evidently, is talking of the overt homosexual, and what a latent homosexual might or might not say had best be left to those whose profession requires that they know. From that medical vantage point, however, Dr. W. I. D. Scott concurs: the last four lines of Sonnet 20 explicitly rule out any overt homosexual relationship,[7] although he does not discuss the *Sonnets* at length.

Dr. Conrad van Emde Boas is the only psychoanalyst who has treated the *Sonnets* in great detail (some six hundred pages' worth) —and with considerable caution.[8] He makes it quite clear that looking back through Shakespeare's works toward his life has sharp limitations. First, he notes that the *Sonnets* and the "double-disguise plays," *Twelfth Night* and *As You Like It,* show the same pattern: a man and a woman are rivals over a "master-mistress." He denies, however, that these writings imply that Shakespeare was physically involved with some boy actor in the company; only an "intrapsychic identification" is implied. Boas is quite willing to accept the "conservative" view (represented, say, by the late Hyder Rollins) that the *Sonnets* are more like formal set pieces or drama than auto-biography. Boas, however, points out that the factual truth or falsity of the poems does not matter; they reveal Shakespeare's unconscious mind equally well whether they are true or invented. He sharply criti-cizes earlier writers (such as Oscar Wilde) who have said Shake-speare was an overt homosexual; such writers, he says, are motivated by their own guilt rather than a disinterested quest after truth. He agrees with the scholarly view that it is obvious from the documen-tary evidence about Shakespeare's life and from the customs of Shakespeare's England that he almost certainly could not have been a manifest homosexual.

Dr. van Emde Boas approaches the *Sonnets* by analyzing those ele-ments in the poems that refer to persons. He compares the descrip-tions of the persons to the mechanisms that psychoanalysis has found behind homosexuality. The first of these is the young boy's shock at the discovery that there are people in the world (women, usually his mother) who seem to lack his physical masculinity. Some-times the boy reacts by preferring in love someone who is intact, as it were, like himself. In the *Sonnets* Boas points to the poet's general tendency to identify with the beloved youth and, in particular, to the notorious Sonnet 20:

> A woman's face, with Nature's own hand painted,
> Hast thou, the master-mistress of my passion;
> A woman's gentle heart, but not acquainted
> With shifting change, as is false women's fashion;
>
> *   *   *   *   *   *   *   *   *
>
> And for a woman wert thou first created,
> Till Nature as she wrought thee fell a-doting,
> And by addition me of thee defeated
> By adding one thing to my purpose nothing.
> But since she pricked thee out for women's pleasure,
> Mine be thy love, and thy love's use their treasure.

A second mechanism in homosexuality is the young boy's over-identification with the "good mother" image, the mother as provider and forgiver. Boas finds this mechanism pervading the sonnets urging the lover to have a child, and also in Sonnets 21 and 40:

> O let me, true in love, but truly write,
> And then believe me, my love is as fair
> As any mother's child . . .
>
> I do forgive thy robb'ry, gentle thief . . .

The third mechanism is a boy's reaction to a brother who rivals him in his mother's love. He gives over his beloved to the brother against whom he feels a resentment so terrible he cannot face it consciously; instead, he shows an exaggerated tenderness. In this connection Boas points to the general triangle situation in the *Sonnets* in which the poet resigns his lady love to his friends.

In general, the homosexual elements Boas finds in the *Sonnets* are: first, the poet's tendency to identify himself with the friend; second, the poet's readiness to take the role of a mother toward the friend and to regard a father as "decrepit"; third, the poet's encouraging the triangle situation and resigning from it.

Finally, Dr. van Emde Boas turns to the facts of Shakespeare's childhood for confirmation. He finds a parallel between the *Sonnets,* the Freud-Jones view of *Hamlet,* and the birth of Shakespeare's brother Edmund (although surely Gilbert would be a more logical candidate) as a successful younger rival to the poet for their mother's love. Hamlet in this view is a projection of Shakespeare himself caught between a father figure and a successful younger rival. Boas dates the triangle episode of the *Sonnets* after 1595 and traces to it Shakespeare's "depression" after 1600. The fact that this depressive period was also one of great creativity suggests that what was bothering Shakespeare in his tragic period was not guilt about his love for his friend or a sense of betrayal, but rather the final loss of his two loves, and (against his friend) a resentment he could not face. Boas supports his view by showing statistically that those sonnets in which the poet adopts a mother role are not the same as those in which he writes of depression.

The point of his book is that, first, it is perfectly clear from the external evidence of the poet's life that he was not a manifest homosexual; it is, however, equally clear from the *Sonnets* that Shakespeare had unconscious (or, better perhaps, childish) impulses which, had he acted them out instead of writing them out, would have constituted homosexual behavior.

Probably no other psychoanalytic angle on Shakespeare has provoked such an angry response from professional Shakespeareans as the notion that the *Sonnets* are homosexual. In this controversy two facts should be borne in mind. First, the psychoanalyst (if he is being careful) is not talking about manifest homosexuality; he is talking about unconscious homosexual impulses, which are quite a different thing. He does not imply, when he says that the *Sonnets* reveal latent homosexuality, that Shakespeare's actual sex life was in any way abnormal—or, at least, unusual. Second, the psychoanalyst would say that virtually all men go through a homosexual phase in childhood, that this is a normal part of a man's development, and that most men carry a residue of this early stage all their lives. Some strongly defend against it. Luckier are those who don't, for, paradoxically, a man needs to accept the feminine component in himself to be a good heterosexual lover—if he cannot love the woman in himself, he cannot love it in another.

In general, this feminine component in a man has to do with his ability to wait, to be passive, to be sensitive and receptive to others —and to inspiration. So far as a writer is concerned, it would be almost impossible for him to create a realistic feminine character unless there were at least some part of his mind that readily identified with women. In short, such cogent defenses of Shakespeare's manifest heterosexuality as Professor Edward Hubler's and such careful probings of his latent homosexuality as Dr. van Emde Boas' coexist quite comfortably: they are talking about two quite different levels of the mind. The psychoanalyst who calls the *Sonnets* homosexual is not implying either that Shakespeare behaved "unnaturally" or that he was in this respect markedly different from other men.

If anything is odd about Shakespeare in this respect, it is his writing about the theme so much; that would suggest he was not easy in his mind about his love for the youth of the *Sonnets*. Such, anyway, is the line Professor Leslie Fiedler takes, relying heavily on the juxtaposition of poems in the collection that preceded the *Sonnets, The Passionate Pilgrim.*[9] Essentially, Professor Fiedler says, the theme of the *Sonnets* is that of Two Loves, not in the form usual to our culture, Wife and Mistress, but rather Boy and Whore.

In the *Sonnets,* the dirty puns and *double-entendres* heap scorn on sex with women; the boy is like a woman in his beauty, but not in infidelity or his genitals (Sonnet 20). *The Passionate Pilgrim* draws not only on the *Sonnets* but on *Venus and Adonis* where the theme comes out even more clearly. This Ovidian erotic poem, says Professor Fiedler, shows exactly what Shakespeare feared most about sex: the encounter of a passive male and an aggressive female. Elsewhere in his works this meeting becomes shameless lust defeating modest reason; *Venus and Adonis* and the *Sonnets* symbolize it as a boy and a woman. Professor Fiedler guesses that Shakespeare longed for a way of being conceived without heterosexual intercourse (as in the banishment of Venus from the wedding masque in *The Tempest* or Posthumus' "Is there no way for men to be, but women/Must be halfworkers?"). Sex with a woman for Shakespeare, and, no doubt, for many of his half-medieval audience, was something to fear and distrust. At the same time it seems clear that Renaissance readers and writers recognized the homosexual basis of a cult of friendship (love) between man and man; certainly the theme shows clearly enough in Ovid's widely read treatments of Hermaphroditus and Orpheus.

The Passionate Pilgrim also draws on *Love's Labour's Lost,* in which woman (Rosaline) leads man (Berowne) away from a society which is pure because it is purely male. In *Two Gentlemen of Verona* and *The Merchant of Venice* women break up male friendships; in *Julius Caesar* and *II Henry IV* political crises produce the same result. In short, woman and the serpent are one, as in Posthumus' diatribe in *Cymbeline:*

> Could I find out
> The woman's part in me! For there's no motion
> That tends to vice in man, but I affirm
> It is the woman's part: be it lying, note it,
> The woman's flattering, hers; deceiving, hers;
> Lust and rank thoughts, hers, hers; revenges, hers;
> Ambitions, covetings, change of prides, disdain,
> Nice longing, slanders, mutability,
> All faults that may be named, nay, that hell knows,
> Why, hers, in part or all; but rather, all.
>
> (II.v.19–28) *

At the end of *Love's Labour's Lost* there is a kind of self-hatred as the male community falls apart; the witty man, his wit denied, must commit himself to the pain and impotence of those in hospitals as though that were the penalty for heterosexual love.

Matching the Two Loves are Two Immortalities—one the immortality of the body through breeding (the "procreation" sonnets); the other the immortality of the soul through the poet's art (19 or 107 among others). These immortalities suggest a cultural context for the male love celebrated in the *Sonnets.* Shakespeare, says Professor Fiedler, was seeking an answer to the old problem of courtly love, long under attack as adulterous and idolatrous. He rescues much of the old apparatus by transferring the love for a married woman to a young male: love still redeems and improves manners; the lover still serves as a muse; and the love is still outside marriage, with sexual consummation avoided. But his device fails: the boy—a woman's son (41)—deceives him with a whore. And Shakespeare himself seems to suffer a sense of guilt about such a love. And yet, although the *Son-*

---

* Of course this speech is ironic in its context. Posthumus' wife has not been unfaithful to him, although he does not know that. Professor Fiedler's point would be that the thought was a live possibility to Shakespeare, not that he necessarily held such a view in daily life.

nets fail in their task of psychological and intellectual rescue, they live as a permanent and beautiful achievement to psychoanalyst and literary man alike. Perhaps that is the only point on which the two agree, though, for Professor Fiedler's oedipal account of their psychology is mostly inconsistent with Dr. Boas' more sophisticated inferences based on the mechanism of conflicting identifications.

ATTITUDES TOWARD THE FATHER AS SHOWN IN HAMLET

Of the plays, the one that psychoanalysts have treated as most revealing of Shakespeare's psyche is *Hamlet*. We have already seen Freud's view, with its elegant logic. (1) Over the centuries critics have been unable to say why Hamlet delays in killing the man who murdered his father and married his mother. (2) Psychoanalytic clinical experience shows that every child wishes to do just that. (3) Psychoanalytic experience also shows that the wish persists in the unconscious mind of the adult, and that wish and deed seem the same there. (4) Were Hamlet, then, to punish Claudius for murdering his father and marrying his mother, he would condemn himself as well; therefore he delays. (5) The fact that the wish is unconscious in all of us explains why centuries of critics could not themselves explain Hamlet's delay.

Freud went on to assume that Hamlet was speaking for Shakespeare himself, and that, in turn, raised a further question: Since oedipal wishes are repressed after infancy, what had reactivated them in Shakespeare's mind? Freud suggested that it was the death of the poet's father, John Shakespeare, but later withdrew the suggestion when he turned Oxfordian.

The late Ernest Jones's *Hamlet and Oedipus* began life as an article in 1910, became the introduction to an edition of *Hamlet,* and finally took the form of a book. It is generally regarded as a classic of psychoanalytic criticism,[10] but, in fact, Jones largely repeats Freud's basic insight, rather more slowly, to be sure, and with a large if somewhat indiscriminate sampling of Shakespearean scholarship.

In essence, Jones added only three points. First, he showed in detail how the son's conflicting attitudes of love and hate toward the father were worked out in the play by splitting or "decomposing" both father and son into different figures: the ghost, Claudius, and Polonius on the one hand; Hamlet and Laertes, on the other. Second, he added another version of the oedipal reading. Freud had argued that Hamlet could not punish Claudius for doing what he, Hamlet, had always wanted to do. Jones added, if Hamlet killed his mother's husband, he would be acting out the first half of the oedipal wish to get rid of the father and take his place with the mother. Hence, against punishing Claudius there stands the whole force of Hamlet's childhood development that put down this oedipal wish. Third, Jones suggested some other reasons from Shakespeare's biography for his infantile feelings about his father having become reactivated around 1601. There was the death of his father, of course, although Jones admits that what evidence there is for the date of *Hamlet* makes it rather more likely that the play was written before, not after, the death of John Shakespeare. There was the death of Essex as a possible stimulus, but there, too, the dates are ambiguous. Finally, with some reluctance, he settled on the hypothesis that Shakespeare had been betrayed (as in the *Sonnets*) by Mary Fitton. "For a psychologist," he wrote, "it is hard to think that Shakespeare never passed through the experience they [the *Sonnets*] describe, which accords so well with the emotion he vividly portrays in all his great tragedies," namely, disillusionment through betrayal.

Another early Freudian who used *Hamlet* as a glass in which to view Shakespeare's psyche was Otto Rank. After a period of twenty years in the bosom of orthodoxy, Rank broke with Freud on the issue of the importance of the shock of birth to later life. Many of his writings on literature, however, date from his orthodoxy, in particular, the massive *Das Inzest-Motiv in Dichtung und Sage*,[11] which first appeared in 1912. (Rank added polemic to his later edition, after the break with Freud, but left his original insights unchanged.) The book originally sought to reinforce the Freudian hypothesis of the universality of the oedipus complex by a wide variety of examples of incest themes from myth and literature. Rank proceeds further to show how the forbidden oedipal relation of mother and son tends to accrete to itself—or, more exactly, to express itself in—other taboo relations: father-daughter, brother-sister, uncle-niece, and so on. His chapter, "*Shakespeares Vaterkomplex*," considers several aspects of the poet's character and also several plays. Of the plays which supposedly show Shakespeare's feelings toward his father, Rank particularly stressed *Hamlet*.

Rank adopted the Freud-Jones view of the play, that *Hamlet* expressed Shakespeare's guilt for the normal childhood resentment of his father which had been reactivated by John Shakespeare's death. Rank's special view of the play, however, was that it expressed not only Shakespeare's feelings as a child, but also his feelings on becoming the father of his own family. So far as Shakespeare's feelings as a son are concerned, the ghost, Rank suggested, represented a projection of the father's accusation and the son's regret for his earlier resentment.

Gertrude, Rank said, represented Shakespeare's feelings as a child that his mother was sinful with his father, and Rank posited a violent reaction by the poet against his mother which led him to marry a woman much older than himself and then to turn away from her and all women toward his own sex (as implied by the *Sonnets*).

Rank also noted that three times in *Hamlet* a conversation between Hamlet and a woman forbidden him is spied upon by father figures: Polonius and the king spy on Hamlet and Ophelia; Polonius and later the ghost spy on Hamlet and his mother. Rank saw these spying episodes as reversals of a common childhood fantasy, the "primal scene," in which a son watches or wishes to watch or imagines himself watching his parents in the sexual act. These fantasies powerfully stimulate the son's desire to "play" the father and also to avenge himself on the father, in Claudius' situation, to kill him "in th' incestuous pleasure of his bed."

At the same time that Hamlet projects Shakespeare's feelings as a son, Rank points out that the play taken as a whole also represents Shakespeare's feelings as he replaced his own dead father. Shakespeare must have felt remorse over his dead son Hamnet; unconsciously, he would, like most men, fear now that he himself was the father, his children would resent him as he had resented his father. Thus, in the play *Hamlet,* Laertes, the eager, loyal son, stands as an example to Hamlet; unconsciously he acts out the poet's feelings of remorse toward his own father, while Hamlet, in delaying, acts out the hostile ones.

Rank selects as one of the most remarkable achievements of Shakespeare's art his mingling in the figure of the ghost his own feelings both as father and as son. As a son, spying on the king and queen, the ghost tries to separate them; as a father, spying on his son and his wife, he cautions Hamlet against harming Gertrude. The ghost combines the son's hatred of the father and love of the mother with the reaction against them—honoring the father, dishonoring the mother. Hence, Rank suggests, Shakespeare with fine poetic intuition altered his source to give both father and son the same name, Hamlet. Finally, Rank laid great stress on the tradition that it was Shakespeare who acted the ghost in performances of *Hamlet* and acted him superbly. Rank argued that every time Shakespeare played the part, he "became" his father and allayed his filial thoughts against the father. Also as ghost, he identified with the son (as against Claudius) and so vindicated his own infantile thoughts against the father. Shakespeare played the ghost so well, Rank says, because he used the role to sustain his own psychic balance.

The Freud-Jones view of *Hamlet* (with or without Rank) has

been repeated again and again by psychoanalytic writers, mostly just in passing, occasionally at length.[12] The basic point, that Hamlet's problem (and through him Shakespeare's) is oedipal, seems to be almost axiomatic in psychoanalysis. There have been remarkably few changes in the theory at least as it is applied to Shakespeare the man.

One such change was provided by Otto Hinrichsen who in 1933 took a *gestalt* view of *Hamlet*.[13] Hinrichsen made an eminently sensible qualification on all such approaches to a Shakespearean play as Jones's or Freud's—approaches that take Shakespeare's characters for real people (Hinrichsen quotes with approval Schücking's notion that Shakespeare is a "primitive") or approaches that take one character as "speaking for" the poet. No single character, Hinrichsen says, can express the conflict in Shakespeare's psyche; only the choice and handling of the material and the interaction of characters can speak the poet's mind. "*Hamlet* is only the showplace of an inner battle." The poet projects himself into *all* his characters. He breaks up the continuum of his own psyche into the sharply defined conflicts of the characters. Artistic characters thus exist only partially, as single psychic factors; they simply do not have the many-sided existences of real people. Hinrichsen's common-sense objection, however, has found little sympathy among psychoanalytic critics.

Nevertheless, one psychoanalytic critic did produce a total view of *Hamlet,* albeit a look through the tragedy to Shakespeare. An English teacher before she became a lay analyst, the late Ella Freeman Sharpe showed remarkable skill in bringing together large numbers of details from a given play. In an early paper on *Hamlet* (1929) [14] she adopted the usual view, but offered a supplement based on Freud's description of the mechanism of melancholia. In *Mourning and Melancholia* Freud suggested that the loss of a loved person is followed by a sort of psychic incorporation of his image which then becomes an aggresive, accusing, relentless force of conscience; all kinds of earlier sins are dredged up and held against the ego. Hamlet, she points out, has recently lost his father, and he is full of self-accusation. Clearly, he is a victim of melancholia or, in a more modern term, depression. But—and this is Miss Sharpe's contribution—"The poet is not Hamlet. Hamlet is what he might have been if he had not written the play of *Hamlet.*" No single character speaks for Shakespeare; they all do. They are all projections of his mind. "He is the murdered majesty of Denmark, he is the murdered Claudius, he is the queen, Gertrude, and Ophelia. He is Hamlet."

What aspects, then, of Shakespeare's mind (confronted with the death of his father) do the several characters represent? The dead king is the good image of the father; Claudius is the bad. The ghost (entombed) is the father incorporated or buried in the mind, a super-ego reproaching the self or ego. Laertes, she says, embodies the sadistic energy of these reproaches from the superego. Gertrude is, of course, the mother; Ophelia is the mirror image of Hamlet, the feminine side of Shakespeare. The tragedy (both for Hamlet and Ophelia) is a suicide according to the mechanism Freud posited for melancholia. On the one hand, Hamlet tries to wait out the time needed for the mind to adjust itself to the loss; he is trying, in effect, to wait out the sadistic urgency of the accusing image of his father represented by Laertes. At the same time, his mind has regressed to the lowest level of infancy in which the father and the mother are thought of as a single parent figure ("one flesh"); the child—and Hamlet—tries to keep these treasures, to incorporate them in himself, literally, to devour them. (This is the mechanism, she says, behind Hamlet's reproaching his mother for her urgency and her appetite.) Poised against Hamlet is Horatio, the man Hamlet wishes he could be: slow, suffering all. The final tragedy is precipitated by Laertes' sudden actions. In short, "Hamlet's death is a dramatized suicide, superego and ego roles being alloted to different characters."

Miss Sharpe's achievement lies in restoring the sense of unity or interplay within the poet's mind. Jones and Rank, working from Freud's earliest insights, stressed the gratification of the poet's unconscious wishes by a single character, Hamlet. Miss Sharpe builds on Freud's later writings, particularly the tripartite structure of the mind, id, ego, and superego. Thus she succeeds in relating the whole play, not just a single character, to the poet's mind. In a later paper, left unfinished at her death, she tries to go a step further in her linking of *Hamlet* to Shakespeare's mind. She posits that the unity of the play is to be sought not only in the purely psychic forces of its creator's mind, but also in the bodily manifestations of those psychic forces.

The theme of procastination is already, she says, implicitly a body metaphor. That is, the unconscious impulses of the adult Shakespeare were disorganized by some oedipal crisis, the death of the father, betrayal by Mary Fitton, or cause unknown. His adult drives regressed to the earlier strata of infancy when the child found his satisfactions not in genital activity but in anal. Then, with a sense of release and exhilaration, corresponding to Aristotle's catharsis, all the impulses are discharged at once and the system cleared.

Miss Sharpe finds in support of this proposition a good deal of imagery associated with anal processes: references to air, for example, to smells and noises, and to the ear (a common "displacement upward" of the anus). She finds also associated with Hamlet himself elements which remind one of Christ's birth from a virgin (references to stars, for example). Another Christlike factor is his being banished, just as Shakespeare left Stratford, and Hamlet's final triumph which is, like Christ's, through his personal defeat.

She sees the play as working out on an adult level a childish wish of the poet's about his own conception. He wanted, as most children do, to be conceived cleanly by a virgin mother, one unsullied by a rival lover, the father. On the other hand, through spying (frequent in *Hamlet*) and by hearing things (poison in the ear), the infant Shakespeare was aware of the sexual way in which children are conceived, but he wished that dirty fate *inter urinam et faeces* onto his younger brother (represented in the play by Fortinbras in the "skirts" of Norway).

Miss Sharpe uses a curious device to relate these various themes and insights. Confronted with imagery of smells and dirt and noises, spying, the themes of procrastination and banishment, the desire to be conceived by a virgin mother, Hamlet's oedipal wish (projected on the ghost) to kill the usurping father, Miss Sharpe, to bring them all together, postulates "as a basic dynamic psychophysical situation of the infant poet-to-be, one in which he was furiously angry and furiously evacuated his bowels." That is, she hypothesizes a traumatic situation with lifelong aftereffects. The child was banished while the parents were left alone together. Fantasying what was going on, the child furiously soiled himself so that his mother picked him up and held him; he thereby won the mother away from the father. She guesses that this pattern may have emerged with the birth of a sibling when the poet was about three—represented in the play by Fortinbras, a "good" son.

Miss Sharpe's suggestion is rather fanciful, indeed startling. Perhaps it could be stated another way, namely, that the writing of *Hamlet* served the adult poet's psychic economy *as* the situation Miss Sharpe postulates would serve the psychic economy of an infant confronted with a rival father and brother.

Ernest Jones himself provided a supplement to the straight oedipal theory in an essay of 1948,[15] in which he considered the two versions given of the elder Hamlet's death (both supplied by Shakespeare or at least not by the known sources). Both descriptions, he points out, combine in their deadliness symbols for the act of love. Claudius' story was that Hamlet Senior had been stung by a serpent while sleeping in the orchard. The phallic serpent goes along with the orchard, which would usually symbolize a woman; King Hamlet, symbolically, was resting in the arms of a woman after love. The ghost's account (repeated in the dumb show) is equally symbolic: he says poison was poured into his ear. Poison, at an unconscious level, stands for any body fluid charged with evil intent. The ear (in this context) represents an orifice below the waist by the mechanism of "displacement upward." The attack by Claudius, the younger brother, on the older stands for the son's attacking the father; as in Freud's original oedipal account of the play, Claudius is acting out Hamlet's wishes. Thus, Jones concludes, to the original reason for Hamlet's delay, his repressed hatred of his father, these images of a homosexual assault suggest a second reason for delay: Hamlet wants to play the woman to his father's love; he fears this feeling and cannot face it. Attributing Hamlet's impulses to Shakespeare, Jones says that all his plays show a readiness to interchange the sexes; this interchanging must reflect bisexual impulses which were a part of his personality.

One of Jones's reviewers, Dr. Harry Slochower, argued that his book should extend these fluid identifications of Hamlet's beyond Shakespeare's immediate personal problems (with Mary Fitton, say) to the general problem Shakespeare shared with all Renaissance men, the shift from firm medieval tradition to fluid personal standards reflected in the play's "language of interiorization moving toward externalization." [16]

At least one other psychoanalytic writer on Shakespeare-in-*Hamlet* has adopted Miss Sharpe's technique of hypothesizing a childhood event to tie the play to. Dr. K. R. Eissler [17] notes that the central incident of the play is the play within the play. He suggests that a play within a play may be like a dream within a dream and make a more clear-cut, less-disguised statement of the theme than the larger work in which it is embedded. On this basis the incident from Shakespeare's childhood which *Hamlet* reflects in the play within the play would be a dream combining the idea of hurting or killing the father with impulses of love toward the mother. And Eissler hypothesizes a childhood situation in which the infant poet-to-be, frightened by such a dream, ran to his parents' bed; there his mother comforted him, but his father awoke and scolded him. As with Miss Sharpe, we can translate and say the play within the play served the adult poet as such an episode might have served to comfort an infant.

As for contemporary influences leading to the writing of *Hamlet,* Dr. Eissler suggests the death of young Hamlet and (with due hesitation about the dates) the death of Shakespeare's father. In fact, he says, the play could have been written *before* John Shakespeare's death, and in that case the theme of delay and procrastination in *Hamlet* would be a wish-fulfilling fantasy staving off the poet's father's death. The contempt for women in *Hamlet,* he suggests, could be traced to Shakespeare's feelings at seeing his son Hamnet survived by his twin sister Judith or his father survived by his mother. Hamlet's death with "flights of angels" may be a hope for Hamnet, who, after all, died before he confronted the troubles of adulthood, such troubles as Hamlet's. Dr. Eissler makes another ingenious suggestion as to contemporary influences on Shakespeare that led to his writing of *Hamlet:* perhaps Shakespeare was thinking of the poisoning of William Underhill, the former owner of New Place, by his son Fulk. Shakespeare went to considerable expense to get a new deed from another of Underhill's sons, Hercules. Maybe this recollection underlies Hamlet's disgruntled simile about Claudius:

> My father's brother, but no more like my father
> Than I to Hercules.

Dr. A. André Glaz, in a highly eccentric study,[18] says his reading of *Hamlet* (see below, p. 179) in view of the intensity of Edmund's lines about bastardy in *King Lear* shows that Shakespeare was deeply concerned about illegitimacy. Dr. Glaz guesses that betrayal by a woman around 1598 threw the poet into a period of depression from which he recovered when he accepted the reality of his own illegitimacy through his mother's confession. Clearly we have reached the limits of psychoanalytic speculation as to the insight afforded by *Hamlet* into the poet's feelings toward his father.

ATTITUDE TOWARD THE FATHER AS SHOWN IN PLAYS OTHER THAN HAMLET

The plays other than *Hamlet*, which psychoanalysts feel show Shakespeare's feelings toward his father, are those involving kings and rulers (one who rules being a common symbol for a father). Otto Rank, for example, in discussing *"Shakespeares Vaterkomplex,"* dealt not only with *Hamlet,* but also with *Julius Caesar.*[19] The earlier play, he says, differs from *Hamlet* in that there is no mother figure present and there is only one father figure, Caesar. Moreover, Shakespeare did not include in the play its source's suggestion that Brutus was Caesar's natural son, and this omission, Rank says, shows that the material was especially charged with emotion for the poet. For these three reasons the question, to kill or not to kill, can become much more explicit in *Julius Caesar* than in *Hamlet.* Brutus is "all son," and to him alone Caesar's ghost appears. Cassius, with his constant talk of suicide, represents one aspect of Brutus, the self-punishing; it is significant that he dies on his birthday. Similarly, Antony embodies the sense of filial piety. Lest it be objected, Rank writes, that these are historical people and therefore tell us nothing about Shakespeare, we should recognize that the poet can give them life only by breathing into them his own feelings.

Very early in the development of psychoanalysis Isidor Sadger suggested that Lady Macbeth projected aspects and problems of Shakespeare's character.[20] Because Duncan resembled her father, she embodies, Sadger said, Shakespeare's love for his father, but also his resentment and his unconscious impulse to get rid of him. (On the theory that John Shakespeare was a butcher, Sadger suggested that the poet would often have seen his father sticking animals with a knife—as Macbeth, in a way, does.) Lady Macbeth also represents a projection of Shakespeare's ambition; the fact that (according to Sadger) the poet gives this ambition to a woman and denies it to Macbeth himself is as though Shakespeare were saying, I am capable of father murder only under a woman's influence. Finally, her suicide projects Shakespeare's own guilt and self-punishment for his feelings. Thus in the first half of the play Lady Macbeth represents a child's unrestrained striving against his parent; in the second half he projects an adult's remorse after the parent's death.

In the article on *Macbeth* which Freud praised and used,[21] Ludwig Jekels argued that the play dealt with the contrast of sterility and fecundity. Shakespeare, he says, identified himself with Macbeth in the role of the bad son who kills or wishes to kill the father (Duncan); he duplicated the role in Macduff who is in his own way a bad son, surly and hostile to the king-father (now Macbeth), whom he finally kills. Jekels guessed that Shakespeare might have left Stratford because his relations with his father got worse as a result of his irregular marriage; like Macduff, he deserted his wife and children—and Hamnet died. In 1601 Shakespeare's father died, and Jekels, like the other analytic writers, saw this event as determining Shakespeare's tragic period. The poet's childish resentment and rivalry of his father renewed themselves, but now as feelings of guilt and remorse for that former hostility; he would have felt that his own son had been punished for his father's bad wishes (as in "Sinful Macduff,/They were all struck for thee!").

When Queen Elizabeth died in 1603, Jekels argues, she must have reminded Shakespeare of his own "barren scepter." Elizabeth was a "bad child" in plotting against such mother figures as Mary Tudor and Mary Stuart. She had, moreover, ordered the execution of Essex, a man, in a psychic sense, almost like a loving son to her. Elizabeth, Jekels says, appears in *Macbeth* as the dual character, Macbeth and Lady Macbeth. Jekels also argues that *Macbeth* must be dated 1606 because Holinshed set Banquo's murder at ten years after Macbeth had become king; ten years after Shakespeare's Hamnet died the poet revived him in the figure of Malcolm.

Finally, Macduff, Jekels said, represents a wish fulfillment on the poet's part for his own resentment of his father. Macduff had a quasi-divine birth like a god of fecundity, Dionysus in particular. Like Dionysus, Shakespeare left his home and returned in triumph. And Macduff was uncorrupted by the mother he had not known; he cancels out, as it were, Macbeth's mother-prompted parricide.

CORIOLANUS AND SHAKESPEARE'S MOTHER

To psychoanalytic critics those plays, such as *Julius Caesar, Macbeth,* and *Hamlet,* in which a king is killed, have suggested Shakespeare's hostile feelings toward his father; *Coriolanus,* on the other hand, supposedly shows the poet's feelings for his mother. As Otto Rank said,[22] this play is to the mother's death what *Hamlet* was to the father's. Like Macbeth, Coriolanus is under the influence of women. Under the impact of his mother's death, Shakespeare regressed to such childish mechanisms as not acting like a man so he could possess and identify with his mother:

> My throat of war be turned
> Which choired with my drum, into a pipe
> Small as an eunuch, or the virgin voice
> That babies lull asleep!
>
> (III.ii.112–115)

In *Coriolanus* as in *Hamlet* Rank saw the father as split into more than one character; Menenius is the honored father, Aufidius the hated. The relation between Coriolanus and Aufidius shifts from hatred to an affection described in almost sexual terms. Coriolanus says to his erstwhile foe:

> Know thou first,
> I loved the maid I married; never man
> Sighed truer breath. But that I see thee here,
> Thou noble thing, more dances my rapt heart
> Than when I first my wedded mistress saw
> Bestride my threshold.
>
> (IV.v.119–124)

And one of Aufidius' servants sneers, "Our general himself makes a mistress of [Coriolanus]; sanctifies himself with's hand, and turns up the white o' th' eye to his discourse" (IV.v.207–209). Such a change, Rank noted, from absolute hatred to absolute love resembles the shift in a boy's relation to his father: hatred turns into love when the boy gives up his aspirations toward his mother.

In a later study Charles K. Hofling suggested that the play and Mary Shakespeare's death together served to "cure" Shakespeare of a preoccupation with his feelings toward his mother.[23] By writing *Coriolanus* he freed himself to return to Stratford and live with Anne again.

Since World War II a good many analysts have studied the early mother-child relationship, and they have found much evidence that inconsistent or hostile mothering in the first year gives rise to massive aggressive drives in the child, and later in the adult. Dr. David Barron (in a study we shall look at in more detail later) argues that this must have been what happened to Coriolanus.[24] The chilliness of Volumnia created in him the vast aggression that made him a successful warrior and, Dr. Barron suggests, the same thing must have happened to Shakespeare—his experience in the first year of life gave rise to a fierce need to achieve independence through self-expression in his plays. Coriolanus, thus, speaks for Shakespeare.

Dr. Rufus Putney, however, argues exactly the contrary.[25] Coriolanus would have acquired at his mother's hands not only massive aggressive drives directed outward, but an implacable superego (aggression turned inward). He judges himself and others with fierce, unyielding severity. But what endears Shakespeare to us is quite different. He is like a Lepidus or the Second Citizen in *Coriolanus,* who insists, "What he cannot help in his nature," one ought not to "account a vice in him" (I.i.41). Shakespeare does not pass harsh judgments on his characters. Rather, he "leaves us with a blissful uncertainty of suspended judgment." He recognizes and forgives a man's subjection to intrapsychic forces he cannot control.

Shakespeare, in short, is just as opposite to Coriolanus as Dr. Putney's view is to Dr. Barron's and their opposition illustrates the risks involved in trying to read back to the author from a single play or character.

ATTITUDES TOWARD SIBLINGS

Mother and father have largely occupied the analytic critics' attention; there are only a few references to Shakespeare's hypothetical relations with his brothers. We have already seen Ella Freeman Sharpe's thesis (n. 14) that Hamlet represents the bad son, Fortinbras the good, and her view that the rebellion she postulates as "a basic dynamic psychophysical situation of the infant poet-to-be" may have been provoked by the birth of a sibling when Shakespeare was less than three. Otto Rank found in *King Lear* a similar pattern of loving son Edgar opposed by hating son Edmund, and interpreted them as representing ambivalence toward the father on Shakespeare's part.[26] Weston A. Gui, in an ingenious (if somewhat zany) analysis of *Midsummer Night's Dream* concludes that Bottom stands for Shakespeare's wish to displace first his father (represented by Oberon), and second his brother Gilbert (represented by the Indian changeling) at the breast of their mother (represented by Titania).[27]

SHAKESPEARE IN A VARIETY OF SINGLE PLAYS

Under the heading of miscellaneous attempts to deduce the Shakespearean psyche from individual plays or characters, three items should be included. First, a recurring problem for Shakespeare, the late Ernst Krist suggested, seems to be a feeling, like Prince Hal's that his father is not all he should be. Kris gently succumbed to a "temptation to detect a neat connection between the artist and one of his characters." "With appropriate reservations" he put forward the idea that at the time Shakespeare was reading about Prince Hal he was restoring the fortunes of the Shakespeare family and purchasing a coat of arms. "The motto chosen is one that might well have been used to characterize Prince Hal's striving for the crown: *'Non sanz droict.'* " [28]

Two writers have used *The Merchant of Venice* to look at Shakespeare. In 1934 T. A. Ross suggested that some of the problems presented by the title character could be resolved by recognizing that Antonio is a "tainted wether," in love with his friend Bassanio, but continent and hence melancholy. He concluded that such an interpretation showed that Shakespeare thought a continent love between two men, a "friendship" in the full Renaissance sense, the most noble and admirable of human relations.[29] E. E. Krapf in 1955 suggested that Antonio's melancholy with respect to Portia and Bassanio stands for Shakespeare's own depression about his two loves of the *Sonnets* deceiving him.[30]

Theodore Reik used his analysis of *The Merry Wives of Windsor* (Falstaff as a child trying to have the mother) to say the comedy reflected Shakespeare's disappointment in his own mother.[31] Dr. L. A. Strong is perhaps touching on a related matter, psychologically, when he points out that Leontes in *The Winter's Tale* has "the form of inferiority complex commonest in Shakespeare, that of readily believing the woman he loves to be unfaithful to him." [32]

Dr. A. Bronson Feldman, pursuing his Oxfordian fancies, has considered *Othello* and *Pericles* as indices to the dramatist's psyche. He suggests, as many other critics have done, that Iago is Othello's evil *alter ego;* that he represents a projection of impulses in Othello's mind to doubt his own virility. These fears lead Othello into a paranoid fear that his impulses to love may be perverted, and out of this fear he projects his own impulses onto Desdemona and kills her for supposedly loving Cassio.[33] About *Pericles,* Dr. Feldman puts forth the idea that the incestuous relations between Antiochus and his daughter represent a transmutation in middle age of the dramatist's (Oxford's) childhood wish to have his mother.[34]

Dr. Feldman has also produced an extended analysis of *The Comedy of Errors* as a revelation of Shakespeare's mind.[35] He selected this comedy because, coming so early in Shakespeare's career, it might suggest the motives behind his turning playwright at all. In other words, the question Dr. Feldman asks of the play is, What impelled Shakespeare to write it? The play opens with "a groundwork of tragedy," Dr. Feldman notes, and he suggests that the apparent gaiety of the play is actually a hysterical effort to evade a real feeling of depression. Dr. Feldman saw the depression as stemming from the poet's unconscious feelings about his marital troubles, particularly the tendency in the play to divide the characters rather sharply into high and low (i.e., carnal) people.

Splitting is of obvious importance in *The Comedy of Errors,* and Dr. Feldman interprets it as related to Shakespeare's thoughts about divorce, a splitting, as it were, on the sea of matrimony. Shakespeare, Dr. Feldman says, translates his own problems with Anne into the marital troubles of Antipholus and Adriana which are essentially a problem of identity, not knowing one's self or one's mate. Shakespeare doubles himself into the two Antipholi; neither twin, however, likes Adriana-Anne. Adriana and Luciana, Dr. Feldman says, are also "twins." Luciana is the ideal bride of anticipation, the "bright Anne"; Adriana is the actual bride, the "dark (*atriata*) Anne." Luciana is the shining aspect of Diana (as contrasted with the gross scullery maid Luce). Ephesus is the home of the moon goddess and of magic, deviltry, and sex, yet the play never mentions the moon (because it was identified with the virgin Queen). The two Dromios are also twins, and they parody their twin masters, perhaps, Dr. Feldman says, symbolizing Shakespeare's servile tendencies. The name "Antipholus" means "anti-follies," representing, according to Dr. Feldman, Shakespeare's belief that he could cure the follies of the world by wit.

The father and mother in the play are projections, says Dr. Feldman, of Shakespeare's attitudes toward his own father and mother.

Aegeon is associated with Syracusa which, Feldman suggests, really means "Sire-accuser." He is, in general, treated rather coldly throughout the play, associated with death and tragedy. Aemilia is the mother conceived of as nunlike, virginal, pure, and white; she is also, Dr. Feldman says, deathly, "abbess" meaning "abyss." (The less pure aspects of the mother he associates with the two sisters.) Aemilia is also the mother-like-a-man of childhood fantasy because "abbess" comes from Aramaic *"abba"* meaning "father." Her masculinity is involved both with killing (i.e., castrating) and death (i.e., sexual "dying"). The sea also links, Dr. Feldman says, drowning and sexuality.

Dr. Feldman sees the action of the play as really the quest for the mother; the central metaphor is that of a drop of water (unconsciously, of semen) seeking the oceanic mother, identified as Diana's city of Ephesus. ("Ephesus," Feldman suggests, is a pun; the city *effaces* the real images of people and replaces them with *lunatic* effigies.) While in theory husbands are supposed to have a divine right, in this play the women dominate. So also the Antipholi never actually commit adultery (and, in exchange for this continence, they are allowed to commit a variety of larcenies and other small bestialities).

Another form of the quest for the mother, Dr. Feldman says, is Antipholus' banging at the door while his twin from Syracuse dines with his wife; it is a version of the child trying to break in on the privacy between father and mother. The theme of gold in the play, Dr. Feldman says, relates to the child being forced to produce his precious feces by the mother goddess. (Shakespeare, Feldman says, thought money crass.) As a reaction against this crassness, Antipholus is transferred from the care of his mercantile father to that of the noble, martial Duke Menaphon; this is a "Family Romance" (in which the child imagines that his "real" parents are rich and powerful strangers), and it reflects Shakespeare's contempt for his father's occupation.

Dr. Feldman interprets the play as a variety of covert and symbolic versions of sexually replacing the father at the mother's breast. Shakespeare divided himself into doubles, one of whom floats away with the mother when the father's ship is split. These doubles end their journeys in the bosom of the mother's church, itself a symbol of maternity. To the extent Shakespeare identified himself with Aegeon, Dr. Feldman says, he sailed the sea of matrimony as captain of a family vessel, and he guided his mast into the forbidden harbor sacred to the great mother, virginal Diana. One of the twins, in fact, loses himself in this sacred mother town. Also, the poet as Antipholus gets a "cake" from the wife while the rival Antipholus (now representing the father) remains outside. The romance with Luciana, Feldman says, is a gesture of sexual promise toward the romantic facsimile of the mother.

For each of these sexual gestures Dr. Feldman finds a rather cruel punishment to match it. For one twin's floating off with the mother, the other twin suffered hardships. For meeting in the church, the twins must face "the melancholy vale," the place of death and execution behind the abbey's ditches. For riding the mother's boat, Aegeon is wrecked at sea; for trespassing on the mother city, he is threatened with beheading (i.e., mutilation or castration). For one twin's losing himself in the mother city, the other twin must go with his "drawn sword to the symbolic castration of a monastery" (*sic*). And for one twin's tricking the mother-wife into a meal, the other must stand exiled from her feeding.

In short, then, Dr. Feldman answers his question, Why did Shakespeare write *The Comedy of Errors?*—he wrote it to gratify his wish to fall together with father and mother into destruction, to return to the womb of the mother as a tomb. Shakespeare, Feldman concludes, wrote the play to save his sanity.

Unfortunately, in later articles on *Othello* and *The Comedy of Errors* Feldman extends this already fairly odd kind of analysis to an even odder purpose: to show the play was written by the Earl of Oxford.[36] Surely, however, the odds against psychoanalysis having any bearing on questions of authorship are overwhelming. One cannot with airy speculations about the psychic life of Edward de Vere balance off the solid documentary evidence that Shakespeare wrote Shakespeare.

The Tempest, most people would say, is Shakespeare's one obviously autobiographical play, but curiously, practically no psychoanalytic writers have relied on it alone. Using *The Tempest* to get at the mind of the colonialist, M. Othar Mannoni [37] notes that Shakespeare could depict that mind in Prospero though he himself had had no experience of colonization—the portrayal shows how there is a colonialist implicit in each of us. The colonial mind (Prospero's or Shakespeare's or anyone's) regresses to a position of dealing with his own forbidden impulses by finding a group of dependents and inferiors in whom he can find those impulses and then, by controlling the "natives," control himself. When Prospero abjures his rough magic, he gives up this way of dealing with his impulses and his wish to be a master. One can fairly guess, I think, that this kind of projective defense was a large part of Shakespeare's ability to write plays—he shows it in Prospero and also in the duke in *Measure for Measure.*

Although Mannoni does not say so, his argument implies that play-writing and directing served Shakespeare as magic served Prospero or the natives a colonial: as ways of managing inner states as though they were "out there." This view of the play becomes explicit in Dr. W. I. D. Scott's Jungian reading.[38] *The Tempest* represents Shakespeare's maturation—he casts down his defensive mask ("persona" in Jungian terms), the wizard, the maker of spells, and he reveals himself as a fully reintegrated personality. "Shakespeare the dramatist has fulfilled his task; he can spend his remaining years as Shakespeare the man."

The writings we have been considering so far have gotten at Shakespeare's psyche by the extended analysis of a single work or character that is assumed to express a basic unconscious wish of the poet. As one reads them, it seems to me, one feels constantly that the evidence (except in the case of the *Sonnets*) is far too meager for the conclusions. A single play or a single character is, after all, only a tiny fraction of Shakespeare's whole achievement. While it is undoubtedly true that each work will reveal his personality, one feels on surer ground when the analyst approaches the author through patterns of action that run through several plays or, even better, through Shakespeare's whole output. As early as 1907, at the Vienna Society, Dr. Eduard Hitschmann and Dr. Max Graf [39] were urging the study of an artist through recurring motifs and characters (the way Richard II occurs also as the melancholy Jaques and ultimately as Hamlet). One of the reasons for the group's enthusiasm for Brandes' criticism was that he showed how periodically, at certain times in Shakespeare's life, certain figures would appear.

SHAKESPEARE IN SEVERAL WORKS

One of the earliest of such studies was Erich Wulffen's analysis in 1911 of Shakespeare's *"grosse Verbrecher,"* Richard III, Macbeth, and Iago.[40] Wulffen's study is scarcely psychoanalytic, but his conclusions bear a certain resemblance to psychoanalytic ones. Richard III, he feels, misbehaved because he felt isolated and lonely. In Macbeth he sees a strongly sexual personality, highly stimulated by the man-women, Lady Macbeth and the three witches. Shakespeare could give these characters life because he was in one respect like them; he, too, had homosexual impulses (evidenced by the *Sonnets*), was highly stimulated by masculine women, and felt isolated from other men. Iago, however, he could not give life to, although he could make us admire him for ferreting out the abnormality in Othello's marriage (his wish to suffer at the hands of Desdemona, as Shakespeare wished to suffer through his two loves in the *Sonnets*). We admire Iago for adapting Othello's wish to suffer to his own wish to cause pain.

Otto Rank, in his study of the incest theme in literature,[41] notes throughout Shakespeare's works repeated references both in language and action to various incestuous desires or killings of near kin. These oedipal impulses, he points out, occur not only in the plays he analyzes in detail, *Hamlet* and *Julius Caesar,* but also in *III Henry VI, Titus Andronicus, Richard II, Macbeth,* and *Coriolanus.* He does not, however, apply these plays biographically to the dramatist' psyche, except as they touch on Shakespeare's relation to his father. The ghost scenes in *Hamlet, Julius Caesar, Macbeth,* and *Richard II* are all to be interpreted, Rank says, as projections of Shakespeare's infantile impulses against his father and his guilt about them (or, put another way, the ghosts are projections of imagined accusations by Shakespeare's father for the son's infantile wishes).

F. Plewa writes about Shakespeare's regicides in Adlerian terms, that is, stressing power, inferiority or superiority, in the social situation as the central fact of mental life. Plewa notes that Shakespeare was a highly favored child, the only one of the senior Shakespeares' first three children to survive into infancy. This, he suggests, is the reason the poet always saw the dethronement of a king as a sin, almost as though the throne were a private right: Shakespeare himself had been a "king," and his brothers and sisters were usurpers.[42]

Theodore Reik compared the sea change spoken of in the death of the father in *The Tempest* to Hamlet's morbid, fleshy descriptions of death (*Hamlet* being written, he assumes, after the death of Shakespeare's father). He compares Hamlet's morbid thoughts to the obsessive patterns of a patient who felt she had to keep thinking of death or else death would get her. Then, as she grew older, her thoughts suffered a sea change; she came to welcome death and to think of a beautiful afterlife. Reik suggests that Shakespeare had the same obsessive thoughts about death, but later in life became reconciled to the idea. The pattern, Reik points out, is common to many people; he gives an example from religion, rotting flesh becoming precious relics. Reik analyzes the obsessive preoccupation as, first, a desire to pursue resentment of the father beyond the grave; and second, a fear of retaliation (much like Rank's analysis of the ghosts).[43]

Hanns Sachs finds an incestuous note in the last four romances which, he points out, all show a young girl at the center of the play and show her, moreover, from the point of view of her father.[44] In *Pericles, Cymbeline,* and *The Winter's Tale* the daughter is restored to the father; but in *The Tempest* the father gives the daughter away

Sachs concludes that these plays express Shakespeare's own feelings toward his daughter Susanna. In *The Tempest* the father leads the daughter to her lover: "This is Prospero's, and was Shakespeare's, last service to his last love."

Sachs also notes that several Shakespearean heroes marry for money: Claudio in *Much Ado About Nothing*; Petruchio in *The Taming of the Shrew*; Bassanio in *The Merchant of Venice*.[45] It is possible, he says, that these represent fantasies in which the poet "extended his successful money operations to the field of marriage where he had actually failed." But this, he concludes, is low and common. "What he dreamt of, probably most intensely in his first years of poverty in London, was about a kind of loving, delicate, and charming woman who would bring into his life ... beauty and refinement and would rescue him from humiliation and ugliness by the sheer love and magnanimity of her soul; just the thing Desdemona does for Othello."

In Jungian terms, K. M. Abenheimer sees the last plays as concerned with the problem of "individuation," that is, renouncing the child's longing for parental shelter in favor of living a life of his own. *Othello, Lear, Cymbeline, Winter's Tale,* and *Tempest,* he says, are all concerned with jealousy or a paranoid estrangement which leads to the hero's isolation. In *Othello* and *Lear* the result is the death of the hero, while *Cymbeline* and *The Winter's Tale* have comic happy endings in which the circumstances of the isolation simply cease. As the title hero, Cymbeline mirrors Shakespeare's problems at the time, but the side actions tend to swamp the interest in the hero. Cymbeline loses his children and true friends because of his unjust banishment of Belarius and his undue trust in his second wife. This same basic motif of "isolation through paranoid folly and reunion" is repeated in Posthumus' loss of his wife and in Belarius' retreat to the woods. Imogen's being *"mollis aer," "mulier,"* "tender air," Abenheimer interprets as Shakespeare's inability to like women at this point except for those born out of the daydreams and thoughts of a man. Cymbeline recovers his lost ones, but only *The Tempest* shows the individual (Prospero) transformed: the magus manages to convert his childish longing for femininity (represented in the Jungian pantheon of the unconscious as the anima image) to an adult longing for woman. That is, he grows away from conceiving of woman (Miranda) as immaterial and spiritual into seeing her as real, wifely, and motherly.[46]

In 1948 Jack Lindsay applied psychoanalytic lore to the fairy lore of Shakespeare's *Midsummer Night's Dream* and *Romeo and Juliet*. Before Shakespeare, fairies in folklore were short but adult-sized earthy folk (perhaps followers of a pre-Christian religion—he cites Margaret Murray's *The God of the Witches*). Shakespeare changed these adult-sized fairies into tiny people

> In shape no bigger than an agate stone
> On the forefinger of an alderman,

and so they have remained ever since in English literature. Mr. Lindsay suggests that Shakespeare was drawing on the sixteenth- and seventeenth-century lore about Tom Thumb with its (quite psychoanalytic) symbolism which sees the baby man as *eo ipso* a phallus:

> I had a little husband, no bigger than my thumb.
> I put him in a pintpot, and there I bid him drum.

Tom Thumb was the child as adult, a child with an adult's sexual powers but without the adult's responsibilities. For Shakespeare, Lindsay says, adult-sized fairies represented the defeat of moral law and the triumph of sexual promiscuity and venereal disease. By making them tiny, he returned their adult sexuality to a pure and satisfying contact with the mother. This temporary regression, released at the end of *Midsummer Night's Dream,* enabled Shakespeare to free himself of his fear and enslavement to his own mother. The end of the play frees the energies of love. We see the pattern again in *The Tempest*—Puck reappears as Ariel, and at the end Prospero-Shakespeare puts down his magic (and phallic) wand.[47]

Dr. Daniel Schneider has suggested that Shakespeare's "secret sorrow," the central figure in his emotional life, was his mother; she appears in the plays in a long series of threatening guises: Gertrude, Lady Macbeth, Desdemona, Juliet, Kate the curst. Similarly, Shakespeare seems to conceive of all his men as either fathers or sons, "smashing taboos, being caught in jealousy, avenging treachery, etc. —Othello and his mother's handkerchief, Hamlet and his mother's 'incestuous sheets,' Macbeth and his bearded witches." [48] Professor Joseph T. McCullen notes (in a nonpsychoanalytic way) that the theme of brother hate and fratricide runs through virtually all of Shakespeare's plays from *Richard III* to *The Tempest.*[49] Gilbert S. Moore points to a similarly pervasive theme—childlessness and an "obsession with genealogy." [50] He attributes it to a preoccupation with mortality and a fear of extinction. All these three themes would relate to recent psychoanalytic concern with aggression and its sources in the early mother-child relationship, as would the work of Dr. David B. Barron.

Dr. Barron, in two recent studies, points out that some of the most violent images of anger in Shakespeare's works link loss of infant, loss of pity, and choking:

> Mothers shall but smile when they behold
> Their infants quarterèd with the hands of war,
> All pity choked with custom of fell deeds,
>   (*Julius Caesar*, III.i.267–269)

or the description of the murderers of the princes in the tower saying

>   "We smotherèd
> The most replenishèd sweet work of nature
> That from the prime creation e'er she framèd."
> Hence both are gone with conscience and remorse.
>   (*Richard III*, IV.iii.17–20)

The association becomes most clear in Lady Macbeth's

>   Make thick my blood;
>   Stop up th'access and passage to remorse . . .
>
>   Come to my woman's breasts
>   And take my milk for gall,
>   (*Macbeth*, I.v.44–49)

the description of Duncan dead as a fountain stopped up, and the appearance of Banquo's ghost to interrupt a banquet. In short, violent rage seems associated with the rage an infant will feel when its feeding is interfered with.[51]

Dr. Barron pursues the point in a detailed study of *Coriolanus*.[52] He begins by noting that Shakespeare added to the materials from his source in ways all associated with hunger and oral dependency. He gives Volumnia lines that show she would rather have her son at war than feeding at home, even a suckling on her breast. She sent him away "when yet he was but tender-bodied and the only son of my womb." Shakespeare greatly amplified the mutiny of the citizens for food, and he provided the epithet "Boy!" that stings Coriolanus to his final fatal burst of rage, as though he could not stand to be the kind of being who is dependent on a mother.

Drawing on recent psychoanalytic research which shows how inconsistent feeding in the first months of life can cause overly strong aggressive drives, Dr. Barron suggests a number of ways in which playwriting may have helped Shakespeare deal with the aftereffects of capricious feeding by his mother. One is his association of rage (in the theater) with interrupted feeding. Further, the mouth is the organ both for eating and speaking: writing mouth-filling speeches may have represented for Shakespeare a self-sufficient creativity. Still further, the mouth is our earliest means for taking in the non-self and making it part of the self—as in the passive receptivity of inspiration in the creative process. Another attitude from the earliest feeding situation that Shakespeare may have worked out in his writings is a sense of the fickleness of time and the faithlessness of woman:

> Past reason hunted, and no sooner had,
> Past reason hated, as a swallowed bait
> On purpose laid to make the taker mad.
> *(Sonnet 129)*

By putting his emotions into an immortal art form, Shakespeare may have resolved the wild fluctuations of emotion he felt in infancy. Again, in later life, Shakespeare may have succeeded in feeding on the esteem of his audience as a substitute for his infantile need to feed on his mother. Dr. Barron suggests that the intensity of emotional expression in the plays may represent the conflict in the adult writer between infantile forces of rage at dependency and heroic efforts of defense later to achieve independence through his own artistic expression.

One final word on the theme of homosexuality: Dr. W. I. D. Scott finds a clue in that certain characters like Orsino in *Twelfth Night* or Antonio in *The Merchant of Venice* seem very important at the opening of the play, but then tend to drop out of sight. He says these characters show homosexual patterns: Orsino's love for a girl-boy is a way out of a mother fixation; Antonio, the older man, loves a younger sonlike man. These characters tend to disappear, Dr. Scott says, because Shakespeare found them too threatening to work with, too close to Shakespeare's own problems as shown in the *Sonnets:* the love of an older man for a younger one or for a "master-mistress." [53]

Most of the earliest studies of Shakespeare the man (our first group) looked at a single play or character as expressing a single experience in the poet's life (the death of his father, son, or mother; his betrayal by the "dark lady"). Later and more sophisticated studies consider a series of plays as revealing a long-term character trait of the poet. These later studies (at least some of them) carry a much greater ring of truth than the first, partly, I think, because they show a greater psychoanalytic maturity. The nature of "character" is a more recent and still rather open question in psychoanalytic theory; there is less room for crudity in considering character, which must involve both impulse and defense, than in simply labeling unconscious impulses. Then, too, it seems possible to move with a good deal of certainty from a pattern in several plays to a character trait of the poet to a childhood reason for such a trait based on clinical observation. It does not seem possible to move with any certainty at all from a single play to an infantile experience and from thence to Mary Fitton, Queen Elizabeth, or George Underhill in the adult poet's life. The obvious next step, then, is to consider traits in all the plays—a Herculean task.

SHAKESPEARE IN ALL THE PLAYS

Nevertheless, three heroic souls have attempted to reveal Shakespeare the man by studying *all* his works. Of the three, the most ambitious was Ella Freeman Sharpe. She evidently planned a very detailed study of all the plays or at least those she saw as critical. Among her papers at her death was a diagram of a "First Scheme of Cyclic Movement" in Shakespeare's plays.[54] Her editor, Marjorie Brierley, describes this diagram as dividing the plays into two large phases. Each phase shows a descent to a nadir and a rise to what was called "Reinstatement of the ideal," against a base line of time. In grouping the plays into this sequence, comedies and tragedies were considered in pairs. Thus, the first phase runs from *Richard III* through *Titus Andronicus* paired with *The Taming of the Shrew*, then through *Romeo and Juliet* paired with *Love's Labour's Lost* to the nadir represented by *Richard II* with *Midsummer Night's Dream;* up from the nadir through the combination of *King John* and *The Merchant of Venice* to the reinstatement of the ideal in *Henry V*. The ideal in the first phase is kingship, and the second phase is marked off from the first by a preoccupation with the coming generation and parent-child rivalry. This second phase descends from *Henry V* through *Julius Caesar* matched with *As You Like It* (and *Twelfth Night*), through *Hamlet* and *The Merry Wives of Windsor*, through *Troilus and Cressida* paired with *All's Well That Ends Well* to *Measure for Measure*. At that point there is a hesitancy, but the curve turns down again and the plays are grouped differently. No longer is the pairing between comedy and tragedy, but between outward-turned and inward-turned aggression. The curve goes down through Othello (who kills Desdemona) and King Lear (who is killed), through Macbeth (who kills and is killed) and Antony (who kills himself) to the nadir represented by Coriolanus (who kills and is killed) and Timon (who, apparently, kills himself). This nadir is labeled "no love." The curve proceeds upward from it through *Pericles, Cymbeline, The Winter's Tale,* and *The Tempest*. "The new note is the next generation and fulfillment through children. *The Winter's Tale* and *The Tempest* are apotheoses of young love in which rivalry [between the generations] is transcended," and this is the ideal reinstated in the second phase.

Miss Sharpe died before she could elaborate her scheme with the analyses of the plays to back it up. It is impressive, though, to note how closely it corresponds to such traditional divisions as Dowden's. Miss Sharpe evidently felt that the rhythm she found applied not only to the whole sequence of Shakespeare's works but also within individual plays.

In her early paper on *Hamlet* she noted the importance of procrastination in *Hamlet* and also that in several of the tragedies the catastrophe is precipitated by some too-sudden action of the hero (*Romeo and Juliet, Hamlet, Othello, Lear*). In her later paper on *Hamlet* (also left unfinished at her death),[55] she noted a rhythm in the play similar to the one she found in Shakespeare's whole creative pattern. That is, at the opening of *Hamlet* the unconscious content (the son's oedipal rivalry with the father) takes us to a relatively sophisticated stage in the child's development as retained in the adult's unconscious; it corresponds to the child's achievement of physical coordination and a fairly advanced degree of mental organization at, say, age four.

Under the pressure of the crisis in Hamlet's affairs, the hero himself and the various images and events of the play as a whole fall back, as it were, to earlier stages of infancy ("deeper" layers of the unconscious). Hamlet becomes more helpless and ineffectual; the action of the play moves toward the activities of a younger child, peering, spying, babbling, an intense preoccupation with food and dirt. Finally, at the end of the play, the action bounds up again with a kind of exhilaration to its original level, but carrying with it material from the earlier, "deeper" stages of infancy.

In more technical language, Miss Sharpe sees the opening of *Hamlet* as presenting a problem in genital terms; the play then regressing to pregenital or partial instincts; the denouement resolving the problem by pregenital activities infused with the creative purposes implicit in genitality. In the terms of the play Hamlet is presented at the opening with a direct oedipal problem; a rival has killed his father and married his mother. Through the middle of the play Hamlet meets this problem by ineffectual activities that do not directly attack Claudius, pretending madness, the play within the play, the duel with Laertes. Finally, within these ineffectual activities he strikes at the king directly.

Miss Sharpe argued in her discussion of *Hamlet* that this pattern of high beginning, regressed middle, and partially recaptured height was not only the pattern of *Hamlet,* but also of any creative work, and of the development of the personality itself (as in Ernst Kris's concept of "regression in the service of the ego"). Her two phases of "the cyclic movement in Shakespeare's plays" show a similar pattern of climax, descent to a nadir, ascent back to the climax. Unfortunately, she did not live to complete the long and detailed analyses of the plays that she would need to substantiate her hypothesis—with one exception. She did make an extended comparison of *King Lear* to *The Tempest* in these terms.[56]

She calls *The Tempest* a sequel to *Lear* in "a cycle which seems characteristic of creative artists." (In the diagram of the cyclic movement of Shakespeare's works as a whole they are on opposite sides of the nadir of Phase II.) She sees the two plays as linked by: the storm; the fact that the central figure is an older man; the central relationship is that of father to daughter; in both plays carnal life is separated from the higher people of the play; the two plays show three themes in common—retirement, ingratitude, and the contrast of revenge as against "saving." On one level, she says, the dramatist is working out in the two plays his attachment to his daughter. On a deeper level, any father's feelings toward his daughter stem from what he unconsciously retains of his childhood desire for his mother.

The ambiguity is particularly strong in *Lear* where the tragic victim is paradoxically both old and childish. The unconscious problem in *Lear,* then, is a problem of infancy which persists in the unconscious of the adult (Shakespeare), but now it can be worked out through resources of language big enough to express the titanic troubles of his or anyone's childhood. The problem is that the child's feeling that he is omnipotent ("They told me I was everything") is followed by his horrified realization that not only is he not "everything"; he is hopelessly outclassed in the rivalry for his mother by his huge father on the one hand and his helpless younger siblings on the other. (Miss Sharpe links the childhood problem embodied in *Lear* to the birth of Shakespeare's younger sisters and suggests that the problem was made particularly acute for the infant poet by the fact that, having been the only one of the Shakespeares' first three children to have survived into infancy, he had occupied a position of especial attention and care.)

The infantile problem appears rather clearly in the opening colloquy between Gloucester, Kent, and Edmund. There is carnal sexuality and the birth of a rival brother (Gilbert?) as a result of it; at the end of the scene child Lear sends both father (Gloucester) and brother (Edmund) away. The play as a whole should be considered (Miss Sharpe says), like this scene, as a sort of *gestalt* all of whose elements grow from the unconscious factors (both adult and infantile) in the poet's mind. The characters should be regarded, not so much as three-dimensional people, but as the personifications of disparate influences from the poet's mind. And the plot is dictated rather more by the unconscious content of the play than by the logic of events.

"Thou mad'st thy daughters thy mother," the Fool tells Lear, and that is their unconscious significance. The three daughters personify three disparate aspects of the mother: Cordelia is the "good" mother; Regan is the "bad" in the special sense of withdrawing; Goneril is the "bad" mother in the sense of one who is actively hostile. (Miss Sharpe says, as Freud did—and for neither author do I see why—that Goneril is pregnant at the opening of the play, and therefore represents that aspect of the mother that gives birth to rivals to the child.) Similarly, the three sons-in-law personify disparate aspects of the father (or to put it in adult *and* infantile terms, three aspects of the rival to woman in Shakespeare's unconscious): France is the father deprived of his wife; Cornwall is the cruel, blinding, castrating father; Albany is guiltless—and ignorant.

Lear's resigning the government suggests Lear's ceasing to govern himself, giving way to the mad and incontinent impulses of infancy. His choice among his three daughters expresses these impulses both on an infantile and an adult level. On the infantile level, he selects the bad mother in preference to the good to act out Shakespeare's infantile feeling that he is sinned against (punished) for sins which are unconscious on his part, particularly sins of incontinence, of failing to govern himself, sins projected in the play onto "retainers" or "knights" (nights?). On an unconscious adult level the old man's choice among his daughters and his rejection by them are reversals of the unconscious and forbidden wishes that Shakespeare must have had toward his daughters, namely, that they would choose and accept him.

The Fool embodies an infant's sense that he was tricked or betrayed: "I was fooled." As Lear says, "They told me I was everything." Lear's going from house to house on a monthly basis, Miss Sharpe suggests, is related to childish fantasies about the monthly cycle in women. (Later, when Gloucester appears with bandaged, bleeding eyes and Lear identifies him as Goneril with a white beard, there is a variant of the earlier fantasy, namely, that woman bleeds because she has been mutilated—symbolized by the blinding.)

Child Lear is locked out while the husband and wife remain within; he hears strange noises of "sport," "hunting" (that is, exploring). He tries to beat his way in with noise: "I think the world's asleep." His reaction is to go out in the storm, a sort of infantile tantrum where physical and psychic stresses merge. He wails his own impotence and

hat the gods or parents, the "servile ministers," will not do his will.
Lear's revenge is a kind of incontinence; he does not govern things,
nd quite literally he wets himself. He regresses, too, to the magical
hought of infancy in which curses and threats are as good as action;
e promises to kill his sons-in-law (rivals) although he knows he
asn't the power.

The Gloucester plot both supplements the main plot and intro-
luces another rivalry, that of older against younger brother. Edgar
epresents a projection of guilt, then flight, in response to his fear at
he frightening wishes of childhood against the father. His feigned
nadness mirrors Lear's acting out the real madness of childhood. The
Gloucester plot, like the Lear plot, fulfills wishes. The father is muti-
ated (symbolized by tearing out the "vile jelly" of his eyeballs); he is
hereby punished both for his knowledge of secrets (about love) and
or his hidden, horrid relations with the mother which rival the child's
pen love and breed more rivals: "The dark and vicious place where
nee he got cost him his eyes." At the end innocent Edgar, innocent
f both the sex and violence associated with Edmund, becomes the
:ader, the father, carrying before him his trumpet.

In the final scenes Lear is restored to the maternal care of Cordelia,
ut she is taken away again, and he "howls" like any dispossessed
hild. Finally, he surrenders ultimately and completely to the father
gures: "Undo this button," and retreats to a purely imaginary pos-
ession of the mother.

The infantile situation, then, which *Lear* expresses begins with the
hild feeling that he is the whole world and can do as he pleases. He
s shocked as he realizes his rivalry with the father (conceived in sex-
al terms) and with a rival brother (who comes in some mysterious
exual way). The child regresses to a tantrum level of magical think-
ng and incontinence. He succeeds in returning in a limited way to
an earlier situation at the breast where a child can scorn the king he
nvies." More crudely, the underlying unconscious situation of *Lear*
; that of an angry child who feels neglected by his mother in favor of
is father and his brother, who runs away and wets, who thereby wins
is mother's attention, but only briefly before punishment.

My brief summary cannot do justice to Miss Sharpe's elaborate
nalysis which, despite occasional misreadings and a generally mad
ing to it, is highly convincing as to infantile fantasies, although
ather less so with respect to the defensive level. Element after ele-
nent of the play falls into place in the infantile conflict she posits, and
ne can only wish she had done more with the resolution of the con-
ict.

Her analysis of the successful counterpart to *Lear*, *The Tempest*, is

much briefer. The comedy, she says, also deals with the theme, "I was fooled," but, where Lear reacted by giving up government both of himself and the kingdom, Prospero resumes it. Prospero is a child also (in the poet's unconscious) but he is a benevolent child who controls his childish impulses (projected as Caliban). "The stimulus for regression in the poet's maturity was the reactivation of the unconscious incest wishes toward his daughters, the buried hostility to the father being transferred to sons-in-law." This is true both for *Lear* and *The Tempest,* but, unlike King Lear, Prospero does not repent—his enemies do. He himself acts as both mother and father; Miranda is symbolically both mother and daughter. A kind of harmony is reached in which Prospero twice crosses over the "waves" of mental disturbance. In short, Miss Sharpe says, *The Tempest* represents the mature poet mastering his infantile sexuality by defensively reinstalling his earlier romantic ideals.

The second of our three writers considering Shakespeare the man in all his works is Dr. Mark Kanzer who provides a somewhat different view of Shakespeare in "The Central Theme in Shakespeare's Works." [57] Kanzer criticizes the emphasis on parricide in Shakespeare's plays by such writers as Rank, Jones, even Freud himself. Like Schneider, he sees as Shakespeare's central theme the fidelity and reliability of woman. In particular, he traces three phases each embodying a somewhat different treatment of the one theme. In the first phase, the "romantic-comic," the plays concentrate on high-spirited, ardent virgins. Two ideas run through the early plays both obvious derivatives of the child's oedipal wishes. First, possession of the heroine (who, psychoanalytically, is the mother) brings death. Second, the alternative to this possession is altruistically to give over the heroine to another man—if pushed to an extreme, this altruism edges over toward an unnatural tenderness toward the other man. In this first period the men in the plays, particularly the young men, tend to be weak and vacillating. As examples, Dr. Kanzer suggests Proteus in *Two Gentlemen,* Claudius in *Much Ado,* the two lovers in *Midsummer Night's Dream,* or Romeo. Like Romeo and Claudio, these young men tend to leave the women they love.

The second, the "tragic" phase, progresses from the first by a pattern well known to psychoanalysts—Freud described it in 1910 as "A Special Type of Choice of Object Made by Men." That is, some men tend to think of women either as idealized virginal figures or as sluts. The tabooed, idealized, virginal (so the child wishes) mother cannot be possessed; only debased women, prostitutes, are allowed. Shakespeare shifts his interest from the virginal heroines of the first phase to more mature, stronger, voluptuous, and treacherous women.

(like Cleopatra) in the second. Examples would be Helena, who in *All's Well* is a sort of mother figure, Isabella who, Kanzer says, is either cruel or unreliable, Gertrude, Lady Macbeth, and so on. There are certain special treatments of the theme: notably Timon's misogyny and Volumnia who identifies with Coriolanus and so satisfies her own urges toward masculinity. Such a mother can be kept only by constant success.

Most of these plays of the tragic period, Kanzer says, show another pattern: the women shift their affections from one lover to another. This reflects Shakespeare's feeling that he was supplanted by his younger brothers (and sisters). Edmund is such a rival, and Macduff suggests the sibling in the womb. The plays of this period show sadistic impulses both toward the brother and the rival. Yet, in this shifting of affections, Dr. Kanzer says, "the dramatist must assume an ambivalent attitude. As son he wishes to take the place of the father with the mother, and as older child he fears the competition of the younger brother. In the resulting conflict he is divided within himself and must solve the problem by permitting the heroine to favor now one, now another of his representative forms while he himself strives to stand apart from the action and derive his satisfaction as dramatist from omnipotent control over the characters created by his fantasy." One thinks of the Duke in *Measure for Measure* or Hamlet with his "Mouse Trap" play. By forcing the heroine into the decisive role, Shakespeare, Kanzer says, shows an identification with women. He mentions the *Sonnets,* the plays in which women appear in men's clothes, the mother's love for a boy in *Venus and Adonis,* or the rape in *The Rape of Lucrece.*

In the final period the virgins reappear and take the center of the stage from the older women of the tragic phase. They are usually shown in a father-daughter relationship. Men are shown as suspicious and unjust, but they are forgiven. Dr. Kanzer notes the incest situation in *Pericles;* Caliban's lust in *The Tempest* he sees as a childish version of Prospero's love for Miranda.

Kanzer also examines two recurring events through the plays: first, plays within plays; second, the behavior of the audience at these "plays." He takes an example from each of the three phases. In *Midsummer Night's Dream* Bottom peers through a hole in the wall; later he finds only bloody clothes. In *Hamlet* the king sleeps after embraces from his queen. In *The Tempest,* dreams of fertility and union are shown before sleep. In short, these "plays within plays" all show exactly the characteristic psychoanalysis predicts: they grow out of childish fantasies about watching the parents' loving and a sleep like death after it.

Dr. Kanzer goes on to consider the various audiences. Hippolyta has a share in the comedy; Ophelia suffers for the crimes of another; Richard III plots against the audience. In *Caesar,* Antony feels contempt for his audience as he enthralls them; Coriolanus refuses to appear to his; Timon throws water (urine) in the faces of his audience and withholds the (fecal) gold. For Miranda, however, "O brave new world." The audience is to be loved. In other words, Kanzer says, Shakespeare's feelings toward his audience parallel his feelings toward women: "The audience is actually a major character and a projected form of the heroine herself."

On the basis of his study of heroines, plays within plays, and audiences, Dr. Kanzer concludes that the character who most nearly approximates Shakespeare is the "complex and histrionic" Hamlet, perpetually impelled to action (supplanting the father), yet perpetually staving it off. "In a symptomatic act which gratifies both conflicting tendencies" Hamlet gets a cry of players and puts on an adaptation of a play. "Shakespeare may have been such a Hamlet, perpetually arrested at the scene in which he sponsors the drama and instructs the players."

Writers such as Dr. Kanzer or Miss Sharpe tend to look at the total configurations of several plays or all of them. The earlier psychoanalytic writers, such as Jones or Rank, tended to look at one character within the play who supposedly speaks for the author. Such a method has obvious affinities to a Romantic conception of literature as self-expression, but it actually stems from Freud's description of the creative process in "Creative Writers and Day-Dreaming." Freud argued that the central figure of a novel or play represented the dreamer in the dream, the ego of the writer. *But* Freud went on to say that in more sophisticated writings this ego tends to split up into a variety of characters. He thus provided a basis for Dr. Kanzer's or Miss Sharpe's approach to the play as a total *Gestalt.* Nevertheless, the classical psychoanalytic approach, considering one character as the projection of the writer, has not by any means proved incorrect nor has it been exhausted as shown by the third of our writers who seek Shakespeare in all his works.

Professor Harold Grier McCurdy, in his study, *The Personality of Shakespeare,*[58] has combined these two approaches; indeed, he has even attempted to quantify them. One must, he says, look at the whole play, but one must also recognize that the principal character is likely to represent the ego of the author, although he insists that there is no way of telling *from the play alone* which elements in it represent conscious factors in the author's mind and which unconscious. He accepts Freud's basic assumptions that (1) a work of the imagination is a wish-fulfilling fantasy, and (2) that the characters are projections of the author's own feelings. He has an interesting way of putting it. As in McDougall's psychology, McCurdy compares the personality to a sort of "shadow community" consisting of the various people whose influence we have absorbed (or, more technically, whom we have introjected). Psychoanalytic terms can in this sense be understood as social relations within this community; identification would be a business merger, say, and a complex would be a gang or clique. Drama, so understood, will lend itself beautifully to the expression of the author's personality, even better than the direct statements of lyric poetry.

Professor McCurdy quantifies this approach to drama by considering the number of lines spoken by the various characters. He tallies this number, which he calls "character weight," for the character who talks most. He then uses it as a base to set the percentage of that number spoken by the second most garrulous character, the third, and so on. Thus in *King Lear* Lear himself speaks 682 lines (Rolfe arrives at 770); Edgar speaks 56 per cent as many; Kent, 50 per cent; Gloucester, 47 per cent, etc. (Professor McCurdy found that the curves were approximately exponential in form, thus corresponding to other statistical studies of literary vocabulary, interactions in small groups, and so on.) A preliminary comparison between such curves for Shakespeare and those for Marlowe shows that Marlowe's are "sharper"; that is, his first-ranking characters tend to outtalk the second-ranking characters more than Shakespeare's top-ranking characters do. One would expect this result, and it tends to confirm the correctness of the procedure. Professor McCurdy also notes that the curves for Shakespeare's histories and tragedies are markedly "sharper" than those for the comedies. (This confirms statistically a conclusion that many other writers have reached independently in a qualitative way, namely, that comedy tends to be more of a hurly-burly of equally important characters than tragedy; hence there is less identification with comic protagonists than with tragic.)

Professor McCurdy's first step is to consider broad types of characters. He finds, first, that the character weight of male characters is four times that for female. He concludes, not unreasonably, it would seem, that Shakespeare was strongly masculine. The character weight for nonlovers is about twice that for lovers in Shakespeare's plays (contrast the novels of Charlotte Brontë, where the relationship is just about reversed). Romantic love seems to be relatively subordinate in Shakespeare's thinking. The total character weight of those characters who survive their play is about twice that of those who die during the play, but if the tragedies alone are considered the character weights of those who die about equal the character weights of those who survive. (Contrast this figure with that for Sophocles: the character weight of those who survive is four times that of the characters who die.) Shakespeare, Professor McCurdy concludes, "loads his stage with death." The character weight for violence is only slightly less than that for all the nonviolent characters: Shakespeare put a lot of violence as well as death into his plays. McCurdy finds no particular tendency for these relations to change as the playwright matured, although there is some decrease in love interest with age.

Considering only the top-ranking characters in these scales of character weight, Professor McCurdy finds that one-sixth of the top-ranking characters are flawless, noble women who ease the sufferings of others. On the other hand, five-sixths of the top-ranking characters are men who tend to treachery, misanthropy, and pride; they have what Professor McCurdy calls "alert, suspicious hostility." He concludes that, if his initial hypothesis holds, if top-ranking characters are projections of the dramatist himself, then Shakespeare had a strong bisexual component in his nature; regardless of the correctness of that hypothesis, Shakespeare seemed to idealize women more than men.

The second-ranking characters tend to be either helpers, opponents, or sexual partners of the top rankers. The scope of these relations is broad, but there are some notable omissions: there are no religious relations, nor any lassitude or passivity allowed for. The themes and relations, then, that interest Shakespeare are the struggle for power and sex. Sex he tends to identify with sensuous beauty, power with intellectual mastery.

Among the themes of the plays Professor McCurdy finds betrayal is the major one, either sexual or political betrayal. If sexual, it involves either a husband or near-husband and a wife or near-wife (not illicit relationships). The form the betrayal takes is: "I was not the victim of the falsehood and infidelity of others; I suffered from self-deception." Professor McCurdy analyzes in this connection *Two Gentlemen, Hamlet, Merry Wives, Measure for Measure, Much Ado, Othello, Cymbeline,* and *The Winter's Tale.* If the betrayal is political, the one betrayed is a ruler who is also cast as a father or a fatherlike man.

The second most common theme—it is markedly more important in *King Lear* and other plays after 1605—is the relation of father and daughter. The handling of the theme follows a three-stage pattern: at first the father and daughter have a close relationship (tenderer and more sexual in the later plays); then she wilfully selects a lover; third, he rejects or gives her up. On a statistical basis, McCurdy finds that fathers and lovers are played off against one another; the more lines the father has, the fewer the lover gets, and the correlation is very high.

A third important theme is the contrast of high figures linked to imagination and fancy with low characters linked to carnal desires. Professor McCurdy notes a number of contrasts: Puck and Bottom; Hal (I would have said Hotspur) and Falstaff; Maria (Feste better?) and Sir Toby; Ariel and Caliban. In the later plays the low character, Parolles or Cloten, for example, gets increasingly sexual—and increasingly controlled, often by women.

The relation of mother and son does not occupy a particularly important place in Shakespeare's themes, except in *Hamlet* and *Coriolanus*. (Other analytic writers, Professor McCurdy feels, have given these plays disproportionate weight. He himself finds no mother love above the third rank on his character-weight scales. Where the theme occurs, the son tends either to be overly dependent on the mother or to overreact against that dependency.)

The relation of father to son, Professor McCurdy says, becomes an important theme only after *Henry IV* (Falstaff being a father figure). The sons work under serious reproaches and demands to justify their existence. In the last three plays, he notes, fathers recover lost sons.

Having described characters and themes, Professor McCurdy goes on to suggest what he thinks Shakespeare's personality was. He finds the poet was a supremely normal, if unusually perceptive, man. He was predominantly masculine and aggressive, not romantic or dreamy. The diversity of his top-ranking male characters, however, suggests that Shakespeare had no clear conception of himself. The occasional rise of tender and romantic feminine components to dominance in the plays suggests, Professor McCurdy says, latent homosexuality. So, he says, does the constant fear of betrayal by women and Shakespeare's hope that he is only fooling himself by believing that women betray. Revulsion against women is translated: recoil of the woman into the arms of another man. (If I may intrude my own view at this point, this corresponds to a well-known formula of defense against strong feelings for another man: "I don't love him; *she* does.") In the later plays this tenderness and femininity are allowed more, he says, but only as relaxation by a man of demonstrated power. Shakespeare apparently waged a constant struggle against this feminine side of his nature and felt a good deal of guilt about it. He also, Professor McCurdy says, seems to have felt guilty about living up to his father's wishes, and he felt guilty, too, about his infantile desires to murder his father, overreacting into grandiose actions of violence and revenge.

Professor McCurdy goes on to relate his insights through the plays into Shakespeare's personality, to the facts and legends of Shakespeare's life. He finds that Shakespeare identified strongly with his father—he seems to have been like him, at least as the two traditions about John Shakespeare would have him, a jolly man and, for a while, a successful one. Shakespeare thus seems to have had a dual image of his father represented, say, by Henry IV and Falstaff. There is the serious, businesslike coat-of-arms John Shakespeare and the Falstaffian clown John Shakespeare who "durst have crackt a jeast" with his son any time. Similarly, Professor McCurdy says, Shakespeare seems to have had a dual image of his mother, Volumnia and Gertrude. One is cold and severe, the cause of her son's defeat; the other is lascivious. Both cause a restraint in the son's relations with other women.

Such figures as Arthur in *King John* or Mamillius in *The Winter's Tale* suggest, Professor McCurdy says, tender feelings toward boys and young men, as do the pairs of friends in the later plays. Perhaps, Professor McCurdy suggests, Shakespeare was compensating for the lost Hamnet. Viola, for example, becomes in a way a son; sons-in-law in the plays become sons. Shakespeare was concerned with money a good deal, and several of his top characters are, too: Petruchio, Shylock, or Timon, who may, Professor McCurdy says, represent Shakespeare's father. Shakespeare seems to have had on his father's behalf dreams of money and revenge on the town of Stratford.

Professor McCurdy closes his book with a fair and accurate critique of his own method. He himself makes very clear the problems involved in linking a hypothetical childhood with the momentary environment of the adult Shakespeare. There are two factors that I think should be added to Professor McCurdy's astute observations on his method. First, his statistical techniques create the illusion of more certainty than there actually is. After a careful numerical analysis, the conclusion is likely to be highly qualitative, say, that certain characters show "alert, suspicious hostility." There is no way of weighting the effect of dramatic conventions nor does the method of counting the lines a character speaks allow for the importance of a character who is talked about; and, even so, there seem to be some unresolved discrepancies between Professor McCurdy's count and the standard one of Rolfe. Second, Professor McCurdy tends to identify characters in the play too readily with characters we know about in Shakespeare's life, for example, Claudius with Edmund Lambert. It seems to me this procedure falls into the fallacy of misplaced concreteness. That is, we know about Edmund Lambert, so we find him in the play. But actually, as can be seen in one's own dreams, it is often rather trivial stimuli that evoke strong unconscious responses; with Shake-speare, it may well have been just someone he saw in the street one day, not Edmund Lambert, that made him characterize Claudius the way he did—or it may have been a combination of a whole range of stimuli. Even so, I would join with Professor McCurdy's eloquent plea for freedom of methodology (at least until there are some con-clusions to argue about).

SHAKESPEARE IN DICTION AND IMAGERY

So far we have been considering writers who looked through the plays to Shakespeare the man by means of character and theme. By comparison, relatively little has been done about looking through the plays by means of language. In many ways nonanalytic studies of im-agery like the late Caroline Spurgeon's *Shakespeare's Imagery and What It Tells Us* [59] or the studies of G. Wilson Knight come very close to psychoanalytic procedure. Miss Spurgeon was seeking to es-tablish Shakespeare's identity as different from Marlowe's or Bacon's; her approach was to treat Shakespeare's images as an unconscious manifestation, a sort of thumbprint inadvertently left behind. Later critics use imagery to discover theme and meaning, but the end prod-uct of Miss Spurgeon's endeavors is a mere catalogue of Shake-speare's images to suggest what he was interested in, what he was fa-miliar with, what, in a sense, sprang most readily to his mind. Sec-ondarily, Miss Spurgeon discusses the occurrence of a central image associated with a particular play, say, disease images in *Hamlet,* or food in *Troilus and Cressida.* This second method leads to the studies of such later critics as G. Wilson Knight whose interpretations of the plays' themes rely heavily on discussions of imagery. With respect to the personality of Shakespeare, Knight in particular leaves us with a chart of Shakespeare's "universe," [60] suggesting a number of his as-sociations in a way very much like that which psychoanalytic criti-cism makes possible.

There is still a third method of quasi-psychoanalytic criticism of imagery in Shakespearean circles, that represented by Professor Ed-win A. Armstrong, who is not only nonpsychoanalytic, but devoutly so. His *Shakespeare's Imagination* [61] deals with image clusters, for example, the famous cluster pointed out by Whiter in 1794 of dogs-melting-candy-flattering. Armstrong lists nine other such clusters in which the mention of one element tends to bring in the others by as-sociation in adjacent lines. (Professor Armstrong being a bird-and-insect watcher, his image clusters run rather heavily to ornithology and entomology, and other clusters, less zoological, have since been pointed out in addition to the ones he named.)

Both Miss Spurgeon and Professor Armstrong attempted to extend their studies of imagery into a description of Shakespeare's personality. Miss Spurgeon's has been aptly described as making the poet into "the troop leader of the Stratford boy scouts." Professor Armstrong's is equally bland. He concludes that Shakespeare's memory combined retentiveness and availability, that he associated quickly and easily, that his emotions are shared by many, that he composed by relaxing and assimilating, then writing furiously. Neither Miss Spurgeon nor Professor Armstrong is burdened by any particular scientific knowledge of the human mind; indeed Armstrong strenuously argues against the existence of an unconscious containing suppressed desires.

In a recent article [62] Dr. Kanzer has called the psychoanalysts' attention to the importance of imagery as a revelation of the author's psyche. He notes, for example, an image Miss Spurgeon spoke of: a snail referred to, not for slowness, but for its tender horns "which were regularly described as bruised and drawn back into the shell." "Perhaps," Dr. Kanzer says, "there is an inner connection here with another striking and peculiar image about short lengths of candle with an evil smell which, when most wanted, had a tendency to go out." Kanzer also quotes Armstrong and F. E. Halliday for the proposition that Shakespeare's images tend to be followed by their opposites; Kanzer points out that this is exactly what one would expect from the lack of negation in unconscious or dream thinking. Dr. Kanzer's article represents plea, however, not completion; so far no psychoanalytic critics have considered Shakespeare the man by any systematic approach to all his imagery.

A few psychoanalytic critics have looked at Shakespeare's psyche by means of a single image. Professor Arthur Wormhoudt, for example (like Armstrong), considers birds in Shakespeare,[63] but from the point of view of Dr. Edmund Bergler's psychoanalytic theories about writers. As Freud and Jones have pointed out, a bird often symbolizes for the unconscious a male member because of the bird's ability to rise. In so far as the child interprets the breast as physically like a male member (see Freud's essay on Leonardo), the bird can also be a symbol for the breast. Bergler, however, argues that writers are preoccupied with the breast and the oral stage in child development; therefore, Wormhoudt hypothesizes that the oral symbolic equation breast=bird should be more common with writers than the genital symbolism.

He takes a number of his examples from Shakespeare. Claudius' "limed soul" at prayer is to be understood, he says, as a phallic impotency which means that Hamlet need not kill him; on a deeper level, the image identifies him with the mother's breast (Claudius often being associated with drink) and Hamlet's refusal to kill him is a defense against a childish impulse to devour and so make the mother's breast once and for all a part of him, to detach it and incorporate it. The "temple-haunting martlet," he says, consciously refers to the irony of trusting as Duncan does. Unconsciously, it is a swallow; in the scene preceding Lady Macbeth has prayed that her mothers' milk might turn to gall, and the nest is built on a castle, which is a feminine symbol: all these things, Wormhoudt argues, show the identification of bird and breast. He notes that many women in Shakespeare are compared to birds, Imogen, Goneril (a kite), Petruchio's Kate (a falcon), Demetrius' Helena (a crow); Lucrece the poet described as a trembling bird, and Shakespeare lavished loving care on his description of her breasts. Wormhoudt makes a general reference to Armstrong's book and says that those clusters also show the bird-breast symbol.

Dr. Sidney J. Baker has examined Shakespeare's sexual images, with interesting results.[64] "Shakespeare," he concludes, "sacrificed few opportunities to scatter sexual allusions and puns." In all, Dr. Baker collected six hundred examples (and I'm sure that someone fresh from a reading of Eric Partridge's *Shakespeare's Bawdy* could find many more). He then catalogued these images according to the aspect of sexuality they represented and the way in which they represented it.

"The interesting point that emerges from an examination of Shakespeare's sexual terminology," he says, "is that, almost without exception, it serves to demonstrate Freud's theory of dream symbolism." That is, the male genital is represented by elongated objects, weapons, machines, musical instruments, or roots; the female genital is represented by containers, circular objects, cavities, ships, landscapes, flowers, and houses. Many animals are used to represent man as a sexual animal. The sexual act itself appears metaphorically as climbing, eating, burning, tilling the soil, play, work, business exchange, or violent action. This last metaphor is the most common one in the whole group: Dr. Baker finds that fully one-fifth of his six hundred examples represent the act of love as violent action, and he concludes that this indicates a strong component in Shakespeare of masculine aggression, an unconscious sadism that would be associated with the anal stage in child development. (Dr. Baker's conclusion would, of course, be much stronger if we knew that his figures, six hundred references to sex, over one hundred of them to the sexual act as violent action, were uncommon, not shared, say, by Jonson or Marlowe or Chapman.)

Dr. Baker finally concludes that Shakespeare must have recognized the significances of the symbols he used; this awareness, in turn, implies a remarkable lack of inhibition in expression. In part, he says, we can attribute this freedom to the times, but Dr. Baker insists that Shakespeare, even for an Elizabethan, was unusually free of guilt and inhibitions about sex.

Perhaps the most interesting psychoanalytic essays at Shakespeare's language are the analyses of particular speeches scattered through Dr. Robert Fliess' *Erogeneity and Libido*.[65] Dr. Fliess uses Shakespeare for the poet's "remarkable" clinical insights; for our purposes, the process works the other way—we find the psychology of Shakespeare's writing from Dr. Fliess' clinical experience. The book deals mostly with the earlier stages of psychological development, the oral and anal phases when the child is interested in the mouth or excretion, and the residues these stages leave in the adult's mind.

What Fliess finds is that in particular speeches the images regress to these earlier stages of child development. The succession of Shakespeare's images, in other words, constantly moves up and down the unconscious scale from the deepest or earliest levels of infantile experience to the highest or latest stages. For example, he quotes *Henry V*, I.i.47–50, Canterbury's description of Henry V's eloquence:

> . . . that when he speaks,
> The air, a chartered libertine, is still,
> And the mute wonder lurketh in men's ears
> To steal his sweet and honeyed sentences.

The passage, Dr. Fliess says, shows a curious mixing of speech with listening. The eloquence of the king's speaking is described in terms of his hearers' listening. In particular, the last two lines of the speech treat *listening* as *oral* stealing. The metaphor, he says, takes the earliest passive and sucking mouth of infancy ("the mute wonder") out of the later, less sensitive mouth of the adult ("a chartered libertine") and projects this early mouth into the ear. The reading applies whether a "libertine" is a freeman or a rake, whether "chartered" means hired or licensed; in either case, the passage compares air to someone involved with activity who is then "still." The two lines, in other words, act out verbally one of the common sublimations in anyone's development: someone listening to a play is feeding on words much as, when he was a child, he sucked in sweetness.

In another case, the speech of Fortinbras' captain in *Hamlet* (IV.

iv.16–22), Dr. Fliess notes how Shakespeare uses the verse rhythms to express thoughts in motor terms. "To pay five ducats, five, I would not farm it," the captain says, and Dr. Fliess comments that the first half of the line marches along with the brisk, sharp military step of the preceding lines, while the independent clause, "I would not farm it," shows a relaxation in the consonants and the rhythm as we glimpse the rural origins of the soldierly speaker. Similarly in Cassius' description of himself and Caesar swimming the angry Tiber, "stemming it with hearts of controversy," a muscular idea is expressed in terms of thought. Such metonymies make an appeal to the unconscious where our childhood persists, particularly that part of childhood when psychic events and physical experiences were all mixed in together so that abstractions are expressed as concrete images.

Thus, Dr. Fliess, in this kind of analysis, comes close to plucking out the heart of the mystery. The late Ernst Kris, as we saw in Chapter 5, found in art a sort of psychological calisthenics. That is, art, he said, systematically leads us back to the seething urges of infancy in our adult unconscious; then, in satisfying art at least, the adult's consciousness, his self-preserving ego, re-establishes its control. While Kris's comments make much sense, and it is easy to see how they apply to the over-all sequence of action in a play, it is rather difficult to see how the texture, the language, the succession of individual words and images, generates this action of release and recapture.

Fliess suggests the way, at least for Shakespeare. That is, the poet's images flutter up and down the mind's levels. A single word evokes a whole spectrum of infantile and adult material, both of impulse and defense. Possibly such analyses explain the tremendous power poetry has to stimulate us, to give us at one and the same time the feeling of the mind's and the voice's sensuous movement and also a feeling of tremendous psychic power in the face of limitless potentialities of experience. The trouble with Dr. Fliess' method of analysis, however, is that it tends to degenerate into mere labeling and with very few labels at that: a particular image can touch us at only one of three levels, oral or anal or phallic.

Even so, I think the trouble can be removed. What is called for is more detailed attention to the interaction of the particular words. In the passage Dr. Fliess quotes from *Henry V*, for example, one could include in the analysis the ambiguities involved in "chartered libertine," the ambiguity in "chartered" which implies both the greater freedom of the adult and the greater restrictions placed on him. The sound of "mute wonder" with its *m* and *n* paves the way for the oral images of "sweet" and "honeyed"; the metaphor of wonder lurking mutely in the ear may be a covert image for birth, particularly for the child's fantasy of birth through the anus (ear). "Air" may be involved as anal imagery also. The vowel shift from "still" to "steal" may play its part in the sudden freeing. In short, the answer to the labeling problem may simply be a more detailed treatment of the individual images. If so, Dr. Fliess' method holds out the possibility of being able to analyze the psychological impact of a passage of poetry as it moves along word by word and image by image.

EVALUATING STUDIES OF AN AUTHOR'S PERSONALITY

The difference between Dr. Fliess' method and the early remarks of Freud, Jones, or Rank about Shakespeare suggests an extraordinary change in psychoanalytic studies of a single author's personality. If this chapter has suggested anything at this point, it must be that there are a great many studies of Shakespeare's personality and that they use rather widely different methods. Clearly, not all of these studies are equally sound. How do we rate these various readings and methods, letting one character speak for the author or all the characters, looking at one play or many, considering action or structure or imagery or diction? There are, it seems to me, four criteria for evaluating psychoanalytic readings of Shakespeare's character: Which kind of psychoanalytic approach are we dealing with, early or late? How much of Shakespeare is the analyst dealing with? How readily do his insights into Shakespeare relate to clinical experience? Is he dealing with conscious or unconscious material? These four criteria call for a good deal of explication.

As for the first—which kind of psychoanalytic approach to character is used—we need to distinguish, as in psychoanalytic literary theory generally, an early from a late approach. Character, as a concept, came relatively late to the psychoanalytic scene. Freud's first concern and that of the earliest psychoanalysts was with particular neurotic symptoms precipitated by particular crises in adult life which interacted with particular events in infancy.

"Character," by contrast, represents the long-term, steady-state personality to which particular neurotic crises may come. It is defined as "the habitual mode of bringing into harmony the tasks presented by internal demands and by the external world" (Fenichel); that is, character is the way the ego customarily deals with the external world, the drives from within, and the demands of the superego.

There are thus two sharply different ways of trying to read the author from his works. The early analysts tried to see in particular plays or characters particular crises in Shakespeare's infantile and adult life. The later analysts try to see in a lot of his work his habitual ways of responding which are his individual "character." (In this respect Miss Sharpe's essays make an interesting bridge from the early approach to the later one.) The two approaches come out with different types of result. The early one tends to produce evidence of instinctual drives or infantile situations which are more or less the same for all men although evoked by particular circumstances. The later approach looks for that habitual interaction of drives and defenses which is individual character apart from the particular circumstances of Mary Fitton or Queen Elizabeth. Of the two methods, the later one seems much the better. We simply do not know enough about the facts of Shakespeare's life to identify any but a few isolated crises. His marriage, the death of his father, mother, and son are about all. We do, however, have a large body of his creative work from which we can quite legitimately infer his character or life style—if that is our objective.

Clearly, then, so far as psychoanalysis applied to discovering the personality of a writer is concerned, it seems to me the best analysis is that which brings together into one configuration the greatest number of elements from the greatest number of works. Therefore, among the various methods we have seen applied to Shakespeare, the shakiest is assuming that one character, say, Hamlet, "speaks for" Shakespeare. Aside from the objection that this procedure sharply and unduly limits the data, we might also ask, Why Hamlet, why not Laertes? One man in his time plays many parts in the psychic economy of a play. King Lear, for example, symbolically plays the role of father, son, and husband in his tragedy, sometimes sequentially, sometimes all at once. Which aspect of Shakespeare does he "speak for"?

The next weakest method is using the action of only one play to look at the author. It is rather striking that those writers who deduce Shakespeare's personality from either a single character or a single plot (Freud, Jones, Rank, Sachs) come out with psychic universals: Shakespeare, they conclude, had an oedipus complex or sibling rivalry or an interest in incest themes. But all men have these things. Other psychoanalytic critics (for example, Miss Sharpe or Bronson Feldman) analyze a single play in great detail. Regardless of the validity of their individual conclusions, they do at least come up with a universal Shakespeare plus a particularized Shakespeare, one, say, with a tendency to use incontinence as a weapon for solving the conflicts all men face.

When the psychoanalytic critic goes still further and considers all the plays as Professor McCurdy does, Shakespeare becomes even more particularized: not only does he have hostility toward the father combined with a tendency to identify with him (psychic universals); he tends to see his father in two rather sharply marked ways, either as a serious, stuffy, money-minded man, or as a jovial old clown. Shakespeare both hates and loves his siblings (universal); in particular, however, he tends to have an oral rivalry. He sees brother figures as either serious, military, idealistic, somewhat stuffy young men busily emulating the conventional ideals of their fathers, or rather rakish, witty, realistic men, linguistically gifted. (Compare Hotspur and Hal, Othello and Iago, Edgar and Edmund, Brutus and Cassius, Claudio and Benedick, and so on.) This contrast in results matches the contrast in the psychoanalytic approaches: the early one concentrates on crises from instinctual drives more or less the same for all men; the later approach finds the special interplay of drives and defenses which makes up individual character.

In short, *the more details the psychoanalytic critic deals with, particularly details of imagery, the more he goes beyond psychic universals to give us a particularized Shakespeare.* The ideal method, then, of psychoanalytic inquiry into Shakespeare's personality (or any other author's) would be to deal with *all* the plays and poems and with every kind of detail within them, especially the particularizing imagery which has been relatively neglected by psychoanalytic critics. This neglect is rather puzzling in view of the theoretical view of Shakespeare's plays as being at one level like an illusion of real events and at another like a dream. It is to the dream level that the analyst primarily looks: yet no analyst would analyze a dream without the patient's associations to the elements of the dream. In the case of Shakespeare, the dreamer is unavailable, but as Dr. Eissler points out,[66] the particular words and images chosen by the poet serve for purposes of analysis as his associations to the incidents of the play.

Surely, then, the next step in psychoanalytic examination of Shakespeare the man must be an attempt to deal with all the details of at least several if not all of the plays. The task, of course, will be monumental, but in this day of computers, mechanical collators, and electronic concordance makers nothing, I suppose, is impossible.

Impossibilities aside, however, it is clear that the best *method* of psychobiographic criticism is that one which will interrelate the most details from the most plays in terms of the later psychoanalytic approach to character. Aside from method, how do we evaluate different conclusions within the same method? Here the problem is not only how many details are interrelated but also how well. That is, how many steps does it take to get from the play to the psychoanalytic structure it is being compared to and how firm are the individual steps?

Contrast the following two readings. The first argues that Lear becomes a child with respect to his daughters and four items of evidence are adduced. First, he chooses to be helplessly dependent on them; second, he demands total, uncompromising love from them; third, the argument makes sense out of the prevailing image (Spurgeon), that of a body subjected to physical stresses as a helpless child's is; fourth, the Fool says Lear has made his daughters his mother. In this reading four rather large elements of the play are interrelated, and in all four cases it is only one step from the play to an oedipal attitude, well known from clinical experience.

The second reading argues that Aemilia in *The Comedy of Errors* is a phallic mother, a common infantile conception. Two items of evidence are adduced: first, "abbess" may be Englished as a she-father; second, the abbess is associated with a stone abbey where her son seeks sanctuary and "wholesome syrups"—the image of rock is a symbol for the male organ, and is related to images of hardhearted mothers who suddenly turn kind in folklore; they are represented as rocks which suddenly gush forth milk. The first item of evidence requires a long step through Aramaic; the second requires us to link a stone abbey to a pointed stone. The steps are unreliable, and therefore the reading is, too.

In short, the criteria for the validity of a psychoanalytic reading are exactly the same as those for any other kind of critical or scholarly reading—how many details does it relate and how readily are they related? One would apply the same criteria, for example, to the contention that such and such a work is a source for a certain play of Shakespeare's: one would ask, How many details from the alleged source are in the play and how much have they been altered? The moral is: Beware the psychoanalytic reading that rests heavily on a single word and requires a good deal of stretching to get from the word to the psychoanalytic interpretation.

The fourth problem in evaluating psychoanalytic readings raises the question of conscious and unconscious. The psychoanalytic critic tosses these words about rather freely, but as Professor McCurdy points out there is no real way of telling from the play alone whether Shakespeare was conscious or unconscious of a given factor in it. Similarly, it is difficult to tell from the play alone whether we are seeing an impulse expressed or a defense against an impulse, whether a given fantasy is a wish or a fear. What the analytic critic really means is that it is likely in terms of clinical experience that such and such a factor in Shakespeare's mind was unconscious or defensive.

In some cases such probabilities approach certainty; in others, not. For example, if *King Lear,* as Miss Sharpe suggests, is the acting out of a childish fantasy of using incontinence to force the mother to giver her love again, chances are that this fantasy is truly unconscious. On the other hand, Shakespeare's tendency to make his villains cynical may have been quite conscious; he might have felt that the characteristic was appropriate to villains, and he may have known very well that he did not like the quality in himself, his father, or his brothers.

One could go even further. Perhaps, as Ernst Kris suggested, a given factor in a play may not represent the author's personality at all but simply his ability to empathize with someone else's.

Clinical analysis of creative artists suggests that the life experience of the artist is sometimes only in a limited sense the source of his vision; that his power to imagine conflicts may by far transcend the range of his own experience; or, to put it more accurately, that at least some artists possess the particular gift to generalize from whatever their own experience has been.[67]

If this were totally true, it would be impossible to read an author's personality from his works; yet, clearly, different authors have different styles and the style must have something to do with the man.

TWO SPECULATIONS

Dr. Kris's qualification on reading the author from his works leads us to the importance of style as contrasted to the particular conflicts of action and character a story or play may represent. For Shakespeare, style includes above all else imagery, and the somewhat limited studies of Shakespeare's imagery lead me to two somewhat digressive speculations: one, a hypothesis about the creative process; the other, a possible method of analysis.

Those writers who deal with the action and character-conflicts in Shakespeare's plays come up with a universalized Shakespeare, while those who deal with a large collection of lines and images arrive at a particularized Shakespeare. This fact suggests a hypothesis, that for Shakespeare, perhaps for all writers, the larger chunks of action: plot, conflict, character configuration, come from the phallic or oedipal stage of childhood retained in the unconscious of the adult; the details of language and characterization seem to come from the earlier oral or anal stages of childhood. This is admittedly an empirical hypothesis based only on the limited studies so far conducted on Shakespeare; particularly lacking is a fuller treatment of imagery.

Nevertheless, if the generalization holds, it suggests some fairly important things about the creative process and about character generally. That is, the poet's mind seems to meet his material first at the level of interpersonal relationships; he reacts to his materials in terms of a family structure. When he comes to write it, however, he dips, as it were, into deeper layers of his unconscious when his mind was centered more on himself and brings up anal and oral associations in the form of particular words and images with which he fleshes out the bare bones of action.

Artistic creation, then, represents a reversal and re-creation of growing up. As we progress from earliest infancy to later childhood, notably to the oedipal phase, we interpret our later problems in terms of earlier conflicts. The first oral conflicts about self and nonself, love and hate, the ability to be passive and wait, will color development at the anal stage. And anal problems of keeping and giving up will tone the child's handling of the oedipal crisis. In literary creativity, "regression in the service of the ego," the writer seems to return, once he has got his plot, to earlier layers of infancy, and then re-enact the developmental process by handling the interpersonal conflicts of the plot with imagery drawn from the earlier pregenital stages. Perhaps, then, the creative process provides evidence for the general psychoanalytic view of a relatively normal character. That is, in the larger chunks of our lives—careers, marriages, relations to parents, and the like—perhaps it is the oedipal or phallic stage that controls. As for what we are in isolation, the particular tone and style with which we approach life, perhaps these things come from a deeper layer, an earlier stage in infantile development.

My second digressive speculation stems from the (to me) rather striking fact that all three of the nonpsychoanalytic critics who have dealt at length with Shakespeare's total patterns of imagery (Spurgeon, Armstrong, and Knight) have resorted to graphic means, charts or tables, to set out their conclusions. This emphasis on graphic method suggests that a topological approach may have something useful to offer in representing many different aspects of a poet's psyche. In fact, one can even visualize a sort of enormous three-dimensional chart of Shakespeare's mind as a diagnostic or critical tool. The middle layer of such a structure would be the words and images of a play (or, as long as we are free to imagine enormous tasks, all the plays). The images would be presented, not in a continuous sequence or line as they occur in the text of the play, but as an area or field of linked clusters, the associational groups as described by Professor Armstrong, but many more of them, and linked together by the bridging of ideas. For example, Armstrong describes two chains of association that Shakespeare seems to have: in one, the key word "pinch" provokes associations to death, cannons, eyeballs, eye sockets, ears, vaults, mouths, wombs, tombs; in the second, the key word "beetle" evokes references to crows or other birds, mice and vermin, night, cliffs, or death. Death bridges these two clusters, and in our hypothetical chart of Shakespeare's imagination one could link the two clusters through this idea.

All of Shakespeare's associational clusters linked together would constitute the middle layers of this vast chart. From this middle layer the chart would show at a higher level the intellectual content of the plays by a series of larger terms, such as life, death, power, and the like (also shown as a "field") which constitute the links among the particular clusters. Such a chart would correspond to Wilson Knight's picture of the "Shakespearean Universe." The map could also reach down to a lower layer of infantile material which would link the various clusters as unconscious configurations. For example, the "pinch" image cluster is a series of hollow images which run from birth to death and are apparently associated with possessing the mother.

In short, such a three-dimensional structure for Shakespeare (or any other poet) would constitute a picture of the conscious and unconscious layers of his mind and the links between them represented by the structure and language of his works. Indeed, in theory, one ought to be able to make such a model for any person from whom a sufficiently large sample of verbal responses could be obtained. In fact, Profesor Charles R. Osgood and his associates have made up visual models to represent the "semantic space" of particular personalities.[68] The Osgood models come out looking like molecules and represent a static personality. A probably better approach would be the "tree diagrams" of transformational linguistics as developed by Professors Noam Chomsky, Morris Halle, and others,[69] which seem to be a very basic model for psychological processes, in particular, processes that psychoanalysis would call "developmental" (if taking place over a number of years) or "preconscious" (if part of a nearly instantaneous thought process). But these are speculations, both technical and digressive, that take us too far afield from what is, after all, the subject of this chapter.

SHAKESPEARE THE MAN: SOME CONCLUSIONS

There is one conclusion it seems perfectly safe to draw from all these studies of Shakespeare's personality: he enjoyed remarkably good mental health. It may seem somewhat puzzling to speak of

Shakespeare's mental health when we add up some of the actual events in his plays (*not* the psychoanalytic interpretations of them): sadistic mutilation, rape, and cannibalism in *Titus Andronicus;* necrophilia in *Romeo and Juliet;* incest and murder in *Hamlet;* blood lust and unsexing in *Macbeth;* sadistic and masochistic fantasies of mass rape and murder in *Othello;* nymphomania, exhibitionism, and torture in *King Lear;* prostitution in *Timon of Athens;* blood lust again in *Coriolanus;* self-wounding and suicide in *Julius Caesar;* obsessive sexual fixation in *Antony and Cleopatra;* homosexuality in *Troilus and Cressida* [70]—if these are the explicit elements of Shakespeare's plays, surely he must have been a very sick man. Paradoxically, no. In our own day, as in Shakespeare's, such is the stuff as dreams are made on, and unfortunately, in our cheery age, they sometimes make up reality, too. These fantasies speak not of sickness, but of life. The man who tries to carry such foul imaginings into reality is sick, of course, as is the man who is frightened by them or unaware of them, who cannot face them squarely. A man who, like Shakespeare, can accept such imaginings and not only come to grips with them, but transmute them into moral, even bourgeois, drama, such a man has an extraordinary strength and beauty of mind.

We can, though, be far more definite than that. If we sift the readings in this chapter according to our four criteria, we can come up with a tolerably clear psychoanalytic picture of Shakespeare's personality. The overwhelming majority of these analytic students of the man tell us that the primary area of conflict in Shakespeare's psyche was the phallic or oedipal stage. The plays and poems express over and over again the two basic oedipal wishes, to get rid of the father and possess the mother.

In particular, though, the plays express conflict with the father (Rank, Hinrichsen, Sharpe, Jekels). The figures that dominate Shakespeare's stage are men, and the leading figures in the plays are almost without exception cast in the roles of fathers and sons (McCurdy, Schneider). The major theme of the plays is an aggressive struggle between men for power and sex (Freud, Jones, Rank, McCurdy). A variant theme involves replacing or supplanting one father with a more satisfactory substitute (Kris). In still a third variant the "sons" of the plays or poems adopt a passive, feminine, submissive attitude toward the "fathers" (Jones). Often the son has to justify his existence, live up to his father's expectations, suggesting a certain sense of guilt for this filial hostility (McCurdy).

The oedipal pattern seems to underlie the important theme of betrayal in the plays (McCurdy, Strong). That is, one could consider the oedipal triangle as a complex interlocking of betrayals: I am betraying my father with mother; she is betraying me with him; she is betraying him with me; he is betraying me with her, and so on. In particular, Shakespeare seems to have been preoccupied with that form of jealousy which says, "No, I was not really deceived by that woman and that man; I only deceived myself" (McCurdy), in effect, saying it is in his power to give up or avoid the situation of conflict. All these various betrayals could represent either a wished-for consummation or a feared outcome of the oedipal situation, and the expression of such fantasies could serve either as an imagined gratification or a self-punishment defensively warding off feelings of guilt.

As one would expect from this oedipal material and the fantasies of betrayal, Shakespeare tends to see woman primarily as a disturbing, seductive, almost demonic influence (Rank, Fiedler, Sadger, Schneider), and a major concern of the plays is with the fidelity and reliability of women (Kanzer). We can fairly guess that Shakespeare saw his mother as a rather seductive and possessive woman, somewhat along Venusian lines, and that this early sense of absolute possession by her and of her suffered a sharp upset when the oedipal conflict emerged. One defense the early plays use is to give up motherliness, to reduce the heroines into virginal, young, and unmaternal women, occasionally a "master-mistress" (Kanzer), whom we can guess represents not only a defeminized woman but a point of identification for Shakespeare: he could imagine himself in such terms loved by both a man and a woman, a pre-oedipal child unambivalently loved by and loving both father and mother.

The last plays with their concentration on the father-daughter relation suggest still another strategy by which Shakespeare handled his fear and his love for his mother: the protective forgiving fathers of the romances (Sachs). Clinical experience shows that a father is likely to behave to a daughter as his mother behaved to him, and we can guess that Polixenes and Prospero image in part Shakespeare's mother. This, then, is another defensive maneuver in the oedipal conflict, identification with the mother (van Emde Boas) in order to love oneself or to be loved by one's father. Still another Shakespearean defense is to give up the woman entirely, out of fear, or as an overcompensation for hostility to a male rival, a father—or perhaps a brother (van Emde Boas). And, finally, Shakespeare may have found in the audiences he wrote and acted for a mother substitute to whom he played both son and lover (Rank, Kanzer).

Shakespeare was, in effect, an oldest child, and one can guess that the birth of his brother Gilbert when he was two-and-a-half played its part both in his feelings of betrayal and his marked propensity for splitting or pairing characters: Antonio and Bassanio, Claudio and Benedick, Viola and Sebastian, Brutus and Cassius, Iago and Cassio,

Macbeth and Lady Macbeth, Coriolanus and Aufidius. Often he writes about two young men competing for a prize only one of them can have: Hal and Hotspur, Richard and Bolingbroke, struggle for the possession of England; Demetrius and Lysander, Troilus and Diomed, fight for a woman; Hamlet and Laertes compete in acts of revenge. One could multiply almost indefinitely examples of these "Two Noble Kinsmen" or "Two Gentlemen of Verona."

The recurring pattern of two young men is only a particular case of a general habit of Shakespeare's: treating his characters as rather sharply divided into high and low or good and evil (McCurdy, Feldman) or following one image with its opposite (Kanzer). We can guess that this represents not only sibling rivalry, but also the competitive struggles of the phallic stage and also still another way of dealing with the oedipal crisis: splitting himself into good son and bad, splitting off good father from bad father and, in particular, the virginal, untouchable mother from the seductive voluptuary who deceives.

What must strike us, I think, about Shakespeare's personality is the astonishingly wide range and flexibility of his defenses in the oedipal triangle we all once faced: he can identify as need be with any one of the three protagonists, father, mother, or child; he seems able imaginatively to condense two figures into one or to split one into two; to project his feelings into any one of the three or introject theirs into himself. These fluid identifications must have helped him as an actor and writer; these defenses no doubt played a considerable part in Shakespeare's success.

So far we have been considering defenses that, in effect, work the oedipus conflict forward toward one or another possible outcome. Shakespeare, however, could also take the conflict back—he could regress to pre-oedipal styles of development, drawing on deeper layers of his psyche for images with which to reinterpret the later struggle (Fliess), and this is perhaps the most important element in his creative abilities (Sharpe). In his writings, at any rate, he shows a tendency to back away from ordinary love between a man and a woman (Fiedler). As we have seen, a key figure for him to identify with was an unsexual, "master-mistress" youth loved by both men and women (van Emde Boas, Lindsay). Shakespeare seems to have felt some guilt for this kind of identification and the guilt in turn gave rise to fears about his own potency (Kanzer). He tends to pull sex back to a more primitive understanding of it as aggression (Baker), and there may have been a basis for this in childhood episodes of spying on his parents and misunderstanding the act of love as fighting (Rank, Sharpe). If so, such spying would have provided a basis for his later interest in watching and hearing plays.

Very little of the plot and character of the plays stems unaltered from the periods of development preceding the phallic stage. There is some use of anal imagery, some preoccupation with delay and procrastination, some tendency to see excretions as weapons (Sharpe); there is some concern with money and a sense of it as "dirty" (McCurdy). Shakespeare seems to have been able to identify imaginatively with anal personalities and concerns, but this phase left no major components in his own personality.

As for the earliest, the oral period, Shakespeare often treats love in terms of food or appetite. We can guess from his tendency to come out fighting that his mother managed somehow in infancy to mobilize a good deal of aggression in him (Barron) and that this perhaps unduly strong aggressive drive allowed him to respond to the oedipal conflict in the way he did. Shakespeare's heroes *do* things; they actively seek to master reality—even if weak, like Richard II, or vacillating, like Hamlet, they do not only think or talk or know. Perhaps this strong aggressive drive urged Shakespeare himself on to master reality by writing and directing plays.

In short, the picture we get of Shakespeare in psychoanalytic terms is that of a remarkably normal man, one facing the universal conflicts, but armed with a rich repertoire of defenses and a great deal of energy at the service of his well-developed ego. At the same time, he must have been sufficiently disturbed by his early conflicts or his reactions to them so that he chose to work them and his life out in terms of plays, symbolic actions instead of real ones. The choice was fortunate for him, and for us.

All the various readings discussed in this chapter, for all their different methods and emphases, would agree on that one thing—Shakespeare's blooming mental health. At first glance that would seem to be the only thing Shakespeare's psychoanalytic biographers could agree on, they talk about so many different matters. Shakespeare would seem to have become a sort of psychological Everyman, a victim of whatever is the psychoanalytic equivalent of medical student's disease, in which the victim shows successively all the symptoms he reads about in the textbook.

It is possible that this result is inevitable, given the basic method of psychoanalytic criticism. That is, the psychoanalytic critic compares to the play a structure or pattern of mental behavior that he has found in his own or someone else's clinical experience. There is, inevitably, a certain averaging that will take place; one will find in Shakespeare's works the pattern that that one brings to them. The more patterns the psychoanalytic critic looks for in the plays, the more, presumably, he will find; and the picture of Shakespeare that will emerge will be that of a many-sided man, not a man with any single striking abnormality. Perhaps such an averaging is inevitable in psychoanalytic criticism, but I do not think so.

Jonson and Marlowe provide us with informative contrasts to Shakespeare. In Marlowe's plays, a central figure towers over the play, dominates the action, and markedly outtalks the other characters. Young Mortimer sums up the type:

> As for myself, I stand as Jove's huge tree,
> And others are but shrubs compared to me.

Personal interactions of real love and hate play relatively minor parts. True, Marlowe was writing these parts for Edward Alleyn and Alleyn was a giant of a man who could out-Herod Herod; but other men who may have written for Alleyn and the Admiral's Men (Greene or Kyd or Chapman or Porter) did not write like Marlowe. A psychoanalytic critic, it seems to me, would not be unreasonable in assuming, first, that this style is particular to Marlowe, and second, that the central figure is not only a part for Edward Alleyn but also a projection of the poet's ego as Alleyn himself must have been.

This ego is conceived (as Professor Harry Levin's *The Over-reacher* amply demonstrates) in terms of a craving or appetite, be it for knowledge or wealth or power or love; Tamburlaine's feast of crowns makes the symbolism of hunger abundantly clear. The Marlovian central character talks a lot; he is likely to launch into verbal tirades, threats, curses, vows, ragings, or set pieces of great formal and sensuous beauty in which the "mighty line" of the verse substitutes for, indeed becomes, the action of the play. Marlowe's language, moreover, is studded with categories and universals; words like "all," "every," "never" sputter through his speeches. These categories, the psychoanalytic critic would point out, are a residue of the two-valued thinking of earliest infancy, either suck it in or spit it out. In short, as C. L. Barber has shown for Faustus,[71] these focal characters, who project the ego of Christopher Marlowe with their boundless appetites, their use of words as ends in themselves, and their sense that they are all-important, give us a clear picture of a man whose adult life is colored primarily by the oral stage of infancy.

Jonson, as Edmund Wilson pointed out long ago,[72] is primarily an anal poet. Jonson's plays tend to be organized not so much around a central character as around a central situation, particularly one in which a person is treated like a thing. The characters of the play come to this nuclear situation and try to get things out of it, much as parents try to cajole or threaten a child into giving up a precious part of itself. Delays, stalling, or proper timing often play important parts in the action of one of Jonson's comedies. His characters tend to be parts of an aesthetic whole rather than "real" people. Jonson also pays a compulsive attention to dramatic rules and to little scholarly details. Language either flows like Sir Epicure Mammon's or comes out in crabbed fits and starts of jargon; indeed, Jonson collected jargons as he collected knowledge. Sexual relations in Jonson's plays tend to be reinterpreted as possession or as money. Money itself and gold recur steadily. Jonson shows a continuing interest in, at one extreme, glitter, at another, heavily dirty realism. In short, Jonson shows that curious chain of associations that the psychoanalysts describe as the anal character: the child's desire to hold on to its bodily productions turns into an interest in collecting other kinds of dirty objects (such as stones, shells, small animals), finally into collecting precious objects: gold, coins, or hard-earned bits of knowledge.

When the psychoanalytic critic calls Shakespeare a balanced personality, then, it is not simply because of his method of looking at personality; there are sharp differences in the personalities of writers when looked at through the lens of psychoanalysis, and Shakespeare is just as clearly not a primarily oral or anal personality as Marlowe or Jonson clearly is. In fact, it is a fair inference that he was a greater writer than the other two, precisely because he was a more fully developed personality.

The psychoanalytic conception of childhood development is rather like—if you will not cry tilt at the crudity of my analogy—a pinball machine. The infant starts at the top and runs a sort of obstacle course past different obstructions. If he gets stuck ("fixated") at a given scoring pin, bumps up against the same situation repeatedly, a large amount of his total psychic energy becomes bound up with that particular kind of crisis.

Another analogy sometimes used (although the best in this kind are but shadows) compares development to water forming rivulets in sandy ground. For each of us a certain quantity and quality of water flows, the energy of our innate or nearly innate drives. This flow of water will form itself into different patterns depending on the environment it finds. Where there is an obstacle, the water tends to dam up and swirl around, become fixated, in that particular spot of conflict, and the rest of the flow is accordingly impoverished. In an ideal personality the water would be free to spread far from its source perhaps in several different directions—we could speak of a "broad" personality or a "deep" one. Real individuals, as opposed to ideal ones, find themselves bound into a series of conflicts. The more diffuse the conflicts, the further along in development they come, the less energy is tied up in each one, and the more the pattern will approach the ideal. This seems to have been Shakespeare's development, as against Marlowe's or Jonson's evident bogging down in earlier stages.

When, therefore, the psychoanalytic critic says that Shakespeare is not a predominantly oral or anal character, he does not mean that Shakespeare does not have these elements in his personality. Rather, he means that they are there in his unconscious mind, but they are followed by later developments. The concept is not unlike Elizabethan humours psychology: the healthy man is one who has all the sicknesses but has them played off one against another in equal balance,

> So mix'd in him that Nature might stand up
> And say to all the world, "This was a man!"

We find in Shakespeare a mingling of orality and anality, homosexuality and heterosexuality, oedipal hatred of the father and post-oedipal identification with him, love of the mother but fear of her betraying, hatred of a brother mixed with love. Such a mixture constitutes an accurate description of health in a psychoanalytic sense, at least when to them is added Shakespeare's uncanny ability to bring not only these phallic conflicts to expression but imagery from still earlier stages of development, combining them in such a way as to produce great works of art that won for their author honor, riches, and (one guesses) the love of women.

All this psychoanalytic jargon, however (for which I hereby apologize to nonanalytic readers), does not tell us what we would really like to know: what he was like, and what was the nature of his creative gift. Perhaps it is not fair to ask psychoanalysis to tell us. We would like a portrait, but psychoanalysis can only offer an X ray. Psychoanalysis can suggest important unconscious forces in an adult, but, in most cases, those do not give us a picture of what the adult is like: to do so is to stretch insight and inference far beyond legitimate limits. Nevertheless, we would like the pudgy monument in Stratford's Church of the Holy Trinity to step down, the stiff face of the Droeshout portrait with its odd wisp of beard to speak to us, and psychoanalysis does give us some hints.

It is relatively easy to say on the basis of his psychobiography what Shakespeare was not (because he apparently had no markedly oral or anal fixations). If so, he was not the kind of man who is compulsive about details and possessions in the manner of a bookkeeper, a scholar, or a miser. He was neither compulsively neat nor compulsively disorderly. He was not explosive and irascible. Neither was he a man of great intellectual curiosity; the itch to "find out" things was not particularly strong in him. He was not the kind of person who "feeds" on others, who needs people around him, who is greatly dependent on company or external supplies of esteem. Neither was he reckless or carefree or sharp tongued.

Saying what Shakespeare was not, however, does not grant our wish to know what he was. We can, though, make an educated guess. If we are willing to take psychoanalytic insights into unconscious elements from infancy and stretch them to guess at overt adult personality traits; if we assume his aggressive drives were defensive against passivity rather than vice versa; if we add in Miss Spurgeon's guesses about his adult interests and some of the less shaky legends about the poet; and if we rely on what we do know factually about his adult life, we can come up with a sketch, admittedly a very speculative one, of a Shakespeare as though we had met and known him slightly, say, at a cocktail party. The picture, not unsurprisingly, turns out rather like the one Stephen Dedalus drew in the library scene of *Ulysses*.

Hazel-eyed and auburn-haired, he was probably a muscular, compact man, fond of sports. One's first impression would be of a sort of Enobarbus, a man's man, aggressive, competitive, at home in the world of men, the kind of man one thinks of as rather puzzled by and a little afraid of women whom he tends to see either as ideal figures (in God-home-and-mother terms) or as mere amusements put on earth for a man's convenience. He would seem not to be a thinking person; politically and religiously he is conservative to the point of naïveté. Professionally, he is a forceful, driving man. He works for and seizes money, not in an avaricious way, but rather as a token of power and social status, two things about which he is somewhat touchy. At the theater, though, he prefers to work as sporadic director of the group rather than alone or as the man ultimately in charge of the company. He enjoys a masculine camaraderie, and he would be thoroughly at home at an American Legion convention or in the locker room of a Westchester country club.

But this is only a first impression. Perhaps your first indication that this is not the whole man would be his remarkable verbal wit, something we don't associate with the golfing mesomorph. He is terribly amusing and clever, fond of jokes, and given to finding the exact word or phrase that sums up the people around him. He is also rather more interested in other people than the self-contained man's man usually is. He does not, however, collect people or depend on them or seek to pry into them; in fact, his feelings toward others are rather difficult to describe, but he seems to like to confront, as it were, the essence of the people around him, to experience (as opposed to "know") what they are really like. He seems to work on the assumption that other people are not exactly what they seem—they are more complicated than that, often made up of two quite inconsistent characteristics as he himself is.

Probably, during your acquaintance, some event would make you realize how this man who seems best suited to be a merchant or a burgess ended up as an actor and poet. That event might be a sudden petulance, perhaps a reluctance to make up his mind, a wish that someone else would take care of it all. Somewhere within this man there is a very tender, gentle person, even weak and wavering, someone who could cry easily, who dislikes violence and cruelty, who submits easily to others, particularly if they impose interest or tenderness on him. His own interest in other people is intense; he seems quite uncannily able to see things from their point of view and to sympathize, even to fuse with them. At times he becomes almost motherly, particularly toward younger men. Where one's first impression was of an aggressive masculine man, confident among other men and unsure of himself among women, this inner man is quite the opposite. He seems much surer of himself among women than among men. He is, in fact, rather a ladies' man (if we credit that William the Conqueror anecdote), his success with women stemming partly from his own sheer love of the texture and flesh of reality, partly from his dual nature, his ability to play as need be the conquering heroic man's man or the distressed poet in need of mothering.

In fact, if you tried to find one word to sum up this two-sided man, it would be that: "play." With this curious and marked discrepancy between the way he first impresses you and the more complex way he turns out to be you can see why he became an actor. You can see, too, why so often his plays contrast the private man and the public one; why he seems to enjoy seeing two sharply different characters in a similar situation, often with one merging into a larger matrix or order, the other thrusting loose from it: Hal and Hotspur, Laertes and Hamlet, Macbeth and Banquo, Edmund and Edgar, and so on. Once we recognize this sharp difference in him between the outer man's man and the more childlike inner man, it becomes clear why, as an actor, he seems to like to play the part of an older, paternal figure, and yet, being an actor, remain dependent on the audience he woos with such subtlety as though it were his love.

Such a sketch of Shakespeare rests on a great many inferences, both in its handling of the evidence about the man and also in extending psychoanalytic inferences about infancy into adult character.* If this be

* To the psychoanalytically informed reader it may be worth a long footnote for me to explain why I am assuming that aggressive masculinity served

a Shakespeare as though we met him at a cocktail party, then the party was out on a limb. The sketch, moreover, whatever it says about Shakespeare the man or Shakespeare the actor, doesn't answer the second question of interest: What was the nature of his creative gift? Why could this man write the masterpieces he did? Nor have the psychoanalytic studies of the plays shed much light on the matter.

If we are willing to accept the idea that Shakespeare was neither a particularly oral or anal personality, but phallic, we can see a basis for his style; we can understand why he writes more richly than Jonson or Marlowe, why his plays seem to span a greater range of human experience than theirs do. On the other hand, this kind of description does not tell us why any of them, Shakespeare or Marlowe or Jonson, was able to write great drama. One answer is "laxity of repression"; another is "capacity to sublimate." But where do these qualities come from? Or do we have simply to conclude that John Shakespeare and Mary Arden were, in that tiresome modern phrase, "successful" parents? Perhaps the answer lies in the rather sharp split in Shakespeare's personality (although I will not venture to say that one could not find the same in the other two playwrights). The dualism in his nature may have enabled him to project aspects of himself as characters or symbols, and, once projected, to dissociate himself from them

Shakespeare as a defense against passive feminine needs rather than passivity as a defense against aggression felt as threatening or overwhelming. Clearly, I think, both styles show in his writings, but which was the visible or "outer" part of his personality?

I think the aggressive was, for several reasons. Had he tried to master aggression by passivity, we would have gotten the picture of a relatively inactive individual given to sporadic nastiness and obstruction, an oral rather than a phallic character. But his contemporaries record a "gentle Shakespeare" (i.e., gentlemanly), and we know he was active in his company, in lawsuits, and in business. The plays abound in images of sports and violent action, particularly the explicit acting out of parricide and fratricide. The plays, it seems to me, probably mirror the man: they are explicitly aggressive in a phallic and oedipal way but at a deeper level uneasily passive (for example, in Shakespeare's constant acceptance and violation of monarchical order). Thus, Shakespeare's application for a coat of arms and his purchase of New Place would show how in life he placed his aggressive, phallic drives toward business success at the service of oral wishes to be accepted into a larger, nurturing social order.

From the point of view of the methodology discussed at the opening of this chapter, notice how (in the absence of a description by his contemporaries) we can surmise a great deal about Shakespeare's visible personality from his works alone. Just one or two items of external evidence are necessary to bridge the gap from fantasy productions to visible personality. But, of course, we cannot check our surmise about personality against external evidence of personality.

and treat them with great flexibility. But this, too, one of the "latest" in psychoanalytic theories of artistic ability, seems rather vague and unsatisfactory. Finally, then, although psychoanalysis has given us some insight into the man, it has not succeeded in telling us Shakespeare's secret. The creative gift remains, as Freud said it would, the heart of the mystery.

[8]

Psychoanalysis
and the Artist

CLOSEST, perhaps, or at least reaching most directly to the heart of the creative mystery is that group of psychoanalytic writers who have dealt with Shakespeare not so much to gain insight into the man or his writings as to use him for a case in point to prove a theory of art. To some extent, of course, all the psychoanalytic critics we have considered have been using Shakespeare as evidence for a theory, but usually a general theory of human behavior, not one about art alone. Their conclusions about Shakespeare, linking him to the universals of human behavior, can be separated out. The writers in this chapter, however, use Shakespeare to prove a theory of art, and their conclusions seem quite inseparable from the theory. These writers tend not to be orthodox psychoanalysts (who seem no longer to feel the need to prove their conception of art); of the nine writers with whom this chapter deals, seven use psychologies which represent more or less marked deviations from orthodox psychoanalysis.

Of these, the most noted is Otto Rank. One of Freud's earliest students, a man more interested in the cultural than the medical aspects of psychoanalysis, Rank broke with Freud in the mid-twenties on the issue of the importance of the trauma of birth and the general theme of separation in the development of the psyche (also on some questions of therapy). Rank's earlier writings on art, notably *Das Inzest-Motive in Dichtung und Sage* and *Der Mythus von der Geburt des Heldens,* are thoroughly orthodox. His writings on art after the break tended to be a *Kunstwissenschaft, an Aesthetik* rather than a psychology of art. In general, Rank's later position treats art as a compromise product of two competing fears in the artist's mind: first, the artist fears death and therefore wishes for immortality—as a result, he tries to represent reality and himself in a lasting form. Second, the artist fears life—and as a result he gets "the will to style," the wish to impose form on matter to produce an idealized reality. Such a broad formulation does not lend itself to the treatment of details, and indeed, when the later Rank discusses a work, he does so in rather broad and general terms. He himself argues that biographical facts are unimportant.[1]

In his discussion of the *Sonnets,* for example, he concludes that "not only are the sonnets in fact self-dedicated—as is creative work of every description—but they reveal that peculiar attitude of the creative instinct toward the creative ego which seeks to glorify it by artistic idealization and at the same time to overcome its mortality by eternalizing it in art." [2] He says that woman becomes, in the *Sonnets* as in the plays, an evil, disturbing daemon, whereas the young friend proves a helpful ideal. The promises to glorify the young friend, to immortalize him, the urgings that he procreate, all these themes of the *Sonnets* are covertly the poet's desire to immortalize himself, an attempt to be symbolically reborn as like himself as possible (i.e., in his own sex) so as to live his own vanishing youth over in his friend's, thus triumphing over the fear of death.

> O, how thy worth with manners may I sing,
> When thou art all the better part of me?
> What can mine own praise to mine own self bring,
> And what is't but mine own when I praise thee?
>
> (39)

As for Shakespeare's works in general, Rank points to a certain lack of realism, representing a triumph over life. He says that Shakespeare's metaphors present a jumble of past and present mixed both spatially and temporally. Moreover, Shakespeare's characters at times seem extended metaphors: Othello is unrestrainedly jealous *like* the primitive; Shylock is inhumanly avaricious *like* the devil of gold himself; Hamlet incorporates old immortality beliefs.[3] Rank sees Shakespeare as writing at an important transition point in literary history. The earlier phase (he is thinking, I suppose, of medieval literature) offers pure narrative on the one hand, and an abstract, conceptual drama on the other. The later phase (including Shakespeare) has actual action on a stage, which Rank interprets as a decline in magical faith in words alone. Shakespeare had to "psychologize" his characters, but the effects of medievalism show in his unfavorable picture of women.[4]

J. I. M. Stewart is another writer who has said Shakespeare stressed the psychological truth of folk tale rather than the literal truth of the realistic novel.[5] Professor Stewart's book sets out to answer such "realist" critics of Shakespeare as Bridges, Schücking, or Stoll, who, he says, argue that Shakespeare's characters and plots are not consistent, not true to human nature, that his characters explain themselves too much, that the plays, in short, are artificial and unreal because of the crudity of the demands made on the poet by the Elizabethan theater. Professor Stewart argues that Shakespeare was indeed sacrificing a literal reality but to get back into psychological reality. The scholars, he says, have substituted their notions of what is likely to be in the plays (based on their suppositions about the Elizabethans) for what is actually there.

In approaching the plays, Stewart argues, one must consider both character and situation in terms of the heightened consciousness that poetic drama gives us of the deepest springs of human action. We must look in poetic drama not to a single character, but to the play as a whole; we must look with an intuitive awareness of the recesses of human passion. Professor Stewart gives many examples of situations in the plays which seem unreal, but which, in fact, tap profound truths about human nature (and not only those made available through depth psychology). For example, he notes that some critics see Angelo's sudden gust of passion for Isabella in *Measure for Measure* as highly artificial; Stewart argues that it is just the opposite, highly credible. "We may feel from the start that he has a share in a good many of those vices which the respectable, self-regarding, and self-righteous may discreetly indulge: as arrogance, rectitudinousness, cruelty, and—in the matter of his betrothal to Mariana—a little sharp practice and self-deception when money affairs go wrong." [6]

In short, Stewart sees the various characters as probable and lifelike but also as projections of Shakespeare's psyche, and he quotes with approval Freud's remarks at the end of "Creative Writers and Day-Dreaming" about the various characters in a sophisticated work representing aspects of the author whom, in a crude work, one single hero would embody. In the last analysis, however, Professor Stewart's book makes more of a literary plea than a psychoanalytic one: "What I have tried to urge is simply this: that in the interpretation of Shakespeare a study of the psychology of poetic drama (which leads us to understand his *medium*) is at least as important as a study of the contemporary climate of opinion (which gives simply *conditions* under which he worked)." [7]

Professor F. L. Lucas's *Literature and Psychology* [8] is also rather more literature than psychology. It is unique, however, in its use of the psychology of Wilhelm Stekel, another deviant from the straight-and-narrow path of orthodox psychoanalysis. In the conventional interpretation of the symbols of fantasy, the psychoanalyst regards a few as having fixed or universal meanings (e.g., a telephone pole "always" represents a phallus), but most symbols (and some say all) can vary their meanings pretty widely, depending on the associations the patient has to them. Stekel regarded most symbols as fixed rather than variable, and he broke with Freud on the matter. Professor Lucas is rather more interested in Stekel as wise therapist, however, than as symbologist. Lucas mostly makes a plea—and who can argue with him?—that critics should use Freud and psychology to learn about men rather than to invent learned nonsense. Thus, Lucas talks about *Hamlet* in terms of some of Stekel's case histories, rather than as oedipus complex or in terms of Stekel's symbology.

At the opposite extreme in dependence on theory is Professor Arthur Wormhoudt's application to Shakespeare of Dr. Edmund Bergler's theories about literature.[9] Bergler (see also Chapter 5) attempts to extend rather freely the emphases of the second phase of psychoanalytic theory into the problem of literature. That is, in Freud's latest writings two different emphases appear: first, he recognized increasingly the importance of aggression as a basic instinctual component of human behavior alongside sexuality; second, he laid more stress on the pre-oedipal stages in psychic development, the periods when the child's interest is concentrated on the mouth or the anus. Bergler pushes these later views to the point of saying that such phenomena of later infancy as the oedipus complex must be understood in terms of the earlier phases—these are the basics, and all later psychic problems grow out of oral and anal matters. Literature, then, does not so much express unconscious wishes, says Bergler, as it expresses defenses against repressed conflicts. The crime every writer defends against, says Bergler, is "unresolved masochistic attachment to the image of his mother," the tendency to take pleasure in the pain of passively submitting to the refusal of the breast. Bergler suggests a number of defenses, the most important being the "autarchic fantasy" —the writer plays both roles, the giving mother and the recipient child, by manufacturing words and identifying them with mother's milk.

Professor Wormhoudt has applied this emphasis on aggressive drives and conflicts from the earliest stages of infancy to the Romantic poets in his book, *The Demon Lover;* there, he also argues that the oedipus complex is not adequate to explain either Hamlet's aggressive hatred of Gertrude and Ophelia or Shakespeare's conflicts. The play does not deal with the oedipus conflict directly, but as a defense for Shakespeare's deeper problem: oral conflict with the mother. One defense the play makes is to shift aggressive feelings from the mother to the father (Claudius), but this is not complete, and Hamlet abuses both Gertrude and Ophelia. Professor Wormhoudt sees the *Sonnets* as expressing homosexual tendencies, perhaps unconscious ones, and he notes that male homosexuals are motivated by a violent rejection of the mother and, as reflections of her, all women. The *Sonnets,* then, he says, prove that Shakespeare could not have been motivated in *Hamlet* by oedipal love for his mother because he had rejected her.[10]

Professor Wormhoudt derives from Dr. Bergler "the five-layer structure of sublimation" which, with great assiduity, he applies to *Hamlet.*[11] He sees art as relying on a quite limited series of possibilities. First, there are "ring" and "finger" symbols. "Ring" symbols are associated with the feeling of the mouth formed into a ring; the finger is what goes into the ring: food, liquids, words, and so on. Second, these symbols will come in visual, aural, or tactile form. Third, they will be projected upward (as light, height, stars, heavens) or downward (as dirt, earth, darkness, or, in general, anality). These projections will either persist and grow into identifications, or the psyche will retreat into self-centeredness.

The "five-layer structure of sublimation" comes in three patterns: first, the establishment of the ring and finger symbols, and their projection into eye and ear; second, the aural and visual ring and finger symbols are projected upward or downward onto the outside world; third, the writer identifies himself with these projections. The quincunx comes in the form of alternating waves of outward projection and inward inhibition associated with the three patterns. Professor Wormhoudt finds these five layers in *Hamlet's* five-act structure (without discussing whether or not there is such a thing as a five-act structure). Much of his analysis is of the characters' names; some of isolated metaphors. In general, Professor Wormhoudt sees *Hamlet* and the *Sonnets* (particularly 73 with its "Consum'd with that which it was nourish'd by," referring, he says, to mother's milk) as expressing writer's block, but Professor Wormhoudt assures us that it is a universal human difficulty (although Professor Wormhoudt seems to have overcome it).

Dr. Bergler himself has contributed an analysis of *Hamlet*[12] in justification of his theories, an analysis considerably more flexible than that of his disciple. Bergler lists seven "paradoxes" in *Hamlet*. (1) Hamlet's indecision seems unmotivated. (2) Oddly, conscience (as personified in the ghost) orders the hero to do something, murder, that conscience usually forbids. (3) The punishment (death) Hamlet suffers for his crime (oedipal wishes) is unusually severe (as contrasted to impotence or castration). (4) Hamlet, in effect, connives in his own death through a surprising naïveté in accepting the match with Laertes. (5) Hamlet does not leave his mother to heaven, but abuses her and seems to regard woman as the chief villain. (6) Throughout the play Hamlet is ambivalent. (7) Finally, the play seems to depict a normal oedipus complex, but the bisexual (*sic*) Shakespeare could not have had a normal oedipus complex.

Dr. Bergler agrees that Freud's basic insight, that Hamlet hesitates because of oedipal feelings, is right, and that this insight resolves the first paradox; but he insists that the others can be resolved only by recognizing that the oedipus complex itself is but an outgrowth of earlier, more profound mechanisms. In earliest infancy writers (and maybe everyone), Dr. Bergler says, have a wish to suffer at the hands of the mother. One way of defending against such a wish is the oedipus complex, a denial, in effect, that one really wishes to be passive to the mother, insisting, instead, that one wishes to possess her sexually and aggressively. This "deeper" paradox of masochism, pleasure in pain, torture for torture's sake, Bergler sees as explaining the other paradoxes he finds in the tragedy. Thus, the ghost speaks for what consciously Hamlet would like to be (the ego ideal); unconsciously, however, Hamlet knows he is just as guilty as Claudius. The discrepancy leads Hamlet to punish himself for not living up to the ghost's commands, but also to enjoy punishing himself (paradoxes 2, 3, and 4). Similarly (paradox 5), Hamlet regards his mother as the dirtier of the villains because she stands as a deeper source of his feelings of guilt than either the ghost or Claudius. Hamlet (paradox 6) and, by implication, Shakespeare (paradox 7) are supposed to resent the father, but this resentment only camouflages the far deeper resentment and rejection of the mother.

In his analysis of *A Midsummer Night's Dream,*[13] Weston A. Gui has allowed for Bergler's theories. He sees, in orthodox Freudian terms, the comedy as Shakespeare (in the person of Bottom) being rejoined to his mother (Titania) and replacing both his father (Oberon) and his brother Gilbert (the Indian changeling). In terms of Bergler's theory that the writer produces words as a milk substitute, one could, he says, consider *A Midsummer Night's Dream* as involved with creating words as a substitute for the moon (the moon being a common symbol for the mother). Gui uses also Dr. Harry Lee's "reconstitution" theory (see Chapter 5) that the writer produces art to reconstruct the mother's body which he (like all children) has destroyed in dreams and fantasies of destruction. Gui proposes that the play as a whole is a "Bottom's Dream," to be sung "in the latter end of a play," or, as Bottom says, " 'Peradventure, to make it the more gracious, I shall sing it at her death.' "

Both Bergler and Gui are working from later psychoanalytic data on development which stress pre-oedipal relations with the parents, particularly the mother, and particularly in that very earliest stage of the child's development (before eight months or so) when he does not yet see himself as an entity separate from his ministering angel. So is Dr. David Barron when he very tentatively concludes at the end of his study of *Macbeth:* "As a preliminary generalization based on this intensive study we can postulate that a supreme creative power such as Shakespeare's is founded upon a strong temptation to regress to magical participation with mother, which must be countered by full confrontation with father, in order to ripen to mature expression." [14] Do we see here the beginning of a confirmation of what was guessed at the end of the preceding chapter? Perhaps these views, even overstated as some of them are, confirm one measure of the greatness of an artist or of his work. The great writer can draw upon all the geological strata of human development, from the earliest union of a "pre-self" with the mother through the rich interpersonal conflicts within the family triangle, and on to the sublimations of the adult personality.

Shakespeare has been pressed into service to prove the artistic theories not just of psychoanalysis but all kinds of psychologies from "psychognostics," an "implicit, intuitive knowledge of human nature," [15] to Marxist psychology which sees the plays in terms of the social stresses of the author's times. [16] Evaluating these treatments of the bard or those like Otto Rank's or Arthur Wormhoudt's which draw on some special psychological system takes two stages, really. The first is an evaluation of the psychology which presumably had best be left to professionals. The second, more within the purview of literary criticism, should be an evaluation of the skill or sense with which the system is applied to Shakespeare. Two questions, it seems to me, are involved. First, how many details from the play or the poem are brought into relation? Second, for each of these details, how many are the steps and how firm are they, that are needed to take us from the detail in the play to the corresponding element in the psychological structure being placed against the play? In short, how much must the play be strained to fit? For all the critics in this chapter except Barron, Stewart, and Lucas, the answer, I fear, is a good deal. These elaborate theories have proved beds of Procrustes rather than ordinary, comfortable second-best beds.

[9]

Psychoanalysis
and the Works

IN THE past two chapters we have considered psychoanalytic studies which take up Shakespeare's works only to look through them to the man or to find them proof of a psychological theory of art. In this chapter we are about to consider psychoanalytic studies which purport to look at the works themselves. Any hope, however, that these critics will analyze Shakespeare's works themselves is necessarily somewhat paradoxical. In the nature of the case, any psychological system must deal, not with works of art in isolation, but with works of art in relation to man's mind. It is hard to see how a psychology could deal with a work of art *qua* work of art, and in practice these writers do not. They begin, as all writers on literature and psychology must, with a congruity between a psychological system and the work in question. Often, a psychoanalytic critic will discover the congruity and leave it at that; the reader may make of it what he will. In effect, though he does not often say such a stodgy thing, the psychoanalytic critic is usually trying to show that the play or poem runs true to human nature as seen by psychoanalysis. That is, the play has in it the same pattern as the clinic, so, psychoanalysis, cross-checked by play and clinic, is right. The better—or more systematic—psychoanalytic critic will go on in one of two ways after establishing his congruity. First, he will apply his insight to the mind of one of the characters as though the character were a living human being. Second, and this procedure is unfortunately rare, he will apply his insight to the audience's mind; the critic will use the congruity to suggest the reason for the effect the work in whole or in part evokes.

Naturally, most psychoanalytic critics, particularly those who are practicing psychoanalysts, are not nearly so interested in elucidating Shakespeare's works as they are in using Shakespeare's works to supplement the clinical evidence for a psychological proposition. Since this is a book about Shakespeare, I have turned these psychological inductions around into deductive reasonings, taking them as the application of general psychological principles to Shakespeare's plays and poems (and, indeed, there is always more evidence than simply Shakespeare for the general propositions involved).

In organizing what turns out to be a very large body of material, I have arranged it play by play, poem by poem, using the simplest and most certain order I know—alphabetical. Within the section on a given work I have arranged the various psychoanalytic studies in order of generality: I have put first those studies which treat the whole work; second, those which deal with a major part, theme, or character (in the order in which the parts appear in the play); third, those which discuss a single speech (in the order in which the speeches occur in the play). Where there is more than one study at a given level of generality, I have arranged them chronologically.

Finally, before pushing into this rather tangled thicket, it might be well to remember a remark of Freud's. One of his students was giving a seminar paper on *Hamlet,* and he began by apologizing for the number of quotations from Shakespeare he would have to use. "Bring as many quotations as you can," Freud dryly remarked. "They will certainly be the best part of your paper."

ALL'S WELL THAT ENDS WELL

Paradoxically, this summary of "Psychoanalysis and the Works" must begin *faute de mieux* with a Jungian study of *All's Well,* for there is no full-fledged treatment of the play from the point of view of orthodox psychoanalysis. Barbara Hannah [1] sees the comedy as working out the individuation of a self, that is, the therapeutic reconciliation of conflicting parts of one's nature, the reconciliation itself being symbolized by the marriage at the end. Thus, the various characters in the play stand for various personages in the drama of the self; the several separations and unions of the characters should be regarded as stages in the process of individuation. Bertram is the ego who must create and enter into the union of male and female elements of character. Bertram's mother the countess, Helena, Diana, and Lafeu's daughter Maudlin, whom Bertram is to marry in lieu of Helena, all develop different aspects of the anima, the buried or rejected feminine aspect of the self. The presence of the mother and Bertram's leaving her show how a son must get over his love for his mother to grow up into real maturity. The central anima figure is, of course, Helena to whom Bertram must unite and of whom Maudlin is another, still more hidden form. Diana is the goddess aspect of the anima who enables Helena to perform miracles, or, at least, the ingenious tricks by which she wins Bertram's affection. Lafeu, the wise old man, represents the animus (the male side of the personality), and the king represents the complex, paradoxical Self. Symbolically, Bertram's coming back to him represents the ego's embracing the whole Self. Parolles stands for the Shadow, the personal (as against the collective) unconscious. He dominates the ego (Bertram), separates him from his self (the king) and from the anima (Helena). The shadow is cunning and deceptive, and it is after Helena converses with Parolles that she herself can become clever and devious. Once the shadow is unmasked, though (in the scenes revealing Parolles' cowardice), he is abandoned and rendered helpless, and the ego (Bertram) takes on some of his attributes (lying). At the end of the play Lafeu takes Parolles into his house, symbolically giving the shadow a place in the psyche as a whole.

Particular events of the play, from this Jungian point of view, symbolize particular elements in the drama of individuation, for example, the medicine that Helena gives the king. "The dearest issue" of her father's practice, "a triple eye," "a medicine / That's able to breathe life into a stone," is the *medicina catholica* of the alchemists, symbolically, any external means that unites the different parts of the self. All the women in the play favor Helena's marriage to Bertram; they are thus representatives of the uniting principle, eros. The men tend to oppose the union and so stand for the dividing principle, logos. Nevertheless, the play as a whole moves toward the union of male and female. Even in the opening lines Lafeu says the countess will "find of the king a husband." The final union or *quaternio* should be king and countess, Bertram and Helena, but it turns out to be Bertram and Helena, Parolles and Lafeu—lopsidedly masculine, it is an accurate picture, to a Jungian, of the collective psyche in Shakespeare's day and ours.

It is possible on the basis of a Jungian reading to guess at an orthodox psychoanalytic one despite the great differences in theory and terminology. With such terms as animus, anima, or shadow, the Jungian hypostatizes into static entities what the psychoanalyst sees as fluctuating, dynamic representations of earlier experience. Presumably, this difference underlies the tendency to apply Jungian analytic psychology to myths, folk tales, and works of art (which are fixed) as against the tendency to apply orthodox psychoanalysis to patients conceived of as dynamically developed and developing individuals. Anyway, where the Jungian sees the countess, Helena, and Diana as representatives of an anima, the psychoanalyst would find in them aspects of or attitudes toward a mother. The king and Lafeu (and Helena's dead father) would be aspects of or attitudes toward a father. The final union or marriage would be the attainment of an oedipally-conceived love object, and the analysis of the play as a whole would proceed along oedipal lines, at least initially.

So, at least, do the fragmentary psychoanalytic or nearly-psychoanalytic remarks about the play. Dr. P. R. Vessie suggests that Helena's effort to make a marriage under royal aegis reflects a deep feeling of inferiority.[2] Professor John F. Adams notes that, in Bertram's challenge to Helena to get the ring from his finger, the ring stands for virginity, her chastity, ultimately her genitals.[3] Otto Rank (in his earlier, Freudian phase) showed that the bed trick by which Helena obtains the ring (and pregnancy) from Bertram is an *inzest-motiv*.[4] The noble Bertram taking to wife the woman he himself has dishonored corresponds to the son whose own birth proves that his mother was dishonored (i.e., had relations with his father). The woman in the dark is taboo, her forbidden quality represented by the dark and the subterfuge; like tabooed women in general, she stands ultimately for the mother.

This oedipal motif, Rank noted, comes out in the very first lines of the play. The countess says, "In delivering my son from me, I bury a second husband," and Bertram (more or less) agrees. Together, they manifest a childhood fantasy: the son longing to take his father's place with the mother; she longing to have him do so.[5] Later, in I.iii, Helena and the countess play with the thought that Helena's lover is her brother. The relation of brother and sister so introduced is a disguised form, in both *All's Well* and *Measure for Measure,* Rank says, for the tabooed relationship of mother and son which thus seems to underlie a good deal of the play.[6]

Dr. Samuel A. Tannenbaum, the physician and bibliographer, notes what he takes to be a "Freudian slip." [7] Parolles, a prisoner and tormented (so he believes) by the enemy, promises to tell them all they want to know: "By my troth, sir, if I were to live this present hour, I will tell true." Dr. Tannenbaum suggests that Parolles has made in "live" a slip of the tongue for "die," so intense is his wish to live.

ANTONY AND CLEOPATRA

In *Antony and Cleopatra* Professor Herbert Weisinger [1] finds confirmation for his somewhat Jungian view of Shakespeare's tragedies as a combination of (1) ancient patterns from the racial memory of the death and rebirth of a sacrificial king, and (2) a sudden leap out of these endless cycles into another mode of experience, Christian order. The structure of *Antony and Cleopatra* shows this combination of pagan and Christian by continuing after Antony's death into the love death of Cleopatra. Through their joint death, God's order, he says, is reaffirmed. Dr. K. R. Eissler's Freudian glance at the play [2] merely notes that Antony and Cleopatra's "dying together" represents a common fantasy, which, as one of Ernest Jones's essays pointed out, stands for the supreme consummation of love.

The external conflict of Rome and Egypt mirrors, Mrs. Cynthia Kolb Whitney suggests, the conflict within the characters who become at war within themselves.[3] Antony, specifically, is torn between his aggressive Roman self and his effeminate Egyptian self (associated with references to eunuchs). In effect, Rome and Egypt represent two different kinds of masculinity. Rome is a harsh fatherland, in which the men see themselves as fathers or sons and care only for masculinity in its aggressive sense. In Egypt, masculinity means a sexual submission to woman represented as Cleopatra or Isis or Egypt (periodically fertile); all these femininities blend into a single seductive mother figure.

Parallel to the external and internal conflict of these two kinds of masculinity are conflicts in time. There are many times when various characters are "not themselves." Virtually every event happens at the "wrong" time, as when Antony loves at a time he should be fighting. Life according to Egypt and life according to Rome are—or should be—separated in time. Psychologically, then, the tragedy is a tragedy of different kinds of masculinity occurring at the wrong times. In effect, grizzled Antony is trying to reach back toward an infant's total union with his nurturing mother, though his whole life span separates him from her. "His being is forever at the wrong time, and hence tragic. This is the tragedy not only of Antony . . . but of everyman."

Dr. Tannenbaum pursued "Freudian slips" throughout Shakespeare to show that writers understand slips of the tongue the same way psychoanalysts do, namely, as the expression of hidden wishes or ideas. He dealt with two such slips in *Antony and Cleopatra*.[4] Cleopatra, as a way of saying to Antony that Fulvia is simply Caesar's representative, fakes a slip of the tongue when a messenger comes. "Where's Fulvia's process? Caesar's I would say? both?" But there is a real slip later, when Caesar says of his false promises to Cleopatra, "For Caesar cannot leave to be ungentle" (some modern editors read "live," although the Folio says "leave"). The line is a bit puzzling, and Dr. Tannenbaum suggests that Caesar hesitated between saying, "Caesar cannot leave to be gentle" and "Caesar cannot be ungentle." His own knowledge of his falsity led him to fuse the idea into a line which reveals the truth. The inadvertency of the slip shows incidentally, Dr. Tannenbaum says, in that the line (as printed in the Folio) has two and a half feet too many in rhythm.

AS YOU LIKE IT

Dr. Conrad van Emde Boas, in analyzing the relation of the *Sonnets* and the "Double-disguise" plays to Shakespeare's psyche, concludes that in *As You Like It* the rivalry between Orlando and Phebe for the master-mistress, Rosalind-Ganymede, makes up one of the patterns of homosexuality found in clinical practice.[1]

Dr. W. I. D. Scott [2] suggests as a Freudian analysis of Jaques that he has an overdeveloped superego that makes him project his own failings on others, criticizing in them faults of which he is himself guilty. A fuller view of the character, Dr. Scott feels, comes from recognizing him as an involutional depressive, a man suffering a depression as a result of the glandular and other changes of the forties and fifties. More specifically, he sees Jaques as paired with Touchstone or Orlando, who are "feeling extraverts" (in Jung's eight personality types); they are the repressed shadows of Jaques's own character, a thinking introvert. Jaques concentrates too much on his own self, but this repression or narrowing is a useful adaptation for one approaching the end of life.

Dr. Tannenbaum finds three slips of the tongue in this comedy.[3] Early in the play Rosalind is in the dumps—her father has died, she has met Orlando, and fallen in love. Celia asks her why she is so depressed.

> *Celia.* But is all this for your father?
> *Rosalind.* No, some of it is for my child's father.

Dr. Tannenbaum argues that she meant to say "father's child," meaning herself and her precarious situation, but because she was longing for Orlando, she referred instead to him, the man she would like to have father her children. Later in the play, when Oliver is describing the way his brother rescued him, he speaks of himself in the third person as "a wretched, ragged man," but at the end of his long description says, "From miserable slumber I awaked," thus blurting out his identity. When Rosalind, disguised as Ganymede, hears her lover was wounded, she swoons; her companion Celia cries, "Cousin Ganymede!" "Cousin" was the form of address she used for Rosalind *in propria persona.* In none of these three cases, though, is it clear that the wording represents a slip—each could well be simply an ordinary utterance—and Dr. Tannenbaum's ingenious readings must remain "not proven."

THE COMEDY OF ERRORS

We have already seen Dr. Bronson Feldman's description of the patterns of oedipal and sibling rivalry in *The Comedy of Errors*,[1] which he referred first to Shakespeare's, then to Edward de Vere's psyche. Otto Rank also found an incest theme.[2] The play's content he sees as oedipal, and he notes in it one of the recurring elements in oedipal stories. While the twins' father, Aegeon, by the end of the play is old and decrepit, "all the conduits of [his] blood froze up," the mother Aemilia becomes young, as though she had just given birth to her sons "this present hour."

CORIOLANUS

The psychoanalysts consider *Coriolanus,* not unreasonably, another oedipal play, although one stressing the relationship of mother to son rather than the rivalry of father and son. We have already seen Otto Rank's treatment of the play, referring it to Shakespeare's psyche.[1] He pointed to Coriolanus' tendency to identify himself with his mother; he saw in Menenius an honored "father" to Coriolanus, in Aufidius a hated "father" who ultimately causes the "son" to be killed.

Dr. Jackson Edmund Towne [2] notes that Shakespeare emphasizes (more than his source did) the subordination of Coriolanus' wife Virgilia to his mother Volumnia. The hero's arrogance toward the common people is really a result of his mother's training. When she urges him to plead with the plebeians in the market place, she foreshadows her later pleading that he desert the Volscians. She makes this last plea good by what is to Coriolanus the most terrible threat of all, that he is not her son: "This fellow had a Volscian to his mother." In short, it is Volumnia who dominates Coriolanus, and it is she who ultimately defeats him.

Charles K. Hofling,[3] following Wilhelm Reich's character types, identifies Coriolanus as a "phallic-narcissistic character," the kind of man who becomes an athlete, an aviator, soldier, or engineer. He tends to be haughty, aggressive, self-confident; his narcissism reveals itself in exaggerated displays of dignity. Such a person is capable of strong attachments to people, and he is likely to show aggressive courage, but he is ridden by many irrational motives. Hofling notes the recurrence of the butterfly image: first Coriolanus' son Marcius torments a butterfly in "One on's father's moods." Later, Cominius describes the Volscians following Coriolanus against Rome as confidently as "boys pursuing summer butterflies." Hofling concludes that "the childhood frustrations of Coriolanus stand—and are shown by Shakespeare to stand—in a cause-effect relationship to the unleashing of furious aggression in adult life."

Coriolanus shows the mob an extreme aversion to begging for votes and to showing his wounds; yet, at another deeper level, Coriolanus identifies himself with the mob:

> Let them
> Regard me as I do not flatter, and
> Therein behold themselves.

Volumnia Hofling sees as a quite unfeminine woman, much concerned with honors and appearances. Coriolanus seems to identify Rome with his mother—he does not want to say he wishes something from her (or the mob), particularly when what he wants is to win the power and authority of the consulship (like a father's). Most of all, he hates to have to ask passively for this power. Aufidius, Hofling suggests, may be a father substitute to whom Coriolanus turns after rejection by the mother. In any case, Coriolanus spares the city when his mother and Rome give up their masculine, aggressive behavior to him and beg. Hofling sees Virgilia as much more feminine than Volumnia, less selfish in her relationship to Coriolanus, more loving to him, and less concerned with honors and appearances. Virgilia, by the end of the play, seems to have had a therapeutic effect on her husband. Coriolanus has reduced his need for revenge against women, and he is more aware of the softer tendencies in his own personality. But when Aufidius calls him "Boy" and "Traitor," Coriolanus falls into irrationality; both epithets are great wounds to his new emotional maturity and his now-real masculinity.

Professor Gordon R. Smith,[4] in another analysis of the character of Coriolanus, compares him to the authoritarian personality described by Erich Fromm and T. W. Adorno. Professor Smith finds a number of correspondences, not only with Coriolanus, but also Menenius, Volumnia, and even Virgilia. The authoritarian personality, for example, tends to ally itself with a "power idol," Virgilia and Menenius to Coriolanus, Coriolanus to Volumnia, Volumnia to Rome. The authoritarian, when he so allies himself with a superior power, is likely to be sadistic: he longs to have absolute power over people or to exploit them, as Coriolanus does the plebeians and Aufidius; Coriolanus also likes to watch others suffer (the plebeians, Rome, his former companions, even Menenius). The authoritarian tends, too, to rationalize his sadistic impulses. Sometimes he says he has his victim's best interests at heart (as Coriolanus and Menenius assure the mob the patricians do). Sometimes the authoritarian says, "I'm so good, I've done so much for you, I have a right to expect you to depend on me"; and Coriolanus constantly asserts his superiority and his past achievements. Sometimes the authoritarian says he has a right to hurt others because they have hurt him or they may, and Coriolanus says these things, too.

Like authoritarians generally, Coriolanus shows contempt for the weak, a lack of insight into himself, an explosive, moralistic aggressiveness, and a tendency to project his own faults on others (he is himself far more fickle than the citizenry he accuses of fickleness). When the authoritarian, instead of allying or identifying himself with higher authority, submits to it, he is likely to do it completely, reveling in his suffering. Toward his parents, for example, he is likely to have the same rigid, stereotyped adoration that Coriolanus has for his mother. Professor Smith finds many other patterns, many more, really, than either Hofling or Towne do for their psychic mechanisms (which, by the way, are different but not inconsistent with Smith's). Professor Smith then goes on (in a procedure far too rare among psychological critics) to show how this play fits in with the middle-class political views of Shakespeare and his audience.

A footnote in Drs. Seidenberg and Papathomopoulos' psychoanalytic study of Sophocles' *Ajax* identifies Coriolanus as another character type, although one related to the authoritarian personality.[5] Sophocles' Ajax and Shakespeare's Coriolanus are both men, they say, who remained attached to their mothers, never fighting out their oedipal battles with their fathers. At the core of their adult personalities they have a passive, feminine identification. To defend against this passivity, they developed tremendous reaction formations of implacable belligerence. Should this defense fail, though, the return of the repressed passivity would lead to total collapse. Thus, once Volumnia's pleas have made Coriolanus "womanish," he completely and passively submits to his lifelong enemy, Aufidius (a father surrogate), whom formerly he could defeat in battle.

Dr. Rufus Putney [6] also considers the man Coriolanus from the point of view of the identifications from which his character developed. Volumnia's seeming affection and pride in her son mask her underlying hatred. Coriolanus adapted to his own rage toward her by displacing it away from his mother onto plebeians or Volscians. He cannot face this anger toward his mother, and thus she can force him to do things by threatening her own death if he does not spare Rome or her own dishonor if he will not flatter the plebeians.

As a result of this aggressive relationship, Coriolanus took in from his mother an implacable, sadistic superego against which his own ego must ever give way. He holds to his mother's principles inflexibly, refusing to flatter the plebeians, even when his mother has herself given up those principles. Because he holds them unconsciously and inflexibly, he is baffled at her willingness and ability to give them up.

Still another recent student of the play, Dr. David B. Barron, sees Coriolanus' "tragic flaw" as tremendous power combined with a fatal dependency.[7] He traces Coriolanus' fall to his mother—the hero is obviously very much under her influence and that influence is of a uniquely destructive kind. She would not allow him to enjoy being dependent on her when he was a child; instead, she sent him off to fight:

When yet he was but tender-bodied and the only son of my womb, when youth with comeliness plucked all gaze his way, when for a day of kings' entreaties a mother should not sell him an hour from her beholding, I, considering how honor would become such a person, that it was no better than picture-like to hang by th' wall, if renown made it not stir, was pleased to let him seek danger where he was like to find fame. To a cruel war I sent him, from whence he returned, his brows bound with oak.

This peculiar mother-son relationship reveals itself in the play's food imagery. Dr. Barron says that Shakespeare's changes from Plutarch greatly amplify the theme of hunger; it is Shakespeare who introduces the idea that Volumnia preferred Coriolanus to be at war instead of sucking at her breast, and he who creates the final, fatal epithet, "Boy!" that stings Coriolanus to his death.

In short, Coriolanus behaves like a man whose mother frustrated his feeding needs as a child and then diverted his resulting anger away from herself onto external enemies. We see Coriolanus repeat aspects of this pattern several times in the play. For example, after the plebeians have turned against him and deprived him of the praise and honor he feeds on, Coriolanus turns away from his "nurse," his "birthplace," Rome (but also his mother), blazing with hostility. His mother finally appears in the Volscian camp and makes him recapitulate his original childhood diversion of hostility away from her (Rome). We can see the pattern at a point of transition when Coriolanus shows a mixture of love and hate to his old enemy Aufidius, the oral element revealing itself in their meeting at a banquet and in Coriolanus' description of his former triumphs against the Volscians as having "drawn tuns of blood out of thy country's breast."

The pattern shows still another form in Coriolanus' relation to the populace. Partly, he plays a child to the citizens as his mother: though his real hostility is to them, he lets them send him off to fight enemies and then, when he returns, he reluctantly lets them feed him praise. Partly, though, Coriolanus acts the role of his frustrating mother to the people as child: he denies them food, puts down their mutiny, and urges them to fight the enemy instead. From a mass of evidence, then, Dr. Barron has brought out a strikingly clear and accurate clinical picture of a man with two conflicting needs: one for achievement (to establish his independence from his mother), but underneath, a deeper need to be dependent, to receive at her breast love, praise, the milk of human kindness.

In short, these eight psychoanalytic critics show a quite considerable consensus about *Coriolanus*. Rank sees the play as an oedipal configuration to be referred ultimately to the mind of the author. Hofling and Smith see Coriolanus' own personality in terms of two related character typologies. Towne, Hofling, Seidenberg, Papothomopoulos, Putney, and Barron see Coriolanus' personality developmentally, as growing out of his relation to his mother, in particular, her frustration of his needs in early infancy to be dependent. Recent psychoanalytic data about the first months of life say this kind of early oral frustration would lead to a permanent build-up of aggressive energy (as in the character types described by Hofling and Smith); it would lead to an inability to tolerate being dependent and to a blurred differentiation of self from love object (Coriolanus' need to prove himself, win an identity, through achievement, countered by his tendency to identify with his mother). Dr. Barron's discussion of the food imagery shows the oral understructure (or lack of it) in Coriolanus' personality and, by returning to the poetry of the play as a whole, takes us back to Rank's original way of looking at the tragedy, as a total configuration to be referred to Shakespeare's own mind.

Thus within this consensus we can see three ways of looking at a play: to the play as a total configuration; to a single character in terms of adult character types; to a single character seen dynamically and developmentally in terms of a more or less hypothetical infancy.

In addition to these studies of *Coriolanus* the play and Coriolanus the character, a few psychoanalytic writers have considered particular speeches. Otto Rank, in his later non-Freudian study of art,[8] picks out Menenius' speech to the mutinying mob, comparing the commonwealth to the human body, as one of the great mythic patterns—he finds parallels in the *Timaeus* and in Assyrian metaphors. While the comparison is traditional in Shakespeare's day, Rank sees it as establishing Shakespeare's place midway in the development from primitive magic to less primitive myth to a still less primitive awareness of these comparisons as mere metaphors.

Two writers have caught Coriolanus' lapse of memory. After the battle at Corioles he wants to confer a kindness:

> *Coriolanus.* I sometimes lay here in Corioles
> At a poor man's house; he used me kindly.
> He cried to me; I saw him prisoner;
> But then Aufidius was within my view,
> And wrath o'erwhelmed my pity. I request you
> To give my poor host freedom.
> *Cominius.* O, well begged!
> Were he the butcher of my son, he should
> Be free as is the wind. Deliver him, Titus.
> *Lartius.* Marcius, his name?
> *Coriolanus.* By Jupiter, forgot!
> I am weary; yea, my memory is tired.
> Have we no wine here?

The indefatigable Dr. Tannenbaum notes [9] that in Plutarch the man whose name Coriolanus forgets is "an old friend," an "honest, wealthy man." Shakespeare makes the man poor, and Dr. Tannenbaum concludes that the reason Coriolanus cannot recall his benefactor's name is that, being a snob, he wishes to forget he is indebted to a commoner, a plebeian. Dr. Towne suggests in passing: "It would be most natural, after a hard fight, for such a man as Coriolanus temporarily to forget the name of one who was really an enemy despite kindness manifested in the past." [10] In other words, we should take Coriolanus literally when he says, "Wrath o'erwhelmed my pity"—he is, after all, a man with a great deal of aggression in him.

And last, Dr. Robert Fliess quotes [11] the dialogue between Aufidius' servants in which they call war a ravisher but peace a great maker of cuckolds; he finds in it an identification of Eros, the life drive to procreate, with Thanatos, the death drive to destroy, and suggests that it gives this mild, amusing conversation a greater force.

CYMBELINE

For those few psychoanalytic writers who have touched on *Cymbeline* it is intimately related to *The Tempest*. Hanns Sachs sees in it the same father-and-daughter theme that he finds in all the late plays.[1] We have already considered K. M. Abenheimer's Jungian study of the play which he refers to Shakespeare's psyche.[2] Abenheimer notes also that Belarius pretends to be the father of the king's sons; in technical jargon he introjects the image of a good father which he sought but did not find outside himself in the king. Dr. Robert Fliess considers Posthumus' jokes with his jailer pending his execution, notes that they talk about it in terms of a feast, and suggests that maybe all governmental executions hark back to survivals of cannibalistic impulses.[3]

HAMLET

Psychoanalysts seem to take to *Hamlet* like kittens to a ball of yarn, and, by way of attempts to straighten out the tangle, there have been at least four partial surveys of the psychoanalytic literature on *Hamlet* already.[1] One reason for this psychoanalytic interest is that *Hamlet* involves a basic psychoanalytic proposition. We have seen in an earlier chapter how *Hamlet* popped into Freud's mind in October, 1897, when he discovered the oedipus complex itself; he first publicly stated his reading in *The Interpretation of Dreams* (1900); but after Dr. Jones's long article appeared in 1910 *Hamlet* seems, more or less, to have become his province. The whole matter of Hamlet's oedipus complex has almost become one of the cornerstones of psychoanalytic theory, and at times the question virtually loses its literary origin. In fact, *Hamlet* has provided the theory for analyzing two unfortunates: a South African Negro confronted with Hamlet's problem [2] and an unfortunate young New Yorker named Gino who stabbed his mother thirty-two times with the proverbial carving knife.[3] At the other extreme the reading can lose its clinical origin and become a kind of allegory as when (so Alberta E. Feynman suggests)[4] Jean Cocteau used the Freud-Jones reading of *Hamlet* to rework the oedipus myth in his play *The Infernal Machine*.

Given such a tangle, the best structure I can offer for this mass of psychoanalytic and near-psychoanalytic readings is to start first with the orthodox Freud-Jones reading as matters stood in 1910 and work out, as it were, in widening circles: first, from Freud and Jones to direct restatements and stagings of their oedipal view. Then we can look at amplifications of the basic Freud-Jones insight which remain well within orthodox psychoanalysis. Widening the survey further, we can consider two kinds of variant readings: those that concentrate on Hamlet's doubts and delays; those that see matricide as the basic problem. As a balance, we shall consider some of the critiques of the Freud-Jones view, those by literary critics and those by semi- or antipsychoanalytic writers from the ranks of existential psychoanalysis, Adlerians, Jungians, myth-and-ritual critics, and Rankians. The iris thus fully widened, we can close down on particular aspects of the play, individual episodes and speeches. (This survey is outlined on pp. 372–379.)

a. The Freud-Jones View

The basic issue of the play Freud and Jones say (and so, they point out, do many literary critics) is: Why does Hamlet delay? As we have seen, Freud puts and answers the question rather neatly. (1) Critics, by and large, have been unable to say why Hamlet delays. (2) Clinical experience shows that every child wishes to murder his father and marry his mother. (3) Clinical experience also shows that this childish wish persists in the unconscious mind of the adult, and that wish and deed seem the same there. (4) Were Hamlet to punish Claudius for murdering his father and marrying his mother, he would have to punish himself as well. Therefore, he delays. (5) The wish in question is unconscious in all of us, and that is why the critics could not say why Hamlet delays.[5]

Dr. Jones also proceeds to his answer step by step.[6] First, he shows that Hamlet does, in fact, delay. Second, he shows (by pointing to the killing of Polonius, the pirate episode, and the final scene) that Hamlet is a man of action who ordinarily accomplishes what he sets out to do. Third, he eliminates the argument that Hamlet is held up by the situation external to himself by pointing to the parallel case of Laertes. Finally, he produces the psychoanalytic answer: Hamlet delays because of the nature of *this* task as opposed to any other. Neither avenging the parricide alone nor his disgust at his mother's swift remarriage explains his reaction. Therefore, it must be the special nature of his task: to avenge his father on his uncle. Claudius' crime, however, corresponds to what psychoanalysis has discovered are wishes common to every child. "In reality [Hamlet's] uncle incorporates the deepest and most buried part of his own personality, so that he cannot kill him without also killing himself."

This much is Freud's, and Jones adds a wrinkle of his own: "The call of duty to kill his stepfather cannot be obeyed because it links itself with the unconscious call of his nature to kill his mother's husband, whether this is the first or the second [husband]; the absolute 'repression' of the former impulse involves the inner prohibition of the latter also."

Thus, as the argument leaves the hands of Dr. Jones, there are two strings to the oedipal bow. First, from the point of view of instinctual drives, Hamlet cannot kill Claudius because he would have to punish himself for (mentally) committing the same crimes. Second, from the point of view of defenses, Hamlet's childhood repression of the wish to kill his father operates in adult life against the killing of Claudius.

Dr. Jones went on to consider the successive changes in the myth as it passed from Saxo Grammaticus and Belleforest through the hands of the unknown author of the *Ur-Hamlet* to Shakespeare. Relying heavily on Otto Rank's formulations in *The Myth of the Birth of the Hero,* he saw a steady increase in disguise or repression of the oedipal content of the myth. In its earliest form Amleth does not hesitate; Hamlet's delay is one form the repression takes. Another form is the decomposing of the original villain into at least three father figures, the ghost, Polonius, and Claudius. Of the three, Polonius introduces a new motif: he is the father who withholds his daughter from a prospective son-in-law, and he thus brings in another group of incest themes.

Still a third form of repression or disguise is the splitting of the hero into a number of brother figures: Fortinbras, Horatio, Laertes, and Rosecrantz-and-Guildenstern. Every one of these changes stresses, Jones says, Hamlet's failure where the original Amleth had succeeded. In a sense, the whole development is summed up in the fact that where Amleth's madness had concealed his secret, Hamlet's reveals it. This steady growth of disguise in the myth, Jones points out, fits Freud's hypothesis about "the secular advance of repression," the idea that the older a society gets, the more it has to repress.

b. Restatements of the Freud-Jones View

Many approving articles, notes, reviews, and whatnot have repeated the Freud-Jones view substantially unchanged.[7] And, of course, there are a great many restatements of the Freud-Jones view in the course of saying what nonsense it is. Some of these attacks are amiably and amusingly satirical.[8] Others are shrill and abusive, for the oedipal view of *Hamlet* seems to provoke that response. Even, for example, the gentle Granville-Barker dismisses all psychoanalytic approaches to Shakespeare as "dirty nonsense," although he hastens to add, "I do not use the 'dirty' abusively, but to connote the more material side of our nature, which was formed, as we know, out of the dust of the earth." [9] Whether the critic is pro, con, or whimsical, there seems little question that the Freud-Jones view of *Hamlet* is very widely known and probably this century's most distinctive contribution to Shakespearean criticism.

c. Stagings of the Freud-Jones View

The most important restatements of any critical position about Shakespearean drama are, of course, restatements in the living theater, and the Freud-Jones view has had its share of those. Theatrical research being what it is, one cannot be sure when the oedipal view of *Hamlet* first reached the stage, but surely one of the earliest such stagings was Arthur Hopkins's 1922 production with Robert Edmond Jones's sets and John Barrymore as Hamlet. Dr. Tannenbaum was moved to a satirical study of Barrymore's apparently heavily oedipal portrayal,[10] particularly as he played the closet scene; but a less critical critic, Mr. Patrick Kearney, waxed enthusiastic about Jones's method of production. Jones used symbols extensively, representing the ghost, for example, by "wavering amorphous lights" as a way of getting at "a child's memory of the father as an avenging giant, magnified by the son's unconscious sense of guilt." "By means of this device," said Mr. Kearney, "the secret, guilty desires of the spectator are aroused." [11]

By 1946 Jean-Louis Barrault's Hamlet was also showing an oedipal tinge,[12] but, of course, the most famous rendition of this kind was Laurence Olivier's. As early as 1937 Olivier had played a Freud-Jones Hamlet, but it was his film of 1948 that froze this treatment for posterity: there can be little doubt that Olivier's film did more to popularize the oedipal view of the play than anything else. Sir Laurence has himself expressed his thoughts in the book about his film.[13] At least one psychoanalytic critic, however, has objected to Olivier's oedipal portrayal as being too obvious. "Does not the prince admonish the actors they should not 'tell all'?" asks Dr. Theodore Reik.[14] "Olivier's Hamlet does. He leaves no doubt in his audience's mind that he had studied Freud." The post-Freudian actor no less than the post-Freudian playwright faces a problem: he cannot let what he knows intellectually about psychological forces affect his characterization. That must come from his own inner resources, or else, as Freud predicted, "we shall be inclined to send for the doctor."

d. Amplifications of the Freud-Jones View Within Orthodox Psychoanalysis

The first of the psychoanalytic expansions of the original Freud-Jones thesis was that of Otto Rank in 1912 in his study, *Das Inzest-Motiv in Dichtung und Sage.*[15] Rank's approach represents an improvement in that Jones tends to spend much of his effort in controverting earlier critics, while Rank spends his on studying the play. His basic view, first, is that the characters and episodes of the play must be taken as projections of impulses in the poet's mind; second, the basic issue in the play is the oedipal one; third, the large number of splits and spinoffs in incident and personnel suggest a good deal of ambivalence in the whole affair. Thus, the political situation and theme in the play become, in essence, erotic; they reflect the oedipal wish embodied in this erotico-political shambles with its two components: first, the wish to kill the father; second, the wish to possess the mother.

There seems, at least in Rank's treatment of *Hamlet,* to be less concern with the second wish. Hamlet feels (as any child in an oedipal phase does) in two contradictory ways about his mother, first that she is (or should be) virginal, taboo, untouchable; second, that she is only too readily available—but not to him. Hamlet, Rank says, projects these two feelings one after the other onto Ophelia. We see Hamlet's real feelings toward his mother only in the closet scene. There, they are watched by Polonius, just as Hamlet and Ophelia had been watched—the watching in both cases projects onto a father figure the son's wish to spy on his mother and father alone together. The finale, in which Hamlet and his mother die together, projects the wish to "die" with the mother, to return to her womb in a sexual way.

The first wish of the oedipal pattern, the wish to kill the father, Rank regards as the crux of *Hamlet.* For one thing, Hamlet's wish that his father be dead has been carried out; the other half of the oedipus wish (that he now possess the mother) has not been. Hamlet's death wish against the father (even if acted out) has been doubly disguised: first, the wish is to be acted out, not against Hamlet's father, but against Claudius (who is, nevertheless, in two ways a surrogate for Hamlet Senior, as uncle and as stepfather); second, the wish is made legitimate as a desire to avenge the father, not kill him.

In effect, because half of Hamlet's oedipal wish has been acted out, his father is half dead; hence Hamlet Senior appears as a ghost. The ghost thus serves to project Hamlet's "buried" oedipal wish and also to prove that his father is dead. It provides an opportunity for further disguise of the original oedipus wish as abundant, even excessive, love of the father (a reaction formation or overcompensation). The ghost also represents the "immortality," the persistence into adulthood, of the son's childhood resentment of the father and also the immortality of the father's inhibiting effect on the son. The fear at the sight of the ghost projects, Rank says, the child's fear at the sight of the parents in night clothes.

Hamlet's real feeling toward his father then (perhaps not so much in the sense of the character's "feeling" as in the projections of a hypothetical feeling through other characters) is one of great resentment. The father has taken his bride away (the Polonius father, that is); the father has taken his mother away (the Claudius father). Claudius' coming between the political election and Hamlet's hopes is really a projection of Hamlet's own erotic wish to come between his parents. Putting side by side the images of the two brothers, Hamlet Senior and Claudius, compares in a psychological sense handsome son to decrepit, depraved father. Hamlet's real feelings toward the father emerge in his sharp, savage, sudden killing of Polonius—significantly, in his mother's bedroom. The fact that Hamlet dies once Claudius is killed is a working out in fantasy of the child's feeling that once the father is replaced there is nothing left to do: "The rest is silence."

The basic pattern, then, of *Hamlet,* Rank says, the reason there are so many splits, decompositions, and projections of character, is ambivalence, both toward the mother and toward the father. This ambivalence, Rank argues, is ultimately to be referred to Shakespeare's becoming the father after his own father's death; he now has some of the feelings of a son and some of a father.[16] In the play this dualism becomes Hamlet's hesitation to commit revenge for what he wished to do himself. The dualism shows also in the contrast between Hamlet's hesitation and Laertes' eagerness to avenge his father's murder. There are three fathers in the play, each representing a different attitude toward the father: Hamlet Senior, the honored father; Claudius, the projection of the son's wish to kill the father; Polonius, the ridiculed father, who keeps his daughter away as the father keeps the mother. There are two sons, Hamlet and his "successful" counterpart, Laertes. The conclusion of the play is to be understood as Hamlet's feeling that life is not worth living once the mother is gone; he can kill Claudius then. His wish to kill Claudius in his incestuous bed disguises the real wish, to deprive him of his sexual power, in other words, to castrate him. It is also another projection of a fantasy about watching the parents' loving: the watching is projected onto the ghost-father who breaks in on Hamlet and his mother.

Rank notes two recurring motifs from folklore. First, in "Das Motiv des Uriasbriefes," a father who wishes to separate his son from some woman (daughter or mother) sends him away with a letter sealing his doom. In *Hamlet,* the interfering father is projected onto the Polonius-Ophelia side of the plot; the letter is transferred to Hamlet's "brothers," Rosencrantz and Guildenstern. Second, in another motif from folklore, Laertes gets some of the elements of the father in the earliest versions of *Hamlet:* the exchanging of swords and the sword wedged (as a trap) in its scabbard: these occur in Shakespeare's *Hamlet* as the exchange in the duel and as Hamlet's hesitation. Rank regards as one of the great triumphs of Shakespeare's art the mingling in the figure of the ghost both the father's attempts to separate mother and son and the son's efforts to separate the Claudius father and the mother.

Rank, as we have seen, refers these insights back to Shakespeare's feelings in 1601. His argument as a whole lacks the simple logic of Jones's. On the other hand, it is much more inclusive; much more of the play is brought into the oedipal situation. The price he pays for this inclusiveness is a lack of consistency. That is, Hamlet's wishes are now fulfilled, now yet to be accomplished; Claudius is now father, now a projection of Hamlet's mind, and so on. But Rank's view of the play is dreamlike, and no questions of realistic consistency are proper. In the unconscious there is no negation, and in dreams—or poetry—we do not choose between alternatives; we take both. Rank's view of *Hamlet* with all its interlocking ambivalences and apparent inconsistencies gives us a far truer picture of the mind in art than Jones's logic does. Rank's method, like Jones's, was to refer the psychoanalytic patterns he found in the play to Shakespeare's (necessarily somewhat hypothetical) mind. Nevertheless, Rank's study represents a considerable departure from Jones's in that he does not treat literary characters as living people. His approach to them as projections of mental impulses allows for much more scope and complexity (oddly enough) than assigning to each of the individual characters the complexity of being human.

We have already seen (in Chapter 7) the late Ella Freeman Sharpe's two papers on *Hamlet* (1929 and 1947).[17] Like Rank, like Jones, like all the early psychoanalytic critics, she unifies the details she considers in terms of the poet's psyche—as with the early Freudians, this procedure gets her into such oddities as the bowel movements of the infant poet-to-be. Miss Sharpe, like Rank, deals with many details of the play (as contrasted with Jones's study of *Hamlet* which dealt with only a few). Miss Sharpe, moreover, deals with a far greater range of details than even Rank does. Where Rank had confined his attention entirely to oedipal matters and incest themes, Miss Sharpe came to grips with particular images, and in discussing those images she drew on Freud's discoveries about pregenital oral and anal phenomena as well as his earliest, more purely oedipal approach. Moreover, she tended to see the play in dynamic terms, as having a beginning and an end, rather than as a more or less static configuration of attitudes.

Another psychoanalytic writer concerned with the dynamics of the tragedy is Erland Lindbäck.[18] Quoting Freud, Rank, Jones, and Symons (see p. 199) with approval, he tries to relate the psychoanalytic reading of *Hamlet* to the dynamics of dramatic development. Lindbäck sees the play as showing the oedipus complex pushing its way to the surface of action. The original appearance of the ghost as an external reality relieved Hamlet of some of his guilt feelings, putting them outside himself, but the subsequent action forces his oedipus wishes back within. At the dramatic climax, which Lindbäck takes to be the closet scene, the second appearance of the ghost allows Hamlet to turn some of his guilt into outward aggression again. But it is not until Laertes punishes him for the murder of a father (Polonius) that Hamlet's conscience is assuaged and he can release his aggression and consummate his revenge.

Rather less systematic than Freud, Jones, Rank, or Sharpe is Dr. Theodore Reik whose essays often take the form of rambling free associations. Within these patterns of free association, Dr. Reik has made some interesting remarks on Shakespeare, and, in particular, on *Hamlet*. In some ruminations published in 1949, Reik noted Hamlet's intense preoccupation with death and thoughts of death.[19] Such thoughts occur to young people, Reik says, as a reaction to aggressive and murderous impulses. That is, when an adolescent's desires are frustrated, aggressive impulses emerge against the authority figures, the parents and teachers, that are doing the frustrating. The young person, however, is likely to feel quite guilty about these impulses with the result that he turns these impulses against himself, so that finally they take the form of an intense preoccupation with the problem of death in the abstract. The adolescent disguises the personal origin of these apparently generalized thoughts, but the feeling of gloom actually atones and punishes him for murder in his own thoughts. "It is not accidental," Reik notes, "that Hamlet's profound meditations on death emerge when he plans to kill the king, and that in connection with it even suicidal impulses occur to him."

Reik pointed out in a later essay the relation of Hamlet's thoughts of death to the mechanism of the whole play.[20] To the child or the primitive—or the adult's unconscious—thoughts are as good as deeds; one can wish, pray, curse, or vow things into being. Thus, if a child merely wishes his father's death, he feels just as guilty as if he had actually tried to murder him. Hence, Hamlet feels (unconsciously) that his ordinary hostility toward his father caused Hamlet Senior's death; Hamlet feels guilty, in other words, even though he knows his uncle did the deed. Out of this guilt for the father's death, a series of defenses can form. One is: "I didn't want father dead; I didn't want to possess mother; in fact, it is she who is responsible for father's death." The mechanism is one of reversal, but with a grain of truth underneath: in a way, the mother was responsible because the son's desire for her brought about the hostile wish against the father.

The defense can go further into the mechanism of projection: "Not I wanted to murder father, but he (another man, thought of as father's rival)—not I desire mother (but another man)." In *Hamlet* this is the projection (as Rank pointed out) of Hamlet's (or Shakespeare's) oedipal wish onto Claudius. The defense, however, can go still another way, into "reaction formation," changing the aim of the drive, or, in Shakespearean language, protesting too much. "I did not want to murder my father—on the contrary, I want to revenge his death and not only do I not desire my mother, I actually dislike her and attack her." And this, too, we see in *Hamlet,* in the prince's scorn for all women and his attack on Ophelia. Rank had noted these mechanisms in part; the point Reik added is that it does not matter whether the father is murdered or not; Hamlet would have felt the same way regardless of the cause of his father's death, for Hamlet is reacting not to reality but to his own unconscious wishes.

In a still later essay [21] Reik linked Hamlet's interest in omnipotent thinking, his constant curses, abuses, and self-complaints to the general idea of attacking with the mouth. This "oral sadism" would be, presumably, another form of Hamlet's general aggression which he translates into a preoccupation with death.

During the time spanned by Reik's essays other analysts had added angles to the psychoanalytic view of *Hamlet.* In particular, a South African analyst, J. Meltzer, argued that Hamlet shows a masochistic wish to suffer. Under the stresses of the total situation, his mind has retreated to this more primitive way of solving his problems, letting them hurt him.[22] Thus Meltzer, like most of the analysts we have been looking at so far, tends to treat Hamlet as a living person.

Dr. K. R. Eissler in his extended analysis of *Hamlet* [23] discusses this and other theoretical problems as well as the play. He concludes that it is all right to consider Hamlet as living because he is a projection of the living Shakespeare. Moreover, Eissler argues, a drama has two levels: at one it is the equivalent of a record of historically true events, a "story" about apparently real people; at the other level, a drama is like a dream in that the onlooker knows more than the characters and in that a central theme is elaborated as if by the dreamer's associations. In other words, Eissler regards a play as having a latent and a manifest content of its own—like a dream.

His essay expounds the latent content of *Hamlet,* first, through the characters, and second, through the psychic development of Hamlet himself. Eissler notes that the three young people of the play have somewhat the quality of siblings. Hamlet, that is, represents an older brother who will be "king," but does not know when; he tends to ally himself (at least compared to Laertes) with the forces of law and order. Laertes is a sort of jealous, impetuous younger brother. With respect to the "sister," Ophelia, their roles are reversed: Laertes is the restraining force; Hamlet the impetuous.

The play has three fathers and two father substitutes; each of them reflects a different fantasy about the father. The ghost is the idealized father; Polonius is the dotard; old Fortinbras is the murdered father; Claudius is the criminal father; Fortinbras' uncle is the sick, bedridden, impotent father. Yet for all these fathers there is only one mother, Gertrude. Eissler suggests that maybe Shakespeare's use of decomposition or splitting of the fathers and condensation of the mother represents aggression toward the one and love for the other. At any rate, there is a good deal of ambivalence toward the father, which shows, for example, in Hamlet's doubts whether the ghost is a spirit of heaven or hell. The ambivalence toward the ghost comes about because he—or it—has erected again the taboo against Hamlet's "having" his mother. Ambivalence shows also in Shakespeare's leaving the question of incest ambiguous. Clearly Claudius' dealings with Gertrude are not scouts' oath behavior, but it is not clear at all whether to Shakespeare, his audience, the other people in the play, or, indeed, to anyone but Hamlet, it constituted incest. The effect of the ambiguity, Eissler says, is to let Hamlet call it incest and us accept his evaluation as the privileged emotional reaction of a child.

This childishness of Hamlet Eissler sees as the key to the play. The hero, he says, develops in the course of the action from child to adult and we can trace the change through the soliloquies. The most childish Hamlet appears in the first. He equates incest and sexuality and refuses to speak; he regards himself (in the comparison to Hercules) as infinitely below his father. In Hamlet's soliloquy after the appearance of the ghost, he erects defenses against the ghost's intrusion into his mind (writing in his "tables," but only trivial matter); the internal and external justifications for what he must do conflict in him. The Hecuba soliloquy serves as a sort of trial action for the killing and establishes a conflict (like an actor's) between external appearance and state of mind. Because of his feelings toward his mother, Eissler says, Hamlet distrusts emotions and tries to find another motive acceptable to him. His distrust of emotions leads him to action on the one hand and devaluation of the ghost on the other. The "To be or not to be" soliloquy continues the thought of the preceding one: What makes a man not act? Fear of death, in effect, fear of losing his manhood, fear of castration. After the soliloquy he abandons Ophelia; his action shows the influence of woman on him weakening, woman conceived of only as saint or slut. In his soliloquy over the king at prayer, Hamlet appears as frankly sadistic; he no longer doubts his own emotionality. Finally, in his remarks on Fortinbras' campaign for an eggshell, he criticizes all his father's ideologies; at last he is free of his fear of death and incest.

In the last scene we see Hamlet having progressed to a degree of independence, Dr. Eissler says, far greater than his father had demanded of him. The final scene presents death and, through "dying together," incest with the mother, and, in Fortinbras, Hamlet's rebirth. Hamlet, in short, has accomplished the task imposed, has integrated himself and shed his childish fantasies—and, in the course of the play, because of the ambiguity in *Hamlet's* historical time, says Dr. Eissler, those fantasies have included nearly all the unconscious fantasies in any man's life, all slipped in more or less unobtrusively.

One may question, it seems to me, Dr. Eissler's assurance in treating a literary character, even so labyrinthine a one as Hamlet, as a living person. One might also question Dr. Eissler's faith in Hamlet's success at the end. On the other hand, this study of the play is most useful for its emphasis on a dynamic *Hamlet,* rather than a series of static attitudes. Another dynamic approach is that of Lora and Abraham Heller.[24] They stress an important qualification to the Freud-Jones view, implicit in it, but one not often stated directly. Hamlet is not a man whose development was arrested at the oedipal phase; if that were true, then he would have been neurotic always and Ophelia could hardly say of him,

> O, what a noble mind is here o'erthrown!
> The courtier's, soldier's, scholar's eye, tongue, sword,
> Th'expectancy and rose of the fair state,
> The glass of fashion and the mould of form,
> Th'observed of all observers, quite, quite down!

Rather, Hamlet has regressed from an adult position to the oedipal level as a result of three shocks: his father's sudden death; his mother's hasty remarriage; the ghost's revelations.

Then, the question behind the question of delay is: Why did Hamlet regress instead of promptly killing Claudius as Laertes, say, would have? Because unconsciously he feels his mother is responsible. "No child is unaware of the tensions and conflicts between his parents. And it is an everyday commonness that the death, especially the sudden death, of the parent with whom the child was identified is often interpreted by the child as a murder by a surviving parent toward whom he has long felt hostility." Earlier, Reik (n.20) had pointed out that even if Hamlet's father hadn't been murdered but had died a natural death and even if the queen hadn't remarried, Hamlet would still have felt hostility toward his mother. She, the Hellers argue, is a shallow, animal woman who never really loved Hamlet Senior. Her "hanging on him" should be regarded as forced and compulsive. Because of this family history, they say, Hamlet delays because his real hostility is not to Claudius but to his mother—even within an oedipal framework. Unfortunately, as Frank Wadsworth points out, the argument rests on a number of readings which are, if not downright erroneous, at least quite debatable.[25]

Still another extension of the Freud-Jones view stems from what is, to many, the most exciting and promising development in current psychoanalytic thought, the work of Erik Erikson. Without contradicting either traditional psychoanalysis or ego psychology as developed by Kris, Hartmann, and others, Erikson radically expands their scope by extending the intrapersonal approach of psychoanalysis into the individual's interpersonal relation to the psychological patterns of his society embodied in the people close to him. We can consider this expansion as proceeding in three directions. First, Erikson has extended psychoanalytic notions of developmental stages in childhood through young adulthood, middle, and old age. Second, he has worked out in some detail the "adaptive hypothesis" of Hartmann and others: he shows specifically how every stage of life, from beginning to end, poses issues the solutions to which will be in varying degree trouble spots or successful adaptations to the tasks life sets us. Third, he has looked intensely at the way differing patterns of child rearing encourage individuals toward the solutions their cultures favor: Luther in medieval Germany, children among the Sioux or in Soviet Russia, women in America, and, the ur-problem of psychoanalysis, Hamlet in Denmark.

Thus, when Erikson turns, in a paper on youth,[26] to Hamlet, he sees him as both facing a developmental crisis and taking from his culture (the Denmark of the play) ways of dealing with that crisis. In particular, Erikson sees Hamlet as a delayed adolescent, facing in his thirtieth year the issues most men work out in their early twenties. The typical task of adolescence, Erikson suggests, is to find something and somebody to be true to; to establish loyalty and fidelity to one identity, repudiating others. Against this need there is "identity diffusion," and, typically, the adolescent can find his own identity only by trying out several roles and rules. Thus Hamlet is *par excellence* the "player," one who tries out different identities.

It is very difficult, however, for Hamlet to achieve from his "playing" a firm identity, for the Denmark he confronts is a morass of infidelity in which playacting seems almost a necessity. All five of the young men in the play who are Hamlet's age, "all sure (or even overdefined) in their identities as dutiful sons, courtiers, and future leaders ... are all drawn into the moral swamp of infidelity, which seeps into the fiber of all those who owe allegiance to 'rotten' Denmark." All five—and Hamlet—find their identities diffused by the world

around them (which includes, Erikson whimsically notes, a caricature of a psychiatrist: Polonius, with his "I have found the very cause
of Hamlet's lunacy").

Confronted with a world that gives him nothing to be faithful to,
Hamlet loses all kinds of aspects of himself (suffers "identity diffusion"). He takes no pleasure in being a courtier (in the "drossy age"
he confronts), nor in being masculine (woman "delights not me"),
nor in being human ("What a piece of work is a man"), nor even in
existing ("O that this too, too sullied flesh would melt"). What does
please Hamlet is the sincerity of Horatio—and of the actors (although he denounces overacting). Yet, despite his love of sincerity,
he becomes himself the actor he feels ambivalently toward. He
"seems," though he detests seeming.

He thus acquires, in Erikson's term, a "negative identity," one
which is not true to the self that came to adolescence. He becomes,
for example, the furious avenger his better ethical sense would not
tolerate. He endorses a bellicose Fortinbras utterly alien to his own
complex, rich self, and the true adolescent, searching for fidelity, dies.
The rites of war that are to speak for him are false and inadequate.
"Thus do inner reality and historical actuality conspire to deny tragic
man the positive identity for which he seems exquisitely chosen."

An Eriksonian view of the play emerges even more clearly in a
paper directed specifically to *Hamlet* by two of Erikson's students.[27]
Neil Friedman and Richard M. Jones offer a supplement to the traditional Freud-Jones view which they regard as "inadequate": inadequate in a psychological sense because it sees Hamlet's conscious
activities as merely defensive rather than socially adaptive; inadequate in a literary sense because it does not see the play as a ritual
function in its own historical context. Ideally, understanding the play
should enrich psychological understanding while psychological understanding enriches the play. To do so, understanding must move from
a psychodynamic view of what goes on within Hamlet to a "psychosocial" view of Hamlet's Denmark.

One should begin with a literary view of the play, for example,
Francis Fergusson's, that all the actions in their various ways light up
the rottenness of Denmark. What is this rottenness? It shows in the
attitudes of the play's various parents toward their children: that they
are to be watched over, seen into, and so controlled. Excessively
watched children grow up into excessively wary adults, and so, in a
"psychosocial" way, the pattern perpetuates itself. Such a child-
rearing pattern would lead to trouble specifically in the child's efforts
to resolve the developmental issue of the anal stage: to achieve
autonomy rather than motivation simply from shame or doubt. One

would expect the young of such a society as Hamlet's Denmark "to grow up with weakened will and blunted purpose."

A later developmental stage, adolescence, presents the issue of fidelity, both in oneself and in others. Thus, Hamlet confronts his mother's hasty remarriage, his uncle as a murderer, and all the rottenness of Denmark with its general infidelity between outward appearances and inner meanings. It is in response to this issue that Hamlet becomes an "actor," spied upon, watched, yet able by his "playing" to buffer the intrusions of the adults around him. "In a society in which sham and pretense are accepted and expected, becoming an actor realizes to its limits the unconscious tendency of that society."

The ghost, in this context, becomes another spying adult, distrusting and therefore to be distrusted. "Pity me not," he says, but invites pity anyway:

> I could a tale unfold whose lightest word
> Would harrow up thy soul . . .

"If thou didst ever thy dear father love," he says, casting doubt on his son's love, as does Denmark's whole system of paternal exploitation. The ghost makes a negative appeal:

> Duller shouldst thou be than the fat weed
> That roots itself in ease on Lethe wharf,
> Wouldst thou not stir in this.

> If thou hast nature in thee, bear it not.

"If," "shouldst," "wouldst"—these conditional and negative appeals signal us that the father does not, in fact, expect his son's loyalty, and therefore he must be hiding something himself.

What Hamlet's father is hiding is the "mutuality" of the oedipus complex, that is, the way the child's crisis in his relations with his parents answers to the corresponding crisis in his parents' development as young adults. The child with his lack of inhibition presents both a potential threat and a potential model to his parents as they develop physical intimacy. They, in turn, with their physical power but psychological inhibition present a threat and model to the child. Ideally, the child could become a rejuvenating influence upon his parents, but in Hamlet's Denmark intimacy between adults has become a kind of showing off, and Denmark finds a substitute gratification in looking into the lives of children, a spying that ultimately robs the child of his separate existence—destroys him. Thus, Hamlet compares Polonius to Jephtha who had a daughter "which he lovèd passing well"—and killed.

In short, according to Friedman and Jones, this parental pattern of spying on children offers three gratifications: "getting in on" intimate things; controlling the children; and thus, at least metaphorically, killing them. Correspondingly, Hamlet delays for three reasons which represent failures caused by this psychosocial pattern at three stages of development. First, the pattern of parental spying and prying has blunted his will (the anal issue). Second, he feels oedipally guilty (the Freud-Jones view), but also, third, he cannot identify with a father he cannot trust because of this pervasive psychosocial pattern (the adolescent issue of fidelity). Understanding the play in this way enriches psychology; psychological insight, in turn, enriches the play.

Such amplifications of the Freud-Jones view are difficult to bring together into a meaningful whole, since they mostly try to deal with a number of details within the play as a way of working out the basic oedipal pattern. The strength of these readings (when they are strong) resides in their handling of details rather than in a single, reproducible formulation. Rank, writing in the earliest stage of psychoanalysis's development, confines himself to the oedipal impulse, while the later writers introduce the idea of defensive ways of dealing with that impulse. Rank goes beyond Jones, though, in showing how the play is not simply a portrayal of a man in a tight spot, but a totality or *gestalt* of competing attitudes and drives represented by the various characters and motifs. Miss Sharpe also deals with the play as a totality of interacting elements, but sees the events and images in the more sophisticated way of later psychoanalysis not only as expressing but also as dealing with the basic oedipal impulse. Like Rank, she sees the play as reflecting a mind, as it were, behind Hamlet's, while others after her have continued Jones's technique of speaking of Hamlet as though he were a living person. Lindbäck discusses Hamlet's problems of outward-directed and inward-directed aggression (his "need to suffer" described by Meltzer). Reik discusses a number of defensive reactions (reversal, projection, reaction formation), and Eissler sees the dramatic development of the play as Hamlet's progression from childish ways of dealing with his problem to an adult one. The Hellers discuss the initial regression, before the play, so to speak, that starts him off at a childish level. The Eriksonian approach treats Hamlet as a real person, psychosocially interacting with a real culture.

While even all these readings do not give a total psychoanalytic picture, they do show the complexity to which Freud's initial oedipal

ulation leads. Certainly no one can say an oedipal reading of
nlet is reductionist, although it is not, of course, the only possible
ading. Indeed, it is not even the only possible psychoanalytic
ading.

e. Variations on the Freud-Jones View: i. Doubting and Delaying

Freud and Jones concentrated on the particular nature of the crime
Hamlet was to avenge and the form his revenge was to take. Even
quite early in psychoanalytic *Hamlet* criticism, some authors concerned themselves with Hamlet's peculiar behavior in response to his
task: his doubting and delaying. Mr. Alan Clutton-Brock suggested in
1922 that Hamlet delays because he wants to forget, that is, repress.
Unconsciously, Hamlet shrinks from killing Claudius because he is
eager, above all, to forget his father's murder as well as his mother's
second marriage, and the more he tries to force himself into action,
the more his unconscious invents pretexts for delaying. (Ernest
Jones, in his review of this book, noted that, while it was influenced
by the oedipal view of the play, it uses only the idea of an unconscious obstacle, not the specific oedipal conflict.) [28]
A fuller development of the idea came in Wilhelm Stekel's book on
doubting. He sees the reason for Hamlet's delay as doubts about his
origin. The possibility that Gertrude had had an affair with Claudius
before Hamlet Senior's death raises the possibility that Hamlet is
really Claudius' son. Were he to take revenge on his uncle, he
would kill his own father. Stekel suggests that this mechanism co-
exists with the Freud-Jones oedipal approach; he sees doubts about
one's origin as at the root of every compulsive doubting: "Every
doubter is a Hamlet." [29]
In an excellent study Professor Theodor Hartwig [30] brings the approach through Hamlet's doubting into line with the oedipal reading.
He stresses the plastic quality of the oedipus conflict, its variations
possible under varying social situations. That is, the oedipus complex
involves *both* hate and love of *both* mother and father. Because of
these competing aspects of the oedipus complex, Hamlet becomes
involved in something like an obsessional or compulsive neurosis; he
feels impelled first to do and then to undo, and he is thus inhibited
from all action toward his goal. In all of Hamlet's actions Hartwig
finds an impulse to act which then dissolves into talking and thinking
about the action instead of performing it. In general, Hamlet insists
on fleeing into an illusion that his will is free, that he must choose and
think about his choice, as a defense against recognizing that he is not

free at all, that his neurotic drives, in fact, prevent him from acting freely. This same ambivalence turns up in other characters, for example, Claudius who speaks of "mirth in funeral and . . . dirge in marriage." Laertes, by letting Hamlet get hold of the poisoned rapier, commits, in effect, a "Freudian slip." A "touch" of guilt brings home to him his own need to be punished.

In a highly eccentric article but one with a grain of sense, Dr. A. André Glaz [31] takes an approach to *Hamlet* not unlike Eissler's. He, too, sees the play as existing on two levels, one the "noisy realistic" drama which is oedipal, the other the self-analysis and catharsis of Hamlet alone, to whom all the other characters are projections. This second drama has the quality of dreams or the unconscious: it ranges freely through time and space; it does not abide by cause and effect; it makes extensive use of symbolism and representation through the opposite. One can see the two levels in the play within the play: the verbal Mouse Trap is the realistic form; the mute dumb show is the dream form of Hamlet's little play.

Hamlet's delays, then, should be understood as fragments of this inner drama. In it Hamlet feels like an illegitimate son so that his oedipus situation is complicated by an unalloyed hatred of his father. And he feels that his mother has betrayed him. He then resolves to act the role of the "real father" himself. Hamlet, in this dream drama, is represented by four people: Hamlet himself, the man facing the problem; Horatio, the conflict-free ego; Laertes, the unsolved oedipus complex; Fortinbras, the integrated personality. Similarly, while the ghost represents the wished-for kingly father, Polonius and the gravedigger show the father-as-clown. Ophelia serves as a younger Gertrude, and her obscene mad songs are Gertrude's confession of adultery. Understood this way, Hamlet after "confinement" in the English madhouse can become Fortinbras as four captains bear off his split self. Although he has some interesting insights, Dr. Glaz's approach suggests, I think, the limitations of treating a drama purely and simply as a dream, and Professor Morton Kaplan has criticized his essay sharply for collapsing all the characters into aspects of Hamlet, then Hamlet into Shakespeare, applying everything discovered (or invented) about Hamlet to Shakespeare without any change.[32]

One final version of the doubting-and-delaying hypothesis: Dr. Karl Menninger suggests, rather laconically and elliptically, that Hamlet is using thinking instead of action (obsessional thinking) as a way of managing aggressive feelings too great for him to handle.[33] He avoids direct aggression, giving, instead, an appearance of thoughtful and thorough consideration. At the same time, though, he achieves indirect aggression through his failure to live up either to his father's injunctions or to Claudius' wish that he take his place as "our chiefest courtier."

e. Variations on the Freud-Jones View: ii. The Theme of Matricide

Concentrating on Hamlet's doubts and delays has led to one variant on the oedipal view, but the principal variant has been to consider Hamlet's delay the result of matricidal impulses instead of parricidal ones. As early as 1912 Erich Wulffen suggested that Hamlet is held back primarily by his sexual feelings for his mother—that is, he himself feels guilty of what Claudius has done. Only after his mother is dead can he finally kill Claudius. The proof of the pudding is Laertes; he has no mother and he can avenge swiftly.[34]

Wulffen did little more than adumbrate an approach to the play through Hamlet's relation to his mother. The real originator of the matricidal view is Dr. Frederic Wertham, most widely known as an attacker of wicked comic books. In a book-length study of a young matricide in New York [35] and a later, shorter theoretical paper,[36] he has set out his reasons for disagreeing with the Freud-Jones view that Hamlet cannot punish Claudius for doing what he, Hamlet, would like to do. Wertham argues, first, that Hamlet identifies with his father, not with Claudius; he expresses love for his father, not the hostility he directs to Claudius. Second, the revenge, as it actually works out, seems more for the adultery than the murder; Laertes even has to remind Hamlet, "The king, the king's to blame." Further, Dr. Wertham insists that *Hamlet* was not written after the death of Shakespeare's father, and he insists that Freud was really provoked to his reading of the play because he wanted to prove that the oedipus complex was universal.

From a psychiatric rather than a psychoanalytic point of view, Dr. Wertham offers as a replacement for the oedipal reading what he calls the "Orestes complex." Hamlet, Wertham notes, has to caution himself against harming his mother:

> Let not ever
> The soul of Nero enter this firm bosom.

Speaking to his uncle, he says, "Farewell, dear mother." Dr. Wertham takes this as a slip of the tongue, showing that Hamlet unconsciously hates his mother, not his uncle. Hamlet's speech, "Those that are married already, all but one, shall live," Wertham sees as applying to Gertrude. Finally, Wertham insists that Hamlet speaks hostilely throughout the play to his mother, not to his father. The real reason for Hamlet's delay, then, is that he is ambivalent toward his mother; one part of him identifies with his father and wishes to avenge him; another part of him identifies with his father as the representative of law and order and looks on revenge as wrong.

In general, Dr. Wertham finds that *Hamlet* illustrates a number of sides of his "Orestes complex." There is overattachment to the mother, which is transformed into excessive hostility by the discrepancy between the way the mother behaves in private and the way society says she should behave. The matricidal impulse needs a final trigger (which it does not get in *Hamlet,* but does in the case history of the young matricide in New York); the mother image comes between the son and a love object. The real basis for the Orestes complex, Dr. Wertham says, is the child's almost boundless hostility toward the mother when he realizes in early infancy that this all-provider can thwart as well as provide. This hostility can extend to all women and also become a hatred of his own sexuality; with it may go the feeling that death is the inevitable punishment for sexual desires. Finally, if the child is deprived of love, he may retreat into fantasy, thereby allowing infantile sexual wishes to come to the fore with a good deal of guilt. In Hamlet's case, these fantasies are the "torrent of erotic pictures which Hamlet hurls at his mother" in the closet scene: he is not only accusing spectator, but active participant.

In short, Dr. Wertham finds or thinks he finds a number of the elements of the "Orestes complex" in Hamlet. One could wish, however, that the textual evidence were stronger in details; one could also wish to see why the Orestes reading rules out the oedipus reading. A child might well resent his mother for making him hate his father. Most of those who have followed the orthodox Freud-Jones approach have found ambivalence toward the mother not at all inconsistent with oedipal wishes toward her, and, in fact, Dr. Jones in the final version of *Hamlet and Oedipus* incorporates Wertham's insight, saying, "Matricidal impulses . . . always emanate from the oedipus complex of which they are . . . an attempted solution." And Ernst Kris adds his considerable authority: the outcome of the oedipus complex must depend also on the mother-child relationship in the pre-oedipal phase. Hamlet's responses stem not only from the repressed parricidal impulses stressed in the early psychoanalytic studies (Freud, Jones, and Rank), but also from Hamlet's dangerously submissive attachment to his idealized father (see below, Jones's "The Death of Hamlet's Father") as well as "the son's unsatisfied longing for, and retaliatory impulses against, a mother who had betrayed her infant." Both of these themes are important to later psychoanalytic thinking about the oedipus complex.[37]

Dr. Henry Alden Bunker, following out the matricidal view,[38] makes the point that the acting out of the oedipus complex in a tragedy requires two things: killing the father and possessing the mother. He finds both only in *Oedipus*. In most so-called oedipus stories the mother is killed (he gives as instances the stories of Orestes, Alcmaeon, Bellerophon, Peleus, Potiphar, and Beowulf, as well as *Hamlet*): killing the mother symbolizes having her in a sexual way for which the son is likely to pay with death or the loss of his manhood. Hamlet Senior's injunction to his son, "Nor let thy soul contrive/Against thy mother aught," Dr. Bunker says, is really, then, a warning not to commit incest with her. (Except for this one symbolization, it would seem that Dr. Bunker's reading of the various stories he quotes does not allow enough room for other disguised forms of acting out the oedipus wish.)

We have already noted (in Chapter 8) two somewhat impenetrable attempts to bring *Hamlet* into line with Dr. Edmund Bergler's theories of oral masochism.[39] In general, the Wormhoudt-Bergler view represents a variant on the matricidal views of *Hamlet*. The hero is defending himself (or Shakespeare is defending himself through Hamlet) against guilt for taking pleasure in being denied by the mother; his defense is to pretend that he loves his mother and that it is really his father whom he hates. Nevertheless some of Hamlet's oral aggression still remains fixed on Gertrude and Ophelia.

Still another matricidal variant on the oedipal reading of *Hamlet* comes from Dr. Moloney and Rockelein.[40] They find at least three reasons why Hamlet's oedipal wishes should make him kill Claudius, not delay: first, Hamlet would want to show himself how he would have saved the king (he would "prevent the crime in retrospect"); second, he would want to deny to himself his own unconscious desire to kill the king; third, he would kill Claudius to prove his own innocence. The oedipal reading, they say, makes the play an unhealthy call for submission to an inevitable fate. The Moloney-Rockelein view is that Hamlet's trouble consists of being psychologically immature; he is passive and submissive, and he fears becoming an adult; he wants to remain a child. They find a good deal of evidence for this view in the text, particularly in the final scene. That is, once Gertrude is out of the way, Hamlet can no longer be a child, so he frees himself from the father by killing Claudius; he becomes the king-adult, but dies happy, escaping adulthood. Moloney and Rockelein find their reading more consistent with the matricidal view than the oedipal; Hamlet's fear of maturity and hatred of the father could come from unconscious rage against the mother.

E. E. Krapf [41] arrived at an ingenious compromise of the matricidal and parricidal views on the assumption that Shakespeare was homosexual: Hamlet delayed because he couldn't make up his mind *which* to kill, the father figure or the mother. One does not expect psychonalytic insight of a rigorous kind from Marcel Pagnol,[42] but he does agree with Krapf that Hamlet is homosexual, not *"un véritable inverti . . . only . . .* quite feminine, that he does not have the reflexes of a man."* Hamlet is "an only son, very handsome of face who loves his mother with an unhealthy love. An elegant and distinguished man who speaks to women of sexual things; an intellectual dreamer who constantly poses. . . . A man who at the age of thirty, still lives among students, and who, in order to return to these indispensable comrades, refuses to be 'our chiefest courtier' and repulses the love of the pure, but voluptuous, Ophelia. . . . Is this completely a man? No, certainly not. Hamlet is for me, without any doubt, a *philosophe d'un sexe douteux* whose role could be perfectly played by a great *comédienne."*

Although he is psychoanalytically not very explicit, Professor Ralph J. Hallman also sees Hamlet's relationship with his mother as the critical one.[43] Hamlet, he says, has lost his emotional bearings with respect to his mother, and precisely because of his feelings toward her he finds the universe itself "essentially base, pointless, and out of joint." "No one rushes headlong into action, even to avenge a father's murder, when facing a purposeless universe."

It seems to me that Professor Hallman opens up the real importance of the matricidal view. That is, Jones accepted the matricidal view if Hamlet's hostile impulses toward his mother are taken as a defensive solution of his oedipal conflict: he need not fear his father for he does not desire his mother—he hates her. But I can also see Hamlet's hostility toward his mother as stemming from a pre-oedipal oral conflict that paved the way for this solution to the later oedipal issue. Then, because his feelings toward his mother reach back to that time in early infancy when she was his universe, his disgust at her (which is reinforced as a defense against his oedipal conflict) can spread to a disgust and depression at all things. Thus, by putting this oral view of Hamlet, Sharpe's anal one, the Freud-Jones, matricidal, and Eriksonian views all together, we can get a total picture of Hamlet as a dynamically developing and adapting human being all the way from infancy to age thirty. Of course, as a purely literary critic would certainly object, that may or may not be a sensible way of looking at a literary character.

It is worth noting that most writers who hold that Hamlet was matricidal regard their view as the only correct one; most psychoanalysts, however, will accept both the oedipal and the matricidal reading, indeed, find a real interaction between them. The situation is both more dogmatic and more confused when we turn to literary critiques of the oedipal view of *Hamlet*.

f. Literary Critiques of the Freud-Jones View

Many more literary critics than psychiatrists have disagreed with the Freud-Jones view and rather more violently. I shall mention only those few, however, who have gone beyond mere invective (for others, see above, notes 8 and 9). Professor Oscar J. Campbell suggests that Hamlet is really the victim of cycles like those of a manic depressive which always give him the wrong emotion at the wrong time.[44] Professor Dupee, reviewing Jones's edition of the play, criticizes Jones for measuring Hamlet (treated as a real person) against a quite hypothetical and nonexistent, well-adjusted man; on the other hand, the scholars, he says, have made Hamlet over into that quite hypothetical and nonexistent, well-adjusted man.[45]

Professor F. L. Lucas, while willing to acknowledge that there is oedipal material in the sources to *Hamlet,* finds in the play itself another mechanism: he feels Hamlet has invested his mother with all his conscious feelings about the way things ought to be. He has made her a part of his own mind, an ego ideal, and he has seen that ego ideal shattered, and that part of himself he must now hate (this is the basis for his melancholia). In other words, Hamlet is torn between love and hate of his mother. By losing her, he has lost also his faith in other women, in humanity, in life itself.[46]

As even this small sample suggests, most literary critics who try to reason against the Freud-Jones view go about it by trying to outdo the psychoanalysts at their own game. An exception is Professor Lionel Trilling. Usually sympathetic to psychoanalytic approaches, he sharply criticizes Jones's work on strictly literary grounds.[47] Jones, he points out, treats the play, not as a play, but as a "mystery" to be "solved." Further, he seeks a solution, not in the play, but in Shakespeare. Trilling's judgment seems quite correct to me, but *contra* Trilling has come Hiag Akmakjian, who defends Jones on the grounds that he is writing, not literary criticism, but applied psychoanalysis. Surely, though, the issue is whether a play is a mystery to be solved, not what label to put on Jones's book. To separate literary criticism from psychology is to say one is "scientific," the other—what? One can see this wish for obscurantist criticism in Professor Leo Kirschbaum's curious argument: the essence of *Hamlet* is mystery, and the best psychological reading, therefore, is the one which leaves that mystery alone.[48]

Professor John E. Hankins continued the literary counterattacks into the alien territory of psychoanalysis by arguing that the Freud-Jones description of *Hamlet* is not at all a normal or usual development of the oedipus complex.[49] Rather, he suggests, Hamlet is inhibited from acting by "fear of matricide" and quite rational doubts about the ghost and the veracity of his message. Professor Robert Reed has put forward the view that external factors are enough to explain the delay (Hamlet's doubts about the ghost, the king's praying, and so on); that therefore what really needs to be explained are Hamlet's self-accusations of delay.[50] In Elizabethan terms, says Professor Reed, the self-rebuke serves as a sop to an overdeveloped conscience. In Freudian terms, and he quotes Freud, Hamlet has made his parents' strictures into an important part of himself, his strong superego. That part of his superego or conscience which his mother gave him (the conscious ego ideal, according to Reed) has collapsed in his disillusionment at her remarriage. That part his father gave him (Professor Reed says this part is unconscious) is now supposed to revenge. But Hamlet's conscious reason finds this ridiculous. Then his self-accusations must be understood as coming from his guilt at the discrepancy between the demands of his unconscious superego (or conscience) and his performance of those demands.

It is a little surprising that there should be any literary critiques of this kind, that is, attacking the Freud-Jones analysis of *Hamlet,* not from a literary but a psychological point of view. With all due respect to my literary colleagues, it seems to me they are somewhat out of their depth, psychologically speaking. Surely criticisms of a psychoanalytic diagnosis as such are the province of the expert—in psychoanalysis. For literary critics not trained in psychoanalysis there are plenty of cogent criticisms of the Freud-Jones view of *Hamlet* that can be made from the point of view of an expert in literary criticism: misreadings, misunderstandings of tone, treating a play as a puzzle, reading back to Shakespeare, treating the characters as real people, and so on. It seems to me the purely literary critic would do well to confine himself to those, if he wishes to object.

g. *Semi- or Anti-Psychoanalytic Views*

As one might expect, the sharpest disagreement with the Freud-Jones view of *Hamlet* has come from the semi- or anti-Freudian psychologies. From the rather murky and Kierkegaardian atmosphere of postwar European psychoanalysis, Dr. Annemarie Dührssen has put forth the view that *Hamlet* is essentially an existential tragedy with no particular relevance to oedipal feelings.[51] That is, in the two persons of Hamlet and Ophelia the play shows the two tragic pitfalls that confront existential man.

Ophelia has been pretty systematically betrayed by the men around her: Laertes, Polonius, the king have all encouraged her to take an attitude of worldly distrust toward Hamlet's professions of love; then Hamlet proved they were right. In short, the men around Ophelia all let her down, and the one woman she knows, Gertrude, seems helpless. Ophelia cannot stand her own nature as a woman, but she cannot face hostile feelings toward men, either, because she longs for love and tenderness (as in her mad speeches). Left only with a harsh sexuality, unable to act for or against the men around her, she goes mad, is misunderstood for the last time by Laertes, and with little else to do, dies.

Hamlet is Ophelia's opposite. He is not passive, as she is, but he is caught between being a man of thought and a man of action. His delay comes about, not so much for oedipal reasons, as because of an early-established conflict in his feelings toward his parents. His relationship to them has been long and ambivalent, but he had finally made his peace with it, when the ghost confronted him with a task calling for full maturity, clarity about his own ideals, and conscious awareness of his own impulses. These things Hamlet most notably did not have, and all his earlier ambivalence was dredged up to delay him. The contrast between the external task and his inner state of psychic and spiritual confusion is what makes Hamlet identify himself with clowns and actors. In short, then, Ophelia's tragedy is that of outer betrayal; Hamlet's, of inner betrayal. Their joint tragedy is the total disillusionment of modern man toward the values put forward by his parents.

Alfred Adler, who chose to break with Freud on the issue of the importance of superiority and inferiority in social situations, argues that *Hamlet* proves his point about the importance of social factors.[52] "There is only one case in which killing can be justified, and that is in self-defense, when our own life or the life of another person is in danger. No one has brought this problem more clearly under the purview of humanity than Shakespeare has done in *Hamlet,* although this has not been understood." In other words, Hamlet was unable to kill the king until he could do it in defense of himself and his mother. (The reading neglects the fact that Hamlet kills Claudius when both mother and son are already doomed; there is no question of defending. Claudius is killed in rage or desperation, not self-defense.)

Another Adlerian, Philippe Mairet,[53] has argued that Hamlet is essentially a spoiled child living with the mother who spoiled him. He delays because he is neurotic. We know he is neurotic because he shows the two essential characteristics of the (Adlerianly) neurotic man: a striving after perfection for his personality and actions; a total inability to lose himself in any interest outside his own immediate concern. The play appeals because all men to some extent feel this conflict between social imperfection and the desire for personal perfection, but are not aware of it, and so cannot explain why the play appeals to them.

Before going on to other nonpsychoanalytic readings of the tragedy it would be well to pause a moment over approaches to *Hamlet* through myth and ritual, for they seem to underlie certain of the psychological approaches. It was Gilbert Murray who, in 1914, first brought to general attention the similarity of *Hamlet* to the year-king myths described by Frazer and others.[54] There are two kinds of year-king myth, says Murray, those that reckon by half-years, summers and winters, and those that reckon by whole years. In the half-year myth, evil Winter comes and slays the good Summer King or vegetation god who then, come spring, rises from the dead and returns to life again. In the whole-year myth, Winter comes and slays the existing Year King, then himself waxes proud and royal (the tragic hubris of summer); then the Avenger of his predecessor comes and slays him in his turn. Murray pointed out that the Orestes and Hamlet dramas both show elements of both these year-king myths. Hamlet, although he is on the side of right against wrong like the good Summer King, nevertheless has a number of wintry aspects: he is black, joyless, furious, alone—an Avenger, "the bitter Fool who must slay the King." And Murray finds the appeal of the tragedy in its resonance with the faint stirrings of such myths deep within us (a more or less Jungian approach).

Dr. J. T. MacCurdy promptly showed how psychoanalysis would apply to Murray's description.[55] The Winter-Summer conflict simply works out in seasonal images the oedipus complex. Both Orestes and Hamlet stay in the mother's home, are antagonistic to the opposite sex, and have one close male friend. Both are psychotic; both hallucinate sexually as in dementia praecox (today one would say schizophrenia), commonly precipitated by oedipal conflicts. Both heroes are, in effect, sons who have succeeded in their oedipal impulses.

On a conscious and (I must suspect) whimsical level, Mr. William Montgomerie sees Nero as the link between the Orestes theory of Murray and the Freud-Jones oedipal theory.[56] Claudius, he says, is like the Roman emperor Claudius; Hamlet is like the matricide Nero. Further, Nero wrote a poem on Orestes and acted in it, and he wrote a poem on Oedipus and acted in it. Q.E.D.

Whimsy aside, Murray's mythic approach seems to underlie certain of the nonpsychoanalytic psychological approaches. In one study, Otto Rank, in his later anti-Freudian phase, argued that Hamlet is a man who wants to do what he must with words, that is, magically, in the fashion of myth, but he has to resort to deeds.[57] The drama represents the quasi-mythological "heroic ideology transforming itself into the poetic." In a more comprehensive (but scarcely comprehensible) analysis,[58] Rank suggests a reason for Hamlet's delay: "his revolt against his father's control over his soul and life." Rank sees the key issue in the tragedy as immortality, and he refers to the primitive belief that the son receives the soul from his father, thereby shortening the father's life. In *Hamlet* the father tries to recover his life by ingesting his son, harnessing him to the father's task. Were Hamlet to kill Claudius, he would serve his father's immortality by "undoing" the murder. Were he to repossess (as it were) his mother, he would serve her immortality by letting her be part of a later generation. To achieve his own immortality, then, Hamlet delays. His disguise of insanity and (in the sources) lack of sexual knowledge serve to liberate him from his father.

And Hamlet has immortality, in a way. He has a dual, a *Doppelgänger,* in Horatio who is "immortal" in that he lives on after Hamlet. Hamlet himself has some of the qualities of the immortal hero: he comes from the sea; he rises up out of Ophelia's grave; he must be killed by a special, poisoned sword. On a more intellectual level, Hamlet shows the root of the conflict, immortality, in his beliefs: he cannot prize earthly living alone, but he cannot believe in a life after death, either.

The Jungians lead off with Miss Maud Bodkin (surely the most sensible of Jungian critics).[59] She endorses the Freud-Jones view of *Hamlet,* but sees more. The most striking feature of the play she finds (as the psychoanalytic Rank did) to be the splitting of different attitudes into different characters, and she sees the play as related to a general psychic pattern which underlies all tragedy—"a certain organization of the tendencies of self-assertion and submission." The death of Hamlet, with its reference to the "angels" of another world, she says, represents the exultation at a sacrifice both by the victim and the audience. The story Horatio is to tell takes on the quality of a sacred text, existing both on a higher plane and in the minds of men.

Peter Dow Webster argues that Hamlet delays because he is a victim of "arrested individuation." [60] ("Individuation" means the result Jungian therapy strives for, namely, to get the patient to give over exclusive reliance on reason and embrace the whole "self" including, or perhaps even stressing, the more chthonic forces the unconscious has to offer.) As against this ideal, Hamlet ratiocinates too much; he can-

not face the revelations his unconscious has for him; he is too concentrated on his conscious mind and pays too little attention to his unconscious. Little textual evidence, however, is brought forward in
support of this view of the play.

It may be quite unfair to list Dr. Harry Slochower among the Jungians, but besides the difficulty of organizing all these critics of *Hamlet,* there is the further justification that his approach seems to be a
combination of orthodox psychoanalysis with a Jungian interest in
myth and ritual. In a review of the latest edition of Jones's *Hamlet
and Oedipus,*[61] Dr. Slochower argues that "Freudianism" should be
extended to technical and social elements of literature, particularly by
paying attention to language, which makes up the associations of the
author-dreamer. These associations, he says, will show how Hamlet
speaks the language, not of Oedipus, but of "Shakespeare's culture
epoch." Hamlet is a later Oedipus, more individual, less conscious,
less able to hide the truth from himself. The fluidity of his attitude
toward "the divinity that shapes our ends," Dr. Slochower says, leads
to a language of "interiorization moving toward externalization, the
moving platform of the scenes, etc. And it is the language through
which we get the motif of displacement, the psychic core of the play."
These considerations, he says, Dr. Jones leaves out, as indeed he
does.

Dr. Slochower's own analysis of *Hamlet* [62] deals with the play on
three levels: as a universal myth, as a Renaissance myth, and as a
description of a personal psychic burden. Prince Hamlet is, in effect,
stuck between the universal and the particular; and in this, Dr. Slochower says, he is typically modern. As for the universal mythic
themes of folklore and legend, Dr. Slochower finds six in *Hamlet.*
First, the bad brother kills the good brother. Second, there is the theme
of "madness," that is, the confusion of tongues as in the story of the
Tower of Babel or the "Dionysian" (*sic*) revels of Claudius. Third,
Oedipus rears his head. Fourth, we see the father as king and God.
Fifth, the union of the father-God with a mortal (even fleshly)
woman leads to the birth of the hero-son. The dismembered (in *Hamlet,* I suppose, disembodied) father-God reappears and urges the son
on a mythic journey. The son goes "underworld" (overseas), is initi-
ated, and returns. Sixth, the play embodies (as with Murray) a seasonal myth: it opens with winter and death and ends with the promise
of Hamlet's rebirth in the figures of Horatio and Fortinbras.

So far as the Renaissance is concerned, these myths appear, Dr.
Slochower says, in a restless, tentative way. The Renaissance he regards as a time involving the uneasy rejection of the past in the person of Hamlet Senior and the uneasy acceptance of individualism in

the person of Hamlet Junior, with a hope that everything will work out all right represented by Fortinbras. This edgy individualism leads to a concentration on the individual, his "privacy and interiorization." Dr. Slochower bears down on the fifth myth, the "mythic journey," as particularly important in the Renaissance. Such a myth has three stages: we start with the hero in a sort of Garden-of-Eden situation which then sours; the hero becomes a "dangerous child." Second, he sets out on a "journey," in the course of which he commits a "crime," which in turn he repents with "madness." Third, the hero returns, bearing with him a re-creation of tradition. The Renaissance hero—Dr. Slochower gives Don Quixote as an example— tends to get stuck in the middle, in the "madness" stage.

As for *Hamlet,* originally, before the play, the hero believed in his mother and his King-Father-God; then he comes to doubt even the ghost. The "journey" is Hamlet's trip to Wittenberg where he doubts and questions through philosophy; his return home is a return to the "Cave of Existence" where, in effect, he undergoes an initiation into the unsavory world of Claudius' Denmark. His hesitations are his madness; he "thinks"; he has "bad dreams." The resolution of the play would be the re-creation of tradition through the twin personages of Horatio and Fortinbras, who are the two poles of Hamlet, thought and action.

This, however, is the large, cultural myth of *Hamlet* within which the individual psychic burden, the individual "journey" of the hero is played out. Dr. Slochower feels that the best answer to Hamlet's individual problems is given by the Freudians. He states the Freud-Jones thesis, noting, in addition, such factors as the "playing" throughout the play and the motif of psychic substitution, the various splittings and displacements. He points out that Hamlet's opening soliloquy shows no particular regret over his father's death, only over his mother's marriage. In the reference to Hercules, Hamlet in effect identifies himself with Claudius, as later in his expounding of Lucianus he identifies with the "nephew of the king." This is part of his "crime" in a mythic sense; the rest is his delay. The ghost represents a superego, a "commander," who gives Hamlet justifiable motives for his dreams and thinking and playing. The mission the ghost gives his son is Hamlet's initiatory test for manhood—the hero doubts his manhood and fails. Hamlet's half-incestuous interview with his mother constitutes another "crime" for which he is banished.

In short, Hamlet has a personal problem, but instead he tries to do all, and, failing, doubts all. Hamlet is caught in the conflict between self and all. He is, in effect, part of what Dr. Slochower sees as the general pattern of synoecoisis throughout *Hamlet:* the use of many "un-" words and the mingling of contraries in language and action, the funeral-marriage, method and madness, acter and actor, play and reality, Fortinbras and Hamlet. The play, Dr. Slochower concludes, is a dialogue with itself, a mingling of universal myth with personal psychic burden.

Professor Herbert Weisinger in his summary of "The Myth and Ritual Approach" to Shakespeare [63] makes a few passing references to *Hamlet*. For Weisinger, the ultimate point of a tragedy must be the leap from the endless cycles of pagan seasonal myths into another order of experience, the Christian. Hamlet tries to do this, but fails; the play, therefore, tries to be a full tragedy, but is not. That is, Hamlet yearns to be acting with justice and full awareness of the ins and outs and rights and wrongs of his actions, but he never comes to this fullness of moral understanding. The fact that he never bridges his own ambivalences shows up in the various fragmented characters: Hamlet-Laertes; Hamlet-Fortinbras; Hamlet as prince; Hamlet as prospective king.

Dr. W. I. D. Scott presents something similar.[64] Psychiatrically, he diagnoses Hamlet as a manic depressive; in Jung's typology, he is "the morally orientated introverted intuitive." Dr. Scott is perhaps of more help when he suggests that a basic side of Hamlet's problem is his failure to develop a satisfactory "persona" or protective front to present to the world (a psychoanalyst would speak of "defense mechanisms"). He failed to develop such a front because he could not identify with his dominating extravert of a father ("Hyperion's curls . . . An eye like Mars"). Such an incompatibility would lead to excessive remorse after the father's death, here, Hamlet's depression. In Freudian terms, Dr. Scott sees the ghost as Hamlet's superego. In Jungian terms, he offers Polonius and Gertrude as parodies of the archetypal Wise Old Man and Great Mother. Ophelia is the anima, Claudius the dark shadow, the ghost the persona, and Horatio the helpful shadow. Like the other Jungians, Dr. Scott tends to see the characters or events of the whole play as projections of a single personality.

This sense of displacement and decomposition in the characters of *Hamlet* seen as splits of a single personality makes a neat ending to this survey of general psychoanalytic opinions on the tragedy, for there is just about as much unanimity on this point among the various commentators as on Hamlet's oedipus complex. Most of the semi- or anti-psychoanalytic readings of *Hamlet* and many of the orthodox ones stress the idea that the outer events of the tragedy simply project the inner conflicts of the hero.

Such a survey as this necessarily makes it seem as though there is more disagreement than agreement. People who disagree with the

Freud-Jones hypothesis write about their disagreement; those who agree have no need to write. And the overwhelming majority of "depth psychologists" agree. In effect, coming as it did, at the very discovery of the oedipus complex itself, the discovery of Hamlet's oedipus complex seems almost like a rock upon which Freud founded his theory. And, in fact, those who disagree flatly with Freud's reading of *Hamlet* make it pretty clear that what they are really disagreeing with is Freud's strong insistence on the universality of the oedipus complex or psychoanalytic experience in general.

All things considered, however, Freud's rock, his interpretation of *Hamlet,* has withstood a good deal of wash and wear from the various proponents of matricidal impulses, dissident literary critics, existential psychoanalysts, Adlerians, Jungians, Stekelians, and Rankians.

There is a beautiful logical simplicity to the Freud-Jones argument. People cannot tell why Hamlet delays in the task of killing the man who murdered his father and married his mother; psychoanalytic experience shows that every child wants to do the same; Hamlet delays because he cannot punish Claudius for doing what he himself unconsciously wanted to do; the fact that this oedipal wish is unconscious explains why people could not explain Hamlet's delay. Not only does the argument have an elegance of logic; it has behind it a mass of evidence both from clinical and anthropological experience and from the play as set forth by Jones, Rank, Sharpe, and Eissler, to name but a few. As we have seen, it can be expanded to a total developmental and adaptive view of Hamlet.

The only serious psychoanalytic competitor to this reading has been the notion that Hamlet is held back by matricidal impulses he cannot admit to himself. The evidence for this view (Wertham's or Bunker's, for example) is much skimpier; and, furthermore, the oedipal view of *Hamlet* incorporates the possibility of matricidal impulses. As for the existentialists, Jungians, Rankians, Stekelians, and Adlerians, their views of the play as outer-inner drama are really collateral, not contradictory, to the psychoanalytic view. As Dr. Slochower's exposition shows, they can accommodate the Freudian view or be accommodated by it. In short, it seems to me on surveying the history of the Freud-Jones hypothesis that its proponents have every right to say, "We have met the enemy, and they are ours; Hamlet has an oedipus complex."

The literary critic, however, has another round to fire at Freud's rock; although it does not go to the oedipus complex as a clinical or theoretical consideration in psychology, it does cut into its application to *Hamlet.* That is, Dr. Jones is treating Hamlet as a living person. While it may be all very well to say that people have oedipus complexes, Hamlet is not "people," but a tissue of words, and tissues of words do not have oedipus complexes. Dr. Jones has tried to answer this objection in the introduction to his *Hamlet and Oedipus,* but all he says is, it is all right to treat literary characters as living people with pasts and futures beyond the work because literary critics do. This is indeed a touching assertion of faith, but I can hardly imagine literary critics doing something simply because other literary critics do. Further, Dr. Jones is talking about nineteenth-century critics; the overwhelming weight of critical authority in the twentieth century is against treating literary characters as real people (see Chapter 10). But this question, to apply or not to apply psychoanalytic experience to literary characters, constitutes a major problem that runs all through psychoanalytic criticism. It had best wait.

At this point it suffices to state simply that there are two large points about *Hamlet* on which psychoanalytic commentators agree, although they represent inconsistent notions of what a play really is. If the play is a realistic portrayal of a man's problem, Hamlet, the psychoanalysts agree, is suffering through an oedipal crisis. If the play is dreamlike, symbolic, not a slice of life, most of the events and characters in *Hamlet* represent splits or projections of inner impulses onto the outer world of the play (but whose inner impulses? Hamlet's? Shakespeare's? or ours?).

So far we have been considering psychoanalytic comments on *Hamlet* as a whole. As for parts of *Hamlet,* a number have attracted special attention, notably: the symbolism of pouring poison in Hamlet Senior's ear, Hamlet Junior's madness, the play within the play, Ophelia's madness, the graveyard scene, Osric, and some particular speeches. We can take the larger topics in their order in the tragedy, dealing with particular speeches last.

a. Poison in the Ear

Otto Rank [65] found this episode a symbol for impregnation; the fact that Hamlet sees the sexual act as animal-like, sadistic, is part of his general infantilism. Ella Freeman Sharpe [66] sees it as the symbolic poisoning of the child-poet who heard the frightening and distasteful sounds of his parents' loving; he, then, in Miss Sharpe's anal reading of the play, let out his own "poison." Ernest Jones [67] devoted a short essay to the problem, and he concluded that the poison symbolically suggested any body fluid charged with evil intent; the ear by the mechanism of "displacement upward" stands for the anus. The ghost's description of his murder is, Dr. Jones says, a symbolic description of a sexual attack by one man on another; Claudius' description, that the king was stung by an adder in an orchard, is a further disguise of the same idea, the serpent being a phallus emitting poisonous semen. The orchard symbolizes the woman in whose arms the king was murdered, and thus Claudius' account is linked to fantasies in which the child imagines himself watching the parents in the act of love, or, in this case, the "sleep of death" afterward. More importantly, as Ernst Kris points out, Jones's analysis suggests Hamlet's "dangerously submissive attachment" to an idealized image of his father.

The differences in these three accounts probably seem somewhat greater than they are. All three agree that pouring poison in the ear symbolizes some kind of insemination. One need not choose between heterosexual or homosexual insemination for, in the unconscious, there is no negation. Rather, both apply; and the fact that the symbol is ambiguous suggests an ambiguity in the play's presentation, one that reaches to an early level of infantile confusions. Similarly, all three writers relate Hamlet Senior's account to infantile fantasies and confusions about the parents' secrets (indeed, the play itself establishes the relation by showing us the poisoning in the play within a play, itself a symbol for watching the parents' secrets). Thus, all three writers see the poisoning of King Hamlet as a childishly confused account of the sexual act.

b. Hamlet's Madness

Hamlet's madness has earned much comment from medical psychiatrists, although from psychoanalysts not so much as one would expect. Dr. J. T. MacCurdy [68] says the content of Hamlet's psychotic delusions identifies the cause and type of his madness. Hamlet is in love with death; he wishes to "die together" with his mother just as he leaps into the grave with Ophelia. These incestuous fantasies are the symptoms of dementia praecox (or schizophrenia)—not that Hamlet necessarily has it, but Shakespeare, out of his poetic instinct, Dr. Mac-Curdy says, has juxtaposed the right "symptoms" with the right "cause." By contrast, a Swedish psychiatrist has diagnosed Hamlet as a manic depressive, the trauma precipitating his illness being his mother's hasty remarriage.[69] There are, of course, many of these essentially nonpsychoanalytic psychiatric diagnoses of, not just Hamlet, but all of Shakespeare's characters, and they are not really relevant to this study.

Surely the most ingenious, though, of all these diagnoses deserves mention: that of Drs. Stern and Whiles who have diagnosed Hamlet's symptoms as a "Ganser state," that is, a particular psychotic manifestation in which the patient is insane but does not know it, and feigns insanity, giving "crooked" answers to questions.[70] Behind the Ganser state there is a motive for feigning insanity, which, of course, Hamlet has. This ingenious suggestion has provoked an answer by Dr. T. M. Davie, that: first, Hamlet is a literary character, not a real person with real diseases; second, such a diagnosis is merely a labeling which explains nothing; third, Hamlet isn't really insane anyway. And there the ingenious suggestion of the "Ganser state" rests.

Dr. K. R. Eissler is doubtless much closer to the heart of the matter when he suggests that Hamlet's madness is really a very human state, somewhere between truth and feigning. His madness, Dr. Eissler says, stands as a composite of all the thrusts toward reality and away from it that any healthy ego faces.[71]

c. The Play Within the Play

The play within the play, oddly enough, seems to have excited far more psychoanalytic interest than Hamlet's madness. As early as 1915 Otto Rank devoted a special paper to *"Das 'Schauspiel' in 'Hamlet' "* [72] showing how the play within the play fits into the Freud-Jones view of Hamlet, a sort of Freudian-within-a-Freudian study. Rank argues that Hamlet's "Mouse Trap" plays in two ways a central role in the hero's procrastination. First, Hamlet uses the play to whet his blunted purpose as a man might drink to give himself courage; in the same way, the ghost's reappearance reactivates Hamlet, and the player's speech stimulates him to unpack his heart with words. Hamlet, in other words, uses the play to make his father's death seem nearer, in order to overcome his own inhibitions by making it seem his father died "within's two hours." Second, Hamlet uses the play as a substitute for action. The play acts out his father's murder, but it also acts out what Hamlet is supposed to do. The player-king represents not only Hamlet Senior, but Claudius, and Hamlet himself appears as the murderer, "one Lucianus, *nephew to the king."* In other words, the poisoning of the player-king serves the prince as a substitute for the deed he himself must do (as, indeed, Claudius in his agitation recognizes).

The fact, pointed out by Rank, that Hamlet identifies himself with the murderer in the play within the play, introduces another element in his delay. Hamlet, Rank says, uses the play as a substitute for the deed itself; his wild exuberance after it is the exuberance he would feel had he really killed either his father or his stepfather. He is triumphing over the father's death; and he has brought his unconscious guilt for it to light. Still more proof that the play works as a substitute is Hamlet's feeling afterward that the way to his mother is now clear, and a fairly obscene way at that, if his remarks to his mother through Ophelia are any indication. His caution to himself, "Let not ever/The soul of Nero enter this firm bosom," Rank says, is a caution against killing the mother (Nero being famous as a matricide); symbolically, his words are a caution against having her sexually, too (as Nero did).

Yet, Rank goes on, this very feeling, "Now that father's out of the way, I can have mother," immediately mobilizes obstacles and inhibitions to having the mother. First, Hamlet sees the king at prayers; he says he will not kill him until he catches him in the same position as Claudius caught his father (surely, Rank points out, a parricidal wish). Second, he goes to his mother's room and kills Polonius; here, Rank says, the inhibiting force of the father shows most clearly: Hamlet can kill this father only because he cannot and will not look at him. Third, his father's ghost appears: the ghost, Rank says, had served to convince Hamlet that the father(s), Claudius and King Hamlet, were dead, but in both cases the fathers reappear. The play within the play is shown up as a mere substitute for the deed, and Hamlet now must really kill, not just "play."

Rank finds still another motif represented by the play within the play, that of peeping or spying. Hamlet strikes Polonius for the father's crucial crime, Rank says, interfering between the son and his mother (or women in general; he had also interfered with Hamlet's relations with Ophelia who seems linked to Hamlet's mother). Yet Polonius' eavesdropping is simply a projection onto a father of a child's wish to watch the parents' loving and to take his father's place in the act. (In dreams, watching a play almost universally stands for such primal scene fantasies.) At the play within the play, "child Hamlet" watches the parents embrace; he takes the father's role—in a sadistic and perverted way—by the "nephew of the king's" pouring poison in the ear (a symbol for insemination). Thus, Hamlet's play acts out the killing of the father and allows the hero to replace the father in his relations with the mother. This fantasy usually excites the child, and it excites Hamlet as we can see by his racy remarks to Ophelia.

In short, Rank finds that all the components of the oedipus complex, the desire to kill the father, to watch his relations with the mother, and to take his place in them, all come together in the play within the play. Rank goes on to apply his insight to Shakespeare (and, by implication, to the audience that identifies with Hamlet): an actor and playwright wins through drama the right to play the part of a father as, unconsciously, he feels he is not allowed to do in life; he becomes observed, grown up, important. Certainly Rank's insight seems sound, although with the *caveat* that he (like Freud, Jones, and the rest) has treated the character Hamlet at least in part as the equivalent of a real person.

Other commentators, most notably Jones and Miss Sharpe and Eissler,[73] have taken over with minor modifications Rank's basic insights: that the play serves as a substitute for the real deed, the deed "in play," as it were; that it has elements of peeping and spying; that in it pouring poison in the ear symbolizes insemination. Dr. Eissler in his treatment of the play introduces another element, the idea that a play within a play is like a dream within a dream. Two dreams in a night, Eissler says, often make up the equivalent of a single sentence. In the case of Hamlet's Mouse Trap, the dumb show constitutes a sort of introductory subordinate clause, and the rest of the play the independent clause. The dumb show's clause is, Eissler says, "Because my uncle killed my father. . . ." The main play within the play's independent clause is, "I [Lucianus, nephew to the king] will kill him the same way he killed my father." The play within the play, Eissler says, shows that Hamlet's chief worry is hostility toward the father; it disproves the view that hostility toward the mother is the chief factor in the play.

More recently, Dr. Alexander Grinstein has devoted a paper to the play within the play as a dramatic technique.[74] Like Eissler, he compares it to a dream within a dream. Dreams being wish fulfillments, Grinstein says, a dream that one is dreaming represents (1) a wish that the subject of the dream had never happened, was "only a dream," and therefore (2) an oblique statement that it did in fact happen, "the strongest affirmation of it." Thus, in *Hamlet,* the play within the play represents the historical reality of the killing of King Hamlet as told by the ghost. Also, Grinstein points out, it must represent the wish that this never took place, the wish that King Hamlet had not been murdered, but also Hamlet's wish that his oedipal desires had not been acted out, that he did not have to suffer through guilt. The same rule holds, Dr. Grinstein says, for Claudius: he wishes (after the Mouse Trap) that he had not killed Hamlet Senior. Grinstein discusses the question much vexed by conventional critics. Why does Claudius not react to the dumb show? and answers, he doesn't because the identity of the murderer is not shown in the dumb show (he is described merely as "a fellow" or "the poisoner"). In the actual play within the play the murderer is identified as a "nephew to the king" so that the actual play foreshadows Hamlet's revenge on Claudius. With respect to Hamlet, the play presages the reality of the ending; at the same time, it expresses his wish that he did not have to kill his uncle. In the business about the dumb show Grinstein seems to me to have executed some fairly fancy footwork; his basic point, though, that the play within the play deals with a wish that something had not happened seems eminently sound and suggests the foreshadowing function of the episode. It would seem to fit in, too, with Rank's point that the play within the play is a "play" for the real deed required.

d. Ophelia's Madness

Ophelia, like Hamlet, has come in for her share of diagnoses, but in her case, the doctors agree. Dr. Ira S. Wile [75] notes that her obscene language is not unknown in the wards of mental hospitals—she is a victim of mania: thoughts she formerly repressed now find expression. "When conscious inhibition is lowered, love is remembered at the sexual rather than the spiritual level." To the same effect, Elizabeth Foulds also declares Ophelia manic,[76] and, on the assumption that Polonius is senile and Laertes unbalanced, suggests the possibility that her condition is hereditary. From a psychoanalytic point of view, she says, the cause of Ophelia's psychosis would be unconscious relief at the death of Polonius, her repressive father who caused her estrangement from Hamlet and blocked her marriage. Once he is dead, she feels relief and elation, shown in her manic behavior. Still more recently, Jean B. Jofen [77] (again) finds Ophelia manic depressive, as one would expect in a previously extravert or social personality.

It is interesting to contrast these psychiatric diagnoses with Professor Carroll Camden's very convincing diagnosis in terms of Elizabethan psychology.[78] Working from Elizabethan texts, he argues that Shakespeare's audience would have seen Ophelia as suffering from erotomania or *passio hysterica* brought on by lovesickness. Her case would be analogous to that of the jailer's daughter in *Two Noble Kinsmen*. Whatever the limitations of Renaissance psychiatry, such a reading at least has some relevance to an audience's response to the play—unlike these modern diagnoses of Hamlet's and Ophelia's psychoses, which would be relevant only to an audience composed entirely of psychiatrists.

e. The Graveyard Scene

Among the other aspects of *Hamlet* that have come in for particular attention, the graveyard scene has elicited a highly symbolic analysis from Dr. Norman Symons.[79] Within the general framework of the Freud-Jones view, the dialogue between the clowns and the tossing about of ball-shaped skulls are really an attack on the father as one who, Symons says, "lays down the law" as the lawyer with his quiddities, then, as Yorick, goes to the lady's chamber. The metempsychosis speeches run together king and father and worms and stink and skulls; the round skulls suggest the sources of the father's power, both mental and sexual. The riddle as to who builds stronger really means as between the father and the mother, who is stronger? The less bright clown suggests that the gallows maker builds stronger. (Hanging, cutting off a life, is a well-known symbol for castration, so Symons identifies the gallows maker as the father who threatens the son's virility.) The brighter clown says the gravemaker builds stronger (who Symons identifies, in accord with Freud's "Three Caskets" essay, as "mother earth," the ultimate mother). Their equivocation about "lying" in the grave is really a covert discussion about "lying" in that ultimate mother.

Symons argues that Laertes, because he identifies himself with Polonius' revenge (as Hamlet is supposed to do for *his* father), becomes identified with Polonius (as Hamlet would be with King Hamlet). When Hamlet and Laertes fight in Ophelia's grave, this symbolizes a struggle (involving fingers) against the father for the mother (literally, *in* "mother earth"). Hamlet's madness and his pouring forth of speech, Symons says, signifies the emission of "golden couplets," eggs, symbolizing an insemination. Hamlet is sent to England, Shakespeare's "mother country," to be cured. Symons' insights are quite ingenious and should probably be considered as close verbal analysis of the kind we have seen practiced by Sharpe and Fliess; like all such analyses, however, they sound very silly (even if sound) unless they are brought into rather close relation to a general picture of the play from a less primitive level.

f. Osric

Anton Ehrenzweig in a mere sentence in his *gestalt* study of artistic vision and hearing [80] makes a point that deserves more than a sentence. He suggests that "comic relief" in Shakespeare's plays is really a much more elaborate disguise of the very deeply concealed content —a comic treatment of unconscious material being, in his view more of a disguise than a tragic treatment. He suggests that in *Hamlet,* Osric is an "angel of death," a projection of Hamlet's suicidal wishes. He is following in this respect Dr. Richard Flatter's *Hamlet's Father,* which argues that Hamlet, in going to his duel with Laertes, knows he is going to his fate. The evidence is his remark: "The point enven-om'd *too!*" (Italics Ehrenzweig's and Flatter's.) Hamlet, Flatter says, seems to have expected that the points would be unbaited; only the extra, the poison, seems to surprise him. (But he learned the point was not blunted when his arm was scratched!)

g. *Particular Speeches*

In view of the amount of attention *Hamlet* has excited in psycho-analytic circles, it is somewhat surprising that more attention has not been paid to particular speeches, but this lack is unfortunately part of the general tendency among psychoanalytic critics to shy away from poetic details in favor of characters and events. An exception is Dr. Robert Fliess,[81] who has produced what surely must be the capstone on all the long comments on whether Hamlet says, "Oh, that this too too solid [or 'sullied' or 'sallied'] flesh would melt . . ." The solid or sallied (which he says means "sallying") flesh, Dr. Fliess interprets as a swelling and pushing up of flesh, an erection; he sees the thought of suicide (self-slaughter) as a symbol for attacking that swollen flesh, for "self-abuse" or onanism; and the melting of the flesh he takes to be the subsequent flow and relaxation. (Like most analyses of imagery as unconscious symbols, the conclusions are rather startling—but that, of course, does not prove them wrong.)

Professor Simon Lesser notes that in Hamlet's language haste tends to be linked to thoughts of sexual gratification [82] in such re-marks as this to the ghost:

> Haste me to know't, that I, with wings as swift
> As meditation or the thoughts of love,
> May sweep to my revenge,

or his comments to himself or Horatio about his mother's hasty mar-riage. In both these contexts it is death that links swiftness to sexual gratification.

Fliess comments that Hamlet's writing the ghost's injunction down in his tables is, first, a substitute for the real act, a displacement; it is also a way of rendering inanimate the voice of his father, replacing the ghost by a lifeless tablet. It is, in short, a way of killing his fa-ther.[83]

Dr. Tannenbaum, in his quest for "Freudian slips," notes Hamlet's misrecall of the Pyrrhus speech:

> Let me see, let me see:
> 'The rugged Pyrrhus, like th'Hyrcanian beast—'

'Tis not so; it begins with Pyrrhus:
'The rugged Pyrrhus, he whose sable arms ...

and so on. Dr. Tannenbaum suggests that Hamlet identifies himself with Pyrrhus (note the "sable arms") and by his misrecall he unconsciously calls himself a Hyrcanian tiger, because he does not really want to do such a barbarous act as the revenge his father has demanded.[84]

Dr. Ira S. Wile sees the "to be" soliloquy as revealing the state of Hamlet's ego. It is full of fear of present events and it seems to wish death and annihilation at the hands of a superego; yet, at the same time, Hamlet's ego fears death lest there be, not annihilation, but punishment.[85]

Theodore Reik, examining his own free associations to a dream, concludes that Hamlet's statement that his father died "within's two hours" really means that *"I feel as though* it had happened just two hours ago."[86] Dr. Fliess compares the dialogue between Hamlet and Ophelia before the play within the play, particularly their puns on "nothing" and "naught" to the convention in classical sculpture of showing uncomplicated "nothings" "between maids' legs," showing women, in psychoanalytic terms, as unmutilated.[87]

L. A. G. Strong notes the player-king's couplet:

Faith, I must leave thee, love, and shortly too;
My operant powers their functions leave to do.

He is saying he will shortly die, and Strong says this means that Hamlet Senior would shortly have died, but Claudius could not wait. His haste is the opposite of Hamlet's delay.[88]

Very early in the development of psychoanalysis, R. S. Miller noted the "protest too much" element in the play within the play. He quotes the player-queen's speech:

Nor earth to me give food, nor heaven light,
Sport and repose lock from me day and night,
To desperation turn my trust and hope,
An anchor's cheer in prison be my scope,
Each opposite that blanks the face of joy
Meet what I would have well, and it destroy,
Both here and hence pursue me lasting strife,
If, once a widow, ever I be wife!

"In her determination that no one shall know her true feelings in the matter of second marriages, she oversteps herself; and her vehement denunciation only serves to show in what directions her thoughts lie."[89]

Dr. Karl Menninger also spotted the player-queen's elaborate statements that others might marry, but not she. Writing much later in the development of psychoanalysis, however, he identifies her remarks as a specific defense mechanism, projection, which he defines as putting off onto some other person our own vices.[90] Then the real queen's realistic, "The lady doth protest too much, methinks," unmasks the player-queen's projection.

It is perhaps fitting that we close this long summary with an insight from purely literary scholarship. Professor Harry Morris [91] argues that in Ophelia's scrap of song, "For bonny sweet Robin is all my joy," "Robin" is an Elizabethan cant term for a penis, thus showing that what causes Ophelia's madness is "sexual frustration." The psychoanalysts are not alone.

To do more than merely sketch out the interrelations of these ninety or so readings would take a book in itself. The point in connection with *Hamlet* is that this is a play which has been heavily discussed and analyzed in terms of the dynamic unconscious, in terms of myth and ritual, in terms of the Renaissance background, in terms of new criticism—in short, it has been studied by psychoanalytic critics and nonpsychoanalytic critics from almost every conceivable angle. While purely literary studies have worked out a fairly coherent and consistent view of the play's intellectual content, the psychoanalytic studies have not by any means worked out into consistency the play's unconscious content.

Psychoanalytic critics have given *Hamlet* a wide, even wild, variety of readings. The basic insight was Freud's: Hamlet cannot punish Claudius for doing what Hamlet himself wishes oedipally to do. Jones added the idea of repression: the full force of Hamlet's repression of his desire for his mother now holds down the wish to kill the father's surrogate, Claudius. Rank added a wide variety of incest motifs, notably those connected with Polonius. Ella Freeman Sharpe pointed to the strongly "dirty" or anal tone of the play and the themes of procrastination and banishment. Dr. Eissler stressed the relatively large amount of splitting and Hamlet's distrust of emotionality. Erikson sees Hamlet's delaying and "playing" as solutions to a psychosocial conflict.

Still other writers emphasized the interest in matricide. Then, the psychoanalytic critics have noticed the pouring of poison in the ear as a symbol of insemination; Hamlet's madness as thrusts first toward the world, then away from it; the play within the play as symbolizing infantile peering and eavesdropping on the parents' secret life; the Mouse Trap as a substitute for the real deed. The graveyard scene has been analyzed as a disguised attack on the father, and particular speeches have been considered for their content in terms of infantile fantasies.

This is indeed an embarrassment of riches. Trying to put all these readings together is rather like trying to make a single white sheet out of ninety irregularly shaped and colored patches. The readings are not particularly contradictory, but they are incomplete; they deal with a corner of the play here and a side there, and their sum is somewhat ragged. For another thing, these various readings have somewhat the quality of a cubist nightmare: they all look at the play from different points of view. One writer will treat Hamlet and all the characters as living persons. Another will say Hamlet is living, but the others are projections or aspects of his personality. A third will consider all the characters projections of Shakespeare's personality. Some writers deal with a part of the play; others try to gulp it all down. And some writers, the most perplexing of all, will content themselves with finding a congruity between psychiatric diagnosis and the play, then dropping it.

Curiously, although *Hamlet* came in on the ground floor of psychoanalysis, psychoanalytic criticism of *Hamlet* has not kept up with subsequent developments in psychoanalysis as a science. That is, the original Freud-Jones insight, Rank's other incest motifs, and the matricidal view represent the earliest concerns of psychoanalysis: the repressed drives from the dynamic unconscious. Most of the readings of particular speeches and particular episodes (spying, poison in the ear, the play within the play) show the influence of the understanding of symbolism gained from 1910 onward. With the exception of Miss Sharpe and Dr. Eissler, however, there is very little psychoanalytic criticism of *Hamlet* that reflects psychoanalysis' more recent concern (from the late twenties on) with defenses as ego adaptations to inner and outer reality.

Curiously, the nonpsychoanalytic critics give us a lead in this direction. Despite their differing preoccupations, a single thread ran through their readings: in *Hamlet,* inner impulses are given outer expression. In psychoanalytic terms, the defensive maneuver that permeates the language, events, and characters of the play is *projection.* We have an intense sense of Hamlet's inner life behind the soliloquies, but the soliloquies themselves are intellectual and dilatory. The key feelings inside Hamlet we do not see directly—instead, they take place as external events. It was clear from Freud's first formulation that Hamlet's oedipal impulses are acted out, not by him, but by Claudius. Rank showed how various attitudes toward the father are projected onto the several father figures; Eissler and others, how

Hamlet's ambivalences show in the character splittings. The play within the play not only expresses, it substitutes for, Hamlet's revenge. This tendency to turn inner life into outward shows underlies Hamlet's fondness for comparisons:

> My father's brother, but no more like my father
> Than I to Hercules.

> What's Hecuba to him, or he to Hecuba,
> That he should weep for her? What would he do
> Had he the motive and the cue for passion
> That I have?

> Look here upon this picture, and on this,
> The counterfeit presentment of two brothers.

> Examples gross as earth exhort me.
> Witness this army of such mass and charge . . .

> . . . by the image of my cause I see
> The portraiture of his.

Hamlet either uses outer events to express inner ones, or he compares inner attitudes by means of "counterfeit" outer representations of them.

The anal tone of the play, noted by Miss Sharpe, has this same projective quality. Hamlet occasionally speaks of himself as dirty,

> O that this too too sullied flesh would melt,

but soon shifts to the "world" which is "an unweeded garden," "a foul and pestilential congregation of vapors," to "the drossy age" or to all men (rather than Hamlet's attitude toward men), as "this quintessence of dust." Thus, *Hamlet* is like *Oedipus* in more than one way. Both are questioning tragedies. Both heroes are experts at intellectual problems, but both, confronted by riddles the answers to which lie in themselves, try to solve their puzzles by sleuthing into external reality instead.

Such projection or externalization is clearest in the case of Hamlet himself, but the other characters do it, too. Claudius' conscience is externalized in the figure of Hamlet, as is Gertrude's; and it is Hamlet, in the closet scene, who gives expression to her inner sensual drives. We learn of Hamlet and Ophelia's love, not from them, but from Laertes and Polonius who seek to inhibit it. Polonius directs everyone else, but cannot control his own speech. And even Denmark, in the opening scenes, defends, not against the real danger, the ghost within, but Fortinbras' threat of invasion from without. It is this constant externalization that gives the play its special tone,

> Of carnal, bloody, and unnatural acts,
> Of accidental judgments, casual slaughters,
> Of deaths put on by cunning and forced cause,
> And, in this upshot, purposes mistook
> Fall'n on th'inventors' heads.

Dynamically, the play can come to its end only when Hamlet has surrendered himself to those external (perhaps fatherlike) forces, which are nevertheless within himself as well. In action, when the queen has been killed and Hamlet himself is dying, he can do his father's bidding. Earlier, he had surrendered within. "We defy augury. There is special providence in the fall of a sparrow. If it be now, 'tis not to come; if it be not to come, it will be now; if it be not now, yet it will come. The readiness is all."

In some such way modern ego psychology would see *Hamlet* as the interaction of oedipal and other infantile sexual impulses (spying, for example) balanced by defenses, chiefly projection, but also splitting, intellectualization, and regression. But whose oedipus impulse? Whose projection? These are questions that haunt psychoanalytic literary studies from the earliest to the most recent.

Shakespeare's. That is one answer which is perfectly and obviously true. Both the impulse and the defense had to be available to Shakespeare for him to write the tragedy. But modern literary criticism would call that answer irrelevant, an "intentional fallacy." There is some truth in saying that the impulse and the defense are Hamlet's, a truth limited, though, by our recognition that the other characters act out his defenses for him: Hamlet is not a real person in a real world, but a character in the contrived reality of a work of art.

We are left with one more possible answer to the basic questions, Whose impulse? Whose defense? Ours. We in the audience once went through an oedipal crisis, and we now find in Hamlet's echoes of our own. In effect, we are projecting our own inner feelings about parents into the play and then "finding" them there, as indeed Hamlet himself does. Perhaps then, as Freud suggested at the outset, this is the secret of the universal appeal of the tragedy: it deals with a universal cluster of impulses, the oedipus complex. But we can add something to Freud from modern ego psychology. The play deals with the universal oedipus complex, but then the play—itself so much concerned with "play"—provides us out of its very own being with a defense or adaptation: we in the audience "play" that the impulses are not those inside us but those we find in the external reality of the play before us.

We do indeed bear Hamlet to the stage, and there, the play's the thing that catches the conscience of us all.

HENRY IV, PARTS I AND II (AND FALSTAFF)

It is a long step down from the nearly one hundred commentaries on *Hamlet* to those on lesser Shakespearean drama. In the *Henry IV* plays, only three topics seem to have engaged psychoanalytic attention: the theme of father and son, mythic or ritual elements, and the character of Falstaff. Two analysts, contemporaneously (1948) but apparently unaware of each other's work, pointed out the father split in *I Henry IV*. Theodore Reik [1] noted simply that because Hal reacts both to King Henry IV and Falstaff as fathers, they represent two aspects of one figure: "They are personifications of emotional potentialities of each other." Reik points to the episode (in II.iv) where Falstaff plays the part of the king; then there is the turnabout when Hal becomes his own father "judging himself and Sir John: a forecast of his own future."

Ernst Kris studies "Prince Hal's Conflict" [2] much more elaborately. Kris begins by pointing out some supposed inconsistencies in Hal's character as he develops from *I Henry IV* to *Henry V*: Hal tells us right at the start he is only biding his time in riot; he returns, however, to the tavern after Shrewsbury in *Part II*; finally, in *Henry V*, he treats his former companions with harsh severity. Kris points out more patterns of fathers and sons in the play: Henry IV's speech wishing that Hotspur were his son, gives him (psychologically) two sons; Hal's turnabout horseplay with Falstaff gives him (psychologically) two fathers; finally, Hotspur has (psychologically) two fathers, the craven Northumberland and the crafty Worcester.

Hotspur's rebellion, then, should be understood as the acting out of resentful impulses toward a father. Hal's harshness to Falstaff when he becomes Henry V is the same, and Hal's speech in *II Henry IV* as he puts on the crown is an attempt to reassure himself (as he tries to do the night before Agincourt) that "since I refrained from regicide and parricide, I am a rightful king." Hal resents his father's regicide (which is, psychologically, parricide); he feels he must remove the taint of it from himself. As a result, Kris says, he develops a strong conscience (or superego) of his own because he cannot trust his father's. Nevertheless, in his roistering, his repressed instinctual drives break through this conscience. Secondarily, since Hal cannot approve of his father, he turns to a substitute, but picks a shoddy old man, whom he rejects when his real father dies, avenging himself not on his father, but on this substitute for his father. Kris's view and Reik's fit together quite neatly.

Myth-and-ritual approaches to the *Henry IV* plays occupy a kind of middle ground between seeing the plays as a total configuration of fathers and sons and considering only the character of Falstaff. In these myth-and-ritual studies, while they are not in a strict sense psychoanalytic, Falstaff nevertheless retains many of his fatherly attributes. For example, J. I. M. Stewart, in his study of Shakespeare as embodying the psychological truths of folklore,[3] considers Falstaff a kind of Fisher King. Although he is willing to accept J. Dover Wilson's view that Falstaff is a descendant of Riot in *The Enterlude of Youth,* Stewart points to a number of folkloric qualities that such an academic source would not provide. Falstaff is "killed" by Henry V's indifference; he dies of the traditional broken heart. He dies, moreover, with the tide, as people do in folklore and Dickens. He is compared to the Manningtree ox and the salted Martlemas beef, slain in the autumn; in fact, he is throughout compared to food. But festivals such as killing an ox on Martlemas, Stewart insists, really commemorate a whole mythology of seasonal cycles and of sacrifices offered to secure a new fertility in the earth. And that, Stewart says, is what Falstaff is. He substitutes for Henry IV in an England "gone waste and barren under the rule of an old, impotent, and guilty king, who must be ritually slain and supplanted by his son or another before the saving rains can come bringing purification and regeneration to the land." Hal's father is this guilty king, guilty of the regicide-parricide against King Richard; Falstaff is his surrogate, who is sacrificed and with him "all the accumulated sin of the reign, all the consequent sterility of the land," to pave the way for the hero-king, Henry V.

The late Philip Williams amplified Stewart's suggestion.[4] To the ritual elements associated with Falstaff, he added Hal's not becoming the hero-king until after he has sacrificed Falstaff; Falstaff's calling Hal "my Jove," and playing a Saturn to that Jove. Williams notes, too, that critics, in speaking of Falstaff, tend to use the metaphor of a king. In connecting Falstaff to Henry IV, Williams adds that both are mistaken for dead by Hal; both are robbed by Hal when asleep; and both die in folkloric terms, Henry IV in his prophesied "Jerusalem," Falstaff with the tide and in Arthur's bosom. Williams notes that Hal has parricidal wishes: people have "said I heark'ned for your death," he tells his father. And Williams points to the thoroughly ambiguous tone of Hal's speech to his father on his having prematurely walked off with the crown. These parricidal impulses, Williams says, explain Hal's ambivalence to Falstaff and his willingness to sacrifice him.

Stewart and Williams, by treating Falstaff as a scapegoat, leave him still close to the psychological role that Kris and Reik found him playing: the father. In a subtle, excellent study [5] Professor C. L. Barber takes Falstaff a step further from his father role and a step closer to the folklore of Shakespeare's England. Barber treats Falstaff as an imaginative reworking of a special kind of scapegoat, a Lord of Misrule presiding over a Shrovetide Carnival along the lines of the Roman Saturnalia: an acknowledged and accepted period of license at the end of which the Carnival ruler must be tried, banished, killed, or run out of town.

Such a reading marks a transition point between psychoanalytic or psychological criticism and the myth-and-ritual approach to Shakespeare currently thriving in orthodox Shakespearean criticism under the influence of Professor Northrop Frye. I have myself suggested [6] that such myth-and-ritual approaches would benefit from a psychological (scientific, if you will) underpinning. In particular, in considering the *Henry IV* plays as versions of a Saturnalia, we would do well to remember Freud's remarks on such festivals in *Group Psychology and the Analysis of the Ego* (1921): holidays like the Saturnalia derive from a temporary, therapeutic abrogation of the incorporated parental demands on the ego; they are a lawful release from the superego (*SE*, XVIII, 131). And surely *Henry IV* deals with precisely those demands of the king-father on the prince-son. Then, rather than parallel *Henry IV* and the Saturnalia, would it not be more meaningful to relate *both* the comedy *and* the festival to a common psychological source: the wish lawfully to escape lawful demands on the ego? Such a third and prior source would bind the festival pattern of the play to the real-father-play-father psychological structure, instead of leaving those two approaches somewhat separate and discontinuous.

It is not difficult, then, to find a continuity between approaches to the *Henry IV* plays as a total psychological configuration and as folkloric ritual. It is rather more difficult to see a continuity between those readings and psychoanalytic examinations of Falstaff's character or our response to him. In fact, these studies of Falstaff seem at first not even consistent among themselves: he is not only a father, but also a child and even a mother.

For example, in "A Note on Falstaff," [7] Dr. Franz Alexander posed himself the same question Freud did: Why do people like the old reprobate? Alexander suggests that in the *Henry IV* and *Henry V* plays Shakespeare has shown in Hal's growth the development of a human male. In overcoming Hotspur, Alexander says, Hal overcomes the objectified form of his own resentful feelings toward his father, the king. In overcoming Falstaff, Hal shows us the growing child overcoming his interest in early forms of instinctual life: eating and drinking for their own oral sakes; passive, narcissistic self-adoration; irresponsibility—and all these, he says, are characteristic of Falstaff. Nevertheless, we still sympathize with Falstaff. Indeed, Shakespeare revives him three times (Alexander points to Falstaff's death and rebirth on the field at Shrewsbury, to his reappearance in *II Henry IV* and in *Merry Wives*). We like Falstaff, Alexander concludes, because he represents the child that remains forever in us and whom we prize, the "narcissistic nucleus of human individuality." This child in us we must retain in our adult selves if we are not to be totally regimented, like termites. We forgive Falstaff, Alexander concludes, because we forgive our own childishness and because he is much more attractive than the destructive, angry, and childish Hotspur in *Part I* or the cold Prince John in *Part II*. Yet, of course, in the end, we must banish him.

Theodore Reik finds Falstaff's gluttony hypochondriacal: "The fear of death . . . drives him to stuff himself with food." [8] Reik goes on to suggest that Falstaff's love for the young prince is motherly and thus, unconsciously, homosexual. Diego Reinoso finds a somewhat different mother—Falstaff's mother.[9] Falstaff eats, he says, to put a protective shield between himself and the world. At a deeper level, Falstaff's obesity represents the fat knight's reaction to "the bad mother imago." He internalizes her, that is, eats her up to get her inside where she won't bother him and where she will wrap around him and protect him; nevertheless, of course, she—or his fat—keeps him subjugated. He thus idealizes, makes a grand gesture out of, this mother-fat at the same time that he denies its external existence. Falstaff's frequent worries about losing his fat are fears that the bad object will appear again in external reality.

Reinoso's reading finds confirmation from an unexpected quarter, the poet, W. H. Auden.[10] Auden sees Falstaff as a presocial being, a man who has not yet developed a superego. He is thus both infantile and yet, having no restraints on him, Godlike. "A fat man," Auden points out, looks like "a cross between a very young child and a pregnant mother," and on the basis of his "own weight and experience," he suggests that fatness in men expresses physically a psychological wish to withdraw from sexual competition. The fat man, by bringing together in his own body both mother and child, makes himself completely self-sufficient emotionally.

Fanciful as these various readings of Falstaff's character may appear, they are not contradictory. To the conscious mind, Falstaff cannot be father and mother and child; to the nonlogical unconscious mind (where there is no negation), nothing could be simpler. Falstaff is a father in that he substitutes for Henry IV; he gratifies those wishes of Hal's that cannot be gratified by his stuffy, businesslike real father. Falstaff is a child, too, in his irresponsibility, in that he serves as the projection of those wishes of Hal's which are inconsistent with the ego ideal of the hero-king, Henry V. And he is also a generalized parent (both father and mother) who gratifies those same childish wishes of Hal's that he himself embodies.

Even so, at first glance, these analyses of Falstaff's character would seem to have little to do with the fathers-and-sons reading of the *Henry IV* plays or the myth-and-ritual one. Once we recognize, however, that the essential thing about Falstaff is his all-encompassing quality, he fits quite naturally into (and out of) the two other psychoanalytic readings. That is, being both parent and child, he is the childish king, the Lord of Misrule, who is a lawful unlawfulness, a morally approved immorality, a Vice who is a Virtue—until he must be put aside when the Saturnalia ends and the prince grows up. In the fathers-and-sons reading, all the other characters are split: Hal and Hotspur, Prince John and Prince Hal, Worcester and Northumberland, Henry IV and Richard II, Shallow and Silence. Only Falstaff is whole, combining in himself attributes that are split in others: responsibility—irresponsibility, strength—weakness, rebellion—loyalty, candor—duplicity, and so on. No wonder he bulks large in these plays: his huge self embracing opposites must balance all the others who are merely halves. No wonder, too, he seems both a part of the play (one "father") and at the same time a character that we habitually lift out of and beyond the play as sufficient unto himself.

Hal's education is to become this "whole man," both the father and the son. So long as he jokes and fools, he is Falstaff's playful "son," but when he becomes the hero-king, he proves a stern father to Falstaff, and, through Falstaff, to his own childish impulses. As the hero-king Henry V, he takes on Falstaff's ability to combine opposites; he brings together high and low, French and English, Scots, Welsh, and Irish,

> As many fresh streams meet in one salt sea,
> As many lines close in the dial's centre;

and it is curious that one can say the same of the psychoanalytic readings themselves. They, too, start from different points but move to a single conclusion.

HENRY V

Aside from incidental remarks in the course of discussing the *Henry IV* plays, *Henry V* has elicited from psychoanalysts only commentary on two particular speeches. We have already seen one (p. 124), Dr. Robert Fliess' analysis of I.i.47–50.[1] In one of his studies of orality,[2] Dr. Bertram D. Lewin refers to Exeter's speech to the King of France, urging him to avoid war,

> to take mercy
> On the poor souls for whom this hungry war
> Opens his vasty jaws.

He sees this phrasing as related to dreams of being devoured which are in turn related to fantasies about falling asleep.

HENRY VI, PARTS I, II AND III

The *Henry VI* plays have received no more attention than one would expect. Otto Rank noted in *III Henry VI* the contrast between the two brothers Edward and Richard on hearing of their father's death:

> *Edward.* O, speak no more, for I have heard too much.
> *Richard.* Say how he died, for I will hear it all.
> (II.i.48–49)

He suggests that the contrast in this early play is like that much later contrast between loving son and hating son in *King Lear*. Rank also pointed to the scene (II.v) in *III Henry VI* which shows a son who has just killed his father and a father who has just killed his son. Not without reason, it seems to me, Rank suggests that we have here an incest motif.[1] Theodore Reik notes that at V.v.61 Queen Margaret denounces her son's killers as "butchers" and "cannibals." Reik notes that we often use the idea of eating someone else as a metaphor for killing him (e.g., *Qui mange du Pape en meurt*),[2] an idea that accords with Dr. Robert Fliess' remarks on the near-execution of Posthumus in *Cymbeline*.

HENRY VIII

Only one psychoanalytically-inclined writer has touched on this play—Dr. Tannenbaum has come up with two Freudian slips.[1] Three gentlemen are talking about the coronation of Anne:

3 Gent.   So she parted,
    And with the same full state paced back again
    To York Place, where the feast is held.
1 Gent.   Sir,
    You must no more call it York Place. That's past.

For since the Cardinal fell that title's lost.
'Tis now the King's, and call'd Whitehall.
3 Gent.   I know it,
But 'tis so lately altered that the old name
Is fresh about me.

Dr. Tannenbaum suggests that Shakespeare was recalling the fallen Wolsey to his audience's mind to contrast to the joy with which the people witnessed the crowning of their new queen.

The second slip occurs later in the play when an old lady comes to announce to the king the birth of an heir:

King.   Now, by thy looks
I guess thy message. Is the Queen delivered?
Say, ay, and of a boy.
Old Lady.   Ay, ay, my liege;
And of a lovely boy. The God of heaven
Both now and ever bless her! 'Tis a girl,
Promises boys hereafter.

The old lady, Dr. Tannenbaum argues, wanted to be able to tell Henry it was a boy—she slips and fulfills her wish, says "boy," but then saying "bless *her*" brings her to a realization of her error, and she tries to make amends by saying a girl holds the promise of "boys hereafter."

JULIUS CAESAR

Julius Caesar has appealed to psychoanalytic critics largely as a foil for *Hamlet*. Otto Rank,[1] for example, considers this play, like *Hamlet,* a drama of murderous impulses toward a fatherlike man, but in *Julius Caesar* these oedipal or parricidal impulses can be acted out—for two reasons. First, there is no mother present to mobilize the hero's inhibitions. Second, the killing is ostensibly purely political. Shakespeare, Rank notes, eliminated from his tragedy, and departed from his source to do so, any reference to the gossip that Caesar was Brutus' father. In *Hamlet,* the father figure is split or decomposed into several "fathers." In *Julius Caesar,* however, the father-king (Caesar) stands alone, and the "sons" are decomposed. Brutus, he says, is "all of a son," that is, he combines the two attitudes of love and hatred of the father. Cassius embodies one aspect of Brutus, the self-punishing side: Rank notes that Cassius is always talking about suicide, and he dies on his own birthday. Antony embodies the filial piety of Brutus; as Brutus says, rather naïvely,

> Our reasons are so full of good regard
> That were you, Antony, the son of Caesar,
> You should be satisfied.
>   (III.i.224–226)

Rank considers that Shakespeare generally uses ghosts to symbolize the immortality, the persistence, of the son's infantile feelings toward the father, and in *Julius Caesar,* he notes, the ghost appears only to Brutus, the "total" son. The defeat of the conspirators, Rank says, really comes from their own remorse.

Ernest Jones [2] also sees *Julius Caesar* as related to *Hamlet,* and he repeats Rank's observations, adding one suggestion of his own. As other writers have noted in the case of *Coriolanus,* cities commonly symbolize or are symbolized by mothers. Thus, Jones sees Brutus' loving "Rome more" as a reference to a mother figure, and so supplies the missing mother figure for an oedipal reading of *Julius Caesar.*

Dr. Harold Feldman [3] has analyzed the character of Brutus, arguing that Shakespeare's development of Brutus' character makes sense of the actual events of history. Brutus, he says, is motivated by unconscious envy of Caesar; he therefore uses reasons to cover over his passionate resentment. He makes himself seem cold and abstract, prematurely sexless. The basis for his envy is self-love, Dr. Feldman says; hence the frequent references to "love" in the play. Feldman agrees with Rank that Brutus fails in the end because he unconsciously wishes to punish himself for having killed Caesar.

Professor Gordon R. Smith [4] has also analyzed Brutus' character, taking the view that Brutus is motivated, not so much by "virtue" as by a wish for "egotistic satisfaction of his will," or, in more technical terms, Brutus is the victim of a tyrannical superego. Idealistic and also rather conscious of his own moral superiority, he quite erroneously thinks he is best fitted to direct affairs, but he makes mistakes when he tries to evaluate external realities. He rationalizes these mistakes rather than deny his superego, his "principles," which really cause his errors by distorting his perceptions.

Dr. Tannenbaum has analyzed from the point of view of *The Psychopathology of Everyday Life* (1901) Brutus' soliloquy in which he gives his reasons for killing Caesar.[5] Brutus opens his speech with "It must be by his death." He has already decided, and the reasons that follow are so "puerile" they betray the fact they are rationalizations, only masking an unconscious wish for Caesar's death.

Two writers have used Antony's splendid speech to analyze the psychology of persuasion, Bernard Ewer very generally [6] and H.

Lundholm in more detail.[7] Lundholm lists three main ways of making people believe something. First, primitive people believe in the reality of what they want to be real. Second, people in general believe what conforms to the reality of what they know. Third, he cites a principle expounded by McDougall: belief can be engendered by a submission to authority. The contrast between Brutus' and Antony's speeches to the mob, he says, disproves McDougall, for Brutus' speech is based on the third principle while Antony's gives much more weight to the first two: he appeals to what the citizens know about Caesar; and he plays on their wishes both to believe that Caesar loved them and to attack the authoritarian Brutus.

Unfortunately, these readings of *Julius Caesar* are sufficiently scattered in method and thin in number as not to give much of a coherent picture of the tragedy as a whole. The Rank-Jones view of the play as an oedipal fantasy is undoubtedly correct, but within the framework of early psychoanalysis. Today we would like to know more about the pervasive defensive device of splitting in the tragedy, which evidently is related to the fundamental theme of the tragedy on a conscious level: separation or division. Professor Smith's view of Brutus as the victim of a tyrannical superego introduces a newer psychoanalytic note and opens the possibility of seeing the murder of Caesar as Brutus' attempt to deal with a tyrannical father inside himself by an assassination outside. Perhaps, then, this is the most fundamental "split" in the play, between inside and outside; perhaps, too, such a reading would relate to the series of events and images that concern "staying home."

KING LEAR

The greatest or next to the greatest of Shakespeare's plays has evoked an intricate variety of psychoanalytic readings, although by no means as many as *Hamlet*. There are two contradictory kinds of readings of the play as a whole, and there are studies on two particular topics, Lear's insanity and the Gloucester plot.

Readings of the play as a whole fall into two quite distinct groups: those which look at the tragedy from a mythic or ritual or folkloric or Jungian point of view; those which look at the tragedy through a realistic approach to the psychology of Lear himself. As we have already seen, Freud himself took both these rather different tacks toward the play. In his "Three Caskets" essay he approached Lear as a kind of child choosing the ultimate mother, mute Death. In a later letter he considered Lear as an old man harboring incestuous desires for his daughters. As we saw in Chapter 6, these two readings, one mythological and folkloric, the other psychological, are closely related. By and large, however, later psychoanalytic writers have not related them.

Those psychoanalytic writers who have looked at the tragedy from the point of view of Lear's mind (considered more or less realistically) group into two categories: those who treat Lear as an old father and those who treat him as a child. (Notice that Freud's two readings also divide this way.) Ella Freeman Sharpe [1] applied her extended analysis of *Lear* to the probing of Shakespeare's psyche, and, for that reason, we considered it in Chapter 7 (p. 111), but if we consider her remarks as they apply to the play directly, her interpretation falls into that category of psychoanalytic readings of *Lear* which consider Lear as a child. She sees the play as an acting out of the child's massive realization that he is not omnipotent: "They told me I was everything." Perhaps the clearest and simplest evidence she offers is Lear's childish, "Howl, howl, howl," which she considers a child's impotent rage. The central motif of the play is thus, "I have been fooled," worked out in the action in general and the character of the Fool in particular.

Another theme in the play is the child's troubled and confused awareness of the parents' secret life together. These primal scene fantasies come out in many details, but notably in Lear's rage at being "locked out" and in the many references to humans as beastly and animal-like. Also, Miss Sharpe finds in *Lear* a number of images relating to the child's wetting himself in anger at his being replaced by another. Lear has regressed to a point in childhood where physical stress and emotional stress are indistinguishable—hence, the central image of the play, a body twisted and mauled like a baby's. Her reading, distressing as it may be in many respects, is nonetheless remarkably complete and persuasive.

Most Freudian readings of *Lear*, however, have concentrated on the king's psyche as that of an old father. One should note, at least in passing, James S. H. Bransom, whose study of the play [2] and letter to Freud prompted Freud to agree with the "last small section of the book," that Lear's problem was that of repressed incestuous love for his daughters. Far more prolific has been Dr. Arpad Pauncz, who has erected an elaborate structure on *Lear:* "adult libido" and the "Lear complex." [3] Dr. Pauncz argues that the older man has problems of transferring his love from one object to another just as the child does, and that these problems appear all through literature. The most notable example, he says, is *Lear,* which instances the "Lear complex," in which the father eliminates his wife and marries his daughter ("marries" in the symbolic sense in which one uses it in speaking of the oedipus complex). Lear, he says, symbolizes all old men, and unconsciously the division of the kingdom signifies the purchase of the daughters' favors.

Finally, through the storm and madness, Lear comes to understand his situation. His fantasies during the storm are sexual: he calls Gloucester blind Cupid and threatens to do in his sons-in-law. After the storm he is quite content to go off to jail with Cordelia —that would be their "marriage"—and earlier, he had decked himself with flowers like a bride coming to the bridegroom. Dr. Pauncz suggests that the essence of the tragedy is that the old man has to woo for love at the summit of his kingly dignity. Ultimately, he reaches happiness, he gets that love, but only at the depths of human existence or actually beyond human existence, in death. This is the universal tragedy of the aged man; it is also the "everlasting symbol of all mankind." Dr. Pauncz has attracted to his idea one noted follower, Professor F. L. Lucas.[4]

J. Meltzer in his remarks on sadistic and masochistic themes in Shakespeare [5] points out that Lear is the absolute ruler, hence an obvious medium for sadistic impulses; he has been turned into a dependent figure totally at the mercy of circumstances (an obvious medium for masochistic impulses). L. A. G. Strong [6] argues that Lear, like a child or a certain kind of neurotic, cannot tolerate delay in his gratifications or "separation in time" from them. Therefore, he hurries too much, both in setting aside the cares and responsibilities of kingship and in thinking ill of Cordelia. "So, at the end, the rescuers come too late." Both Meltzer and Strong, in effect, give other versions of the father-become-child reading.

Still other writers on *Lear* have looked at the tragedy as a whole, rather than simply or mostly at Lear himself, and inevitably this looking at the tragedy as a whole seems to lead to a myth-and-ritual approach, as it did for Freud himself. Theodore Reik found support for Freud's view in Victor Hugo's phrasings about the play.[7] Hugo spoke of Cordelia as Lear's mother, of her "nourishing" him, and of Lear after her death as "his child's orphan." Thus, his wording shows that Hugo unconsciously recognized the latent psychoanalytic significance of the story.

Writing from his point of view that the psychological truth of Shakespeare's plays is the truth of folklore rather than the truth of photographic portrayal, J. I. M. Stewart says [8] that the violence and obscenity of the tragedy inhere in its total problem (as they do, say, in that of *Romeo and Juliet*). That is, the sensualist, Gloucester, loses his eyes; the man of will loses his reason. The essential problem of *Lear* is the mind divided against itself, Lear and his Fool. Professor Herbert Weisinger [9] considers the tragedy from his point of view that Christian tragedy should represent a leap out of the cycles of pagan fertility and seasonal rituals into another—a Christian—order of experience. *Lear,* he says, fails on this score, for the old king comes to self-awareness in Act IV, but the play proceeds to the slaughter and debacle of Act V. Professor William Frost has considered the opening of *Lear* as a ritual, but in a rather less psychological way.[10] He gives ritual a larger sense as any situation "predictable in important aspects," or, generally, any formal situation. The opening of *Lear* is a stiff, formal ritual of this kind, but it directly conveys the folkloric quality of the plot, and the general movement of the play should be seen as Lear and Cordelia's moving beyond ritual in the final scenes through a real human relationship. Professor Frost, in other words, comes to the opposite conclusion from Professor Weisinger's.

Naturally enough, the Jungians have stressed the folklore angle. Maud Bodkin [11] interprets Lear's love contest and Gloucester's choice between his sons as splittings of two different aspects of the child: one wholly loving, loyal, and affirmative, the other wholly hostile, cruel, and grabby. Lear himself becomes a superhuman figure, going beyond one man's troubles to take upon himself the world's burden. He becomes a sacrificial victim, an image from the collective unconscious. (Miss Bodkin suggests that as the ego gets weaker such images get stronger, emerge, and take over.) Lear dies with the cry of hope on his lips; he and those around him exult in the moment of sacrifice. After his death there is the grave's holy peace; he has become a kind of Christ figure. In a later study,[12] Miss Bodkin points to Lear as an archetype of man in his godlike, kingly role, although Lear in particular shows a singular lack of divine wisdom.

Another Jungian reading is that of K. M. Abenheimer,[13] who sees Lear as the tragedy of self-love: the king, he says, has a "narcissistic longing to discard the burden of being a self-reliant ego without losing the sovereign independence of the ego." In short, he wants the perfect mother; he tries to make his daughters his mother and to become a child again himself, basking in limitless love. Poor Tom o' Bedlam symbolizes defenseless man, what Lear would have to risk and overcome were he to conquer his narcissism. The storm scenes, too, show the nakedness and pain the narcissist fears. Goneril and Regan are narcissistic also. They are (as the cocktail-party phrase goes) "castrating women," women who wish to deprive men of physical power and social superiority. Blinding, particularly the tearing out of the eyes, is, as many analysts have pointed out, a symbol for the destruction of one's manhood—castration. Cordelia, on the other hand, Abenheimer sees as standing for sanity and mental health.

As with Hamlet's insanity, Lear's has attracted rather less attention than one would perhaps expect from psychoanalytic writers. Henry Somerville [14] has diagnosed it as mania. In a fuller treatment,[15] John Donnelly regards Lear as not insane at the opening of the play (although unusual), but passing into schizophrenia or a schizophrenic episode (with disorientation about time, place, and persons) as a result of his incestuous attachment to his daughters. When he is rejected by all three of them his mind gives way to the sexual fantasies that identify his disease.

As for the Gloucester plot, the only point which seems to have attracted attention is the sibling rivalry. Otto Rank [16] noted that here, as elsewhere in Shakespeare, a loving son is paired off against a hating one. Choosing the wrong son cost Gloucester his eyes (his blinding being a symbol for the loss of his manhood). The two sons, he suggests, represent ambivalence toward the father, and he notes, slyly, that the "good" son "pays the price of the father's life." Professor F. L. Lucas points out that *both* plots in *Lear* deal with sibling rivalry.[17]

If we put aside such fragmentary readings, the analyses of *Lear* as a whole fall into three kinds: first, statements of the play's element of folklore; second, statements that Lear as a human being is childish and narcissistic; third, that Lear as a human being suffers from unconsciously sexual impulses toward his daughters. These last two points represent a realistic portrait of what old men go through, and in this sense we could regard the tragedy as a prosaic study in geriatrics in the manner of modern realistic drama, a tragedy of in-laws, in which the superannuated father insists on living with his married daughters. Balancing this realism, however, is the folklore of the play: "Once upon a time there was an old, old king, and he had three daughters. The older two were harsh and ill-favored, but the youngest . . ." and so on.

There is another bifurcation of psychoanalytic readings of *King Lear:* between those that treat Lear as a child and those that treat him as an old man. This second split we can reconcile psychoanalytically—in fact, Ella Freeman Sharpe has made the appropriate point: an old man's love for his daughters is the last stage in the long development of the child's feelings toward his mother. As Goneril says, "Old fools are babes again." The second split, reconciled, suggests a way of reconciling the first as well. That is, both in style (folkloric and realistic) and in portrayal (Lear as child, Lear as old man) the tragedy hovers between age and infancy, between an old man's foolish or bitter beliefs about family affairs and the magic of childhood thinking as expressed in fairy tale and folklore.

The psychoanalytic readings, then, seem to reveal an inner emotional foundation for the play's intellectual "meaning," which (so I have suggested elsewhere) is the tension between fact and value. For example, the old men of the play call on the traditional, medieval view of nature where fact and value come together in the hierarchical order of the universe. The other forces in the tragedy demonstrate Edmund's "goddess," nature red in tooth and claw, a nature of expedience and raw, hard fact. One is the nature of a child's or a foolish old man's beliefs; the other is the nature of an old man's bitterness. Despite their seeming disparity, the psychoanalytic readings put the intellectual issue of the play in emotional terms.

MACBETH

For other psychoanalysts as for Freud, *Macbeth* has proved nearly as stimulating as *Hamlet*. There are many readings, but the total picture is much clearer. The reason seems to lie in the play itself, its pervading unreality of witches, ghosts, omens, and prophecies. Where approaches to *Hamlet* divided sharply (even within a single study) between treating the play as a realistic portrayal of events and treating the play as a split and fragmented dreamlike fantasy, the psychoanalytic writers treat *Macbeth* only as fantasy—except for the character of Lady Macbeth.

Otto Rank set out in 1912 the psychoanalytic axiom about the play: Macbeth's killing of Duncan represents hatred and resentment of a fatherlike authority.[1] Within this framework, Rank says, Duncan and Banquo merge into a single figure, Banquo's ghost constituting a threat of retaliation on Duncan's part as well as on his own. Banquo's ghost projects the son's (Macbeth's) fear of retaliation from his own son when he, in turn, is a father; the ghost sits in Macbeth's place because Macbeth has taken the father's place. The ghost also stands (as, Rank says, all of Shakespeare's ghosts do) for the persistence or immortality of infantile feelings about the father. Lady Macbeth embodies or projects Macbeth's ambitious wish, and it is significant that it is she who recognizes Duncan as the father.

> Had he not resembled
> My father as he slept, I had done't.—My husband!
> (II.ii.13–14)

It is still another part of the incest pattern, Rank says, that the suspicion for the deed falls on the sons of the king.

Another early psychoanalytic reading of *Macbeth* is that of Dr. Isadore H. Coriat.[2] Although it purports to deal only with Lady Macbeth, his monograph really touches on several aspects of the play, albeit somewhat eccentrically. The witches, he suggests, represent a kind of hypnotic suggestion to Macbeth, "rapt withal," which he, in turn, passes on to Lady Macbeth, whom he loves because she enables him to project outward such wishes as that to kill Duncan. Although she enables Macbeth to project outward, Lady Macbeth herself plays the role of a figure of repression. She transforms her own "sexual complex" into an "ambition complex," as a substitute for her lost (*sic*) children. Similarly, she transforms more of her sexuality into what Dr. Coriat calls a "murder complex." Again, she is cast as a repressor in the banquet scene, which reveals to us Macbeth's epilepsy(!).

Her sleepwalking, Coriat says, is "monoideic somnambulism," in which one set of ideas becomes isolated from the main stream of consciousness and takes on a life of its own. At gaps in consciousness, such as sleep, this cluster of ideas takes over. When sleepwalking, the subject seems to see and hear these images clearly; in each somnambulistic episode the subject repeats the same words and gestures; the subject is apparently oblivious to his (her) surroundings; finally, when the attack is over, the normal personality returns, but there is a gap in consciousness. Coriat quotes one Pfeil as to how the sleepwalking scene should be acted: "The movements are erratic and much more energetic than in the waking state: never slow, gliding, or languid as though drunk with sleep. It would be most correct, and for the audience, most realistic [an audience of psychiatrists perhaps], should Lady Macbeth rush hastily across the stage with an impetuous run—neither gliding nor tottering." Lady Macbeth's hand washing, Coriat interprets (as Freud did) as an obsessional attempt to wash off guilt.

After Lady Macbeth's suicide, the real role of the witches, Coriat says, becomes clear. They are, he says, "erotic symbols, representing, although sexless, the emblems of the generative power in nature. In the 'hell broth' are condensed heterogeneous materials in which even on superficial analysis one can discern the sexual significance."

Whether or not influenced directly by Rank and Coriat (or Freud or Jekels, see below, whose first essays on *Macbeth* appeared in 1916 and 1917), this psychoanalytic reading of the tragedy achieved a staging at the hands of Arthur Hopkins and Robert Edmond Jones in 1921. According to Mr. Patrick Kearney,[3] Jones used a huge white cone of light representing the witches as a recurring background, "a phallic symbol" which represented "the life energy which in Macbeth

—to whom fate had given 'a barren scepter and a fruitless crown'— could produce only mocking apparitions." In this context, the cauldron became the well of man's sexuality out of which all his desires and fears come. Mr. Kearney asserts that these things were "powerfully brought home to the unconscious of the spectator," but notes, quite astutely, that the device ultimately failed because symbols need to conform to representational reality so they will be accepted at face value, carrying their secondary message hidden. At least, I would say, there has to be some defensive disguise or displacement of the symbolic "message."

Rather more satisfactory than either Rank's or Coriat's is Ludwig Jekels' extended analysis of *Macbeth,* one article of which appeared in 1917 (and influenced Freud's treatment) and the other in 1933.[4] Like most of the early psychoanalytic commentators on Shakespeare, Jekels insists that the play tell us about the author's psyche. As we have already seen in Chapter 7, Jekels tries to use *Macbeth* to fix up a plot around the dramatis personae of Shakespeare's biography: Queen Elizabeth, Sir Thomas Lucy, the Earl of Essex, Hamnet Shakespeare, and the rest. He is on much surer ground when he is simply pointing out congruities between psychoanalytic theory and *Macbeth.*

Jekels does, however, take a ritual turn before diving into depth psychology. Quoting Karl Simrock, he notes that Macbeth has many of the attributes of a "hibernal giant, whose reign comes to an end when the May festival begins and the green wood comes marching," that is, Birnam Wood. Similarly Macduff has the quality of a demigod because of his special birth. As one would expect from these folkloric elements, Jekels says, the play as a whole is concerned with the succession of generations, the tragedy of the son taking his father's place.

Psychoanalytically, Duncan, who is actually a father to Malcolm and Donalbain, is like a father to Macbeth, Banquo, and Macduff, who are also his "sons," at least his subjects. The first part of the play deals with these "sons'" doings toward a "father"; the second deals with a second father-king's actions toward his "sons." During the first half of the play Macbeth acts the role of a son who replaces the authority of his father by force and substitutes himself. The motive for this father murder is Lady Macbeth, the "demon woman" who creates the abyss between father and son. (Jekels very astutely notes that Lady Macbeth is accomplice only to Macbeth's crimes as a son, not after he becomes the king-father.) Behind Lady Macbeth as instigator stand the three witches who are her surrogates and, like her, neither clearly female nor clearly male. Like the three Fates, Lear's three daughters, or the Three Caskets (as in Freud's essay), the witches represent past, present, and future in terms of the three relations of man with woman: the mother, the beloved, and Mother Earth. The witches give Macbeth the "borrowed robes" of Cawdor, symbol of treason against the "father."

After the death of Duncan, Macbeth takes over the part of the father-king, but, unlike Duncan, he proves a bad father, killing one "son" (Banquo) and trying for the other (Macduff). The problem now is hostility against the son, and Banquo's ghost, Jekels says (as Rank said), represents the hostility of a son who now faces the bad son become bad father. Macduff, he says, is a "bad son," too; he rebels against the king-father, Macbeth, does not attend the coronation, refuses to come to the banquet, and uses "broad words." He does all this, Jekels says, as a parallel to Macbeth, who showed openly the traditional hostility of son for father, yet Macduff's own open hostility is followed by the death of all his own children (notably his son). Macduff proves again, in the logic of the unconscious, that "the bad son makes a bad father."

Jekels points to other parallels between Macbeth and Macduff. Macduff is rather indifferent to Duncan (before his death); Macbeth murders Duncan. Lady Macbeth incites the son-Macbeth against the father-Duncan; Lady Macduff incites her son against the absent father. Macbeth, Jekels concludes, represents in a symbolic, dreamlike form Macduff's relatively ordinary actions. Macduff, he says, is "the true hero." Banquo is the opposite of Macduff: he protects his son whereas Macduff leaves him to be killed. "A bad son," Jekels concludes, "not only sacrifices his son, but, in so doing, also forfeits the blessing of continuous descent." Jekels sees Macbeth as essentially a play about the preservation of the clan, and the son is thought of mostly as a means to this end.

In the second paper Jekels uses *Macbeth* to verify a purely psychoanalytic hypothesis, that, in dreams, neuroses, parapraxes, and drama "there prevails a tendency to give a twofold expression to any important, or, as we may say, central psychic constellation, so that it appears in consciousness in two guises, which are generally quite different from one another." In the case of *Macbeth,* he says, Macbeth represents a dreamlike, extreme version of the bad son and bad father; Macduff represents a quite toned-down, ordinary version of the bad son and bad father. Both Macbeth and Macduff act out guilt: they each did something wrong. Where Macbeth murdered by commission, Macduff murdered by omission—he left his family behind "in that rawness" to be killed. And both Macbeth and Macduff pay for their wrong with childlessness.

Macbeth, however, acts out a version from the unconscious (in this older terminology), with its drastic no-compromise approach, while Macduff acts out a version from the "preconscious," much closer to the muted acting out of impulses in everyday life. After analyzing a dream and the case history of a neurosis, Jekels goes on to conclude that the sense of guilt in drama is given a duplicated expression: in one hero (Macbeth) it finds resigned recognition; in the other (Macduff), it is recast in socially productive form. In dream and neurosis, the sense of guilt cleaves the personality asunder. But in drama, the sense of guilt leads to unification of the self. (It is for this reason, Jekels says, that drama so stresses unity and "the unities.")

Jekels, it seems to me, has hit on something important here. Drama, he is suggesting, brings unconscious material to consciousness in two forms: one stimulating, frightening, even overwhelming to the ego, the other, socially productive and ego syntonic, more extensively disguised and defended against under the pressure of guilt imposed by the superego. Then, in an artistic unity, drama welds these two outcomes to themselves and to the original unconscious material. He is describing, in effect, the relation of artistic unity to dramatic catharsis: in the double-plot tragedy (maybe in all tragedy), a well-unified play points the way, as it were, suggests the line of defense we in the audience are to take against the forbidden drives being acted out. In a terminology older than Jekels' or mine, tragedy uses incidents arousing pity and fear with which to effect the catharsis of pity and fear. But we are digressing from *Macbeth* . . .

Arguing against "realist" critics of Shakespeare and on behalf of a psychic realism, J. I. M. Stewart [5] sees *Macbeth* in psychological terms as dealing, first, with the fascination of horror, blood, murder, and the other gruesome aspects of the tragedy, and second, with uncertainty about the consequences of action; both these factors play conspicuous roles in the childlike primitive mind which is our own unconscious. A French author, M. Jankélévich, suggests that Macbeth has, in effect, two selves, a normal self with a normal conscience, and a satanic self out of the world of dreams.[6] Lady Macbeth personifies this second self; she is the projection of Macbeth's wishes for kingship. To some extent, once Macbeth has decided to kill Duncan and even more after the actual murder, he has destroyed his normal self; he has given his life over utterly to his satanic self. He has murdered sleep, and his life becomes a series of hallucinations, the air-drawn dagger and Banquo's ghost.

Dr. Daniel Schneider, in an amusing attempt to analyze *Macbeth* in the terms of a "how-to-write-a-play" book, comes to a similar dualistic conclusion.[7] Schneider sees two themes in the action: the murder of Duncan and the magic prophecies of revenge. Together they make a single idea, "Ruthlessness leads to its own destruction," but, and this is Schneider's important point, the theme must be understood not as a conscious, reasoned conclusion, but as a fearful fantasy.

In this fantasy Macduff and Lady Macbeth project unconscious feelings about the family. Lady Macbeth is a woman who wants to become the ruling power, to have all the strength and potency of a man; the blood on her hands, Schneider insists, is the blood of her own femininity which her fingers are now powerless to wash away. That very blood suggests the thing that made her an unwilling woman; the loss of a fancied masculinity now becomes the loss of the brain which guides those ambitious fingers, a kind of ultimate loss of power.

Macduff symbolizes the avenging son (in a way, suggests Schneider, of Lady Macbeth, for he was not of woman born and he, like her, has no children left). He attacks this half-masculine, bloody (castrating, if you will) "mother," because, out of her hatred of all men, she denies him birth, denies him sons, denies him his heritage. Macbeth has become, in effect, merely a tool, a stabbing male in her hands.

The revenge formula, Schneider sees as "she who murderously covets and seizes the [potency] of the father loses her own potency (is castrated) by guilt and her accomplice is destroyed by the rage of the magically protected son." Schneider sees the "pivotal character," as Macbeth and Lady Macbeth, a single figure embodying the union of opposites. The "point of attack" is the point at which the prophecies are given and the audience's preconscious mind becomes engaged and involved in the magical thinking which is the essence of the tragedy.

Schneider goes on to consider the play scene by scene. The opening appearance of the witches announces the theme of magic; the following scene, the theme of rebellion. In the third scene we see the witches fully as masculinized women, projections of Lady Macbeth, who confront Macbeth and his duplication in Banquo. Banquo's question to the witches suggests the ambivalence toward the king-father; Macbeth's feeling that the witches gave him the robes of Cawdor suggests the rational mind's ambivalence toward and partial dependency upon magical thinking. Cawdor's death (I.iv.) then continues the theme of revenge-retaliation. Lady Macbeth's first appearance (I.v) shows her as castrator of Macbeth—he is merely her tool. Schneider sees the scene in terms of an unconscious feeling that the woman who covets her father's power (his phallus) will castrate her husband (deny him children) and use him as a tool. The dramatic conflict at this point is whether to act or not to act on the basis of a feeling of magic omnipotence (the child's feeling he is all-powerful) against the strictures of the conscious awareness of reality.

The following scenes, leading up to the murder, Schneider says, state fully both the oedipal conflict and the conflict between an unconscious, childish sense of omnipotence and an adult, conscious attention to reality. Act II brings in the prophecy theme again in the person of Banquo and the discovery of the crime by Macduff. In Act III, when Macbeth accuses the witches of giving him a "fruitless crown," he is displacing his hate for Lady Macbeth onto the witches. In the same vein, his second scene with the witches brings on images of birth, particularly the theme of the magically protected, avenging child. Finally, in Act V, reality closes in on the dark fantasies: Lady Macbeth goes mad (a kind of ultimate mutilation). The theme in the final scenes is "all or nothing," a final statement of magical, either-or thinking against the gradations of reality. In short, then, the unconscious *effect* of *Macbeth* stems from (1) feelings toward a "castrating woman," and (2) puzzlement about the difference between the world of magical thinking and reality.

Meltzer, in his glance at sadistic and masochistic themes in Shakespeare,[8] points to Macbeth as one who projects outward onto witches and prophecies his own wishes to suffer. Macbeth himself, he says, is "a magnificent example of the sadistic-masochistic poles in a dissociated personality." L. A. G. Strong [9] notes simply that Macbeth shows a characteristic of many neurotics: inability to delay gratification. He cannot wait passively for the guerdon promised by the weird sisters.

While Rank, Coriat, and Jekels all stressed the father-murder side of the tragedy, they also pointed out that Lady Macbeth symbolically projects as well as realistically instigates Macbeth's crime. She plays, in effect, seductive mother to Duncan's role as father. Dr. David B. Barron has investigated Lady Macbeth's mother role from the point of view of modern psychoanalytic knowledge of the early, oral mother-child relationship.[10] In *Macbeth* woman is treacherous, particularly in a feeding way. That is, both Lady Macbeth and the witches feed Macbeth "intoxicating dreams of glory." But, at the same time, the most violent images in the tragedy arise at points of obstructed or interrupted feeding: Banquo's bloody ghost breaks up a banquet, Duncan's murder is described as a stopped-up fountain, and, of course, Lady Macbeth says:

> Make thick my blood;
> Stop up th'access and passage to remorse . . .

or:

> Come to my woman's breasts
> And take my milk for gall, you murd'ring ministers . . .

or:

> I have given suck, and know
> How tender 'tis to love the babe that milks me:
> I would, while it was smiling in my face,
> Have plucked my nipple from his boneless gums
> And dashed the brains out . . .

Because of this "inconsistent mothering," to use an anticlimactic term from pediatrics, Macbeth identifies with Lady Macbeth. Thus, Dr. Barron brings new life to Freud's suggestion that they are "like two disunited parts of a single psychical individuality." Where Freud saw them as symbolic halves, Dr. Barron describes them as a composite personality like a mother and son who have failed to achieve separate identities.

Macbeth's identification with Lady Macbeth as an overpowering mother has two effects. First, identified with a woman, he doubts his own masculinity and tries to "rise" in a variety of senses as a way of proving his own identity. Most obviously, he becomes king—in effect, Lady Macbeth diverts his aggression toward her for withholding "the milk of human kindness" to a quest for the blood of Duncan. Less obviously, Macbeth kills the Macduffs as a displacement of his own envy of Banquo's potency; another displacement is his terrible curse that

> the treasure
> Of nature's germens tumble all together
> Even till destruction sicken.

The second and more important effect of the merging of Macbeth's identity with Lady Macbeth's is to blur the differentiation between self and object so that Macbeth is drawn away from the real world and engulfed in a dream life. Outside stimuli can "make" him act, for they are part of a world that smothers and strangles him. Having killed Duncan, he fears guiltily that he will be devoured, as by Banquo at the banquet. Macbeth must eat up his enemies before they eat him, even as Duncan's horses "eat each other." Murdering the Macduff family is, symbolically, an effort to create a man with an identity; Macduff, standing alone, has an identity unblurred by relations with others.

Dynamically, the end of the play shows masculine figures coming to cut Macbeth loose from the maternal world in which he is "cabined, cribbed, confined, bound in/To saucy doubts and fears." In effect, by encountering the "father's," Macduff's, opposition, the "son" Macbeth can differentiate himself from his mother and learn to distinguish his own impulses and forces from those of his environment. No longer can Macbeth say "I bear a charmèd life"—but, rather, "Before my body, I throw my warlike shield." And what, then, is the significance of the prophecy that none of woman born shall harm Macbeth? Macbeth was goaded to murder by the destructive influences of women (the witches and his wife). The man who is to destroy Macbeth must be free of the slightest taint of woman, even birth.

Dr. Barron's reading may sound far fetched to the nonpsychoanalytic reader, but it is common knowledge in ordinary literary criticism that food images abound in *Macbeth*. Barron's oral reading makes sense out of them and indeed makes sense both psychoanalytic and literary out of the play. Many, many facets of the play bear his reading out. In effect, Dr. Barron is showing beneath the oedipus conflict pointed out by the first psychoanalytic writers on *Macbeth* an earlier, oral understructure that shapes the form of the phallic or oedipal conflict later in development. The result is that psychoanalysis can offer a comprehensive view of the dynamics of *Macbeth*.

Nonpsychoanalytic psychological analyses have not been so comprehensive. Professor F. L. Lucas [11] notes simply that Macbeth's witches are symbols of mental forces luring him to commit new crimes to make sure of his punishment for old—they project, in other words, Macbeth's longing to be punished and so to free himself from an overpowering guilt. Otto Rank (in his post- and anti-Freudian phase) treats Macbeth [12] as a hero of words rather than of deeds, driven by fantasies and speeches and "witches." Professor Weisinger [13] feels that the play does not reach the full scale of ritual tragedy, for Macbeth's ambivalence toward himself, his immaturity, tells us at the outset he will not rule Scotland well.

Lady Macbeth all by herself is sufficiently fascinating to attract almost as much attention as the play as a whole, and, in particular, she has come in for the kind of realistic analysis of character that the rest of *Macbeth* has not evoked. Frieda Mallinckrodt (following Isadore Coriat's book—see n. 2 above) [14] analyzes Lady Macbeth (as Freud did) as a divided personality. On the one hand, she is an intensely masculine woman, with a strong hatred for her father such as one would expect to find in men. (Like all the analysts, Dr. Mallinckrodt identifies Duncan as a father substitute because Lady Macbeth says he resembles her father.) All her masculine energy is stored up; it can only be worked out vicariously through her husband. Yet, says Dr. Mallinckrodt, Lady Macbeth also has a feminine, loving side to her which is frustrated by the death of her children (*sic*). She shows this feminine side in her tenderness (*sic*) to her husband. Before the murder, the masculine side of Lady Macbeth determines her behavior; after the murder, when she has no hope of children, Dr.

Mallinckrodt says, her feminine side overwhelms her with remorse and she falls ill.

Isadore Sadger [15] analyzed Lady Macbeth's behavior in terms of the general mechanism for sleepwalking. The sleepwalker unconsciously seeks a loved one, often the loved one of infancy. For example, sleepwalking children will frequently try to crawl into bed with the loved parent. In Lady Macbeth's sleepwalking, she is looking for Macbeth's bed; five times in the sleepwalking scene she repeats, "To bed." Often, Sadger says, a sleepwalker will adopt mannerisms that tend to identify him with the loved one he is seeking. So Lady Macbeth does when she reverses her earlier notion that "a little water clears us of this deed" to share Macbeth's fear that their hands will never be clean. Similarly, the very disturbance of her sleep identifies her with her insomniac husband. At the same time, Macbeth really stands for her father to whom her affections are bound—the reason she seems to have so little sexual feeling toward Macbeth. When she holds the candle, she makes herself into the image of the parent looking at a sleeping child, and when she says, "Come, come, come, come, give me your hand," she adopts the tone of a parent speaking to a child.

R. S. Miller notes simply the similarity between a female patient with a washing mania and Lady Macbeth.[16] Caroline Shrodes, Justine van Gundy, and Richard W. Husband [17] offer a view of Lady Macbeth's sleepwalking as a defense, specifically, reaction formation (an exaggerated expression of whatever virtue is the opposite of the vice one feels guilty of). Lady Macbeth covers up her guilt through seemingly irrational but persistently repeated acts, here, washing herself clean again after a dirty deed.

Dr. Robert Fliess [18] also interprets Lady Macbeth's sleepwalking defensively, as an obsessional attempt to "undo" Duncan's murder by hallucinating the conversation with her husband previous to it. Her preoccupation with the amount of blood in "the old man" provides further evidence for Dr. Fliess' contention that in unconscious symbolism castration is distinguished from death by the amount of blood. Limited bleeding symbolizes castration; bleeding without limit (like Duncan's) stands for death.

One detail has come in for a psychoanalytic interpretation, the same one that caught De Quincey's ear, the knocking at the gate. Dr. Henry Wexler [19] calls the Porter's speech a "dream scene" balanced against the dreamlike world of the murder scene. The Macbeths are momentarily involved in self-reproach to which the Porter is a kindly devil, while the knocking is more ominous. It symbolizes the "awakening" of the self-preserving conscious part of the mind to something other than the raw, murderous demands of the id as dreamed in dreams, the ego awakening to a fear of retribution, in other words. The "knocking" is ignorant of the murder, for in unconscious reasoning the sense of guilt arises whether the murder was actually done or only imagined. Just as Lady Macbeth is Macbeth's *alter ego* (Freud's suggestion), Wexler points out that the Porter may be his *alter* super-ego. The symbol of entering through doors occurs commonly in dreams and fantasies; usually it symbolizes birth, but it can also signify death entering, as in folklore or in *Macbeth*.

Only one speech has been analyzed. The vigilant Dr. Tannenbaum has spotted a slip of the tongue.[20] Lady Macbeth has just finished reading Macbeth's letter that tells her of the prophecies; she is planning murder when a servant appears to say, "The king comes here tonight." "Thou art mad to say it!" she blurts out, thus, says Dr. Tannenbaum, revealing her inner knowledge that Duncan would indeed be mad to trust himself to her. Then she tries to cover her slip with:

> Is not thy master with him? who, were't so,
> Would have informed for preparation,

as though hers was only the consternation of a good housewife confronted with an unexpected—and important—guest.

Briefly, *Macbeth* seems to operate on two levels. At the phallic or oedipal level, the tragedy deals with two sons murdering two fathers: Macbeth murdering Duncan, Macduff murdering Macbeth. In Macbeth's crime a "mother" (be she Lady Macbeth or the bearded witches) is both the instigator and the projection of Macbeth's hostile wish against the king. That mother, moreover, seems almost to have usurped a good half of Macbeth's masculinity. The half-masculinity of Lady Macbeth, the food imagery, and the magic and fantasy that pervade the tragedy take us back to a more primitive level—the oral stage. Macbeth and Lady Macbeth represent a child and a mother, each imperfectly differentiated from the other. Out of this blurred relation of self and object the oedipal conflict springs: Macbeth tries to achieve an identity by hostile action against his environment; Lady Macbeth turns that hostility from herself toward Duncan.

While there are not so many psychoanalytic readings of *Macbeth* as of *Hamlet,* the final picture makes much more sense. It seems to me that the reason for this coherence is that there has been relatively little effort to deal with *Macbeth* as an illusion of reality. Rather, starting with Freud's own comment on the characters, that Macbeth and Lady Macbeth are the divided halves of a single personality, each unintelligible without the other, psychoanalytic critics have been content to consider the characters as projections of psychological impulses rather than portraits of those impulses in "real" people. The witches, ghosts, and prophecies of *Macbeth* would seem almost to force this kind of reading, and it is no bad thing.

MEASURE FOR MEASURE

In this problem comedy the ever-alert Otto Rank detected an incest motif in the bed trick.[1] Angelo is slipped a maiden he himself dishonored in lieu of the sister, Isabella, who is ostensibly devoted to her brother. Rank says this is a rearrangement of an incest situation: the girl in the dark is the "dark," tabooed mother, whom the son has himself dishonored, his own birth proving the fact that she has had intercourse with a man. The incest taboo is transferred to the brother-sister relation and expressed in terms of Isabella's chastity. Indeed, she almost says as much:

> Is't not a kind of incest, to take life
> From thine own sister's shame? What should I think?
> Heaven shield my mother play'd my father fair!
> For such a warped slip of wilderness
> Ne'er issu'd from his blood.
>
> (III.i.139–143)

Hanns Sachs analyzed the play as a whole, although rather more in a literary than a psychoanalytic vein.[2] Angelo he sees as a sadistic type, hostile to ordinary love, who prefers to adopt the role of a punisher. His unconscious desires, however, bob up when Isabella appears. The problem of the play, Sachs not unreasonably says, is that the judge commits the same crime as the criminal (the same thing is true, he points out, of *Oedipus Rex*).

In *Measure for Measure* the matter is complicated by the fact that the crime takes place only in intention; something rather different takes place in fact. Thus, Sachs says, the ultimate theme, from a psychoanalytic point of view, is the problem of guilt for *thinking crimes*. Angelo's actual crime is the same as the slanderer Lucio's, and he is punished the same way, by being forced to marry a woman he cannot respect. The function of the indifferent, intractable Barnardine is to caricature the duke's and Isabella's coldness to life which is like Angelo's coldness. At the end, the duke forces (*sic*) Isabella to marry him—the same crime Angelo had threatened. The point of the play, Sachs says, is that we are all sinners, and only mercy helps. The play as a whole hovers between tragedy and comedy because of its theme: comedy deals, Sachs claims, with bad intentions without acts; tragedy deals with bad intentions acted out. The comic ending persuades us that mere intentions don't matter; at the end of a comedy the superego (the duke here) is, in effect, told that it has no business making us feel bad for mere thoughts, and this, Sachs says, is what happens in the comedy of *Measure for Measure*.

Dr. Robert Fliess [3] notes two elements in the play. First, when Isabella says her brother is not prepared for death, she compares her brother to a fowl in the kitchen—again, Fliess points out, governmental executions (as in *Cymbeline*) seem to be socially approved cannibalistic impulses. Fliess also tries to deal with the scansion of Isabella's speech to Angelo in relation to the psychic regressions involved, and the attempt, while interesting, seems no more successful than any of the other attempts to analyze *Measure for Measure* from a psychoanalytic point of view.

THE MERCHANT OF VENICE

Perhaps because many psychoanalysts are Jewish, *The Merchant of Venice* has received a great deal of attention, more, proportionally, than some of Shakespeare's more important plays. Because of this fairly substantial treatment, we can see quite clearly the basic schism in psychoanalytic criticism. That is, some authors talk about the characters and events in symbolic and folkloric terms, while others look at individual characters as realistic portraits (and, of course, a third group considers particular speeches). We can take them in that order.

Looking at the play as symbol and folklore, Freud, as we have seen, devoted an essay to "The Theme of the Three Caskets." Even before Freud's essay, however, the assiduous Otto Rank had detected an incest theme: [1] Portia, he said, was the daughter of one of those jealous fathers out of folklore who force all kinds of things on young men who try to liberate the imprisoned daughter. The father wants her for himself. Freud's essay then suggested that the three caskets symbolize the three aspects of man's relation to woman: the mother, the beloved, and Mother Earth, a mythological view not unrelated to Rank's incest motif.

Ludwig Jekels used *The Merchant of Venice* to illustrate some of his general points about the theory of comedy. [2] He pointed out, first, that the money debt stands for a moral debt or guilt—as it commonly does in dreams and literature. The guilt in this case is that one which Jekels says is common to all comedy, the projection of guilt onto a fatherlike man for the wishes a sonlike man feels guilty about. The "son" in this case is Bassanio; the "father" is Antonio(!). Jekels in assigning them these roles relies heavily on one source (in which Bassanio is Antonio's adopted son)—and on the theory he is trying to prove. The pattern of the comic action, Jekels says, in this as in other comedies, is to reduce the father to a son, and the mark of Antonio's becoming a son is the fact that Shylock threatens to cut off a crucial, life-giving part of his body.

Otto Rank,[3] in his later phase, considered the play as illustrating his thesis that Shakespeare gives us a humanized, motivated version of older legendary material. Shakespeare, for Rank, represents a transition from a "spiritual" era to a "sexual" one. Thus, Shylock is a traditional "money Devil"—but humanized. Rank sees the three caskets test as symbolizing the religious requirement in some cultures that a man abstain from intercourse the first night after marriage. He relies on analogizing the barrier imposed by the three caskets to testing the suitor by means of a sleeping potion in one of the sources, the story of Giannetto in Fiorentino's *Il Pecorone*. That is, the caskets "stand for" a night with Portia. In effect, the story transforms a man's spiritual anxiety about marriage into sexual resistance on the part of the woman.

Theodore Reik has produced a relatively full analysis of the play; although, because he arrives at it by rambling free associations, it is scattered. Not unless one puts the pieces together does it appear as an entity. Reik makes two points, the first being that the play has much aggression in it. In part, he reaches this conclusion by analyzing the nature of Shylock's cruelty [4] (and we will consider his analysis when we get to studies of character).

Portia, Reik says, reminds him of certain female patients of his who put him through miniature riddle ordeals; he concludes that Portia herself has a streak of cruelty (which may be either a drive or a defensive effort to overcome pressures to be passive and feminine).[5] Portia, he says, is cruel to Shylock and to her suitors, and even to Antonio in so theatrically waiting to the last minute to get him off the hook. Her cruelty is disguised in that the riddle ordeal is set up by her father, but its significance is the same: the woman regards herself (compare Freud's essay) as a riddle to be solved; failure to solve this riddle means that the man is not really a man (in the play, he cannot marry, and in that limited and symbolic way loses his manhood—is castrated). The caskets symbolize the riddle of woman; so also do the rings which Portia and Nerissa give their husbands-to-be.[6] They are symbols not only of faithfulness, but also of the genital of the woman whose love Bassanio seeks to win. Music, of such importance in *The Merchant of Venice,* plays its part in this atmosphere of aggression.[7] Music itself, Reik says, is a sound or scream that has become song. Thus, music serves as a defense against too-powerful aggressive impulses. It "sublimates and masters our violent drives and has the magic force to defend us against the evil dangers within ourselves, as it originally banned the menace from without us" (when it was a simple scream). In short, Reik finds a lot of aggression in the comedy.

Reik's second point is that Antonio and Shylock are "splits," which allowed Shakespeare to express ambivalent attitudes, emotions that contradicted each other in the mind of the poet himself.[8] Shylock's wish to cut off a pound of flesh, Reik says, symbolizes by "displacement upward" a wish to cut off Antonio's life, his manhood. As such, it is linked to Shylock's Jewishness. That is, circumcision is also a symbol, although a milder one, for castration. Consciously, Reik says, the Christian looks at the Jew as a money-grabbing figure; unconsciously, however, the Jew seems to him, in the practice of circumcision, to grab at something else—the Christian fears the Jew will damage him bodily. In *The Merchant of Venice,* Reik says, the insistence on the pound of flesh is a disguised request that Antonio be circumcised—become a Jew; this demand for flesh is the reason Shylock is made a Christian at the end—the *lex talionis* is our unconscious sense of justice.

Shylock is "Jewish" in another way: he keeps crying for vengeance and saying that Jahweh will get it for him. Shylock, Reik concludes, is a symbol for the vengeful father-God of the Old Testament.[9] Antonio, on the other hand, is the "tainted wether," the lamb of God. He is sad. He lays down his life for his friend. He is, in short, Reik says, pure *caritas,* pure Christ. And as a figure to be mutilated, cut to pieces, "castrated," he resembles the mythical figures of Osiris, Attis, Adonis (and Christ)—the dying gods. Mythological as this is, Reik regards it as a psychoanalytic study. Two points do have psychoanalytic relevance and are new with Reik; first, he points out the pervading presence of aggressive motifs both oral and anal; second, he identifies Shylock as a father figure.

E. E. Krapf interprets the comedy in the light of anti-Semitism.[10] Shakespeare, he says, set out to write an anti-Semitic comedy, then found himself ambivalent toward Shylock. At first the plot was simple: Shylock was trying to cut Antonio's life off, but he ends up himself cut down. At first Shakespeare identified with Shylock's victim, Antonio; but then, Krapf says, when Shylock was on the block, the poet identified with Shylock against Bassanio and Portia. By a curious (and unhappy) extension of Freud's essay relating the Three Caskets to the Three Fates, Krapf concludes that Portia represents

Atropos, and that, together, Bassanio and Portia constitute the mother of our earliest fantasies, the mother not yet differentiated from the father, a mother with a phallus.

Krapf relates his ideas to anti-Semitism, concluding that the anti-Semite projects onto the circumcised (i.e., castrated) Jew his fear of such a masculine, dangerous mother; in support, Krapf notes that anti-Semitism runs more against Jewish men than Jewish women. The man who attacks Jews attacks, therefore, mutilated men, men like women; he also, Krapf says, attacks the bad children (of the God-father) who deserve to have their masculinity taken away; and thus the anti-Semite identifies with the masculine, fatherlike (castrating) mother. Jews, says Krapf, are easy victims because they themselves feel guilty of matricidal impulses, having banished mother goddesses from the pantheon. Krapf also goes on (as we have seen in Chapter 7) to say that Shakespeare's identifying with Antonio shows a longing to become the passive love or victim of the father—Shylock. Thus, Shakespeare shows a "negative oedipus complex," in which the son identifies with the mother, an element in homosexuality. Antonio's melancholy, or depression, Krapf says, is Shakespeare's own as he moves into the period of the great tragedies.

Scattered through Dr. Robert Fliess' study of the early forms of sexuality is another fairly extensive analysis of *The Merchant of Venice*.[11] Fliess finds a great deal of mouth imagery in the play. The whole pound-of-flesh plot he sees as related to childhood fantasies about suckling. That is, in childhood one is allowed to suck liquid from the breast, and this is a kind of consummation, but one is denied the ultimate consummation of putting inside oneself the very source of food; one cannot eat the breast itself, in other words. In *The Merchant of Venice* we find this situation reversed: one is allowed to cut the flesh off Antonio's breast, but not allowed to get the liquid, the blood. The same fantasy shows, Fleiss says, in Portia's legalism. The play says at one level that you are allowed to eat from your victim, but not to kill him. At a "deeper" level, the play is saying, you can have the flesh, but not the liquid; if you try to eat the breast, you are punished by not being able to suck from it.

Another oral mechanism Fliess finds is Antonio's melancholy. According to psychoanalysts, the mechanism of melancholia is as follows: deprived of a love object, the subject incorporates it into himself. Once "in him," however, the loved one turns into a tormenting, accusing conscience, and the end result of the accusations is that the conscious mind submits to the unconsciously present accuser. Thus Antonio is melancholy, suicidally indifferent to his own fate. His casual signing of the bond, Fliess says, stands for the ego retreating and giving in to the accuser, the conscience represented by Shylock. Antonio is a suicidal melancholic incorporating (devouring) the figure of the harsh parent—and as so often in unconscious phenomena, we find this situation in the play, but reversed: Shylock, the accuser, tries to devour Antonio. Shylock, then, represents another oral factor—oral, sadistic cannibalism.

Fliess also finds non-oral elements in the play. The exact measuring of the flesh, the haggling legalism, the need to be "quits" with the other—these all have to do with delivering something as precious as one's own body; they are anal traits. The taboo on the charging of interest which plays an important part in the comedy, Fliess suggests, is derived as a repression of a common childhood feeling, that one's feces are an intimate and precious part of the self. The child has to learn that they are not living, and later, as his attitudes toward this precious part of himself develop into his attitudes toward money and other valuables, he insists (or did in earlier times) that these inanimate objects not "breed." The taboo against breeding money might represent, Fliess says, the repression of still another common childhood idea, namely, the child's confused belief that children are conceived in and delivered from the anus.

Considerably less concrete (and therefore less troubling) is A. Fodor's study of the play: [12] before proceeding to some fairly empyrean speculations on Judaism, the Renaissance, and a "secular oedipus complex," Fodor says something that, oddly enough, no one before had come right out and said about *The Merchant of Venice:* simply that Shylock represents a bad father, and Portia a good mother.

If we put all these readings together, separating the wheat from the sizable quantities of chaff mixed in, a tolerably complete picture of the comedy develops. As literary critics have repeatedly pointed out, *The Merchant of Venice* is built up out of two worlds, Venice and Belmont. Venice is hard-boiled, commercial, realistic, and predominantly masculine; in fact, three times women have to disguise themselves as men in Venice. Presiding over this world as a kind of malignant deity is the father, Shylock. It is he who establishes this atmosphere of competition, aggression, of having to pay a price for a favor, for everything. It is he who makes Venice a place of risk and chance in which love must mask itself and hide and hoard and steal. Only when you get out from under his spell can you throw money away (as Jessica does).

Belmont is just the opposite. It is a woman's world of romance and folklore and love, full of riches and bounty and giving. There are risks and aggression, but if you solve the riddle of woman (the only obstacle left by the absent father), then you win the woman and risk relaxes into music. Song and feasting—in Belmont the mouth is always full, while in Venice one is forced to squeeze out of oneself precious possessions, which are, nonetheless, dead and forbidden, as you are, to "breed."

Confronted with these two worlds, one niggardly and anal, one bountiful and oral, is the twin figure of Bassanio-Antonio, one a "mother's child," the other a "father's child." Bassanio, the mother's child, does indeed solve woman's riddle and pledge fidelity. In return he gets a bounty that has all the power of mother love:

> For you,
> I would be trebled twenty times myself,
> A thousand times more fair, ten thousand times
> More rich.

This love is such a bountiful investment, it even triples itself on the spot (Nerissa and Gratiano, Lorenzo and Jessica).

The sad Antonio, on the other hand, is subjected, as if by a father who hates him, to hostility, risk, danger—no wonder he is melancholy. His crisis comes when the father prepares to mutilate him and sacrifice him to his wrath (even as the gentle, melancholy Christ was the victim of Jewish Jahweh's wrath). The comedy acts out the wish that this bountiful mother love which "is not strain'd./It droppeth as the gentle rain from heaven. . . . It is twice blest," redoubled and multiplied in every way, will pre-empt the father hate. Indeed, as events work out, this bounty puts the father's child in charge of the hateful father; it gives to the mother's child the mother herself as a "bedfellow" who has slept till then, not with any man, but only with a masculine disguise of herself.

The psychoanalytic view of the play "grows," as it were, into the literary one, in the same way that its different psychoanalytic strata grow one from another. The earliest, deepest level of the comedy is oral: Belmont, "beautiful mountain," the bountiful mother breast; Venice, withholding and niggardly. The next stratum, growing from this sense of withholding, develops anal (and oral) attitudes toward possessions. In Belmont, money is wooed and freely given to the wooer like mother's milk. In Venice, money is withheld or forced to breed in an unnatural way or made the equivalent of flesh to be cut off. The next psychoanalytic stratum is the phallic or oedipal level, where the contrast becomes that between a loving mother, Portia, and a castrating father, Shylock.

If we think of the play as an interaction of impulse and defense-or-adaptation (in the modern psychoanalytic manner), the impulse is to "have" in oral, anal, and phallic senses; the play grants this wish in a Belmont way and a Venice way. But the wish is modified by two adaptive maneuvers. First, good ways of having and being had (Belmont) are isolated from bad ways (Venice)—you cannot have both. Second, the characters are depersonalized into "things," caricatures, really, that can be had: father and mother, justice and mercy, Jew and Christian, and so on. It is only a short step from such a reading to the central themes of the play in a purely literary sense: the different kinds of "mettle" pointed out by C. S. Lewis have to do with the depersonalizing; my own suggestion elsewhere that the comedy pleads the need to accept risk in the venture of life, breeding, represents another version of the psychoanalytic theme of "having."

So long, then, as we consider *The Merchant of Venice* in fairly abstract, symbolic terms, the comedy makes a great deal of psychological sense. The picture becomes much less clear when we shift to those psychoanalytic studies that treat the characters as real people. Very early Isadore Coriat analyzed Shylock's character.[13] He found the three characteristics which psychoanalysts associate with those people whose psychic development was repeatedly irritated during that period of childhood when a lot of attention is focused on the process of defecation, anal characters, in other words, who react to events in later life as though they were being forced or had been forced to deliver some very precious part of themselves. Such a person, Coriat says, likes children because of their association with a purity and innocence which he feels he has lost, and also because he is compensating for his own resentment. Indeed, Shylock does show a certain tenderness to his child and perhaps to children in general. Second, in accordance with the psychoanalytic thesis that later attitudes toward precious externals like money are outgrowths of earlier attitudes toward precious internals, Shylock has one of the most outstanding characteristics of the anal-erotic personality—a tendency to hang on to money and to feel that the possession of money against superior authority is the equivalent of power and control. Third, Shylock is a hateful, irritable, explosive man, and these are also characteristics one expects to find in the anal-erotic personality.

Reik would agree with Coriat that Shylock was cruel and sadistic, but Reik points to Shylock's use of food similes ("bait") to describe the flesh he wishes to cut from Antonio. "Shylock," Reik says, "is starving in this voracious hunger of vengeance." [14] He is not anally sadistic (as Coriat says); he attacks with his mouth. And Fliess, as we have seen, stands on Reik's side, having pointed out the many images of food and biting (see above).

238 PSYCHOANALYTIC VIEW OF SHAKESPEARE

Readings that consider the play as a total configuration come to a consensus; readings that look at the characters as real people conflict and seem more subjective. That is, although Fliess and Reik seem to contradict Coriat, both sides have considerable evidence to support their view (there is much more to be said for Coriat's anal sadism than he himself says). Are the readings, then, really inconsistent? No—in two senses. Realistically, aggression from the earliest or oral stage of infancy tends to carry over into the next stage, the anal. We can hypothesize a childhood for Shylock compounded of oral frustration followed by sharp demands in bowel training. But that does seem a bit off. Alternatively, we can retreat from considering Shylock as a real person with a "real" childhood to seeing him simply as part of the totality of the play. This comedy, as we have seen, works with both oral and anal "having," both libidinal and aggressive "having." Shylock, then, is both oral and anal, but in an aggressive way, while the Belmont world is both oral and (in its music and money) anal, but in a libidinal way.

There is a second character whom psychoanalysts have looked at in a realistic way: Antonio. T. A. Ross [15] poses a number of questions: Why does the title character appear so little? Why does the opening subject of his depression peter out? Why does he give so freely to Bassanio, dropping his own troubles to talk of Bassanio's love? The answer, Ross concludes, is that Antonio is homosexually in love with Bassanio, but is continent. That is why, Ross says, Antonio calls himself a "tainted *wether*." Shakespeare, Ross decides, regarded continent homosexuality as noble and admirable, and therefore he shows Antonio in Act V as the most noble character of the play.

E. E. Krapf, as we have already seen, also regarded Antonio as homosexual, specifically in his adopting a submissive, passive position toward the "father," Shylock.[16] L. A. G. Strong sees Antonio as suffering from a true depression and also hints at a homosexual motif.[17] Graham Midgley offers a relation between this reading and the play as a whole.[18] The comedy, he says, is a twin study in loneliness, dealing with two "outsiders"—Shylock and Antonio. "As Shylock is to Venetian society, so is Antonio to the world of love and marriage." Antonio is an outsider because he is an unconscious homosexual in the male, heterosexual world of Venice. He is in love with Bassanio; he himself is left with no mate at the end; and he is melancholy throughout because his very love for Bassanio drives him to help his friend find a heterosexual relationship.

Dr. W. I. D. Scott also sees Antonio as homosexually attracted to Bassanio—unconsciously.[19] He suggests that this character type (introvert-feeling in Jung's taxonomy) is particularly given to the kind of depression Antonio describes in the opening lines of the play. Here again there is contradiction in the readings of the characters as living people. Is Antonio consciously or unconsciously homosexual? Toward Shylock or toward Bassanio? The character readings seem to conflict, and the evidence from the play is skimpy. Yet these readings do not really contradict each other: the difference between conscious and unconscious homosexuality is a slight one, especially in a play where no overt homosexual behavior appears. And thus it is not really necessary to establish which particular person Antonio is homosexual "toward."

Further, these realistic readings, consistent or not, fit into the play as a totality. If Belmont is the mother world consecrated to heterosexual love, and if Venice is the father world, almost by definition, love in Venice must take the form of passive homosexual submission to the father. It is worth remembering, too, that the one heterosexual romance in Venice (Jessica and Lorenzo) takes the form of a flight from Venice, and that the women characters disguise themselves as men in Venice (Jessica, Portia, and Nerissa).

Even so, as in most psychoanalytic studies, we find consistency and consensus when the critics look at the play as a whole in a fairly abstract and symbolic way, but a tendency to conflict and contradict when they look at the characters as individuals. When critics look at individual speeches, there is less scope for contradiction because the thing analyzed is so small.

For example, Dr. Tannenbaum finds a "Freudian slip" in a remark of Launcelot Gobbo's to Shylock.[20] On the evening Jessica and Lorenzo are to elope, Lorenzo's friends have invited Shylock to dinner so as to get him out of the way. His erstwhile servant, Gobbo, comes to fetch him.

Launcelot. I beseech you, sir, go. My young master doth expect your reproach.
Shylock. So do I his.
Launcelot. And they have conspired together, I will not say you shall see a masque, but if you do, then it was not for nothing that my nose fell a-bleeding on Black Monday last at six o'clock i' th' morning, falling out that year on Ash Wednesday was four year in th' afternoon.

The passage is, to say the least, a bit obscure, but Launcelot's "reproach" for "approach" hints at the conspiracy to elope and the father's natural "reproach." Shylock answers literally and Launcelot goes on, "And [if] they [the feasters] have conspired together"—and, of course, the feasters have. Tannenbaum sees this as a slip of

the tongue which threatens to give the elopement away and which
Launcelot then tries to cover by speaking of the masque and other
gibberish. The reading seems a bit forced, however.

The classic Freudian slip in *The Merchant of Venice* occurs when
Portia speaks to Bassanio before he chooses the casket:

> Beshrow your eyes!
> They have o'erlooked me and divided me;
> One half of me is yours, the other half yours—
> Mine own I would say; but if mine then yours,
> And so all yours!

Otto Rank pointed out in 1910 that Portia, by her slip, reveals what
she should have kept hidden—her love for Bassanio. Freud repeated
Rank's statement in 1912, as R. S. Miller did in 1915.[21] Dr.
Tannenbaum, however, objects, claiming the line represents no slip at
all.[22] He notes that Freud and Rank read Portia's "Mine own I
would say," as though it meant, "I intended to say." Actually, he
argues, it means, "I should or ought to have said." In other words,
Portia simply states her love for Bassanio quite openly, noting at the
same time that it isn't proper for her to be doing so. Portia, says
Tannenbaum, is open throughout with Bassanio and is so here. Dr.
Tannenbaum's position seems at least possible, and this miniscule
dispute, therefore, suggests one generality: how important the conception of the character as a whole is to what a modern actor would
call the "motivation" of a particular speech.

Dr. Robert Fliess, we have seen, has analyzed the play as a whole
in terms of oral and anal images. In the course of his analysis he
looks at one speech in considerable detail—a rather rare proceeding
in psychoanalytic criticism.[23] Shylock is justifying in court his insistence on the bloody forfeit of the bond:

> You'll ask me why I rather choose to have
> A weight of carrion flesh than to receive
> Three thousand ducats. I'll not answer that;
> But say it is my humour. Is it answered?
> What if my house be troubled with a rat
> And I be pleased to give ten thousand ducats
> To have it baned? What, are you answered yet?
> Some men there are love not a gaping pig,
> Some, that are mad if they behold a cat,
> And others, when the bagpipe sings i' th' nose
> Cannot contain their urine; for affection,
> Master of passion, sways it to the mood
> Of what it likes or loathes. Now, for your answer:

As there is no firm reason to be rend'red
Why he cannot abide a gaping pig,
Why he, a harmless necessary cat,
Why he, a woollen bagpipe, but of force
Must yield to such inevitable shame
As to offend, himself being offended;
So can I give no reason, nor I will not,
More than a lodg'd hate and a certain loathing
I bear Antonio, that I follow thus
A losing suit against him. Are you answered?
                                        (IV.i.40–62)

Shylock, Fliess says, is refusing to justify his "humour," his pleasure, in short, his childish irrationality; but he refuses by dismissing his action as childish and irrational.

Shylock compares his sadism to the childish impulses or behavior of others, for example, the fact that some men "cannot contain their urine." The speech begins and ends with exactly the kind of question-and-answer dialogue that a child might give a parent in response to a scolding: "See? So-and-so does it, too." Within the play, Shylock's impulses ("Hates any man the thing he would not kill?") have all the infantile violence of the child-in-us, and he justifies them in terms of grisly childhood fantasies that themselves would provoke a wild reaction on an infant's part.

Shylock's images are those of irrational horror. The first is the rat "troubling" the house. The house is a common symbol for the body, and the rat gnawing at a hole down in the bowels of the house, gnawing, perhaps, at some precious object, money, say, or some edible hidden down there . . . the image is enough to provoke a whole wave of emotions surging up from the unconscious. Fliess sees the image as related (like the theme of usury) to the child's fantasies that his feces are in fact little animals. The gaping pig—the meat of the pig being taboo to Shylock—again creates a phobic attitude. Beholding a cat, soft, furry, feminine—Fliess suggests the image recalls another kind of fear, a boy's fright at his first glimpse of the seemingly mutilated genitals of the opposite sex. As the pig's mouth is poised against the rat's hole in the depths of the house, poised against the cat is her masculine counterpart, the projecting bagpipe, later described as 'woollen." The bagpipe outside sings in the also-masculine nose and lungs inside.

All the images so far, Fliess notes, have mouths save the last, which introduces the idea of losing control in another way. That is, the rat, the pig, the cat, even the asking, all deal with gobbling, gnawing, unrestrained oral behavior; the bagpipe introduces unrestrained wetting. And all represent to Shylock a justification of his own moral incontinency.

The two kinds of incontinency find a parallel dualism in the reduplication of the speech itself; it goes, question, rat, pig, cat, bagpipe; answer, pig, cat, bagpipe, answer. Fliess would agree with more conventional criticism that we have here the balance and summing up of a practiced pleader, but he also finds an infantile note. This reduplication, he says, is a much enlarged and sophisticated form of the infant's reduplicating syllables, "ma-ma," "da-da," and so on. Fliess suggests that the first half of Shylock's speech is to be understood as passive experience like the first syllable of the baby's babble; the second half represents, he says, responding to and mastering the experience: "You'll ask me . . ." "Now, for your answer." In short, Fliess argues that Shylock's speech shows he is engrossed in childish fantasies about his own rational mind being overwhelmed by archaic, unconscious impulses and dragged under by the resulting incontinence and loss of control. Father Shylock has begun to be turned into a child by the action of the comedy.

This kind of analysis will, no doubt, seem farfetched, and probably in some of its particulars it is. Nevertheless, Dr. Fliess' study of the unconscious effect of the passage (which, of course, does not compete with or contradict a reading of its conscious content) fits both the general atmosphere and the particular situation of the play. We have noted the atmosphere of aggression, the comedy's preoccupation with hoarding and money, its use of ordeals; at the moment of this speech, the hero is being menaced by a terrifyingly unrestrained parent figure. Images of irrational fear, fantasies of devouring, reason overwhelmed by unreason—these enrich the effect of feared sadism at this point in the play. Although the reading of any particular image may seem strained, even fantastic, it is not so when placed in the context of hundreds of similar and related images. In other words, just as the conventional critic of Shakespeare finds the informing principle of the whole at work in each specific speech, so the psychoanalytic critic should be able to find the nuclear fantasy of the whole play shaping the images, symbols, diction, and style of each speech.

THE MERRY WIVES OF WINDSOR

Except for remarks on Falstaff (in connection with the *Henry IV* plays), *The Merry Wives of Windsor* has stimulated only one extended psychoanalytic comment.[1] Theodore Reik sees in Sir John's adult adventures in love a recapitulation of childhood episodes. "Since

I pluck'd geese, play'd truant and whipp'd top," Reik quotes the fat knight, "I knew not what 'twas to be beaten till lately." In the episode of the fat woman of Brainford, "A little boy emerges behind the figure of the old Falstaff, and the situation of being abused, beaten and thrown out of the house presents a childhood experience." Reik interprets the element of diguise as a wish that the old woman *ought* to be beaten; the child who was beaten wants the mother to be treated the same way, and the old woman is really a mother figure.

Mrs. Ford, on the other hand, represents the "good," the desired mother. Putting Falstaff in the dirty linen and dumping him in the river, Reik ingeniously suggests, is simply a reversal of a common childhood difficulty—being taken from a warm, pleasantly dirty cradle and being thrust into a bath. The third episode, Falstaff disguised as Herne the Hunter watching the dance it is forbidden to watch, Reik says, suggests the child's fantasies about watching the parents' sexuality he is forbidden to watch. The horns shifted from Master Ford to Falstaff constitute a reversal of the wish to cuckold Ford. So also does the final line, "He [Master Brook-Ford] tonight shall lie with Mistress Ford." It is, of course, Reik concludes, not Falstaff's childhood that confronts us in *Merry Wives,* but Shakespeare's own; the comedy, he says, is to be interpreted as the child Shakespeare's own early disappointment with his mother. He expresses it in this play particularly because he was writing it—so the legend goes—at the command of that motherlike woman, Elizabeth I.

A MIDSUMMER NIGHT'S DREAM

K. M. Abenheimer suggests (from a Jungian point of view) that this comedy [1] "is the vision of a state outside time and society and morality; the world presented is an ecstatic state of liberty where no action has irreversible consequences and all is mere play." It is, he says, a world of nature spirits as opposed to the human world of tragical consequences and moral demands. Weston A. Gui [2] has a more intricate analysis from a Freudian rather than a Jungian point of view. *A Midsummer Night's Dream,* he suggests, not unreasonably, is about dreams; there are six experiences described in the play as "dreams," although, since Bottom is the only one who sees the fairies, his must be the key dream. In Bottom's dream ("I have had a most rare vision"), he is transformed into an ass and finds himself sitting in Titania's arms, she twined around him like ivy around the fingers of an elm. He receives love of a quite motherly kind. He gets food, for example, honey and nuts. His dream, furthermore, "has no bottom," and this Gui interprets as meaning that Bottom is living again a childhood bliss before any responsibilities about cleanliness. Bottom also gets his large, erect ears scratched—the tension of his itchy, tickling hair is relieved by rubbing—and this Gui interprets as a physical, sexual satisfaction. Yet these delicious, sensuous delights are broken off for Bottom.

Another frustration throughout the play is the moon which, Gui says, symbolizes the chaste, unattainable mother—yet never does she shine in *A Midsummer Night's Dream*. Mixed into Bottom's dream is still another disturbing element, the chase of the four lovers, which Gui interprets as sexual pursuit and their appearing and disappearing as fantasies about love between the parents. Bottom himself is partly transformed into an animal, and this, Gui suggests, resembles other transformations, satyrs or sphinxes; this transformation, too, he says, symbolizes the transformation of humanity into animality in the sexual act. Plays are still another symbol for fantasies of watching the parents love, and the "tragical mirth" of Pyramus and Thisbe with its violent action, bloodied clothes, darkness, and mistaking works the imagery out further. Gui finds significance in the names of the players, too. In short, he sees the comedy as Bottom's replacing (temporarily) both a baby (the Indian changeling) and the father (Oberon) in the mother's arms, she feeding him. But, alas, it remains only a dream. Only in the fairy world does Puck retain the position of honored child with Titania and Oberon. In the "real" world Bottom stands in humble suit to the lawgiver and lover Theseus and the chilly Hippolyta. As we have seen in Chapter 7, Gui relates his insight to Shakespeare, his brother Gilbert, and his father.

Building on Gui's somewhat unsteady foundation, Dr. Donald F. Jacobson [3] produces a reading of the play as a working out of psychoanalytic insights into feminine development. Titania's stealing the changeling, he says, corresponds to the common fantasy of young girls that they steal a baby from their mother. From the changeling's point of view, the question, whose will he be, raises the issue of sexual identification: Will he be a knight of Oberon's train or will he be crowned with flowers by Titania? And Titania, to bring the play to a happy ending, will have to give up her effort to feminize the boy.

Most of the picture of feminine development, though, appears in the plot of the young lovers. There, Demetrius serves as a surrogate for Hermia's father, while the taller Helena represents a mother figure. Although Helena and Hermia (mother and daughter) were as close as "a double cherry" when Hermia was a schoolgirl, Hermia breaks away as she seeks a male, "non-incestuous" lover, Lysander. The ending in which the couples are properly matched represents a giving up of oedipal wishes. Demetrius (father) can marry Helena (mother) with no objection from Hermia (daughter). Hermia, in return, gets Lysander. The play as a whole, Dr. Jacobson says, shows how a woman must give up her oedipal wishes to mature: the child's ties to parents must give way to later loves.

Professor Morton Kaplan [4] has sharply criticized Jacobson's and Gui's readings as "ratiocinative exercise and sterile criticism," adding no insight, literarily and psychoanalytically unsound. While I agree with Professor Kaplan that both readings are grossly overstated, I do feel they point the way for a proper psychoanalytic study. Conventional literary criticism would point to the theme of transformations, also to the hundred and fifty or so references to "eye," "seeing," "looking," and so on. Just on the thematic level, this confusion of vision with transformation raises the question, Is what I see and love "out there" or is it merely my own delusion "in here"? The psychoanalytic critic would recognize the oral themes of self-object differentiation and incorporating through the eyes. At a higher psychoanalytic level, the play deals with an oedipal theme: winning a man or woman tabooed by the king-father through transforming either oneself or what one loves or the parental environment. In dealing with these psychological issues, the recurring defensive or adaptive mechanism the play offers is regression to a "wood" (or madness) of childhood imaginings where self and object are not clearly differentiated, there to effect the appropriate transformations.

It should be possible to achieve the kind of understanding of the play that sees it on a dynamic continuum from oral phase (self-object differentiation) through phallic (primal scene and oedipal themes) to the meaning and morality, the adaptive level, that concerns conventional criticism. But there is no such reading yet.

Two writers have touched on particular details from *A Midsummer Night's Dream*. Ernest Jones, in a fascinating essay analyzing some paintings in which, at the Annunciation, the Madonna is apparently fertilized by words or wind entering her ear,[5] quotes from this comedy:

> . . . we have laughed to see the sails conceive
> And grow big-bellied with the wanton wind;
> Which she, with pretty and with swimming gait
> Following (her womb then rich with my young squire),
> Would imitate . . .
>
> (II.i.128–132)

Boats being a common feminine symbol, the image of the fertilizing wind would seem to support Jones's symbol cluster. Similarly, Dr.

Harry B. Lee [6] quotes Shakespeare's famous description of the poetic imagination:

> The lunatic, the lover, and the poet
> Are of imagination all compact.
>
> (V.i.7–8)

It supports, he says, his own description of the creative process: the writer falls into a destructive, depressed mood; he then (as poet) recreates the object he has destroyed in fantasy; finally, he finds himself a lover at harmony again with the real persons around him.

MUCH ADO ABOUT NOTHING

Shakespeare's comedy of honor has evoked but one psychoanalytic comment—and that from a Jungian. Dr. W. I. D. Scott [1] suggests that Don John is a "psychopathic personality," that is, a man incapable of affection and with no moral basis for behavior. (A definition more usual in America would be a character with a missing or defective superego.) Dr. Scott attributes the villain's failure in development to his being brought up in the shadow of Don Pedro's condescending glory.

OTHELLO

With psychoanalytic as with conventional critics, the focal problem in *Othello* has turned out to be whether to treat the play realistically or not in view of the peculiarities of Iago. Because *Othello* presents the problem of Shakespeare's realism so precisely, this tragedy more than any other reveals the basic schism in psychoanalytic criticism— and the possibility of bridging it. That is, two sharply divided bodies of criticism have grown up. The first treats the play as a realistic portrayal of realistic people who can then be diagnosed as though they lived, breathed, and freely associated. The opposite point of view sees the play as antirealistic, a folkloric interplay of competing types and impulses. Then a third, relatively recent, group of critics bridges these two positions. We can consider treatments of the play in order of generality: first, the antirealist view embracing the whole play; second, the realist view character by character; third, the bridging group. Then we can turn to studies of particular details or speeches.

a. The Antirealist View

These psychoanalytic critics focus on the unrealism of Iago—he is too villainous—or Othello—he is too trusting. As early as 1922 Otto

Rank (whose psychoanalytic criticism always has a folkloric or anti-realistic quality) noted that Othello can be so naïve and trusting because his own jealousy has been split off and represented separately from him in the figure of Iago.[1] Miss Maud Bodkin, writing in 1934, made the argument more explicit.[2] Following a famous essay of Professor G. Wilson Knight's, Miss Bodkin argued that the essential thing about Othello is his tendency to idealize things, just as the essential thing about Iago is his tendency to corrupt things. Miss Bodkin added the psychological touch: Iago should be regarded as the projection of the wisdom and experience that Othello's romantic vision ignores. In effect, Iago voices Othello's own doubts which his idealizing has served to repress. Othello's refusal to bring his doubts into the open takes the visible form of his failure properly to check Iago's story. Iago thus becomes (from Miss Bodkin's Jungian point of view) the devil archetype; she cites for proof Othello's frequent use of the word "devil" once Iago has him in his spell. Iago corrupts the idealist's vision, and Othello becomes possessed, impatient now for the destruction of what he once loved.

Miss Bodkin notes a further element of projection. She adopts Jung's idea that in each of us there are two psychic personages, the animus and anima, representing (respectively) our masculine and feminine sides. Othello and Desdemona, she says, are animus and anima. They are the archetypal man-woman relation, each finding an aspect of self in the other. Desdemona is a "fair warrior" and she finds the warrior in herself in Othello's tall tales. Each, in short, finds in the other essential man or essential woman.

In 1949 J. I. M. Stewart stated the "antirealist" position most explicitly.[3] Answering E. E. Stoll's contention that Othello is "airy artifice," Stewart pointed to the theme of the "calumniator believed," hoary in myth and folklore and holding an honored place in psychological reality. We all have low and baseless suspicions, Stewart says, and we often project them on a fictitious instigator; these are the facts underlying the conventional stories of the calumniator believed. "Iago's villainy draws its potency from Othello's own mind; it is invisible to others because it is, in a sense, *not there;* the devil in the play, like all devils, represents a projection upon some comparatively neutral or insignificant thing; Iago is a device of Othello's by which Othello hears a voice that he would fain hear and fain deny." In the same way, Stewart says, the double-time sequence in *Othello* has a psychological instead of a naturalistic truth, for the real theme of *Othello* is the mind divided against itself (like Lear and his Fool), and it is something we have all felt. "Iago is unreal, and Stoll is right about him. Othello is unreal, and Stoll is right about him also. But the two together and in interaction are not unreal. The two together make your mind, or mine."

More recently Professor Herbert Weisinger,[4] finding in *Othello* Shakespeare's most perfect amalgam of myth and drama, treats Iago as the external symbol of the evil in Othello. At the end of the tragedy, by his failure to kill Iago and in his own remorse, Othello, in effect, accepts the evil in himself and no longer externalizes it. But by consigning Iago to torture, Shakespeare fails to realize the full Christian "leap" that should climax a pagan, ritual tragedy.

The antirealist point of view at least shows agreement on one thing —that Iago projects something in Othello, although there is some disagreement as to what he projects: jealousy (Rank), ability to doubt (Bodkin), suspicions (Stewart), evil (Weisinger). But these four things do not diverge remotely as much as the realistic treatments of even a single character.

b. The Realist View: Iago

Psychoanalytic critics have come up with two diagnoses of Iago. One focuses on his sadism or agression, the other on his relation to Othello. As early as 1914 Isadore Coriat called Iago "an unconscious sadist" (although I wonder how unconscious we need make him).[5] Professor F. L. Lucas feels Iago's villainy stems from jealousy—he feels he is less loved than others, notably Desdemona and Cassio; but then Professor Lucas dismisses his own suggestion as "too subtle for any audience." [6]

L. A. G. Strong, however, makes much the same suggestion.[7] Iago, he says, "has a motive and a strong one." Acutely sensitive, he feels all those "honest Iago's" as patronizing. He is more jealous than most men would be at Cassio's promotion.

Professor Marvin Rosenberg argues that Iago is a projection "of emotional drives that run deep in humanity generally." [8] The theme of *Othello,* he says, is betrayal, and Shakespeare needed a betrayer. In creating Iago, he gave him two sides: the face he shows the world in his speeches and the face he shows the audience in his soliloquies. Shakespeare, Professor Rosenberg says, must have thought this second side quite important, for he put in a number of soliloquies which destroy suspense without advancing the action. On the outside, Iago seems to be, though passionless, quite perfectly human (he is not, therefore, Rosenberg says, the devil of some critics' readings). Inside, though, we see a man boiling with hostility and Dr. Rosenberg quotes the late Karen Horney (not often quoted in literary studies) for the psychiatry to support his description.

We cannot, says Professor Rosenberg, find a motive for Iago's villainy just from his relation to Othello, for Iago spews hatred not just on Othello but on everyone within reach. While his outward actions show no passion, only cool, villainous control, his soliloquies show a man seething with angry passion at everyone and everything. Iago, he suggests, has repressed all positive feelings of affection and replaced them with a child's furious fantasies of great power and salacious sexuality. Iago is, in short, the "vindictive" personality as described by Karen Horney whose only way of proving his worth to himself is by dominating someone else. He is an ulcer type, eating himself out with his corrosive aggression which "Doth (like a poisonous mineral) gnaw my inwards."

Professor Rosenberg finds confirmation for his reading in the theatrical record of successful and unsuccessful characterizations of Iago by actors. Iago, when acted, tempts us to laughter as a defense against recognizing that his (oedipal) impulse to destroy the marriage of a noble older man and a beautiful woman is all too much our own. He tempts us, too, to find an outside source for the villainy in him— and in ourselves; but he is no devil or vice or split of Othello. He is all too human. In short, Iago's real trouble, his neurosis, is that he keeps his aggression inside, away from other people; and Shakespeare, Professor Rosenberg concludes, shows it by resorting to soliloquies to characterize him.

The other realist view of Iago (despite Professor Rosenberg's strictures) looks primarily at Iago's relation to Othello. Dr. Martin Wangh [9] in 1950 set forth the idea that Iago is homosexually in love with Othello. He notes that Iago somewhat implausibly accuses Desdemona of lecherous feelings toward, not just one, but several men. Iago, moreover, feels that Othello has had not only Desdemona, but Emilia. Dr. Wangh argues that these facts can be explained only by saying that Iago is projecting his own love for Othello onto women. The formula of defense is, "*I* don't love him; *she* does." When Iago says that Desdemona feels love for Othello, Cassio, and Roderigo, he unconsciously means that he himself does. Dr. Wangh notes that Iago interrupts Desdemona and Othello's "rest" three times.

The mechanism of Iago's jealousy, he says, is essentially an oral one, as shown by the dream he invents for Cassio, an oral dream of kisses linked to a "raging tooth" (the "raging," suggests Dr. Wangh, is a passionate excitement and the tooth a well-known phallic symbol). The handkerchief, Dr. Wangh says, is white, charged with beauty and mystery, "spotted with strawberries." Quoting cases of fetichists, he suggests that the handkerchief symbolizes a breast, that this is the reason Iago seizes on it to work out his essentially oral jealousy.

Professor Gordon Ross Smith neatly and wittily discusses Iago, beginning with an exposition of the psychoanalytic method of handling character and concluding with further evidence to fill out Dr. Wangh's interpretation.[10] The idea that Cassio "hath a daily beauty in his life" suggests another figure in Iago's feelings toward other men. Similarly, when Iago says he works only for himself, that represents another defense on Iago's part: "I love only myself, so I don't love Othello." Iago's apparent illogic and his suspicions of Cassio with Desdemona show a "will instead of a reason to believe," and suggest that a pathological mechanism is operating. The strawberries on the handkerchief Professor Smith sees as symbols for the glans penis, a further element in Iago's homosexual fantasies. He goes on to suggest the relevance of his (and Wangh's) reading to the play as a whole. For one thing, it gives force to Edwin Booth's interpretation of the temptation scene as a courtship and marriage, kneeling, mutual vows and all. Second, this kind of reading gives the play a central idea familiar to a modern audience. Finally, it gives the tragic outcome a causal base.

Booth was, of course, pre-Freudian, but the notion that Iago is homosexual (like Hamlet's oedipus complex) has gotten a twentieth-century staging. According to Professor Rosenberg,[11] in 1937 Sir Laurence Olivier interviewed Dr. Ernest Jones to find a characterization for Iago along the lines of the oedipal Hamlet. Jones suggested that "to his mind the clue to the play was not Iago's hatred for Othello, but his deep affection for him. His jealousy was not because he envied Othello's position, not because he was in love with Desdemona, but because he himself possessed a subconscious (sic) affection for the Moor, the homosexual foundation of which he did not understand."

Accordingly, Olivier as Iago and Ralph Richardson as Othello played the climax of Act III, the exchanging of vows, as virtually a love scene. Iago became a gay, almost flirtatious character—and the performance laid a large egg. The characterization puzzled all the reviewers and only a physician seemed to get the point. Dr. James Bridie wrote the New Statesman and Nation to protest their hostile review and argue that the performance was "perfectly clear." [12] Iago's perverted sexual character put his mental and physical forces at odds, driving him into sadism and mania. His conflict expresses itself in "pathetic" rationalizations and smutty talk—"the picture [was] horrifyingly accurate."

Whether or not the homosexual Iago comes across on a stage, the two realistic views of the man (as homosexual, as pathologically aggressive) represent different emphases, but they do not conflict. That is, a defense against homosexual impulses might well take the form of an almost overwhelming aggression—as, in effect, Jones's remarks make clear.

c. The Realist View: Othello

For critics who wish to look at the tragedy as a fairly literal portrayal of life, *Othello* poses one problem only: Why is he jealous so easily? Caroline Shrodes, Justine van Gundy, and Richard W. Husband answer simply, Othello is ambivalent toward Desdemona. He cannot separate his love of Desdemona from his hatred for her, nor can he summon his intellect to moderate his passion. In his personality, emotion and cognition are separated. Emotionally, therefore, he tends to have "an all or nothing response." [13]

Why is Othello jealous so easily? Dr. Theodore Reik says [14] he has seen the same kind of jealousy in white patients, so it cannot simply be the fact that Othello is a Negro. Rather, jealousy depends on lack of self-esteem; the jealous man cannot believe anyone could love so base a thing as himself. Othello's jealousy stems from a "permanent and ineradicable doubt of himself," not from a racial problem. And Iago (here Reik shifts to an antirealist view) represents Othello's "hidden self with its concealed doubts."

Dr. Enrique Racker [15] also finds a narcissistic fixation or failure at the roots of jealousy in general and Othello's in particular:

> O curse of marriage,
> That we can call these delicate creatures ours,
> And not their appetites! I had rather be a toad
> And live upon the vapor of a dungeon
> Than keep a corner in the thing I love
> For others' uses.

In effect, Othello needs to be loved more than to love. Other elements common in jealousy, says Dr. Racker, are oral sadism (as described in *Othello* by Dr. Wangh); latent homosexuality ("I don't love Cassio; *she* does, and I find him hateful"); the projection of one's own impulses toward heterosexual infidelity onto an innocent partner (Freud noted this fact in the tragedy). And, finally, most jealousy has an oedipal element: when I take a wife, I have robbed a wife from my father, and I will myself be robbed.

> Look to her, Moor, if thou hast eyes to see:
> She has deceived her father, and may thee.

Dr. A. Bronson Feldman [16] also finds in *Othello* a series of the mechanisms of jealousy as described psychoanalytically: a homosexual current, castration fear, a paranoid tendency. But Othello shows one feature more clearly than the others. Why does he not confront Desdemona's father directly? Why does he agree to go off on a ship

separate from his bride of a few hours? And what about the lines in
which Othello asks that Desdemona accompany him to Cyprus:

> I therefore beg it not
> To please the palate of my appetite,
> Nor to comply with heat—the young affects
> In me defunct—and proper satisfaction.

Or what about:

> Haply for I am black
> And have not those soft parts of conversation
> That chamberers have, or for I am declined
> Into the vale of years—yet that's not much . . .

Othello's jealousy, Dr. Feldman argues, rises from doubts of his own
virility—in effect, he fears that he is not a man, that he has been castrated. And then (as Reik did) Feldman adds in an antirealist note:
Iago is Othello's evil *alter ego;* he voices Othello's unconscious fears
and feelings. L. A. G. Strong also sees Othello's jealousy as coming
from inner doubts,[17] those that arise because he is a Negro. Othello,
Strong says, believes that Desdemona is unfaithful because he cannot
believe that he, a colored man, could hold her.

In a later essay [18] Dr. Feldman looks at five Jacobean tragedies of
jealousy and comes up with a somewhat different mechanism: the
split of affectionate and sensual aspects of love. Othello's jealousy
springs from a long contempt for the opposite sex that turns love into
simply glutting a sensual sadistic impulse. As against this sensual
side, the jealous man grovels in self-abasement before an idol of impossible desire, derived from his infantile reverence for his parents.
Toward this idol he is utterly servile, but bitterly angry should anyone
else seem to be in possession. The jealous man also affects a superiority in imitation of his idol—and Dr. Feldman finds in all five of these
Renaissance tragedies of jealousy this mechanism. There is, however,
not a great deal of evidence in *Othello* for this point of view except
for Othello's violent swing from thinking Desdemona "my soul's joy"
to calling her a "whore," a "devil."

Still more recently Professor John V. Hagopian [19] sees the basis
for Othello's jealousy in his age and in his willingness to postpone the
consummation of the marriage. Othello is simply not sexually satisfying to Desdemona; he knows it; he feels insecure about it and thus
falls an easy prey to Iago. Professor Leo F. McNamara replied to Hagopian with the usual literary objection, that such a reading fails to take
into account Renaissance and medieval conventions.

It is difficult for me to see what conventions are involved, and I would simply summarize this realistic point of view on Othello as saying in a variety of ways that Othello's jealousy proceeds from some inner weakness, a fear of impotency, homosexuality, castration, or a lack of self-esteem.

d. The Realist View: Desdemona

Ever pale beside the mighty black and white of Othello and Iago, Desdemona has elicited relatively little psychoanalytic criticism. Dr. Theodore Reik suggests it may be useful to regard her love as more defensive than a direct gratification of drives.[20] Love, he says, can be regarded as a reaction formation to envy. "I envy that person; I want to be like her; I want to *be* her" becomes "I love her." So with Desdemona. On hearing stories of Othello's valorous adventures, "She wished/That heaven had made her such a man." But this becomes love. In a later study [21] Dr. Reik quotes in support of his view the late Professor Harold C. Goddard for the proposition that Desdemona is a strong, masculine woman, "half the wooer." Desdemona almost takes the initiative in the courtship. In effect, says Reik, she wishes to be a man as brave, as noble as Othello, and Dr. Reik guesses at an element of penis envy. Yet, ultimately, she is feminine in that she gives up the wish to *be* such a man in favor of the wish to *have* such a man.

L. A. G. Strong also sees her as behaving defensively, although in a somewhat different way.[22] She suffers from an inner sense of guilt because she has betrayed the standards of her father and her society in choosing Othello. Her behavior just before his final accusation shows "an unconscious readiness for what is to come."

e. Bridging Realism and Antirealism

The antirealist critics treat Othello and Iago, in essence, as Freud did the Macbeths—as divided halves of a single personality. Iago is the doubting half, Othello the trusting half. The realist critics diagnose Othello's jealousy and Iago's villainy, finding the causes of their actions as though they were real people with real behavior problems. Reik and Feldman, although basically realistic, represent one kind of compromise: Othello is real and can be diagnosed; but Iago is an unrealistic projection of Othello's unconscious weaknesses.

There is another kind of compromise: those critics who bridge the realist and antirealist positions by moving from the analysis of the characters as though they were real to the analysis of the play as an ordered—not realistic—artistic totality. J. Meltzer, for example, finds [23] Othello's personality (realistically considered) rather precariously achieved: he needs external supplies of self-esteem to sustain his basic narcissism and simply cannot afford to give of himself in love. Thus, he marries late; he marries a not-very-sexy woman who is not likely to upset his resistance to sex; the marriage night is interrupted, and so on. In effect, much of the narrative deals with an evasion of sexuality, and Iago, Meltzer suggests, is a projection of the neurotic's cunning in meeting and countering the demands of sex. The narrative as a whole, then, represents an inversion or externalization. The tragedy substitutes incompletely motivated external actions for powerful internal compulsions. In effect, Othello's inner problem becomes the external events of the tragedy.

W. H. Auden [24] finds a similar pattern of inside and outside, but centered on Iago. Iago, suggests Auden, only seems motiveless. Actually, he needs to play God, to show the weaknesses of others because he has a deep sense of his own insufficiency. In effect, he is a practical joker.

In the case of Cassio, Iago deals with a ladies' man who is not a seducer, a man unsure of his masculinity in masculine company. Once Iago gets him drunk, he loses his manhood: "What remains is bestial." To Othello, his marriage means he is accepted in Venice (his suicide speech proclaims his allegiance to Venice), but unconsciously he still feels himself an outcast Negro. Out of his insecurity he becomes too eager to believe and trust, too credulous. Desdemona secretly, unconsciously, looks down on Othello, but cannot face this fact. (Mr. Auden derives this unexpected idea from what amounts to Desdemona's free association. In the Willow Song scene she speaks of the "proper man," Lodovico; then her mind turns to adultery.) Time after time Iago reduces these people to things he can manage by playing on fears and desires they are unconscious of but which we in the audience know. His aim is, in a backhanded way, therapeutic —he makes unconscious conflicts conscious. But he is the therapist who kills instead of curing: "Work on, my med'cine, work!" In effect, then, in this view of the tragedy, Iago represents a split for all the major characters; for all of them he is the projection of buried aspects of their personalities. Thus, Mr. Auden moves from a realist view of Iago, Cassio, Othello, Desdemona, to the recognition of a not-so-realistic pattern that informs and shapes the action as a whole, here, a kind of lust for knowledge, in us as well as Iago, a desire to see coldbloodedly what will happen, to see the weaknesses in others as a cruel therapist might. Mr. Auden's readings of character would lead quite naturally into such things as the imagery of seeing, of reports, and other sensory, navigational ways of governing one's life, or the crucial question: "Who can control his fate?" Mr. Auden, then, has found a bridge across the gap between realist and antirealist critics of the play by turning to the mind of the audience, what we know or don't know as we see the play both realistically and as a nonrealistic ordered totality.

Dr. André Glaz also provides a bridge.[25] From a diagnostic, realistic point of view, Iago is an " 'as if' personality," a character type defined by Dr. Helene Deutsch: a schizoid personality who behaves "as if" he had feeling contact with other people, but breaks down once these relations start to shift from facile, childish identifications to real object relations calling for a real personality structure. As Iago says, "I am not what I am." In addition, he makes others act like what they are not. He makes Cassio a drunkard, for example. In this sense, Iago identifies with Othello. Their two figures merge, as when Othello says, "By heaven, he echoes me," or "Iago becomes me" (F1; usually emended to "beckons").

If Iago is unstably identified, Othello is too firmly anchored to his early identifications with his parents. He is the type known as a "moral masochist," a man with a deep need to suffer in atonement of supposed faults. His deep sense of guilt finds outward expression in his blackness. Once seen this way, the whole play falls into reversals. "Honest Iago" is dishonest. Bianca (white) is a whore. Black (guilty) Othello is really white, innocent Othello. White Iago, incapable of feeling guilt, is guilty, and so on. In other words, to spell out Dr. Glaz's reading, out of the several personalities, seen realistically, emerges the not-very-realistic pattern of the play as a whole; everything is the opposite of what it seems. Not the least of these opposites is the possibility of moving from a realistic view of the play to a not-very-realistic pattern of reversals.

f. Particular Speeches and Details

Dr. Robert Fliess [26] notes that Iago uses an image of horses to describe to her father Othello's and Desdemona's marriage: "You'll have your daughter covered with a Barbary horse; you'll have your nephews neigh to you; you'll have coursers for cousins and gennets for germans" (I.i.112–114). The horse, Dr. Fliess claims, symbolizes in myth and legend a love object barred by the incest taboo, one to be regarded with loathing. The fact that Othello is a Negro symbolizes the same thing. For these two reasons, Othello, much older than Desdemona, constitutes a kind of father to her in the special sense of a forbidden love relation, one surrounded with taboos. (It is curious that only in this rather limited way have psychoanalytic critics found an oedipal element in the tragedy.)

Dr. Tannenbaum, the *aficionado* of "Freudian slips," analyzes the crucial one in this play, the loss of the handkerchief.[27] Othello himself points out that the handkerchief symbolizes his love for Desdemona. Then, at the very moment she feels his love waning, she loses the handkerchief—surely there must be an unconscious factor. To bring it out, however, the business must be properly staged:

> *Desdemona.* Why do you speak so faintly?
> Are you not well?
> *Othello.* I have a pain upon my forehead, here.
> *Desdemona.* Faith, that's with watching; 'twill away again.
> Let me but bind it hard, within this hour
> It will be well.
> *Othello.* Your napkin is too little;
> Let it alone. Come, I'll go in with you.
>
> (III.iii.282–288)

Dr. Tannenbaum suggests that Othello's "it" probably does not refer to the handkerchief, for then Othello would be calling her attention to the fact the handkerchief had fallen, and the loss would not take place. Rather, as Othello speaks of his pain, the cuckold's horns spring to his mind (actually, Dr. Tannenbaum suggests, he has a headache because his sleep the night before was interrupted). The thought of cuckolding irritates him, and he brushes the handkerchief aside on the line, "Your napkin is too little." Desdemona then puts her hand to the spot, but Othello says, "Let it alone," that is, the pain or his head. And Desdemona blots out all memory of the dropping of the handkerchief because this is the first time Othello has snapped at her, and in a Freudian way she wishes to and does "forget" it.

Dr. Robert Fliess also analyzes the temptation scene,[28] finding several infantile fantasies, notably the idea of watching Desdemona and Cassio couple like animals (related to a child's fantasies of watching the parents behave like animals together): "It is impossible you should see this." Iago then moves on to the inverted false dream, and, like Dr. Wangh, Fliess notes that the dream moves from a phallic image (the "raging tooth") to a succession of gnawing images (for example, "As if he pluck'd up kisses by the roots") and closes with a curse (another orally sadistic gesture) against Othello. He notes that Iago links the handkerchief to this oral imagery when he says that he saw Cassio wipe his beard with it. Fliess agrees with Wangh that the handkerchief is a breast symbol. He cites evidence from the play for the proposition that the handkerchief was crumpled and compares the handkerchief to patients' dreams of something crumpled, which he found were dreams of the breast. He finds further confirmation of the breast hypothesis in that, independently, both Cassio and Emilia decide "to have the work ta'en out," that is, to make the one handkerchief into a *pair*. He finds further "mouthing" in Iago's making Cassio drunk, and he concludes from these oral elements that the basis for both Iago's and Othello's jealousy of Cassio is the hatred for a rival nursling sucking from the breast of a virgin mother.

Professor Kenneth Burke,[29] who in a general way regards Othello, Desdemona, and Iago as expressions of one "inseparable integer," considers Othello's line, when (after it is lost) he asks for the handkerchief:

> I have a salt and sorry rheum offends me.
> Lend me thy handkerchief.
>
> (III.iv.51–52)

Professor Burke maintains that, as in a dream, an unimportant fluid, rheum, stands for a more important body fluid. Twice before in the play "salt" has been used in another sense:

> A knave very voluble; no further conscionable than in putting on the mere form of civil and humane seeming for the better compassing of his *salt* and most hidden loose affection.
>
> (II.i.244)

> It is impossible you should see this,
> Were they as prime as goats, as hot as monkeys,
> As *salt* as wolves in pride, and fools as gross
> As ignorance made drunk.
>
> (III.iii.404)

Hence, "salt" having a sexual sense, the "salt and sorry rheum" may represent the very fluid of Othello's desire, a pollution that can only be removed by this special handkerchief. In that context, the handkerchief comes to symbolize Desdemona herself, treated as "private property" that can be owned like a handkerchief.

J. P. Emery [30] has suggested some reasons for Othello's falling into a "traunce," which Iago says is an epileptic seizure. For one thing, the fit represents a flight from an appalling reality (or what Othello takes to be reality) into unconsciousness. For another, an epileptic seizure resembles a sexual ecstasy, and it is rather striking that Othello, who has just visualized Desdemona with Cassio "on her," should then himself alone have an emotional, orgasmic seizure, as though his fantasy aroused him sexually.

Analyses of particular passages for unconscious symbolism (although they may often seem implausible) represent another kind of bridge between what is going on "inside" the character (considered realistically) and the over-all, nonrealistic ordering, thematic and psychological, of the play as a whole. Analyses of passages link the play-as-portrait to the play-as-dream. Not unsurprisingly, it is in the psychoanalytic readings of *Othello,* the play that poses the problem of realism most exactly, that we can see most clearly the two ways to look at a play realistically and antirealistically at the same time: moving from the individual psyches of the characters to the psychological pattern of the play as a whole, first, through the mind of the audience, second, through particular details and speeches. But more of this anon.

PERICLES

The facet of *Pericles* that has most caught the psychoanalytic eye is the incest between Antiochus and his daughter which Pericles confronts in the form of a riddle. It may have been Dr. Max Kahane, in a discussion [1] of a preliminary section of Otto Rank's *Das Inzest-Motif,* who first called it to Rank's attention. Rank [2] pointed out that it is an almost classic statement of a recurring motif in folklore: the jealous father sets his daughter's suitor a riddle to solve (as in *The Merchant of Venice*). Hanns Sachs notes that the theme of *Pericles,* the return of a daughter to her father, runs all through the last plays. [3] The prolific Dr. Feldman suggests that since the princes slain as victims of Antiochus and his riddle are punished by the jealous father, the princess herself must represent the dramatist's mother. [4] In this, as in other Shakespearean plays (*The Comedy of Errors,* for example), the dramatist presents love in terms of food, another maternal motif. The twice-repeated image of the green treetop, Dr. Feldman says, is a phallic symbol. Unfortunately, his conclusions from these various insights are Oxfordian, nor do the other writers say enough about the play to make a coherent picture.

The only reading of the play to bring large segments of the action together is Dr. W. I. D. Scott's Jungian one. [5] Pericles, before he recognizes Marina in the final act, is suffering from stupor brought on by schizophrenia. The original cause was Pericles' horrified awareness of Antiochus' and his daughter's incest. Pericles responded to his discovery by a series of irrational acts because, in fact, he had been horrified to discover the possibility of incest in himself. Later, he fears that the sight of the nubile Marina will arouse these same guilty feelings, and he wishes her dead. Then Cleon tells him she is really dead, and he sinks into a stupor.

He can be revived from the stupor only by the assurance that Marina is so totally and absolutely pure that such incest would be impossible. Yet even after being aroused, he still suffers hallucinations (music, the voice of Diana) until he recovers his wife Thaisa. Symbolically, in the union of father, mother, husband, wife, and daughter, the various parts of Pericles' personality come together. In Jungian terms, Pericles cannot solve the war in himself between conscious and unconscious which was begun by Antiochus' incest until he forms a right relationship with his anima (Thaisa-Marina).

The reading is interesting in that it does bring together large portions of this rather scattered play. Unfortunately, though, there is little textual evidence for these assertions, and there is a good deal of wandering back and forth between the events of the play as external realities and as mere projections of Pericles' personality.

RICHARD II

It is hardly strange that the psychoanalytic critics find Richard II a quite neurotic character. Shrodes, van Gundy, and Husband see his breaking the mirror as a regressive, exhibitionistic response to frustration (not unlike an adolescent's throwing spitballs in the classroom).[1] L. A. G. Strong sees him as showing the neurotic's typical inability to tolerate delay.[2] He wishes to speed up gratification, and then he has to defend or pay back his attempts to speed up time by tardinesses, such as his coming back from Ireland a day late.

Rather more extensive is Professor James McPeek's analysis.[3] He finds three elements. First, Richard shows a strong streak of self-love: childish, full of self-pity, he loves to exhibit himself for the admiration of others (as in the mirror scene). Second, Richard is given to fantasies of omnipotence: he identifies himself with the sun and insists that the forces of nature are on his own side; he makes prophecies and preaches his own infallibility to Gaunt and York; he is interested in psychology as a means of controlling others; he likes rhetoric and ritual for their own sakes. Third, Richard's fantasy in prison is of a rebirth into airy nothingness. All these characteristics occur together in what Ernest Jones called the "God complex," and indeed, Richard identifies himself with Christ (although his Christian love turns sharply to hate when he is crossed—still another aspect of the God complex).

Two small details in *Richard II* have achieved psychoanalytic comment. Dr. Tannenbaum notes a Freudian slip.[4] The Duke of York is talking to the queen: he sends a servant to his sister-in-law, the Duchess of Gloucester, but the servant tells him he had called there earlier in the day and "An hour before I came the duchess died." York turns to the queen:

> How shall we do for money for these wars?
> Come sister—cousin I would say—pray pardon me.
>   (II.ii.105)

He calls his queen "sister" because, Dr. Tannenbaum says, the death of his sister-in-law is uppermost in his mind (or, we could guess, as a way of bringing her back into his presence).

The other detail that has come into the psychoanalytic purview is the little scene in which York pleads for the death of his son Aumerle—there are, needless to say, oedipal overtones. M. P. Taylor [5] has suggested that York is attempting to punish himself for his own guilt-ridden desertion of Richard II. York, he notes, equates his son's dishonor with his own:

> Mine honor lives when his dishonor dies,
> Or my shamed life in his dishonor lies.
>   (V.iii.70–71)

And Aumerle's mother says he is like his father: "He is as like thee as a man may be." Aumerle, in other words, stands for York.

Yet these five comments are not enough to give a coherent account of the play as a whole.

RICHARD III

There is somewhat more richness in the psychoanalytic treatments of *Richard III*. Not unsurprisingly, Otto Rank finds the play full of incest motifs.[1] Richard's killing of Anne's husband and father constitute two; then Richard by marrying her becomes, in effect, both husband and father to Anne, thus filling the other half of the oedipal pattern. Stanley's leaving his son behind as a hostage Rank takes as a disguise for feelings of revenge and hostility toward the son. In general, at the end of the play, the whole idea of civil strife is described in terms of incest killings:

> England hath long been mad and scarr'd herself:
> The brother blindly shed the brother's blood,
> The father rashly slaughtered his own son,
> The son, compell'd, been butcher to the sire.
>   (V.v.23–26)

According to Rank, the comparison sums up a basic pattern in Shakespeare's writings, the eroticization of political situations. In Shakespeare's use of the ghosts of the murdered victims, Rank says, we see a symbolization of the persistence into adult life of the son's infantile hostility against the father. Richard defeats himself, Rank says, through the guilt aroused by these visions.

From an Adlerian point of view stressing social factors, a criminal psychologist has analyzed Richard as an antisocial type (surely an understatement!). Dr. Charles Adler [2] sees Richard as a spurned child. Rejected by his mother, he turned to his father and strove to overtake his three older brothers. He sought success in acquisition and boldness. Egocentric, ambitious, more afraid of women than men, he tried to conquer his murdered opponents even to the point of possessing their women (Anne). Yet, even so, there are undertones of residual social feeling; Richard picks a bad moment to propose to Anne so that if he were refused he could blame it on social circumstances. Outwardly successful, Richard is inwardly always disappointed and insecure. The eclectic Ira S. Wile [3] sees Richard as perfectly exemplifying Adler's concept of organ inferiority. An organic deficiency (understatement as applied to Richard Crookback) leads to an inferiority complex and a compensatory reaction—a superiority complex. Sex becomes subordinate to the power motive (as in the wooing of Anne). Thus Richard represents the Adlerian "will to power" and "masculine protest."

Professor Murray Krieger has recently restated Freud's original insight, namely, that Richard turns sexual desire into lust for power, power into sex; each becomes the excuse and means to the other.[4]

Richard sufficiently dominates the play so that analyses of his personality virtually exhaust the play's possibilities. Even so, some writers have considered particular elements within the play, particularly the dreams. Ernest Jones [5] quoted the lines before and after Clarence's beautiful oceanic dream to show how Shakespeare knew the "appalling intensity" of the nightmare experience:

> As I am a Christian faithful man,
> I would not spend another such a night
> Though 'twere to buy a world of happy days—
> So full of dismal terror was the time.
>
> (I.iv.4–7)

> I, trembling, waked, and for a season after
> Could not believe but that I was in hell,
> Such terrible impression made my dream.
>
> (I.iv. 61–63)

Dr. Robert Fliess offers a far more technical comment on the dream: one based on the phenomenon of heard speech in dreams.[6] In discussing the occurrence of direct quotations, heard speech, in dreams, he hypothesizes that it comes from the superego (which indeed tends to manifest itself in auditory rather than visual terms—the "still, small voice" of conscience).

The ordinary dream represents the fulfillment of a pleasurable wish from the id distorted by the superego reduced to the role of a censor. Clarence's dream Dr. Fliess sees as representing an important variant. It is a "punishment dream" and hence represents the fulfillment not of an ordinary pleasurable wish, but a sadistic thrust from the superego which is masochistically enjoyed by the ego. There are, thus, two direct speeches in Clarence's dream:

> The first that there did greet my stranger soul
> Was my great father-in-law, renowned Warwick,
> Who spake aloud, *"What scourge for perjury*
> *Can this dark monarchy afford false Clarence?"*
> And so he vanished. Then came wand'ring by
> A shadow like an angel, with bright hair
> Dabbled in blood, and he shrieked out aloud,
> *"Clarence is come—false, fleeting, perjured Clarence,*
> *That stabbed me in the field by Tewksbury:*
> *Sieze on him, Furies, take him unto torment!"*
>   (I.iv.48–57)

In the first speech, Warwick's, we hear the voice of the superego (in the form of the parental father-in-law) threatening punishment. In the second speech we hear a representative of the dreamer's ego ("A shadow like an angel") masochistically invoking punishment. The second speech is more complex—it has a visual element. In it ego and superego join in affirming visually and aurally the dreamer's existence and identity: "Clarence is come." The superego element shows in the auditory hallucination and the self-observation; the ego element shows in the self-preservatory affirmation of the dreamer's identity and continued existence.

From so highly technical a point it is almost a pleasure to relax with one of Dr. Tannenbaum's Freudian slips.[7] Queen Elizabeth is inquiring about the well-being of the two princes in the tower:

> *Queen Elizabeth.* Master Lieutenant, pray you, by your leave,
>   How doth the prince, and my young son of York?
> *Lieutenant.* Right well, dear madam. By your patience,
>   I may not suffer you to visit them;
>   The king hath strictly charged the contrary.
> *Queen Elizabeth.* The king? Who's that?
> *Lieutenant.*   I mean the Lord Protector.
> *Queen Elizabeth.* The Lord protect him from that kingly title!
>   (IV.i.13–19)

Dr. Tannenbaum suggests that the lieutenant, Brakenbury, in speaking thus prematurely of Richard as the king, falls into a Freudian slip, but, being derived from the source, that it cannot be laid to Shakespeare's intuition about such things.

The last dreams, the night before the Battle of Bosworth Field, have indirectly drawn forth a comment. Gerald H. Zuk has considered Richard's final feelings of guilt (represented by his dream of his victims).[8] He sees Richard as a type of those who are "defeated by success" (Freud suggested Lady Macbeth was another such). So long, Zuk says, as Richard is plotting against a superior, he is successful. Once he becomes the leader himself, he falls apart. What has happened, Zuk suggests, is that once a forbidden wish is fulfilled (to replace the fatherlike authority of the king), the rebel's ego is overwhelmed by forces of conscience previously repressed.

From such scattered observations it is difficult to piece together a coherent psychoanalytic picture of the play. One thing seems clear: the play as a whole deals with the interaction of power and sexuality or, to put it another way, politics is understood as family conflict. Perhaps it is this dualism that underlies the others so sharply drawn in this early play: good and evil; natural and supernatural; inside and outside; words and things; people as souls, people as objects, and so on. If so, then the dual speeches in Clarence's dream would carry out the same mannerism, and also the formal dualism of the final dreams which promise defeat to Richard and triumph to Richmond. In this sense, the basic dualism of the play becomes Richard's attempt to master (through magical words or political power) what cannot be mastered that way: his physical self and his family constellation.

ROMEO AND JULIET

It is mildly surprising that *Romeo and Juliet* should not have caused more of a psychoanalytic stir with its interrelations of parents and children. Very few psychoanalytic commentators have spoken of it, however.

The first was Dr. Karl A. Menninger, who looked at the mistimings on which the tragedy depends.[1] He said *Romeo and Juliet* was a dramatic exposition of impulsiveness combining with hate to become self-destruction (as in "purposive accidents"). Romeo's impulsiveness causes Mercutio's death when Romeo suddenly intervenes in the fight between Mercutio and Tybalt. He causes his own banishment when he impulsively kills Tybalt. Again, suddenly returning from Mantua to Verona and rushing to conclusions in the tomb, he causes his own suicide and Juliet's. Such impulsiveness, says Dr. Menninger, arises from ill-controlled, partially disguised aggression. Very similar is L. A. G. Strong's 1954 comment on the play: [2] Romeo suffers from a neurotic inability to tolerate separation in time and space, and thus from his neurosis stem the mistimings, the too-soon's and too-late's that make up the tragedy.

In 1944 Theodore Reik commented on the theme of romantic love.[3] In general, from the chill standpoint of psychoanalysis, instantly, romantically, wildly falling in love constitutes an emergency defense against a situation in which one is in a great and general rush to get away from oneself and change personalities. Romeo, in other words, falls in love to escape a dangerous despair, a depression stemming from his rejection by Rosaline, and he happens on Juliet at just the right moment. Romantic love involves finding in someone else one's ideal of oneself, hence, a wish to be like, really to be this person. Such a wish gives rise to feelings of envy, hostility, and possessiveness, and love is the reaction against that envy and hostility.

In *Romeo and Juliet* the feud between the Montagues and Capulets stands for these hate elements in love, which in turn crop out in Juliet's ambivalence after Romeo has killed her cousin Tybalt. The interest in Romeo's name ("My name, dear saint, is hateful to myself") represents another mechanism in love, Reik says, the wish to destroy one's self and rebuild it out of the loved one:

> Romeo, doff thy name,
> And for thy name, which is no part of thee,
> Take all myself.

In general, Romeo has devalued his image of himself, and therefore must project his ideals and aspirations for himself outward onto someone else, namely, Juliet. Such a person "upon whom is projected ideals and aspirations, and not real values," harks back to one's childish love for an all-powerful, all-loving parent, whom one could not judge in real terms; such a lover therefore constitutes an "incest object," a forbidden love, just as Juliet is tabooed by the families' feud. Romeo's love, says Reik, is really a quite childish shifting back and forth between a regression to narcissism and a childish identification with the loved one.

Joseph L. Vredenburg has restated [4] Reik's insights, and Dr. Robert Fliess has also commented on the play as an instance of childish love, although only partially.[5] Fliess analyzes two speeches for the infantile tendency to see love objects in partial terms. For example, he treats the interview between Juliet and the nurse after that worthy lady has delivered her message to Romeo (II.v). The nurse, he says, is about twenty-eight or thirty-three, an energetic, loving person, not by any means aged. In her dialogue with Juliet, she complains first of a headache, then of a backache; she reminds Dr. Fliess of various female patients who had difficulty in accepting their femininity *in toto,* feeling it confined rather to some part of the body, usually the pelvis. The nurse is more interested in dinner than in Romeo, and Dr. Fliess finds in the juxtaposition another tendency to treat sex in partial terms, in this case, as simply oral.

Dr. Fliess also analyzes Mercutio's conjuration of Romeo:

> He heareth not, he stirreth not, he moveth not;
> The ape is dead, and I must conjure him.
> I conjure thee by Rosaline's bright eyes,
> By her high forehead and her scarlet lip,
> By her fine foot, straight leg, and quivering thigh,
> And the demesnes that there adjacent lie . . .
>   (II.i.15–20)

Mercutio recognizes that Romeo has surrendered himself or, in a psychoanalytic sense, has transformed his love of himself into love of Rosaline, and is therefore "dead." Mercutio tries to rouse Romeo by presenting Rosaline in partial terms, foot, leg, lip, and so on, separately. In both Mercutio's speech and the nurse's the loved one is considered piece by piece.

Although Dr. Fliess does not discuss the play as a whole, his readings bear an obvious relation to any over-all consideration. That is, *Romeo and Juliet* is a play of fragmented loves: the splitting up of the Capulets and Montagues, of Juliet and Paris, of Juliet and Romeo, of Romeo and Rosaline, and so on. Furthermore, the play makes much of the contrast between Mercutio's or the nurse's earthy approach to love and the idealism of the young lovers. In short, the tragedy as a whole is one of love taken in partial terms.

Dr. Fliess speaks of Mercutio and the nurse as though they were real people, and much of this book probes that particular issue: How realistically ought we to consider the people and events in Shakespeare's stylized plays? As a way into this question I have myself contributed an analysis of Romeo's little three-line dream: [6]

> *I dreamt my lady came and found me dead*
> (Strange dream that gives a dead man leave to think!)
> *And breathed such life with kisses in my lips*
> *That I revived and was an emperor.*
>   (V.i.6–9)

The dream is wholly and totally realistic in the sense that a psychological analysis shows it has all the properties a real dream has. It is sleep preserving; it is built out of "day residue"; it is a wish-fulfilling fantasy both in terms of Romeo's adult world and his hypothetical childhood at stages oral, phallic, and oedipal. But what sense does it make to speak of a "realistic" dream in so highly stylized and formal a work as *Romeo and Juliet?*

More of an answer will come in Chapters 11 and 12, but my suggestion in the essay was (and still would be) that a feeling or an idea that something is "realistic" seems objective, but isn't. Saying something in a play is "realistic" says as much about one's own perceptions as about the play, for realism, like beauty, is in the eye of the beholder. Yet, obviously, saying Romeo's dream is "realistic" is not so subjective or idiosyncratic a response as saying his dream is just like one I had three weeks ago. To talk critically about Romeo's dream one must sort out what in the perception that it is "realistic" is purely subjective and what is available to others. One can do this sorting by a verbal test: see whether the psychological description of the event (or character) can be phrased in words that apply to the total work, be they ordinary language or the technical terms of psychoanalysis.

For Romeo's dream, the word that links the dream (analyzed as though it were a real dream) to the stylized play around it is "reversal." Romeo's dream prophesies (by reversal) his own death, "Thus with a kiss I die." It is also a wish fulfillment which reverses his present precarious and loveless situation: he becomes an "emperor," a father, reversing his usual passivity. By his remarks on his own dream (that it is "strange") he becomes himself the ridiculing critic of his own passivity and dreaminess, again a wishful reversal of his usual situation, where others laugh at him for his dreaminess. As for phallic symbolism, his dream gives him an inexhaustible potency, in which intercourse simply produces new erections. Finally, at the deepest oral level, the dream turns Romeo's own death into being newly born: he becomes the emperor-child-father whose mother thrusts life into his lips. In short, analyzed as though it were a real dream, Romeo's dream operates at every level by the process of reversal. And such a psychological understanding accords even with the innocent theatergoer's: to him, too, this happy dream, coming as it does just before Romeo learns of his love's death, must seem a reversal.

But the tragedy as a whole—its psychological effect—is also a reversal, for what is *Romeo and Juliet* but the most exquisite expression of the child's inverted wish for love, "Wait till I'm gone. Then they'll be sorry." All through the tragedy we find oxymora and reversals. Friar Laurence sums up the theme:

Naught so vile that on the earth doth live
But to the earth some special good doth give;
Nor aught so good but, strained from that fair use,
Revolts from true birth, stumbling on abuse.

The action of the tragedy is the young love of Romeo and Juliet reversing their elders' old hate. "My only love, sprung from my only hate!" says Juliet, and then, at the end, the prince says:

Capulet, Montague,
See what a scourge is laid upon your hate,
That heaven finds means to kill your joys with love.

Even analyzed with all the armamentarium of modern psychoanalytic interpretation as though it were a real dream, Romeo's dream still fits into a highly stylized and formal tragedy: this is the paradox of literary realism.

Further (if I add my insight to the five preceding ones), the theme of reversal, swinging back and forth between diametric opposites, suggests a hypothesis about Shakespeare's early style. Both *Richard III* and *Romeo and Juliet* are early plays, and both show the same style: the magical use of words; sharp contrasts of good and evil, black and white, light and dark, or love and hate. If *Richard III* be an effort to master erotic problems by political action, then *Romeo and Juliet* represents an effort to master by erotic action a political problem (or quasi-political: the families' feud understood as a problem for Verona and the prince). It is possible that we have here a clue to the dualism and reversals characteristic of early Shakespeare (think of *The Comedy of Errors,* for example). Perhaps the crudities of the early plays represent attempts, so to speak, to divide and conquer—in psychological terms, to master ambivalence by splitting the love and hate, isolating them, and so gaining control over the various fantasies involved. But such a speculation takes us far beyond what has actually been established about the psychology of either *Richard III* or *Romeo and Juliet.*

THE SONNETS

Since the *Sonnets* are almost always treated by psychoanalytic writers as autobiography, we have already in Chapters 6 and 7 heard from almost all of the commentators: Freud, van Emde Boas, Feldman, Rank, and Wormhoudt. Although nonautobiographical psychoanalytic comment is sparse, there is, nevertheless, one extremely unusual study of the sonnet form *qua* form, which naturally discusses

Shakespeare's sonnets.[1] Psychoanalysis has considerable difficulty dealing with matters of pure form (for example, music), for such things are abstract and nonverbal, while psychoanalysis is preeminently a verbal science, at its best when dealing with images, symbols, and the like.

To convert the abstract eight-and-six form of the sonnet into images, Professor Clarissa Rinaker adopts a technique perhaps born of desperation: she analyzes the images critics use in talking about the sonnet form. The octave seems to suggest to most critics a kind of entrance, while the sestet represents an ebbing and flowing back. On this basis she finds that the sonnet forms a rhythm of ebb and flow, in and out, a rhythm almost sexual. For example, critics are likely to say things like "The emotional pitch of a sonnet cannot be long sustained, but should not be cut shorter either." Sonnets are often spoken of as penetrating the ear, and the sonnet is traditionally a vehicle for stories of love, often of forbidden love. These facts suggest to Professor Rinaker that the sexual rhythm of the form is linked with the ultimate forbidden love—the oedipus complex.

The traditional Petrarchan sonnet is divided into two and then divided into two again (4,4,3,3); this pattern suggests femininity, but also the duality of feelings, the ambivalences involved in this earliest affair with the parents. Shakespeare varied the traditional form, and a Shakespearean sonnet, "Instead of a union of two answering parts . . . has a steady and more prolonged forward movement through three quatrains with alternating and changing rhymes *abab cdcd efef,* and a sudden climax with the concluding couplet *gg.*" Both the Petrarchan and Shakespearean types work out oedipal feelings in an abstract form, and both suggest a rhythmic tension and climax, but the Shakespearean form seems to involve more masculine force and drive than the other. (The couplet dangling at the end may represent another "masculine" element.) The Petrarchan form seems to concentrate on moving toward and away from the mother's body, but the Shakespearean type, Professor Rinaker concludes, represents an identification with the rival father.

At the opposite end of the psychoanalytic spectrum from this purely formal analysis is Professor Gordon R. Smith's analysis of Sonnet 143, dealing purely with content.[2]

> Lo, as a careful housewife runs to catch
> One of her feathered creatures broke away,
> Sets down her babe, and makes all swift dispatch
> In pursuit of the thing she would have stay;
> Whilst her neglected child holds her in chase,
> Cries to catch her whose busy care is bent

> To follow that which flies before her face,
> Not prizing her poor infant's discontent—
> So runn'st thou after that which flies from thee,
> Whilst I, thy babe, chase thee afar behind;
> But if thou catch thy hope, turn back to me
> And play the mother's part, kiss me, and be kind.
> So will I pray that thou mayst have thy *Will*,
> If thou turn back and my loud crying still.

Professor Smith notes that the sonnet equates mature heterosexual love with the infantile love of child for mother. The poem, in other words, states an oedipal attachment and relates it to its mature counterpart; in particular, it conveys the feeling of helplessness in the lover as related to a child's feeling that he is helpless.

It is interesting to contrast these two radically different psychoanalytic readings with one of the rare behaviorist studies of literature. Professor B. F. Skinner's article on alliteration in the *Sonnets*,[3] distinctly not psychoanalytic, suggests what a behaviorist approach to poetry as "literary behavior" is like. Skinner analyzes the alliterative pattern in one hundred of the sonnets and concludes that the occurrence of alliteration is no greater than would occur by chance. He quotes Lewis Carroll's Duchess for Shakespeare's "philosophy of composition": "And the moral of *that* is, 'Take care of the sense, and the sounds will take care of themselves.'" In short, the behaviorist concentrates on measurable "behavior" rather than such supposedly imponderable factors as meaning, whether meaning be thought of in terms of form or content.

THE TAMING OF THE SHREW

Professor F. L. Lucas argues that Kate, in *The Taming of the Shrew*, has a masochistic need to be punished.[1] Theodore Reik suggests that Petruchio is really the tamed and deceived one—like the tinker Sly.[2]

THE TEMPEST

By contrast *The Tempest* seems fairly overrun with psychoanalysts. Otto Rank set out the basic insight, that Prospero is a jealous father, putting (as fathers do in myth, folklore, and life) obstacles in the way of his daughter's suitor.[1] Hanns Sachs probed the uncharted jungles of allegory.[2] Prospero, he says, is Shakespeare; the island is poetry ("noises that hurt not"), Miranda is art, Caliban is the rough style of the older Tudor dramatists, the clowns are Shakespeare's imitators, and Ferdinand is young John Fletcher. This, however, is hardly psychoanalytic criticism—or any kind.

Sachs is in safer territory when he stresses his psychoanalytic insights. *The Tempest,* like the other late plays, deals with a father-daughter relationship; it differs from the other romances in that here the daughter is given away, although Prospero commands abstemiousness. Shakespeare, Sachs says, embodied what he thought were his own weaknesses in the minor characters. He gave sibling rivalry to the villains and his animal nature to Caliban, who, in so far as he is a fish, is also a phallic symbol. The whole play, Sachs says, is about freedom and service; Prospero throws off servitudes, but he performs one last service for his daughter by leaving her to her lover.

K. M. Abenheimer supplies a Jungian reading of the play.[3] *The Tempest,* he says, like the other late plays, is concerned about problems of individuation, becoming an adult. The single figure of Prospero combines a human being with an archetype of the magician. On the human level, Prospero is neither an extravert (the Jungian term referring to one who turns to the outside world for satisfaction) nor an introvert (one who turns inward to himself). Instead, Prospero rejects both possibilities and expects his brother to treat him protectively like a child. When his brother betrays him, he is isolated on the island; symbolically, he isolates himself from society. He introjects the roles of both father and mother with respect to Miranda and so insulates himself from emotional reactions.

On the island, the various figures represent the personages of Prospero's psyche (conceived in Jungian terms). That is, Ariel is his anima (the feminine component in the unconscious): Ariel was derived from the mother figure Sycorax; he is bisexual (like the hero of the *Sonnets*); Prospero uses terms of endearment to him which thinly veil a feeling of possessiveness. In short, Abenheimer concludes, Ariel is an image of a kind of asexual parent. Miranda is like Ariel, but potentially a real woman. Caliban is Prospero's "shadow" (a Jungian term meaning the unconscious, but particularly the "dark reflection," the obverse of whatever trends the person emphasizes in his conscious mental life). Caliban shows the bestiality Prospero has repressed, and Prospero does not like him because he will not be repressed; that is, unlike Ariel and Miranda, he will not submit to Prospero's demands for gratitude. The ship's company represents people separating themselves from security and shelter (unconsciously the parents) and so maturing. The king suffers and repents; Gonzalo represents the good father; Ferdinand shows a healthy development toward individuation—he avoids Prospero's isolation; Antonio and Sebastian rebel against parental authority, committing an imaginary attack on the father; Stephano and Trinculo are like Caliban, shadow figures from Prospero's unconscious.

In the action of *The Tempest,* Abenheimer says, Prospero is transformed by the storm. His isolation is undone; his shadow, Caliban, and his anima, Ariel, are released. He is free to love. This much on the human level—at the same time, Prospero is a magician archetype. This recurring symbol in myths refers to a figure who enslaves the anima and controls the conscious mind (roughly the equivalent of magical thinking and omnipotence-of-thought fantasies in psychoanalytic terms). At the end of the play Prospero renounces magic, but, Abenheimer asks, is he really cured? Has he really become a fully developed independent human being? No. Prospero at the end of the play is too aloof. His attitude toward women shows no change. He is, in short, still possessed by the magician archetype. Abenheimer concludes with the idea that the appeal of *The Tempest* lies in the fact that paranoid problems are so common in our culture.

Dr. Harry Slochower sees *The Tempest* as a resolution of the *Hamlet* problem—or its dissolution.[4] *Hamlet* he considers an attempt to achieve an individualism which failed by becoming mere "play," because Hamlet, unable to cope with himself, tried to change the universe. Ferdinand, Slochower says, is a successful *Hamlet. The Tempest* turns all of reality into a play; the real world of politics and usurpation is given over for nature and the harmless elements replace the real world of politics and usurpation.

Theodore Reik, returning us to more explicitly Freudian readings,[5] sees Prospero and Caliban as splits of an ambivalent attitude toward the father. On the one hand, Prospero is noble, all-powerful, the victim of usurpation; on the other, he is a lecherous beast. They are Hyperion and the satyr again.

M. Othar Mannoni treats *The Tempest* as a study in colonialism.[6] In his brilliant analysis of the psychology of colonialism, Mannoni argues that the colonial situation does not create the colonial or settler mind—rather, there is a colonialist implicit in each of us. The colonial is, after all, an adult: he brings his own psychic needs with him, and it is these that create the colonial situation. The colony is simply a place where what was latent in a competitive society can become manifest.

The settler, typically, is a man of considerable powers, yet hobbled by feelings of guilt and inferiority (perhaps from an overly powerful father). A competitive society inevitably places some men in an inferior position: if such a type is one of them, society aggravates his feelings of inferiority. To cure the situation, he seeks power over others. Then, because this is not readily possible in a competitive society, he regresses to a solitude—a desert island in the world (or in the mind) where he can deal with his inner conflict externally by managing others; where he can acquire an almost magical power over monstrous animals or dependent natives, inner states now perceived as outer realities. The natives, in turn, find themselves cast in the role of dependents and inferiors, and they, too, react by regression. They become the obedient child, like Ariel or Friday. Or, if faced by exploitation or abandonment (the breakdowns of dependency), the native becomes the rebellious child, Caliban (or the cannibals in *Robinson Crusoe*).

The Tempest shows this colonial pattern, argues M. Mannoni, and, moreover, because Shakespeare himself had no colonial experience, it also shows how these patterns of dominance and dependence are potential in all of us. From what Prospero tells us of his former life in Milan, he could not accept either himself or other people or society as it in fact was. Instead, he retreated into a solitary quest for magical powers. Dethroned by a younger brother in alliance with the King of Naples (a father), Prospero recaptures his father status on the island: he bullies Ariel and Caliban.

In the first scene on the island we see him put aside his magic robe and try to treat Miranda as an equal, but he can't, and he soon lapses into bossing her as well. Toward Ariel he shows the absolute authority of a father, while Caliban ("got by the devil himself") is the unruly and incorrigible son he disowns.

Although it is Prospero who incestuously faces Miranda on the island, it is Caliban who embodies the forbidden desires and tries to rape her. Prospero's response is irrational, says M. Mannoni: you tried to violate my daughter, therefore you shall chop wood—instead of getting rid of Caliban or trying to correct him. The irrationality of Prospero's response suggests he has managed his own guilty desires by finding and punishing them in the dependent and inferior Caliban (So, M. Mannoni argues, colonials regularly do—certainly the highly sexualized racism of our own South bears him out.)

The action of the play is the renunciation of power and domination, and playing a symbolic role in this movement is Gonzalo's speech on the ideal commonwealth (which to many critics, as to me, has seemed an odd excrescence on the play). Gonzalo's Utopia images a regression like Prospero's to a magic world of childhood, but in Gonzalo's golden world the leader has no magic power. In fact, he is a doddering, impotent father, more than a little ridiculous. In effect, Shakespeare has re-created the *Hamlet* situation in *The Tempest:* brother ousts brother, the father is guilty, while another father is doddering and impotent (Gonzalo-Polonius). Revenge is thought instead of acted—a regression due to loss of real power. In *The*

Tempest Prospero reluctantly gives up his power (rather than simply lack it as Hamlet does). He hesitantly surrenders his daughter, releases Ariel (after just one more task), abjures his magic, and prepares to return to Milan where he will be Duke in name only, powerless, every third thought his grave, the very picture of the dispossessed colonial returned to his native land to die. In essence, to a man with the yearning to be the master of a colony of inferiors, accepting others as equals and the world as it is means in an all too painfully real sense giving up magical powers.

Professor Leo Lowenthal also approaches *The Tempest* as a sociological document, but, further, as an allegory of the structure of the psyche seen psychoanalytically.[7] Such "extra-human" characters in Shakespeare's works as Ariel and Caliban should be thought of, he says, as visible manifestations of psychic processes—like the gods in Homer. Prospero's relationship to his extra-human helpers can be understood as the ego's relationship to other psychic structures. Caliban is the id, primarily concerned with nourishment, resisting the performance of any useful work, promiscuous, irrational, equating freedom simply with creature pleasures. Ariel, on the other hand, is the superego, constantly engaged in considerate acts; he represents the aspirations, moral and aesthetic, every human being has. Prospero himself is the ego, ever trying to reconcile the other two psychic forces in an effort to master reality.

Professor Lowenthal's sociological description of the triad comes, it seems to me, somewhat closer than his psychological allegory to the action in *The Tempest.* That is, Caliban represents a wish to escape into a lethargy and apathy of unproductive behavior. Ariel represents an illusion of complete independence. Without a Prospero, both would perish.

Dr. W. I. D. Scott refines the id-ego-superego allegory.[8] He says Prospero confronts Caliban as an id, but Ariel as an ego ideal (a "thou shalt" as against a "thou shalt not," though derived, like the superego, from parental identifications). In Jungian terms, Caliban is the "shadow," reinforced by Antonio and Sebastian at a more subliminal level. Miranda is the ideal of womanhood, the anima, and Gonzalo is the archetypal wise old man.

As for particular details in *The Tempest,* a number of psychological critics have brought forth glosses. Alfred Freiherr von Winterstein, in one of the earliest studies,[9] notes the attachment of father and daughter and suggests that the flight from Milan covertly symbolizes a flight of father and daughter together away from the mother. Dr. Robert Eisler proposes that the fishy Caliban is a sexual symbol or phallic demon.[10] L. H. Allen sees in Prospero's putting Miranda to sleep (I.ii.186) one of a number of hypnotic gestures in the comedy.[11] Among others, he lists Ariel's "cure" of Alonso, Antonio, and Sebastian. Ariel, he says "hypnotizes" them into murder; then Ariel holds them and wakes them. Ira S. Wile [12] notes that Ferdinand and Miranda fall in love at first sight. He concludes that such a thing is possible if the parties are psychologically prepared, and he concludes that they were in *The Tempest.* Miranda, he somewhat indignantly says, had no such thing as a father fixation or an Electra complex; she just lived near her father. Moreover, he points out, she crosses him as she falls more in love with Ferdinand. Dr. Tannenbaum notes that Miranda is forbidden to divulge her name to Ferdinand, but when he bluntly asks, "What is your name?" she replies:

> Miranda. O my father,
> I have broke your hest to say so!

—"as pretty a *lapsus linguae,*" says Dr. Tannenbaum, "as may be found anywhere in literature." [13]

It might seem that this handful of readings is scattered like buckshot; actually, they come close enough together (even the Jungians) to define a target. They focus on three points. First, Freudians and Jungians alike seem to agree that the imaginary figures, Ariel, Caliban, and Sycorax, are projections of unconscious aspects of Prospero's personality, and although they name them differently, the aspects would seem to be the same. Second, all seem to agree that the play deals with the relationship of father to daughter which is, in turn, a working out in later life of the relationship of child to mother. Prospero's giving his daughter away seems to be, by everybody's standards, a gesture toward health. Third, and most important, despite their differing psychological orientations, all the critics agree that *The Tempest* is a play about the transformation of a mind (usually considered to be Prospero's, which in turn stands for Shakespeare's own). This transformation or individuation takes place through "play" (like Hamlet's) or dreaming or hypnosis. Although different interpreters find different degrees of success in Prospero's transformation, in all the interpretations it is a step toward freedom, surely a fitting enough conclusion for a play whose last three words are "Set me free."

TIMON OF ATHENS

An Adlerian, F. Plewa, approaches the play from the point of view of social forces in the emotional life of the individual.[1] In *Timon,*

Plewa says, Shakespeare shows that ostentatious benevolence and hateful neglect spring equally from the same root—vanity.

Although medical diagnoses of Shakespeare's characters (in the manner of Bucknill and Somerville) are not part of this study, I shall mention two of Timon because they coincide with a hint of Freud's. A. H. Woods [2] and W. I. D. Scott [3] both find Timon to be a man suffering from paresis or dementia paralytica, brain damage resulting from syphilitic infection. Woods sees Timon's generosity as a symptom; Scott relies on the prevailing imagery of prostitution and venereal disease.

As for particular details, Dr. Robert Fliess quotes I.i.206–211: [4]

> *Timon.* Wilt dine with me, Apemantus?
> *Apemantus.* No, I eat not lords.
> *Timon.* And thou shouldst, thou'dst anger ladies.
> *Apemantus.* O, they eat lords; so they come by great bellies.
> *Timon.* That's a lascivious apprehension.

The "lascivious apprehension" in question Dr. Fliess identifies as a common childish imagining that links eating to procreation: the child imagines that the female "eats" the male and so conceives.

TITUS ANDRONICUS

Out of the many mutilations in this early tragedy, Otto Rank picked the episode where Titus kills his son Mutius in anger and later must cut his hand off for it.[1] Rank compares this and the play in general to the group of folk tales in which the father amputates parts of the daughter when she refuses to give in to him. The folk tales, Rank says, relate, first, to the father's incestuous impulses toward the daughter, and, second, to the fantasy that a woman is a mutilated man. Similarly, J. C. Flügel [2] sees the play as a theme and variations on the castration complex—even the rape of Lavinia. Rape, notes Flügel, can symbolize the "castration" of the mother, here followed by cutting out her tongue, again symbolizing the castration of the penis the child in earliest innocence imagines for its mother. Flügel notes also that many of the details and references in the play remind one of the myth of Tereus and Procne, notably dismembering bodies and serving the sons up to be eaten by the father.

Perhaps following Flügel's mythic suggestion or the play's reference to Philomel, William H. Desmonde notes the following elements in *Titus:* [3] a struggle between two princes for kingship, followed by the death of the old king; a human sacrifice to propitiate a dead soul; marriage by capture in which the son is killed; a rape near a pit; a cannibalistic meal. These elements he identifies as ritual fragments. The struggle for kingship, the eating of Demetrius and Chiron, and the proclaiming of Lucius as emperor, he says, all correspond to features of the Feast of Tantalus. They could also be a re-enactment of what Freud called the "primal crime" in which the horde of brothers rose up against, slew, and feasted upon the father. In such a case they would be related to the slaying, dismemberment, and eating of Dionysus. The rape in or near a pit is an element in Persephone rituals. All together, Desmonde concludes, the various elements in the plot of *Titus Andronicus* make up parts of the Lesser and Greater Eleusinian Mysteries. Shakespeare, he says, could have gotten at this esoteric lore through some Roman source such as Ovid. The recurrence of these themes, however, does not simply imply that Shakespeare was fond of folklore; rather, it stems from the recurrence in every generation of the oedipal situations narrated in the myths.

Professor Gordon R. Smith has considered the character of the villain.[4] He finds Aaron the Moor has simply two layers: he does evil without cause; he loves his child and its color. Professor Smith finds he resembles a hardened felon described by the European criminologist Hans Brennecke. As a result of the birth of a child, the man felt remorse, confessed, but then resumed his criminal career. In effect, his repressed father love was released, but there was a later re-repression of his love feelings. Aaron, however, shows only love for the child, no remorse. The reason, suggests Professor Smith, is that he became what the people around him wanted him to be—a black devil. Hence he felt no guilt, no reproach from the superego. His child, being black, he justifies and accepts just as he justifies and accepts his own color. In other words, both the good in him (love for his black child) and the evil spring from his color.

J. C. Flügel, in addition to suggesting the general importance in *Titus* of the theme of castration (see above), comments on one particular speech.[5] In an aside while discussing the significance of speech as a symbol for genital creativity and the tongue as a creative member like the phallus, he quotes Marcus' speech * in the final scene:

> You sad-fac'd men, people and sons of Rome,
> By uproars sever'd, as a flight of fowl
> Scatter'd by winds and high tempestuous gusts,
> O, let me teach you how to knit again
> This scatter'd corn into one mutual sheaf,

* Flügel assumes (following Capell) that the speech is all Marcus', although the quartos and folios assign parts of it to others.

These broken limbs again into one body;
[Lest] Rome herself be bane unto herself,
And she whom mighty kingdoms curtsy to,
Like a forlorn and desperate castaway,
Do shameful execution on herself.

*   *   *   *

(*To Lucius*) Speak, Rome's dear friend, as erst our ancestor,
When with his solemn tongue he did discourse
To love-sick Dido's sad attending ear
The story of that baleful burning night
When subtle Greeks surpris'd King Priam's Troy.
Tell us what Sinon hath bewitch'd our ears,
Or who hath brought the fatal engine in
That gives our Troy, our Rome, the civil wound.
My heart is not compact of flint nor steel;
Nor can I utter all our bitter grief,
But floods of tears will drown my oratory
And break my utt'rance . . .

Marcus uses images of mutilation and dismemberment ("broken limbs," for example) to describe civil strife, particularly that caused by divisive speech ("By uproars sever'd"). While the "body of the state" is, of course, a Renaissance cliché, the passage does bear out Flügel's point: that confused speech tends to symbolize castration. Indeed, Flügel says, the reference to Sinon directly images castration, for, he says, Sinon castrated himself as part of the stratagem of the wooden horse (I have no idea what account of the Trojan war he bases this assertion on). Sinon aside, the penetration of the horse into the city and the subsequent sacking of the city symbolize the rape of the mother ("our Rome" of which we are "sons"), the punishment for which is castration.

We may grant that the theme of castration is at least important, but aside from that observation psychoanalytic writers have not given a cohesive account of the play. But then perhaps the less said about *Titus Andronicus* the better.

TROILUS AND CRESSIDA

There is but one psychoanalytic comment on this provocative and difficult play. Fritz Wittels [1] gives Shakespeare's Cressida (along with Delilah, Helen of Troy, Cleopatra, Lucrezia Borgia, and Brunhild) as an example of the woman of destructive beauty, the narcissistic woman who cannot turn her love to objects outside herself. "They conquer—they cannot be conquered; they possess—they cannot be possessed."

TWELFTH NIGHT

One would expect *Twelfth Night,* with its girl-disguised-as-boy motif, to have excited a good deal of psychoanalytic interest, but not so. There are no treatments of the play as a whole, only of parts, especially the characters.

Ira S. Wile translates Olivia's statement that Malvolio is "sick of self-love" into psychological terms: Malvolio is a narcissist.[1] Actually, however, as Professor Melvin Seiden suggests,[2] the picture may be more complicated. So far from being "sick of self-love," Malvolio may suffer from the lack of same. With his work ethic, he represents the policeman, the superego, of the *Twelfth Night* world. He must deny the antisocial drives of the other characters and in general put down the natural man. To do so, he must learn to deny them in himself; he must be sharply self-critical. If he really loved himself more, he would love his policeman's work less. As it is, he lacks a confident air of authority; his attempts to rule reveal self-hatred and a sense of inferiority.

L. A. G. Strong sees the various characters as using fantasies to protect themselves.[3] Orsino is "the perpetual adolescent," the man who will not grow up. He uses a "shadow love" for an inaccessible woman as a defense against real love. Olivia uses her vow of mourning for her brother as a defense against love that would "shake her spirit to its depths," as when she becomes infatuated with the disguised Viola. Malvolio uses a dream of power and conquest to compensate for a position too low for his gifts—at least, as he sees them.

Dr. W. I. D. Scott [4] suggests that Orsino is suffering from a mother fixation, and that is the reason he dotes on Olivia who here acts as a mother substitute (older, according to Dr. Scott, dominating, and unavailable). Viola, the girl-boy, exactly meets his needs. She matches his own preheterosexual stage of development.

Dr. Scott argues that Olivia's self-assigned seven years of mourning for her brother is not simply a device to put off Orsino. Rather, she is frigid and would have behaved the same way with another suitor. Perhaps because her brother was an older, dominating man, she sees men in power as taboo. Her desire can only be awakened by a very young man, to whom no taboo attaches.

Three speeches have produced particular comment. For example, Malvolio is conjuring up images of himself as ruler of the estate: "I frown the while, and perchance wind up my watch, or play with my —some rich jewel." Dr. Tannenbaum [5] notes the slip (as, indeed, others had before him): Malvolio reaches by force of habit for his steward's chain, then suddenly realizes this normally dignified gesture does not fit his present fantasy. Dr. Tannenbaum adds the idea that his referring to his watch may have led him unconsciously to the chain.

Dr. Robert Fliess [6] picks out the dialogue between Viola and the clown at the opening of Act III. Their "dallying with words," he suggests, stems from infantile sources: the tendency to treat words as things (but surely this could be said of many of Shakespeare's wit sallies). More interesting are his remarks on:

> *Viola.* Hold, there's expenses for thee.
>
>   *   *   *   *
>
> *Clown.* Would not a pair of these have bred, sir?
> *Viola.* Yes, being kept together and put to use.
> *Clown.* I would play Lord Pandarus of Phrygia, sir, to bring a Cressida to this Troilus.
>
>   (III.i.49–59)

He notes that the dialogue relates two common infantile fantasies (which appear also in *The Merchant of Venice*). Since money has for adults the precious value a child attributes to feces, the notion that money can breed would seem to be related to childhood fantasies that feces are living things. The idea of money breeding may also be linked to the child's anal confusions about the facts of life and where babies are made.

VENUS AND ADONIS

It is hardly suprising that the mythological *Venus and Adonis* has received a Jungian comment. Venus, says Peter Dow Webster,[1] is a universal mother figure, a symbol for the genital sexuality represented by the two horses and repudiated by Adonis. At the end, we see Venus in the role of mother, forgiving and loving. Webster links the poem to Bergler's thesis that the writer writes as a defense against his own wish to be caused pain by the mother.

THE WINTER'S TALE

This romance, which conventional critics interpret in terms of seasonal myths and rituals, from a psychoanalytic point of view is an incest play (as, indeed, from a psychoanalytic point of view the rituals are). Otto Rank notes in old Leontes' casting youthful eyes at Perdita an incest motif.[1] In effect, the mother-wife has become young again and is desired in the daughter. The recovery of Hermione and her (in effect) second marriage with Leontes disguise the incestuous wish to marry Perdita. Rank compares Shakespeare's heavily disguised treatment with Greene's *Pandosto,* where the motif is more openly developed.

K. M. Abenheimer notes, "It seems rather symbolic that the mother-fixed youth (Mamillius) has to disappear for good, for this is the problem in all the three late comedies, how the mother fixation can effectively be conquered without paranoid sham solutions." [2]

In another (more or less) Jungian treatment, L. A. G. Strong [3] sees the statue symbolism as crucial. That is, Leontes has an inferiority complex and for this reason believes his wife is unfaithful to him. In effect, his unjust and jealous suspicions freeze his wife's affections— she becomes a statue. Then it is not until Leontes can welcome back the rejected feminine side of his nature (in the form of Perdita) that Hermione can "thaw" back into warmth and love.

Clearly, the particular topic of Leontes' jealousy challenges any psychological reading of the play. J. I. M. Stewart, who argues the general point that where one part of a Shakespearean play seems not to make naturalistic sense, the total configuration makes a psychological sense, applies this view to Leontes' sudden and improbable jealousy which starts the action.[4] Stewart quotes Freud to show that there are three kinds of jealousy: first, "normal"; second, projected (in which one projects one's own impulses to infidelity on the partner); third, delusional (which is a radical defense against tender impulses toward another man: "I do not love him; *she* loves him"). Leontes' jealousy, he says, combines the projected and delusional forms. He cites J. Dover Wilson for the proposition that Camillo had assisted Leontes in "covert immoralities" plus two passages from the play. Leontes says to Camillo:

> I have trusted thee, Camillo,
> With all the nearest things to my heart, as well
> My chamber-councils, wherein, priest-like, thou
> Hast cleansed my bosom, I from thee departed
> Thy penitent reformed.

And later, the king asks one of his attendants,

> How came the posterns
> So easily open?
> *Lord.*   By his [Camillo's] authority,
> Which often hath no less prevailed than so
> On your command.
> *Leontes.*   I know't too well.

Professor Stewart would seem to be reaching a bit here, and needlessly so, for the impulse alone could trigger Leontes' irrational jeal-

ousy. That is, either having been unfaithful himself or having wished
to be, Leontes projects the impulse on his wife. The delusional element stems from Leontes' "twinn'd boyhood" with Polixenes. There
must have been in their close friendship tender impulses; these are reactivated by Polixenes' visit; and Leontes "projects upon his wife the
desires he has to repudiate in himself." To justify his delusions, Leontes picks on the mild flirtations permitted by ordinary courtesy. Because his jealousy is irrational, it is dangerous to dispute it, as
Camillo finds. In short, Professor Stewart concludes, Shakespeare
sacrificed literal truth to give the play the "demonic quality" of myth
and folk tale, highly appropriate to a winter's tale.

W. H. Auden puts the matter more succinctly: "Leontes is a classical
case of paranoid sexual jealousy due to repressed homosexual feelings." [5] That is, Leontes is defending against his own sexually tinged
affection for Polixenes by saying, "I don't love him; she (Hermione)
does." As he says to her at the trial, "Your actions are my dreams."

Dr. W. I. D. Scott follows Stewart in his psychoanalytic account of
Leontes' jealousy.[6] Scott adds evidence by pointing to Leontes'
speech (very obscure and troubling to commentators) which expresses his mounting jealousy as a perfect unconscious description of
the process of paranoid projection. ("Affection," Dr. Scott correctly
points out, here means "affect" or "feelings.")

> Affection, thy intention stabs the center!
> Thou dost make possible things not so held,
> Communicat'st with dreams—how can this be?
> With what's unreal thou coactive art,
> And fellow'st nothing. Then 'tis very credent
> Thou may'st co-join with something; and thou dost,
> And that beyond commission, and I find it,
> And that to the infection of my brains
> And hardening of my brows.
>   (I.ii.138–146)

The speech says feelings can contradict one's ordinary notion of possibility; feelings can speak with dreams (that is, the unconscious).
Feelings can build on nothing, and thus it is easy to accept the fact
they can act with something (here, the skimpy evidence of Hermione's infidelity). They therefore go beyond actual fact or conscious
control ("commission"), destroying my ability to reason. Other
meanings for the speech are possible, but, read this way, the speech
shows Leontes' unconscious awareness of what he is doing, namely,
projecting his paranoid jealousy (although he rationalizes his projection).

Although Dr. Scott agrees with the Freudian readings such as Stewart's, he goes further, bringing in a Jungian regeneration. (Surely there is a final irony in this long summary's both opening and closing with Jungian accounts.) Following the critic John Vyvyan, Scott takes the scenes in Bohemia as allegorical of a religious or Jungian cure. In this reading all the characters and locales are to be understood as aspects of Leontes. Bohemia, in particular, is the world of the soul, and the sea around it is the defenses unconsciously set up. Perdita and Hermione constitute the pure and good anima archetype, while Paulina is Leontes' superego, or, in Jungian terms, his "helpful shadow." We are left, as we began, with the basic dichotomy of psychological literary criticism: Are the characters and events of a play to be considered as realistic portrayals of personalities? Or are they to be considered as projections and aspects (not necessarily realistic) of a single psyche?

"This," said Chaucer's Friar, "is a long preamble of a tale." In the course of the past four chapters we have looked at well over four hundred comments on Shakespeare's works, ranging from whole books to single sentences, some applied to Shakespeare's personality, some in the service of theory, some straighforward explications of the works. As we agreed at the outset, to many people all this will seem an index and obscure prologue to the history of lust and foul thoughts; to others, I hope, it will suggest the positive contribution that psychoanalytic criticism may make and, to some extent, has made. So far as Shakespeare is concerned, the psychoanalytic critics have given us a moderately clear picture of the poet's personality, scattered insights into twenty-two plays and two poems, and, in addition, full accounts of eleven major plays. To come out with that net profit, I have been sifting wheat from chaff as we went along, while we were still close to the individual plays and their interpretations: what remains is to make the criteria explicit.

In all this mass of commentary one glaring omission will immediately strike the literary historian—the psychoanalytic critics, virtually without exception, have failed utterly to take into account the role of convention, for example, in the shift in Shakespeare's last plays toward romances of reconciliation, centered about the relationship of father and daughter. While changes in the audience's tastes or in conventions could explain such a trend, perhaps the literary historian tends to overrate convention. Surely Shakespeare was enough his own master, both financially and as a writer, to toss a convention aside had it not fitted his own needs as a poet and his feelings as a father. Equally certainly, however, the psychoanalytic critic tends to overrate the effect of the individual psyche and underrate the importance of convention. Shakespeare's works—or any writer's—must inevitably represent an interaction of his single mind with the collective mind of his day expressed in the conventions and tastes of his audience. The psychoanalytic critic should try to explain what conventions accomplish, why something appeals in 1610 but not in 1600. But psychoanalytic critics have up till now, as Ernst Kris complained, passed by such questions as form or the effect of culture on expression.

Granted, then, that this omission weakens some of this large body of criticism, what are the other criteria for evaluating a psychoanalytic reading? We can put the question in two halves: How do the various types of psychoanalytic readings rank? Given two readings of the same type, how does one choose between them? For example, as we saw at the end of Chapter 7, other things being equal, a study which deals with all the work tells us more than a study which deals with only a part; although, of course, one can put a series of partial studies into a coherent view of the whole (as we did with *Coriolanus, Hamlet,* the *Henry IV* plays, *Julius Caesar, King Lear, Macbeth, Merchant of Venice, Othello, Richard III, Romeo and Juliet,* and *The Tempest*).

Character studies necessarily deal with only a part of the play and are therefore less useful than studies of the play as a whole. Indeed, character studies, as we shall see, may be useful at all only in that they identify "latent impulses" of the character which may be considered as stimuli to or projections of latent impulses of the audience. To deal with all the play, a psychoanalytic study would have to deal at length with the poetry—and unfortunately very few do. Finally, those analyses which can show a unity, a resolution of the playwright's or audience's unconscious impulses and defenses, have done more than those which merely identify them (although whether or not there is such a thing as a "unity of affect" is ultimately an empirical question).

As for evaluating two different studies of the same kind (total or partial), we need to decide: How farfetched is the link the critic makes between the play and psychoanalytic theory? For example, to use Hamlet's remark to Claudius, "Farewell, dear mother," to support his matricidal reading, Dr. Wertham must construe Hamlet's nasty little joke as an unconscious slip. Coriat suggests that the weird sisters have hypnotized Macbeth. Lowenthal sees Ariel as a "superego," although Ariel only once makes a moral statement and never commands Prospero, his "ego." Such readings involve a wrenching of the play to reach the psychoanalytic "law." Contrast Rank's handling

of the play within the play as a "peeping": watching stage plays almost always has this symbolic meaning in dreams; the reading, therefore, is not farfetched at all.

The temptation is strong, however, for anyone new to the psychoanalytic description of the mind to reject such a reading because the
psychoanalytic idea itself seems farfetched. (Naturally.) For example, Hamlet's mother says of him after his tiff with Laertes at Ophelia's grave:

> And thus a while the fit will work on him.
> Anon, as patient as the female dove
> When that her golden couplets are disclosed,
> His silence will sit drooping.

Miss Sharpe glosses the lines as an anal simile. Gertrude's image, in
its unconscious aspect, depicts Hamlet first with a "fit"; then, anon,
"His silence will sit drooping." As for the "golden couplets," the twin
fledglings, children commonly confuse the act of giving birth with the
act of elimination, and we have already seen several times the close
link in the unconscious between things precious and the common
muck. Miss Sharpe's reading, although fragmentary, does interrelate
all the words it deals with and in turn relates the single image to the
play as a whole: Miss Sharpe finds a whole series of body metaphors
in *Hamlet,* particularly anal ones, and a recurrent contrast between
purity and physical birth. She sees the total action of *Hamlet* as a
body metaphor: first, the waiting and hesitating fits and starts, then
sudden action and relief. Her reading, in other words, fits the play as
a whole, and it is not, in the literal sense, farfetched.

Even so, any sensible man would say it is a crazy reading. In other
words, any "sensible" man would fall into the temptation of rejecting
the reading because what he really rejects is the psychoanalytic description of the mind it involves. We find it hard to believe that children (and the child in us) fantasy a great deal about their bodies and
those of parents and siblings, particularly the parts of those bodies
adults are not supposed to think about—much. We find it hard to accept as normal and virtually universal in childhood such lurid fantasies as the belief that the mother has a phallus; the confusion of
womb and anus, giving birth and defecation; the fear of castration;
and particularly the child's fears and fantasies about his parents' sexual intercourse. Even harder to accept is the idea that the child in us,
our unconscious self, still thinks about these things, still reacts to reality in ways shaped by these grotesque drives and fantasies. Our very
adulthood is predicated on the belief that such fantasies do not exist
in us, on repression and defense, in other words. Our whole adult be-

ing resists this kind of reading. Yet the evidence from couch and clinic for these propositions is at least powerful, if not downright overwhelming. We would do wrong to give in to wishing truths away, least of all the most painful truths of self-knowledge.

If we grit our teeth, then, the criteria for evaluating psychoanalytic readings come down to two. Does the study take into account all the play or only a part? How farfetched is the link the critic makes from the play to the psychoanalytic interpretation (*not* how odd the psychoanalytic interpretation seems)? Applying these criteria leaves us with a long series of insights into the plays, even many of the scattered ones being worth while.

For example, Otto Rank says that Shakespeare tends to eroticize political situations, to reunderstand them as family conflicts (the castration theme of *Titus Andronicus* being a variant). Rank is telling us something quite interesting about the poet and also about our reactions to the early history plays. Rank's insight (that the bed tricks in *All's Well* and *Measure for Measure* dramatically represent taboos and inhibitions) also suggests a factor in our response or Shakespeare's use of dramatic "tricks" both to express and evade defenses. Similarly, Dr. Feldman's account of *The Comedy of Errors,* while its eccentricities render it only fragmentarily sound, nevertheless shows an oedipal problem resolved by a splitting which both solves the conflict and punishes the participants—another important hint at the function of dramatic "gimmicks." J. I. M. Stewart's explanation of Leontes' jealousy as a defense against his own femininity seems sound. He suggests not only an aspect of Shakespeare's interest in betrayal but also the way this one "unmotivated" element in *The Winter's Tale* related to the theme of woman so important throughout that romance. In *Midsummer Night's Dream,* recognizing the primal scene element in the lover's chase and alternation relates that middle plot to the Bottom-Oberon-Titania triangle; it also brings the middle of the play together with the play within the play at the end and the nuptial theme which brackets the play as a whole. Gordon R. Smith's oedipal reading of Sonnet 143 and Robert Fliess' analyses of pregenital imagery in the verse show us in action the poet's "laxity of repression" or "regression in the service of the ego."

In short, even the scattered insights, when they are sound, open our eyes to new affective relationships within and without the plays and poems. Naturally, still more insight becomes possible when we turn from these fragmentary interpretations to those plays about which psychoanalytic critics have written enough so that we can see the play as a whole. We can see, for example, in the early plays, *Richard III* and *Romeo and Juliet,* Shakespeare's almost crude use of splitting into sharp dualities of good and evil, love and hate, black and white apparently as a defensive device to master sexual drives and drives toward power. The plays' situations of fear or other strong emotions come about when these drives directly conflict or coincide, in other words, when the splitting fails in some way. One can guess that behind this defensive maneuver lies a wish or need on Shakespeare's part to separate a father's power from a mother's sexuality. *The Merchant of Venice* shows this splitting of father and mother most clearly: between the castrating father in the masculine, aggressive world of Venice and the bountiful, giving mother in the feminized, libidinal world of Belmont.

After the sharply dualized early plays, the plays of the middle period fall into two groups: those which stress power struggles among men, typically fathers and sons (*Julius Caesar,* the *Henry IV* plays), and those in which a woman's presence eroticizes such a power struggle—the woman's presence seems either to disarm the conflict, turning it into romantic comedy, or to make a serious play more terrible yet (*Hamlet, Lear, Othello, Macbeth, Troilus and Cressida*).

The *Henry IV* and *Henry V* plays instance *par excellence* the father-son pattern: Hal by his "low" conduct rebels against his father, but he also defensively fights for his father against "rebels" outside the family circle. Falstaff represents both a substitute father and a narcissistic, gluttonous baby. Hal achieves the status of hero-king when he himself becomes the king-father in the image of his true father, but tempered with some of Falstaff's childish sense of fun. In effect, he himself becomes the combined father and child. *Julius Caesar,* too, deals with the rebellion of "sons" against a father who then takes his revenge; Shakespeare returns to the early device of splitting, but here seems to be saying it doesn't work. Precisely the difference between Brutus and Cassius, the fact that they are split, not one, defeats them (by contrast with the unity-in-self achieved by Prince Hal).

It may seem odd to link Lear to Falstaff, but to judge from the psychoanalytic readings, the foolish knight is an avatar of the mad king. Both seek omnipotence: "They told me I was everything." "Banish plump Jack and banish all the world." Both are old men, "fathers," who yet seek to have, as a child would, "all th'addition to a king," "the laws of England . . . at my commandment." Lear's situation, however, is eroticized in a way that Falstaff's is not. He combines in himself a child's wishes both dependent and incestuous toward his daughter-mothers, and this inner conflict brings him down. Shakespeare repeatedly reveals a feeling that women are somehow deadly, dangerous, for which his tendency to idealize and ennoble women (as pointed out, for example, by Alfred Harbage) is an almost-too-obvious defense.

Macbeth shows this fear most clearly. A "son," prompted by half-masculine "mothers," kills a father (Duncan) and becomes a father (king) himself. Then sons "unknown to woman," "none of woman born," kill that bad son-become-father. Such a feeling, that the influence of woman is dangerous, seems to grow from the classical oedipus conflict, but even more deeply from the son's effort in the feeding situation of earliest infancy to achieve an identity separate from a destroying mother, one who might turn her love for the babe that milks her into hatred that dashes its brains out.

Coriolanus also shows this oral root—the infant hero longing to prove his identity separate from a frustrating mother becomes the adult boiling with hostility, trying to find the right context for it and, in the process, trying to find his own identity. His mother's words, "This fellow had a Volscian to his mother," strike at that very identity; they are what finally drive him to death.

Othello is another middle-period play in which the presence of a woman eroticizes and makes more terrible what might have been simply an aggressive struggle between two men. From the point of view of character, Othello doubts his own virility, while Iago unconsciously seeks a woman in his master. In a less realistic way, Iago projects Othello's doubts while Desdemona projects his feminine self. The psychoanalytic picture is not unlike the problem of omnipotence that dogs Lear and Falstaff: Othello is defeated by the outward embodiments of an inner effort to have it both ways.

Hamlet, too, deals with this problem and the dangerous eroticization of a struggle between father and son by the presence of a mother. Here the psychoanalytic readings are particularly numerous and rich. They show, first, the oedipal pattern of the play, then the way in which that conflict (be it Hamlet's, Shakespeare's, or ours) is split and projected onto a variety of fathers and sons. But this effort to push the inner crisis out into various kinds of "play" fails catastrophically.

The Tempest handles in a final way the same pattern the psychoanalytic readings find all through Shakespeare's plays: the aggressive conflict between men and the libidinal danger from women. The oedipus complex takes the form (as in *Lear*) of a father's love for his daughter. Initially, Prospero combines in himself the father possessing the daughter-mother and also the father-as-ruler avenging himself on those who would steal his power or his love from him. As in *Hamlet,* the inner conflict pushes its way through splits and projections to the outer reality of the play—the island. There, the father-teacher-king-magus controls it, and by this outer control achieves an inner one: he gives up his libidinal attachment to his daughter and foregoes his opportunity for vengeance on his "sons." In a very literal way, he is set free from the schism that runs through all of Shakespeare's works.

But what about the schism in the psychoanalytic studies of Shakespeare? When we bring a series of psychoanalytic comments together this way, it becomes all too painfully clear that there is a split right down the middle of psychoanalytic criticism. This split, in fact, appeared in Freud's very first analysis of Shakespeare, in that letter of October 15, 1897, in which he pointed out the oedipal nature of Hamlet's task. *Oedipus Rex* Freud treated in terms of a totality, the several characters and events working out a general psychoanalytic pattern. *Hamlet,* however, he saw as a realistic portrayal of a particular man going through a particular crisis. Realism and antirealism— Freud's inconsistency at this crucial juncture may reflect his special preoccupation with "poetic license" and his feeling that writers are in some sense preternaturally powerful beings, but the same inconsistency runs through all subsequent psychoanalytic criticism, not only of Shakespeare but of other authors as well.

One kind of psychoanalytic criticism uses psychological knowledge to explain character, motive, and the like realistically: Lady Macbeth's sleepwalking and handwashing; Othello's uncertainty about his virility and Iago's homosexual jealousy; Hamlet's oedipus complex. The other kind deals with the relations among the parts of the play (high plot and low, for example) and treats the play as the projection and interaction of different psychic impulses and defenses: Macbeth and Lady Macbeth as "divided halves" of a single personality, two complementary kinds of oedipal crime and oedipal guilt; Othello and Iago as dovetailing kinds of self-deception; *Hamlet* (the play, not the prince) as working out an over-all pattern of regression from an oedipal crisis. The first method, essentially realistic, is drawn to the realer aspects of the plays, in particular, the characters; the second method, essentially antirealistic, is drawn to the more folkloric aspects, the ghosts and prophecies, Iago or Ariel, as projections of psychic impulses much the way criticism has always thought of the gods in Homer or Euripides. We have come, in other words, to an old crux in conventional Shakespearean criticism—between those who see Shakespeare as a realistic dramatist and those who see him as still close to the medieval traditions and the style of folklore.

One could, I suppose, rationalize the two by quoting Marianne Moore's famous definition of poetry as presenting "for inspection imaginary gardens with real toads in them," but I fear the methods are too far apart for a simile to bridge them. One view, the realist's, assumes that Shakespeare shows us pictures of real people; the opposite method assumes that Shakespeare does not so much depict real people as aspects of real people. In other words, one group of psychoanalytic critics assumes that the life of a Shakespearean play lies in the lifelikeness of its separate parts. The other group sees the life of the play in its totality. Unless we can make some sense out of this inconsistency, we can make no sense out of psychoanalytic criticism.

[*Part III*]

CONCLUSIONS:
PSYCHOANALYSIS,
SHAKESPEARE,
AND THE
CRITICAL MIND

[*10*]

Conclusions Logical

THE basic question that cuts psychoanalytic criticism of Shakespeare down the middle is: whether to treat a play as a realistic portrayal of psychological events outside itself or as itself a psychological event. These two approaches would seem mutually exclusive. It would seem that, logically, the psychoanalytic critic cannot have it both ways—he must choose. But which? To decide, we need to look at the three kinds of psychoanalytic criticism.

There is a fourth kind—you might call it the here-a-phallic-symbol-there-a-phallic-symbol school. When, for example, a Shakespeare class comes upon a passage like this from *Othello:*

> Behold, I have a weapon.
> A better never did itself sustain
> Upon a soldier's thigh,

and some student puts up his hand and says, "Professor Weltschmerz, isn't that a phallic symbol?" and the rest of the class goes, "Ooh" with psychic lights flashing, bells ringing, and sirens sounding as though something very profound had been said—nothing very profound has been said. The student has not made clear to whom Othello's sword is a symbol or what such a symbol would accomplish in the play. In short, he has abandoned the first axiom of psychoanalytic criticism.

The first thing the psychological critic must recognize is that psychology as such deals not with literature, but with minds. There is no justification whatsoever for bringing psychology into literary criticism except to relate the work of literature to some mind, at least in practical criticism—I am leaving aside what we might call metapsychoanalytic metacriticism, the discussion of such general issues as art and neurosis or the nature of tragedy. In practical criticism, the analysis of particular works, any psychoanalytic proposition must involve two steps: first, a statement showing a congruity between the literary work and some psychoanalytic description of mind in general; second (the one our phallically minded student forgot), a statement relating the psychoanalytic description of mind in general to some mind in particular. Usually, the psychoanalytic critic need not spend much ink on this second stage, but he must let us know where he stands on the matter. Otherwise all he writes becomes mere sound and fury, signifying nothing.

Once we recognize this basic fact about psychoanalytic criticism, that it must refer to some mind, we are in a position to make sense out of this large body of psychoanalytic criticism of Shakespeare. For Shakespeare's plays and narrative poems there are three possible minds to which the psychological critic customarily refers: first, the author's mind; second, a character's; third, the audience's. Referring to one of these minds, it seems to me, leads to a bona-fide method; the other two tend to confusion.

READING TOWARD THE AUTHOR'S MIND

The first and most obvious mind to which the psychoanalytically inclined reader turns is the author's; the studies we considered in Chapter 7 and many of Freud's comments in Chapter 6 did just that. Here, surely, is a sensible procedure, provided we recognize its limitations. What the psychoanalytic critic does is bring together Shakespeare's works and the few biographical facts and rumors that bear on his personality into a coherent picture of the dynamics of the author's psyche. Chapter 7 showed a quite remarkable amount of agreement among critics dealing in quite different ways with this evidence and, while a majority vote proves nothing, such a consensus does suggest that the question is at least rightly posed. The psychoanalytic critic looking at the author is simply saying, first, that there is such a thing as a distinctly Shakespearean style; second, with Burton and Buffon, that that style is the man. Shakespeare's choice of subject matter, his images, his ways of representing character, his own developing skill, all these seem just as individual as his thumbprint, and there is little doubt we can, by using psychoanalytic explanations of personality, read back through the works to Shakespeare himself.

Necessarily, however, psychobiographical evidence about Shakespeare from his works is mixed. The style is the man: it is also the culture. To draw any conclusion from the plays about Shakespeare himself, as Ernst Kris has pointed out,[1] one must take into account causes such as literary sources and conventions that coact with the author's imagination to make the plays. By and large, psychoanalytic critics looking at Shakespeare's personality (e.g., Jones) have taken sources into account (although often in rather eccentric ways), but not conventions. For example, psychoanalytic critics often note that in a half-dozen of Shakespeare's romantic comedies girls dress up as boys; they conclude that Shakespeare had at least latent homosexual impulses. But, as we can see from the Induction to *The Taming of the Shrew*, Shakespeare's audience apparently saw nothing reprehensible in a lord's dressing up his page as a woman to greet "with kind embracements, tempting kisses" the deceived tinker Sly.

In fact, since all Elizabethan women characters were played by boys, the embraces of Romeo and Juliet and Antony and Cleopatra all would have put on the stage so intimate a contact between man and boy that even a modern audience might flinch. Because there were no actresses, disguising a girl character as a boy was a natural device, quite conventional in romantic comedies and common to many dramatists besides Shakespeare. The psychoanalytic critic who says Shakespeare was latently homosexual has lost track of convention. He is drawing a conclusion about Shakespeare when properly he can only draw a mixed conclusion about Shakespeare among other Elizabethans, that he—and they—were more tolerant of contacts between two males than a twentieth-century magistrate would be. To draw any conclusion about Shakespeare from the viewpoint of his own culture, one would have to subtract the effect of convention from the plays, and this, by and large, the psychoanalytic critic has failed to do.

There is another trouble with the "psychobiographical" method. The end result of such a study is, as we saw in Chapter 6, a description of Shakespeare's style, concerns, sensibility, perhaps even his personality, but not his works as such. Professor Leon Edel's biographical studies of Willa Cather and Henry James have shown how fruitful such psychological insights can be for the purposes of practical criticism. Nevertheless, these insights in and of themselves make, not literary criticism in the modern sense (analysis of the work), but literary biography in the manner of Sainte-Beuve.

Further, in the case of Shakespeare, we cannot verify such biographical conclusions. Among modern authors (as with James), the biographer can occasionally amass data enough about the man to make psychoanalytic interpretations of his personality as certain as those that a therapist could make with a living patient. More usually, though, we cannot find out, even among living authors, what Freud tactfully called "the intimate side" of an author's life on which psychobiography must rely. So far as an author of centuries past is concerned, any conclusions we reach about him by reading through his works to his personality must remain highly interesting, perhaps highly useful, but ultimately unprovable: a Shakespeare-in-his-works who is as different from the Shakespeare one might actually meet as an X ray is from a portrait.

READING TOWARD A CHARACTER'S MIND

The second mind to which the psychoanalytic critic can relate the work is a character's. By far the greatest part of the remarks of the critics in Chapter 9 (and Freud's comments) follow this procedure; they show that what a character says or does matches some psychoanalytic description of personality. For example, Iago's strange behavior fits the psychoanalytic description and explanation of paranoia; Hamlet acts like a man suffering from oedipal feelings; Lear behaves as though he had unconscious sexual impulses toward his daughters; and so on. But among the writers using this method of psychoanalytic criticism we do not find at all the kind of unanimity about a given character that we found in discussions of Shakespeare's personality. These differences of opinion among equally competent observers equally backed by textual evidence suggest that somehow the question they ask of the text has been wrongly put.

This method of psychoanalytic criticism makes one basic and all-too-often tacit assumption: that we can talk about literary characters as though they were real people. Certainly, if that is so, it makes more sense to use modern, scientific psychology to elucidate character than mere intuition or some sixth sense or a college professor's limited experience of human nature. But does it make sense to talk about literary or dramatic characters as though they were real people? Apparently, most psychoanalytic critics (and many orthodox Shakespeareans) seem to feel that it does.

In fact, Ernest Jones, in the Introduction to his *Hamlet and Oedipus*,[2] discusses the question and concludes that it is all right for the psychoanalyst to treat Hamlet as a living human being because this is what literary critics themselves do. And recently Professor Louis Fraiberg has made the point that literary critics should treat Hamlet as a living person because the psychoanalysts do [3]—thus bringing us back where we started. But, Dr. Jones to the contrary notwithstanding, as a plain matter of fact, most literary critics do not—any more —treat literary characters as real people. This reticence comes as a surprise, I find, to psychoanalysts, philosophers, actors, and, indeed, to some literary critics. Perhaps some instances are needed.

THE CRITICS' REJECTION OF "CHARACTER"

L. C. Knights created the *locus classicus* (for Shakespeare, anyway) in 1933 in an essay, "How Many Children Had Lady Macbeth." [4] He pointed out that discussion of such a question about a character simply does not make sense in terms of modern critical procedure: "We start with so many lines of verse on a printed page which we read as we should read any other poem," considering particular words, ambiguities, images, and so on. "In the mass of Shakespeare criticism there is not a hint that 'character'—like 'plot,' 'rhythm,' 'construction,' and all our other critical counters—is merely an abstraction from the total response in the mind of the reader or spectator, brought into being by written or spoken words; that the critic, therefore—however far he may ultimately range—begins with the words of which a play is composed."

In another essay, "How Many Complexes Had Lady Macbeth?" I argued, as I am arguing now, that Knights' considerations apply to psychoanalytic as well as ordinary studies of character.[5] Older and wiser heads, however, have said the same: "Shakespeare's characters," writes Kenneth Muir, "are not real people: they are characters in a play, called forth by the role they have to act, and determined by the plot." [6] "Shakespeare is making a play, not people," says Kenneth Burke. "Whereas it has become customary to speak of Shakespeare's figures as of living people, the stupidest and crudest person who ever lived is richer in motivation than all of Shakespeare's characters put together." [7] "It does not occur to us today," states the *pontifex maximus,* Edmund Wilson, "to try, as was at one time a critical fashion, to examine the creations of Shakespeare as if they were actual persons about whom it would be possible to assemble complete and consistent biographies." [8]

It is not, however, simply a matter of critical method, but also of historical fact. Professor Elmer Edgar Stoll (and many other scholars of Elizabethan drama) [9] have shown again and again over recent years, in a great variety of different contexts, that plot, staging, and acting in the Elizabethan theater were so closely bound to a series of conventions as simply to rule out the notion that the characters are the lifelike portraits nineteenth-century critics thought them. C. S. Lewis quite delightfully recounts his experience with this kind of character criticism, an experience I share with him as do, I think, most of the critics of this generation:

When I tried to read Shakespeare in my teens the character criticism of the nineteenth century stood between me and my enjoyment. There were all sorts of things in the plays which I could have enjoyed; but I had got it into my head that the only proper and grown-up way of appreciating Shakespeare was to be very interested in the truth and subtlety of his character drawing. A play opened with thunder and lightning and witches on a heath. This was very much in my line: but oh, the disenchantment when I was told—or thought I was told—that what really ought to concern me was the effect of these witches on Macbeth's character! An Illyrian Duke spoke, in an air which had just ceased vibrating to the sound of music, words that seemed to come out of the very heart of some golden world of dreamlike passion: but all this was spoiled because the meddlers had told me it was the portrait of a self-deceiving or unrealistic man and given me the impression that it was my business to diagnose like a straightener from Erewhon or Vienna instead of submitting to the charm . . . To one in my position the opposite movement in criticism came as a kind of Magna Carta. With that help I have come to one very definite conclusion. I do not say that the characters—especially the comic characters—count for nothing. But the first thing is to surrender oneself to the poetry and the situation. It is only through them that you can reach the characters, and it is for their sake that the characters exist. All conceptions of the characters arrived at, so to speak, in cold blood, by working out what sort of man it would have to be who in real life would act or speak as they do, are in my opinion chimerical.[10]

The nineteenth-century method came about, essentially, as an attempt to assimilate Shakespeare to the tradition of the novel—as Mr. Laurence Lerner notes:

A great deal of the development of English literature over four hundred years has been by way of a shift from moral abstractions to individuals as units of characterization. Instead of taking (say) a vertical cross-section through humanity (all the pride, or all the malice), the method of the novelist is to take a horizontal one (a bit of pride, a bit of malice, a limp and a fondness for cats) that corresponds to the uniqueness of a single person. Since the change was both cause and effect of the rise of the novel, it is natural that critics whose outlook is formed on the novel should consider it sheer gain, and should, with their Whig Interpretation of literary history, have singled out for praise among the Elizabethans what seem anticipations of later methods of characterisation. We know better nowadays: there is no need, now, to apologise for treating *Othello* as a poetic construct rather than a photographic version of human behaviour.[11]

"Poetic construct" is the key phrase.

The original error arose from failing to recognize that a play is an ordered and structured work of art, not like everyday reality. This order and structure impose changes on the literal representation of reality. For example, the characters must speak verse—and, as a result, a variety of nineteenth- and twentieth-century critics have labeled Macbeth, Othello, Iago, Richard II, or whomever, as "great poets." But surely this is nonsense—"If characters in poetic drama speak poetry," notes Dr. Leavis, "we ought to be able to notice the fact without concluding that they are poets." [12] The poetry, notes G. Wilson Knight, should make us "rather see each play as an expanded metaphor, by means of which the original vision has been projected into forms roughly correspondent with actuality, conforming thereto with greater or less exactitude according to the demands of its nature. . . . The persons, ultimately, are not human at all, but purely symbols of a poetic vision." [13]

Unfortunately, as some of these quotations imply, the older approach is not yet dead: high-school teaching and middle-brow criticism for the dailies and weeklies thrive on, in Professor Kirschbaum's words, "the inveterate, unswervable naturalistic-psychological approach," "the a priori 'romantic' notion that every Shakespeare character is as real in unity, depth, and complexity as the reader of this book." "I find it," he goes on, "blatantly on the surface or hidden below it, even in the writing of sophisticated modern critics. I perceive its menace in my students at every class meeting," [14] and so, I might add, do I. Students aside, though, this naturalistic approach simply does not make critical sense.

So far I have quoted only critics dealing with Shakespeare. One would think there would be more sense in regarding the characters in a modern naturalistic novel as "real people," but not so. Even here the modern critic (quite properly, I think) objects. "A novel, like a poem," writes Dr. Leavis, "is made of words; there is nothing else one can point to. We talk of a novelist as 'creating characters,' but the process of 'creation' is one of putting words together." [15] C. H. Rickword, another of the Scrutiny critics, puts the matter with particular accuracy:

The form of a novel only exists as a balance of response on the part of the reader. Hence schematic plot is a construction of the reader's that corresponds to an aspect of that response and stands in merely diagrammatic relation to the source. Only as precipitate from the memory are plot or character tangible; yet only in solution have either any emotional valency. [16]

Criticism of the novel, writes Mark Schorer, "must begin with the base of language, with the word, with figurative structures, with rhetoric as skeleton and style as body of meaning. . . . A novel, like a poem, is not life, it is an image of life; and the critical problem is first of all to analyze the structure of the image." [17] And, lest we think this attitude represents only Western formalism, we should note that from a totally alien point of view the best of the Marxist critics, Georg Lukács, states flatly, "The live portrayal of the complete human personality is possible only if the writer attempts to create types." [18] For a Marxist, characterization must show "the real intrinsic totality of the decisive driving forces which determine the social process."

In short, realism, as Karl Mannheim said, "means different things in different contexts." The one thing it seems not to mean is a literal, photographic portrayal of reality—in fact, I doubt if such a thing is possible, since every portrayal, by the mere fact of its being a portrayal, involves the intervention of some personality. Artistic portrayals of reality inevitably depend on the dialectic between reality itself (and who even agrees on that?) and the particular representation of reality made by the artist. So, at least, we would conclude from Professor Harry Levin's many studies of the novel or Erich Auerbach's elaborate analysis of realistic description from Genesis to the present.[19] And, as E. H. Gombrich has shown, the same dialectic applies to the visual arts (where, if anywhere, utter fidelity to some reality "out there" should be possible). Realism, concludes Gombrich, comes down simply to "giving no false information." [20]

When we turn from critics to artists we find again the same sane recognition, that artistic realism simply does not duplicate reality. For Shakespeare, Edgar Allan Poe makes the point most explicitly:

> In all commentating upon Shakespeare, there has been a radical error, never yet mentioned. It is the error of attempting to expound his characters—to account for their actions—to reconcile his inconsistencies—not as if they were the coinage of a human brain, but as if they had been actual existences on earth. We talk of Hamlet the man, instead of Hamlet the *dramatis persona.* . . . If Hamlet had really lived, and if the tragedy were an accurate record of his deeds, from this record (with some trouble) we might, it is true, reconcile his inconsistencies and settle to our satisfaction his true character. But the task becomes the purest absurdity when we deal only with a phantom.[21]

More generally and more beautifully, Virginia Woolf says: "It seems that men and women are equally at fault. It seems that a profound, impartial, and absolutely just opinion of our fellow creatures is utterly unknown. Either we are men or we are women. Either we are cold or we are sentimental. Either we are young or growing old. . . . Such is the manner of our seeing. Such the conditions of our love." [22]

If this be true in life, how much more so it is in art. "It is essential," writes T. S. Eliot, "that a work of art should be self-consistent, that an artist should consciously or unconsciously draw a circle beyond which he does not trespass: on the one hand actual life is always the material, and on the other an abstraction from actual life is a necessary condition to the creation of the work of art." [23] And, surprisingly, Proust:

> None of the feelings which the joys or misfortunes of a 'real' person awaken in us can be awakened except through a mental picture of those

oys or misfortunes; and the ingenuity of the first novelist lay in his understanding that, as the picture was the one essential element in the complicated structure of our emotions, so that simplification of it which consisted in the suppression, pure and simple, of 'real' people would be a decided improvement. A 'real' person, profoundly as we may sympathize with him, is in a great measure perceptible only through our senses, that is to say, he remains opaque. . . . The novelist's happy discovery was to think of substituting for those opaque sections, impenetrable by the human spirit, their equivalent in immaterial sections, things, that is, which the spirit can assimilate to itself. After which it matters not that the actions, the feelings of this new order of creatures appear to us in the guise of truth, since we have made them our own, since it is in ourselves that they are happening, that they are holding in thrall, while we turn over, feverishly, the pages of the book.[24]

To the same effect, E. M. Forster whimsically contrasts "those two allied species, Homo Sapiens and Homo Fictus." Homo Fictus differs from "his cousin" in that he comes into the world more like a parcel than like a baby—offstage and put into storage until he can take part in the action. Food for Homo Fictus is more social than nutritious and sleep is minimal: "He is never conceived as a creature a third of whose time is spent in the darkness." Homo Fictus is much given to dying—or getting married—at the ends of books, and he is tirelessly concerned with human relationships. But most important, "we can know more about him than we can know about any of our fellow creatures." Forster offers "a definition as to when a character in a book is real . . . when the novelist knows everything about it."

For human intercourse, as soon as we look at it for its own sake and not as a social adjunct, is seen to be haunted by a spectre. We cannot understand each other, except in a rough and ready way; we cannot reveal ourselves, even when we want to; what we call intimacy is only a makeshift; perfect knowledge is an illusion. But in the novel we can know people perfectly, and, apart from the general pleasure of reading, we can find here a compensation for their dimness in life. In this direction fiction is truer than history, because it goes beyond the evidence, and each of us knows from his own experience that there is something beyond the evidence, and even if the novelist has not got it correctly, well—he as tried.[25]

But perhaps the simplest statement is Matisse's answer to a lady who, visiting his studio, complained, "Surely, the arm of this woman is too long." "Madame," replied Matisse, "you are mistaken. That is not a woman, that is a picture. *Avant tout, je ne crée pas une femme, je fais un tableau.*" [26]

Finally, from the camp of psychoanalysis itself Freud three times discussed this problem of the realism of plot and character.[27] In his analysis of Jensen's *Gradiva* he pointed out the possibilities of error in treating characters "in all their mental manifestations and activities as though they were real people and not the author's creations, as though the author's mind were an absolutely transparent medium and not a refractive or obscuring one," and, similarly, he questioned treating "Rebecca West as if she were a living person and not a creation of Ibsen's imagination, which is always directed by the most critical intelligence." But for both, he concluded simply that if they appear psychiatrically correct, why, then, they appear psychiatrically correct. In his introduction to the "Dora case," however, he seems to imply that literal, photographic correctness is the exception rather than the rule:

I must now turn to consider a further complication to which I should certainly give no space if I were a man of letters engaged upon the creation of a mental state like this for a short story, instead of being a medical man engaged upon its dissection. The element to which I must now allude can only serve to obscure and efface the outlines of the fine poetic conflict which we have been able to ascribe to Dora. This element would rightly fall a sacrifice to the censorship of a writer, for he, after all, simplifies and abstracts when he appears in the character of a psychologist.

In short, from the point of view of the critic, or the artist, or the psychoanalyst, one cannot—or should not—talk about literary characters as though they were literal, photographic portraits completely faithful to some "external" reality—at least not without qualms and cautions.

JUSTIFICATIONS OF ''CHARACTER''

Nevertheless, a number of orthodox as well as psychoanalytic critics have tried to justify treating literary characters as though they were real people. One line of argument says that the author is trying to show real people (that is, after all, what a play is—people on a stage). But this is to marry a *petitio principi* to the intentional fallacy. We do not know what the author was trying to do except by what he has done; presumably he was trying to show us what he does, in fact, show us—characters in a play, simplified versions of people, that may or may not resemble real people. Shakespeare, in particular, as about half the psychoanalytic critics have shown, wrote especially close to the tradition of myth and folk tale in which the characters are "two-dimensional" and the actions (like Shylock's bond, Lear's love contest, or Leontes' fit of jealousy) frankly motivated by thematic significance rather than "character."

Other psychoanalytic critics (K. R. Eissler, for example) have tried another line of justification, one they share with the great apostle of character criticism, A. C. Bradley. The psychoanalytic critic, they say, is entitled to treat literary characters as real human beings because they are projections of the author who is a real human being. But this reasoning, too, seems to me unsatisfactory. It is perfectly clear that Hamlet is not Shakespeare, and while Shakespeare undoubtedly had an unconscious, that fact, without some severe logical contortions, will not give Hamlet one.

Another, more subtle defense is that of Maurice Morgann whose book on Falstaff established (in 1777) a century and a half of this character-mongering (as it has been called). We can treat Shakespeare's characters as real people because "he boldly makes a character act and speak from those parts of the composition which are *inferred* only, and not distinctly shewn. This produces a wonderful effect: it seems to carry us beyond the poet to nature itself," so that we can consider the characters, "rather as Historic than Dramatic beings." [28] Morgann's argument is paradoxical indeed: precisely because Shakespeare slurs matters of motivation (precisely because his characters are not quite realistic), we "can" treat them as real people. But this is like saying that once the magician has successfully fooled me into thinking the lady was sawn in half, I "can" go on thinking she was sawn in half. Of course, I *can,* but *should* I? And that is the question our psychoanalytic critics of character raise.

Most writers and critics of today would answer simply, if resoundingly, No. We ought to recognize, instead, that literary personages exist only as words and what we call their "character" is only an inference or abstraction from the text. Falstaff, for example, speaks and does a certain number of things and the other characters say a certain number of things about him. This is all the reality Falstaff has. When we say, "Falstaff is a glutton" (or even, "Falstaff eats to incorporate the hostile mother imago") we make him more than he in fact is. By so abstracting, we add to our data about Falstaff by implying he has a continuous existence whereas he actually exists only in a set of discrete words and actions in a set of separate plays. We imply, in other words, that when Falstaff encounters a new situation, for example, when he begins collecting that "competence for life" that Henry V allows him, he will spend a lot of it on food and drink as he has in the past.

The trouble is that it is impossible for Falstaff to encounter a new situation, for he has—can have—no reality apart from the words and actions associated with him in the several plays in which he appears. When we use a word like "glutton" which implies the same kind of continuous reality that ordinary living people have, we commit the fallacy of misplaced concreteness—at the very least we have attached to Falstaff a label which can be rather misleading. As T. S. Eliot's psychiatrist says in *The Cocktail Party:*

> What we know of other people
> Is only our memory of the moments
> During which we knew them.

If this be true of real people, as surely it is, then it is much more true of literary characters. But we assume a continuing existence for the people we know. I suppose we are entitled to do the same for a literary character. But how much should we add to the moments in which we know, say, Falstaff?

DEGREES OF ERROR ABOUT "CHARACTER"

As with most things, there are degrees of error about "character" resulting from these labels appropriate to real people, and, to evaluate psychoanalytic criticism, it is useful to distinguish them. In the most extreme form of the error, the critic insists on a past for the character before the opening of the play—as Dr. Jones does: "As a child Hamlet had experienced the warmest affection for his mother." "The precise nature of his original feeling for Ophelia is a little obscure." (To say the least!) Jones in his Introduction insists absolutely on his illusion: "No dramatic criticism of the personae in a play is possible except under the pretence that they are living people. . . ." "In so far and in the same sense as a character in a play is taken as being a living person, to that extent must he have had a life before the action in the play began, since no one starts life as an adult." [29] In other words, fictional oaks from fictional acorns grow.

There are other ways of going beyond the play besides going beyond it into a past or future that exists in neither fact nor fiction. One can go beyond a play within its own time. I am thinking of such traditional arguments as the nineteenth-century one (but repeated today) that if Hamlet simply killed his uncle and then announced that he was avenging his father's murder, the citizenry would have attacked Hamlet and sanctified Claudius. Here we have turned not to an *Ur-Hamlet* but an *Un-Hamlet,* a play that never existed and never will.

Such statements are, unfortunately, all too common in psychoanalytic criticism of Shakespeare. For example, Dr. Jones says of Hamlet "By refusing to abandon his own incestuous wishes he perpetuate the sin and so must endure the stings of torturing conscience. And ye killing his mother's husband *would be* equivalent to committing th original sin himself, which *would* if anything *be* even more guilty. So of the two impossible alternatives he adopts the passive solution of letting the incest continue vicariously, but at the same time provoking destruction at the King's hand." [30] The conditional verbs I have italicized imply that it is possible for Hamlet to have acted differently from the way he did; Jones is saying Hamlet had a choice. This is putting on critical blinders with a vengeance—the choice was all Shakespeare's, not Hamlet's, and to imagine other ways Hamlet could act is to write another play, not to discuss this one.

Almost all statements about "motive" fall into this error. Motive is what prompts us to action, and the word implies its converse: no motive, no action. To speak of Hamlet's "motives" is to imply another play in which Hamlet acts differently. A similar objection attaches to the statement that a character is "inconsistent," as Professor Dupee argues in connection with psychoanalytic readings of *Hamlet;* we are then measuring the character by some hypothetical other version of himself who acts differently, more in accord with a living human being.[31] The actions of a dramatic (or literary) character are facts, givens, which cannot change; any statement that implies that the character can act differently or be different implies a fallacy.

Most psychoanalytic criticism of Shakespeare, however, tries to show, not inconsistency, but consistency of character, probability in the old Aristotelian sense. When, for example, we are told that Iago is homosexually inclined toward Othello, that Shylock is anal erotic, that Brutus is the victim of unconscious envy of Caesar or a tyrannical superego, the critic is trying to say that Iago, Shylock, or Brutus is acting in a human or lifelike way in the circumstances in which he exists. Yet, consistency in this sense simply begs the question. It is not at all clear whether by probability and consistency we—or Aristotle—mean what is human or lifelike under such circumstances in reality or what is probable and consistent in terms of the internal logic, the *mythos,* of the tragedy as a whole.

Such readings toward consistency are likely to prove confusing for another reason—they imply a continuity of existence and action that the dramatic character simply does not have. That is, any time we use psychological vocabulary, be it the technical one of psychoanalysis with words like "anal erotic" or simply our everyday words for human personality ("Brutus is an idealist," for example), we push aside a crucial distinction. Homo Fictus does not function in the formless world of everyday reality but in the highly ordered world of a work of art. A psychological vocabulary describes men choosing actions in the real world, but dramatic characters do not exist in the real world nor do they choose. Homo Fictus and Homo Dramaticus do not so much what Homo Sapiens would do in similar circumstances, but what it is necessary for them to do in the logical and meaningful realities of the works of art in which they live.

We can see the difficulty very clearly by playing a game of switching characters. How, for example, would a heroine from Dickens fit into a novel of Dostoevsky? How could a character from Homer fit into Virgil, from Shakespeare into Shaw, from Faulkner into Hemingway, from Antonioni into Fellini, from *Peanuts* into *Pogo*—one could go on indefinitely. The point is simply that "character" is shaped by the artistic reality of which it is a part. It makes no sense to lift "character" out of the atmosphere which gives it life. And if it makes no sense to move characters from book to book or play to play, if even so adaptable a fellow as Autolycus could not fit into the world of Falstaff, it seems a little silly to apply to them both a psychological vocabulary from still a third world in which neither of them could be!

In short, my criticism is a verbal one, that the psychoanalytic critic of Shakespearean character applies psychoanalytic words in a context where they do not belong, to an imitation of nature, not nature itself. As Aristotle pointed out long ago, the artist hovers between *mimesis*, making like, and *harmonia*, the almost musical ordering of the events he depicts. Professor Harry Levin says:

Art is always an imitation, never quite the real thing. It cannot represent without symbolizing. By its devices of synecdoche or metonymy, it gives us the part for the whole or the attribute for the object. It never gives us a perfect replica; on the other hand, it never gives us a complete abstraction. . . . In the dramatic moralities, Vanity is a highly feminine creature and the Vice is full of boyish mischief. Life itself is bound to be mixed up with any artistic representation of it; yet even the "slice of life" of the naturalists had to be framed by symbolic conceptions. . . Generally speaking, art seems to oscillate between two poles, the symbolistic and the realistic—or, we might say, the typical and the individual.[32]

The psychoanalytic critic of character neglects the element of *harmonia*, the symbolic conceptions that must modify the mimetic.

He confuses us—and we often confuse ourselves—by using word appropriate to everyday reality for the sharply modified reality of a play or poem. Perhaps we need new words, a word for "motive," for example, that does not imply a freedom of choice; a word for "consistency" of character that means consistency with the patterns of the play world, not the real world; adjectives for character that imply existence for only the two hours' traffic of the stage instead of adjective like "idealistic" or "anal erotic" which imply existence for the canonical threescore-and-ten years. We can—and should—make explicit in remarks like, "As a child Hamlet had experienced the warmest feelings for his mother," the two tacit assumptions of psychoanalytic criticism of character: first, that the critic is treating the play as reality; second, he is generalizing from the discrete events of the play. It is legitimate to say, "Hamlet acts within the play as a real man would act if as a child he had experienced the warmest feelings for his mother and if he were to find himself in the special world of *Hamlet* the play." Confronted with such an explicit—and cumbersome—statement, we will not, presumably, lose sight of the text. If, however, we simply attach labels from everyday life like "idealist" or "anal erotic" and then think in terms of the labels instead of the text, we step off the text onto the airy nothings of a purely imaginary world, as, indeed, all too much of psychoanalytic criticism of character does.

There is still a further question about the "pretence," as Dr. Jones calls it, that the persons in a play are living people: Is it useful? I can think of only one case where the pretense has some claim to be appropriate, namely, for the actor or director who is trying to make the play "come alive." Rightly or wrongly, we have been conditioned to expect from the viva-voce stage a succession of "interpretations," and for the actor and director the psychological labels and the pretense that the play is reality may have some purpose. Yet even here, as Shakespeare's misnamed "realist" critics insist, we are imposing on the bard a naturalism from our own time which is quite alien to the almost folkloric conception of his plays. There is, after all, a weight of evidence that Shakespeare wrote his plays for an acting style which is not only not realistic (in a twentieth-century sense) but, like the stage and costumes of his day, consciously timeless, anti-natural, ceremonial, reaching for the universal rather than the particular so prized in the nineteenth- or twentieth-century naturalistic theater.

I realize that by insisting too precisely on a distinction between plays and reality, literary characters and real people, I may seem to some to be cutting art off from life. Actually, I think it is just the other way around. The critic who insists on the lifelikeness of Shakespeare's plays makes them into mere partial representations of something that happens more fully in life. They become a half reality, a Platonic imitation of an imitation that should be driven to the county line of any sensible republic and ordered to move on so the citizenry will participate more fully in the real world. The critic who insists that art copies life makes art second best. He plays into Platonic (or, for that matter, Freudian) descriptions of literature as a narcotic substitute for reality and leaves us with a conscious self-delusion (such as Ernest Jones's "pretence" that we must take the portrayal for the reality).

On the contrary, a play, it seems to me, is a very real thing, very full of life. Not only do I not wish to cut art off from life; I wish to say it is heightened life, a hyper-reality to which we react more directly, more purely than to everyday reality. Let us, as C. S. Lewis suggests, get away from the elaborate intellectualizations of character-mongering and notice the things a child or peasant would. We can see Shakespeare's works this way only, however, if we consider them not as shaky attempts at an adult's realism, but realities themselves to which we react with a special and wonderful childlike intensity.

THE THIRD "WAY" OF PSYCHOANALYTIC CRITICISM

The question we should use psychoanalytic psychology to answer, then, is not, How are Shakespeare's characters "like" real people, but, rather, Why *do we react* to these admittedly fictional people as though they were real? In other words, instead of insisting that Shakespeare has made an imperfect representation of reality, let us grant that the bard has practiced a magic on us that goes beyond reality and ask in all humility how it was done. We should use psychology to understand poetry as poetry, not to mix poetry up with reality. We should use psychology on our own real and lively reactions to the play rather than on the characters' fictitious minds.

The critic who treats a literary character as a human being makes the tacit assumption that an author finds or invents a reality and then copies it, thus ranking, as we have seen, art second best. On the other hand, the critic who treats the work of art as itself an indivisible whole makes the tacit assumption that the work is to be savored as a reality itself, not as a filtered version of some reality other than itself. In psychological terms, the critic who looks at a single character in isolation assumes that a literary work portrays the stimuli and responses of some fictitious people; the reader who looks at the work as a total configuration considers it as itself the stimulus to the very real responses of very real people—the audience. In other words, the issue is: Is Shakespeare writing realistic plays about realistic people, or is he dealing in the demonic wisdom of poetry and folk tale?

This difference about what the author is doing carries over into the question of what the audience is doing: what kind of covenant, what gesture of "as if" an audience makes when it watches a play. Dr.

Johnson held that we credit a drama "with all the credit due to a drama," that is, we recognize that it is a fiction but credit it as "a just picture of a real original." [33] Coleridge held that "we pass no judgment either way," but rather make "that willing suspension of disbelief for the moment, which constitutes poetic faith." [34] And this is the fundamental question that divides the psychoanalytic approaches to Shakespeare—When we see a play, do we agree to believe (Johnson) or simply not to disbelieve (Coleridge)?

As between these two approaches, the agreement to believe, in other words, to pretend plays (or any work of art) are real, will fit naturalistic theater and fiction well enough; but it will not accommodate a whole host of other genres that the suspension-of-disbelief approach will: myth, folk tale, lyric poetry, surrealist and abstract painting, or music. In folk tale, for example, we clearly do not treat ghosts and witches as real; rather, we do *not* treat them as *un*real.

Similarly, the suspension-of-disbelief approach corresponds to the general psychoanalytic explanation of the way art seduces its audience: because the ego's function of reality testing is, as it were, diverted by "meaning" and by artistic "play," our unconscious responses are free to come through. The more we consciously tell ourselves, "This is not reality, but a play," the more the ego suspends its function of belief or disbelief, and the more we are free to respond unconsciously.

READING TOWARD THE AUDIENCE'S MIND

Thus, we have considered—and rejected—two of the minds to which psychoanalytic readers have referred Shakespeare's works. As for Shakespeare's mind, we found that the method leads to biography, not critical analysis, and, more important, that in the nature of this case, at least, the biography could never be verified; the critic's hypothesis about Shakespeare's personality from his plays must remain just that and no more—hypothesis. As for character analysis, we found a tacit and quite suspect assumption that plays can be treated as like the everyday world.

Thus, deviously, we arrive at the third mind to which the psychoanalytic critic can relate Shakespeare's works, our own, and here, it seems to me, the psychoanalytic critic finds, if I may put it that way, bedrock indeed. He is dealing with a real mind, not, in Jones's phrase, braving the ordinary literary critic "by investigating the unconscious mind of someone who never existed." When he deals with our reaction, the psychoanalytic critic is dealing with the work of art as what it is—a work of art, not reality. And when he deals with the audience's mind, as opposed to Shakespeare's, he can put anything he says to the test (at least if he confines himself to a modern audience).

This third approach, relating Shakespeare's works to the mind of their audience, we can call the "newer" view, although I must confess that designating the first two approaches as older and the third as newer is a gross oversimplification; I am really just trying to prejudice you in favor of the last. In the huge body of psychoanalytic criticism of Shakespeare we find this so-called newer view represented in some of the earliest writings (those of Freud and Otto Rank, for example) while the older view goes about yet, scotched but not killed. Nevertheless, there is some justification for the distinction.

The "newer" approach relates both to newer developments in psychoanalytic theory and to newer views of Shakespeare. Freud's first and basic discovery was the dynamic unconscious with its freight of unsavory wishes. By 1925, though, psychoanalysis was concerning itself increasingly, not so much with the earliest or deepest part of the unconscious as with the various unconscious or preconscious strategies of the reality-oriented part of the mind (the ego) to direct and channel those earliest, dark wishes which, if allowed direct gratification, would ultimately prove self-destructive. In psychoanalytic terms, interest shifted from the id to the ego defenses. This approach to the problems of the individual leads quite naturally to considering a literary work not as a single wish but as a community, a *gestalt* of interacting and competing unconscious impulses and defenses or adaptations.

Further, this so-called "newer" psychoanalytic approach follows on the newer, antirealistic, anti-biographical trends in Shakespearean criticism. Looking through a Shakespearean play to the author's biography is a nineteenth-century pastime. Similarly, looking at the characters as real people or the play as a historical reality, staging Shakespeare with real rabbits hopping about on real grass—these are nineteenth-century approaches to realism. In our own sublimely enlightened century critics play down Shakespeare's realism and consider, instead, the formal interrelations among the various parts of the play. And this is what the newer psychoanalytic approach also leads to.

The difficulty with this newer approach is that there just isn't very much of it—at least with respect to Shakespeare. The theoretical justification for this newer view has all been worked out; in fact, it occurs in two of Freud's relatively early essays. In "Creative Writers and Day-Dreaming" (1908) he suggested that it was only in crude literature, kitsch, that a single character gratifies a simple wish of the author. In more sophisticated literature, he said, the ego of the author tends to be split up among several characters. In "Psychopathic Characters on the Stage" (1905) Freud dealt with the relation of tragedy to the mind of the audience, that is, with the question of catharsis. Ernst Kris's *Psychoanalytic Explorations in Art* has elaborated the conception in terms of ego psychology; Simon Lesser's *Fiction and the Unconscious* has set it out in more literary terms; and you will find my own brief summary in Chapter 4.

In practice, however, as opposed to theory, there is very little of this criticism of affect. Much of what there is deals with works of literature such as myth or folk tale where there is no particular author to tempt the psychoanalyst: Freud's analyses of the folklore in "The Theme of the Three Caskets" (1913), for example, or "Medusa's Head" (1922). This affective approach is commonplace in the gothic realm of cartoons, comic strips, advertising, movies, or television where the critic always faces the problem of emotional appeal. We can hope this approach will extend in Shakespearean criticism if for no other reason than that Shakespeare was once—in some quarters still is—a popular artist. The line between *Romeo and Juliet* and *I Married a Teen-Age Necrophiliac* is not so sharp as some middlebrows would have it. Indeed, affective criticism may be the only instance in literary history where a critical technique has made its way in the hard-boiled world of commerce (as motivation research in advertising and sales campaigns) before it could find a place in the gentler world of letters. To some extent, the critic who deals with works of art as myths studies their appeal, though by "myths" I do not mean Jungian archetypes, which, for the purposes of literary criticism at least, tend to be a dead end, mere labeling. The proper use of myths and rituals in analyzing literature calls for an approach jointly to myth, ritual, and literature, both literary works and literary conventions, all understood as stimuli to affective responses. The notion that mythic elements alone serve as the stimuli to the emotional response flies in the face of experience. "The drama," as C. L. Barber happily puts it, "controls magic by reunderstanding it as imagination." [35]

THE THIRD "WAY" WITH SHAKESPEARE

A few of our psychological commentators did discuss Shakespeare's works from the point of view of affect: Freud's remarks on the appeal of *King Lear* or Falstaff or Richard III, for example, Franz Alexander's later study of the appeal of Falstaff, or W. H. Auden's essay on *Othello*. But, for the most part, in dealing with respectable literature, where there is a proper author with a real mind to be considered, the psychoanalytic critic finds the temptation to turn back to the author's mind too strong to be withstood. Here, however, theory rescues us. According to the psychoanalytic view of art, the audience makes an act of re-creation which parallels *mutatis mutandis* the author's original act of creation. If so, then we can salvage many, if not all, of those analyses of Shakespeare's works which considered them in relation to the mind of the author and also many of the ambiguous ones which just showed a congruity between one of the plays and some psychoanalytic description of the mind without going on to say what mind they were talking about. That is, we can use such studies as those of Ella Freeman Sharpe, Ludwig Jekels, Hanns Sachs, K. R. Eissler, J. I. M. Stewart, the early studies of Otto Rank, and a number of Freud's remarks.

All these studies have this in common: they proceed by establishing a congruity between part or all of a play and some psychoanalytic description of the mind, but *instead of considering the play as a realistic portrait of realistic people responding to psychic stimuli, they take the play itself as the real—not necessarily realistic—stimulus to a real response* (Shakespeare's or ours). In other words, these studies consider the play as a total community of associations to and symbolizations of unconscious material. Naturally enough, this kind of approach evolved most directly in Shakespearean criticism at those points in the plays where they are least realistic, where it is most difficult to treat the play as a realistic portrait of people and events, for example, where characters are apparently unmotivated or where ghosts appear. Thus, we can see the approach in Freud's conclusion that Lady Macbeth's reactions are inexplicable and his decision, therefore, that Macbeth and Lady Macbeth are "two disunited parts of a single psychical individuality," "not completely understandable . . . until they are brought once more into a unity." Otto Rank, considering the necessarily unreal ghosts of Julius Caesar or Hamlet's father, treats them as symbolizations of a dual wish toward the father. First, they represent a quite literal wish to "see the father dead," second, a wish against the "immortality" or persistence of infantile wishes toward the father, a wish, in other words, that these infantile attitudes were as questionable as a ghost and could be laid to rest like a ghost. Maud Bodkin answers the traditional question, Is Iago realistically drawn?, by suggesting that Othello embodies a pure impulse to idealize; Iago embodies the pure impulse to corrupt and debase which has been split off from the hero.

Thus, deviously, we have arrived at a way of understanding the psychology of Shakespeare's works: namely, to consider the play or poem as a configuration, a multiple projection or symbolization or stimulus of unconscious impulses of the audience, interacting through such primary thought processes as identification, condensation, displacement, and the like. It is worth noting that this affective approach, unlike the biographical, does not demand that we consider dramatic and literary conventions separately from the rest of the play: they are as much a stimulus to the affective response of the audience as anything else.

We have by indirections found directions out; by considering what psychoanalytic criticism of Shakespeare is, we seem to have found what it might be and, I think, should be. The difficulty is one of premises. The psychoanalytic critic must recognize that he is relating the play to some mind; he is describing congruities between the work of art and psychoanalytic descriptions of the mind. The best mind he can work with is not the author's, not the character's, but the audience's, ultimately, his own. In other words, the wise psychoanalytic reader will recognize what psychoanalytic theory posits, namely, that a play does not simply depict the stimuli and responses for some hypothetical and imaginary people—it *is* the stimulus to the response of some very real people, the audience, among them, the critic himself.

If we are logical, we will cast all criticism of character into outer darkness. But, in criticism, as in life, logic alone rarely makes much sense, and what you have been reading seems now to me purely and simply wrong. More exactly, it is a correct answer to a question wrongly posed in the first sentence of this chapter: "whether to treat a play as a realistic portrayal of psychological events outside itself or as itself a psychological event." I have included this chapter not so much to get you to go through a dialectic I have been through (though partly that); I have included it because it seems to me, even if wrong, a not-unreasonable conclusion you might draw from this book. This rejection of character criticism does, after all, sort out and clarify the critical problem. It does provide a clear-cut way of evaluating psychoanalytic criticism. It does seem logical, even somewhat commonsensical. It does rest on a massive support from contemporary critical authorities. You could do worse than settle for this conclusion. But I have come to think you could do better by correcting this chapter with the next one.

[11]

Conclusions
Not So Logical

THE time has come to put logic aside and resort to that much more difficult tool, common sense. Psychoanalytic criticism, for all that it is psychoanalytic, is also criticism. To see what it is that psychoanalytic critics are doing or failing to do, we need to establish what it is that orthodox criticism does. Any critic, conventional or psychoanalytic, is first and foremost a member of the audience himself: he experiences the work of art initially as anyone else does. He then becomes a critic only by doing something more, something usually called "the critical act." That act has two quite inconsistent sides: one, objective, descriptive, even scientific; the other, interpersonal and persuasive. Although these two sides differ sharply, even seem inconsistent (one being objective, the other subjective), rare indeed is the critical statement that does not do a bit of both.

THE CRITIC'S TWO ROLES

The interpersonal side of criticism is the one we know best: the critic playing his traditional role as handmaiden to the Muse. In effect, the critic acts as a teacher, using his own experience as a member of the audience to enter actively into the literary transaction that runs between author, work, and audience. Into this transaction or process the critic insinuates his opinions, insights, biases, philosophy, or what have you.

Occasionally, where an author reads and heeds his critics (as Tennyson, for example, did), the critic intervenes in the relation between author and work, in the creative act itself. More usually, the critic conveys to the audience his opinions or insights and so changes what the audience brings to the work of art. He affects the audience's reaction just as any other part of the audience's collective and individual experience does. "Interpretation," T. S. Eliot has written, "is only legitimate when it is not interpretation at all, but merely putting the

314

reader in possession of facts which he would otherwise have missed." [1] These "facts," I take it, could include historical data, dictionary information, stories about the author, or insights into symbolism, structure, and meaning. Any one or all of these, if "taught" to an audience by a critic, can play a part in the audience's perception of a work of art. In this interpersonal role of the critic as teacher, the critic becomes a man speaking to men, not generally, as the writer himself does, but critically in so far as the men he speaks to are involved in a literary transaction.

Once he goes beyond simply being in the audience and starts behaving like a critic, whether he says so or not, the critic is always involved in observing, deducing, and describing the literary process in a scientific way. He must be, because what he chooses to say in his role as a teacher derives from what as an objective researcher he finds are important forces in the interaction of author, work, and audience. To decide what forces are important, he must have an understanding of the literary transaction (explicit or not) which is objective, descriptive—in its essence—scientific.

I know it seems ugly to speak of criticism as "scientific," but the term really cannot be avoided. Criticism is not only the literature of art, writes Professor Harry Levin, "it is also—in spite of itself and inadequately—a branch of science, in so far as it devotes itself to the empirical investigation, the systematic organization, and the objective interpretation of the facts pertaining to its subject matter." [2] And Matthew Arnold went even further, insisting that the main function of criticism is "to see the object in itself as it really is," though, later, he recognized the dual nature of criticism in his more famous definition, "a distinterested endeavour to learn and propagate the best that is known and thought." [3] Whether we speak elaborately of empirical investigation, systematic organization, and objective interpretation or simply of learning about literature, literary criticism must be, in some part of its being, scientific.

And so it has always been. Plato's strictures on the moral permissibility of art, Aristotle's notion of catharsis, or Longinus' of the sublime all rested on a variety of psychological assumptions. Similarly, the prescriptive rules put forward by neoclassic critics: obey the three unities; do not mix comedy and tragedy—these built upon a faculty psychology of audience response. Coleridge derived his theory of the sympathetic imagination from Hartley's associationism. In our own day I. A. Richards relies on a syncretistic psychology to back up his thesis that literature communicates states of mental organization.

So far as Shakespeare is concerned, Romantic critics such as Sainte-Beuve stressed information about the man because they assumed (or found) that the literary transaction of their day took place between author and audience, by-passing the text. Other nineteenth-century critics talked about Shakespeare's characters because they assumed that what the audience was really reacting to was a photographic portrayal of people and events. And twentieth-century analysts of Shakespeare's imagery are really making statements about what the audience responds to when they point out, say, images of disease and rotting in *Hamlet*. The myth critic finds a license in the analytic psychology of Jung for pointing out atavistic myths in Shakespeare. In every criticism, a psychology is—must be—involved. The most cerebral and semantic of "new critical" analyses, the most painstaking of literary histories, the most impressionistic record of visceral reactions, all proceed on some psychological assumption.

Persuader and scientist, teacher and researcher, the critic's two roles are logically quite inconsistent with each other. In one, he stands outside the literary transaction dispassionately observing it. In the other, he actively enters in, changing the audience's participation. But logic does not govern here. In practice, critics are always doing both, although not perhaps at the same moment. The ordinary reviewer for a daily or weekly (as against a quarterly), even if he confines his criticism merely to recommending a particular piece, mixes these two roles: he tacitly assumes that there is some probable reaction of pleasure or displeasure to the particular piece and that he somehow knows it. Then, his recommendation changes our expectation and perception. He may be far less sophisticated, but he is not doing anything fundamentally different from Aristotle, who predicted that one kind of tragedy would be more likely to purge pity and fear than another.

The critic of imagery who "scientifically" attributes the effect of *Hamlet* to images of disease and rotting is saying at the same time that he can get an audience to respond more fully to the tragedy by making it sensitive to these recurring images. The myth critic assumes in a descriptive way that the audience, at some deep level of its being, resonates to the vestiges of myth and ritual; then he fulfills his own assumption by enabling his own readers to respond by means of a sonorous vocabulary of crops, seasons, planets, and dying gods. And curiously, this dual role of the critic persists even if he never communicates his view to other members of the audience. He is, then, his own audience; he affects (defends against?) his own involvement in the work by his own uninvolved observation of that involvement. Or, if he does not, he is not behaving like a critic but just like another member of the audience.

Now, how does the psychoanalytic critic fit into this dual role? We have seen that there are three kinds of psychoanalytic criticism. Clearly, when the critic refers his psychoanalytic insight about the work to the author's mind, he describes scientifically the creative side of the literary process. When he refers his insight to the minds of the audience, he describes scientifically the responsive side of the literary process. But what, if anything, do psychoanalytic statements about character describe in a scientific way? And in what sense does the psychoanalytic critic ever enter into and affect the literary process itself? All too often the psychoanalytic critic seems to be probing away quite cut off from the investigations of traditional Shakespearean criticism, particularly those, like the modern concern with imagery, theme, and meaning, that have most profoundly affected audiences.

We need to "place" psychoanalytic criticism in the literary process, and, to do so, we need to bring together the particular insights we have been considering in the second part of this book and the larger theoretical picture of the literary process in the first part.

THE LITERARY CONTINUUM

In the simplest model of that process, an author, out of his inner and outer experience, writes a text to which his audience, out of its inner and outer experience, responds. In the earlier psychoanalytic picture, the artist responded to an unconscious wish from within and disguised it so as to express it in a text. The audience in some way stripped off that disguise and responded to the unconscious content hidden within.

The later and more sophisticated psychoanalytic view would see the formal disguise as analogous to a defense (and adaptation): it has its own special unconscious determinants, and it molds the form of the impulse even as the impulse in turn molds the defense. We need to think of a complex feedback between impulse and defense rather than simply of an unchanged impulse clothed in an essentially separate disguise. So with the audience: it responds not just to the unconscious material but to that material in terms of the defenses embodied in the formal texture of the work (identification, projection, and so on—see Chapter 4). We need to recognize a dual feedback, between author and text, between text and audience.

When we move from a simple text (as, say, a lyric) to a text with a narrative element (epic, drama, or novel), the situation becomes still more complex. We are no longer dealing with a text alone but a text *cum* imagined event. In that cliché among writers, the characters "take on a life of their own": to some extent, the imagined events dictate the form of their expression in the text. At the same time, as we saw in Chapter 10, the internal logic or *mythos* of the text shapes the event described. We have to think, then, of a three-way interaction or feedback: between the author's original intention modified by the event's own vitality, further modified by the logic of the text, these latter two also modifying each other.

The audience's act of re-creation parallels the author's act of creation. From the textual expression, the audience imagines an event (which will not be exactly the same as the one the author imagined), and this event takes on in the mind of each member of the audience a life of its own from that man's experience. This "life of its own," in turn, will affect his perception of the text. Yet, the text, because it is a *fait accompli,* controls, even as it is controlled by, the imagined event. And it is to this interaction of text and event that each member of the audience responds in the complex terms of his own character and experience.

Part of that experience is whatever criticism he may have read, be it psychoanalytic or conventional. He may have heard from a literary historian that Elizabethan audiences regarded avenging a father as a Christian duty or that they knew Jews only as caricatures in pop cult: if our hypothetical member of the audience has heard this and in part believed it, he will respond to *Hamlet* or *The Merchant of Venice* accordingly. A myth critic may have told him Falstaff has many of the qualities of a Lord of Misrule; and again he will carry his notions about that ubiquitous figure of mythology to his next meeting with Sir John. The orthodox critic, when he acts as a teacher, enters the complex system of interactions and feedbacks which is the literary transaction at the point of audience experience. It is not usually very clear why, in an objective (or scientific) sense, he should be introducing Elizabethan rituals or audience reactions to a twentieth-century playgoer's response, but at least it is quite clear that that is what he is in fact doing. The teaching function of orthodox criticism shows much more clearly than its scientific underpinnings.

THE ROLE OF PSYCHOANALYTIC CRITICISM

For psychoanalytic criticism, just the reverse is true: the science of it is clear, but its active role in the literary process much less so. Many psychologies have served in the past as the scientific foundation for literary criticism, but until Freud there was virtually no truly scientific theory of personality. Even now, sixty years later, psychoanalytic psychology is the only one we have that meets both the demands literature makes on a psychology. First, and this would seem reasonably obvious, a psychology for literature ought to be true, and psychoanalytic psychology does have considerable scientific support (not as much as academic psychologies, but more than Jung's analytic psychology, its only rival in the field of literature). Second, a psychology to be useful for literary purposes should be able to discuss our emotions, those aspects of ourselves most personal and individual and therefore most relevant to literature; psychoanalytic psychology does so, far more than either academic or Jungian psychology presently can. Since literature demands a psychology of personality and since the psychoanalytic psychology of personality seems, in large part at least, the most valid scientifically, we have no choice, no matter how odd the psychoanalytic picture of man may sometimes seem.

Scientifically, then, psychoanalysis makes a strong claim on our belief, but what relevance does its scientific description of the literary process as lived in particular works bear to the real response of an audience? What is the teaching function of psychoanalytic criticism? The critic, be he orthodox or psychoanalytic, is above all a member of the audience himself. As he is a critic, though, he is also a dispassionate observer of the literary process (which, of necessity, includes himself). Then, third, he is a teacher to the degree that he passes on his observations or interpretations of this process (including himself) to the audience (which, again, includes himself). The observing side of criticism and the interpersonal side are no more separate for the psychoanalytic critic than for any other kind, but, for him, the teaching side seems less relevant. Indeed, it involves a certain risk.

That risk becomes all too abundantly clear with post-Freudian writers such as Eugene O'Neill or Tennessee Williams or Arthur Miller. They seem to create plays using Freud as a kind of combination larder and cookbook from which the playwright takes complexes and castrations, devouring mothers and damning fathers, as though one could concoct *grande cuisine* by mixing cans off a shelf. A knowledge of psychoanalysis, however, need not be so harmful to true creativity —there are, after all, artists who have managed to read Freud without drying up the wells of creativity within: Joyce and Faulkner in fiction or, in drama, Beckett and Ionesco. These writers succeed where others fail; presumably, for the same reason, psychoanalytic insights into the *modus operandi* of the literary process need not destroy audience reactions.

Yet there is a risk and fear associated with spreading scientific insights into the literary process. Some well-meaning souls would say 'twere to consider too curiously to consider so; asking—even worse, answering—such questions will only spoil our enjoyment of Shakespeare. Such people expect the magic to vanish when the reader is told that the horror of *Macbeth* is based on primal scene fantasies or that our glee at *The Merchant of Venice* comes from the good mother's triumphing over the harsh father. The artist's bag of tricks once exposed, these good people seem to say, both artist and works will be shown up as the Autolycan con games they are, the tawdry alchemy of the firm of Face and Subtle, or the razzle-dazzle of Felix Krull; much better to be blissfully ignorant.

Such fears, though, are surely unwarranted, for psychoanalytic criticism seems not to have this effect. Speaking for myself, I can say that I enjoy the experience of *Macbeth* or *Hamlet* just as much as I did before learning the psychoanalytical tricks these tragedies turn. My wonder at Shakespeare's artistry is, if anything, greater than it was before. Nor do I know of anyone else whose already-existing enjoyment is spoiled by understanding the work of art, certainly not by understanding its intellectual content, but, oddly enough, not even by understanding its emotional content, either.

Actually, there is a good theoretical reason for this state of affairs. The modern literary critic, in essence, simply points to the work of art and says, "See? This is how it all works together." The psychoanalytic critic (when he is being affective) points to the work and says, "See? These are the things with which the work creates its effect on you." The conventional critic tells us how it *means,* the psychological critic how it *moves* us. Both the work's meaning and the conventional critic's telling us how it means involve intellectual knowledge. That knowledge some people will use as a defense against the raw experience of the work of art. For those who already need the defense, conscious knowledge of any kind will serve, insights from conventional as well as psychoanalytic criticism though, admittedly, psychoanalytic insights have a special kind of lurid fascination.

Even so, the crucial thing is the need for defense, not the kind of knowledge that happens to be available to satisfy that need; and short of a farreaching overhaul of personality (from therapy, for example), nothing will change that need. For those who do not need to defend against the work of art, be they ordinary members of the audience or a Faulkner or a Joyce, knowledge will affect only the way they consciously see the work, not the unconscious or preconscious roots of emotional response. Those who do not need to defend will not. Those who do need to defend will, and they will use any kind of knowledge that comes their way to intellectualize their response.

Such a defensive maneuver involves some loss of impact and probably represents a block to an artist's creativity or an audience's re-creativity. It is not, however, all bad or "sick"—but simply another kind of response for a certain kind of character structure. I suspect, for example, that most, if not all, critics share this need to defend against the direct impact of a work of art—otherwise, why would they go beyond mere experience to perform "the critical act"? If so, this defensive need lies behind all our scientific understanding of the literary process.

Did not Freud himself say, "Some rationalistic, or perhaps analytic, turn of mind in me rebels against being moved by a thing without knowing why I am thus affected and what it is that affects me"? And like him, "Je résolus," said Baudelaire, "de m'informer du pourquoi et de transformer ma volupté en connaissance." To criticize, said Henry James, is "to appreciate, to appropriate, to take intellectual possession, to establish, in fine, a relation with the criticized thing and make it one's own." James is wiser in these words than Arnold and Eliot, who seem to think that criticism can be a dispassionate endeavor. It cannot. Criticism inevitably involves all three of the critic's roles: member of the audience himself; dispassionate observer of the literary process (including himself); active participant affecting at least his own and maybe others' reactions. The two sides of the critical act we so carefully separated at the opening of this chapter cannot really be separated. They blend in their own common denominator—the critic himself.

The psychoanalytic critic is scientific, and he also teaches—but how? So far we have only said how he does not or need not block our emotional response. But then how does he affect the literary transaction when he conveys his psychoanalytic insights? To answer that question, we need to look back at the three particular kinds of psychoanalytic criticism, for it is in these three kinds that the critic's insights will take form. But now it must be clear, these three kinds cannot be separated any more than the two functions of the critic.

In Chapter 10 we saw how necessary it was for the critic to refer his insights to the mind of the audience (including himself) instead of the nonexistent mind of one of the characters. Now we see that when he does so, when he does look at the audience response, part of that response is to the characters as though they were real people. To talk about the character's mind is to talk about the audience's; to talk about the audience's is to give the character a mind. Where we went wrong in Chapter 10 was in saying that some reactions to a work of art are permissible, desirable, licit, sensible, and others not. "Ought" has no business here. So far as the audience *qua* audience is concerned, almost any reaction is reasonable and proper if not, indeed, necessary. How else could I enter a play reality except by relating it to my own highly personal and idiosyncratic world? How else could I react to a character except by relating him to people I have known or been? But only those reactions make sense *for criticism* which either, one, are relevant to the actual literary process and thus to the critic's scientific function, or, two, can be made meaningful to the other members of the audience and thus to the critic's teaching function.

In the complex of feedbacks among author, text, imagined event, audience, critic as audience, as teacher, and as researcher, to talk about one of these is to become enmeshed in them all. The psychoanalytic critic of character, so sharply cut down to size in Chapter 10, here earns his place in the story, and we can answer the first question this chapter asked: What is the psychoanalytic critic of character "scientifically" describing?

When the critic of character finds homosexual jealousy in Iago, an oral identity crisis in Coriolanus, or an oedipus complex in Hamlet, he necessarily implies that these states of mind were possible for Shakespeare and also that they are possible for us in the audience. When he lifts the character out of the contrived reality of the play and looks at him as though he lived in the differently complicated real world, he is only doing systematically what all of us in the audience do preconsciously—respond to the characters as real people. Psychoanalytic analysis of character does not logically conflict with psychoanalytic criticism of the play as a totality: it simply represents a different accent, a stress on a different side of the audience's reaction. That reaction involves an interaction between entering the world of the play and bringing the characters out of the world of the play and making them one's own. The psychoanalytic critic of character is "scientifically" describing the way he himself has brought the characters into his world.

Dr. Johnson held that we credit a drama as a just picture of a real original, while Coleridge announced his famous "willing suspension of disbelief," translated into modern psychological terms, a suspension of the ego function of reality testing. Logically, these two contradict each other: we cannot respond to a play as both a just portrayal of a reality outside itself and something to which notions of realistic accuracy do not apply. But we can see we do both when we recognize the complex series of feedbacks which is the literary process. The text controls and informs the imagined event it portrays—Coleridge is right. Yet that imagined event "takes on a life of its own" and shapes and informs our perception of the text—Johnson is right. Again, we have, not a schism, but different sides of a single two-way street.

In the same way, the psychoanalytic critic of character who finds, say, an oedipus complex in Hamlet the prince will find, if he looks at *Hamlet* the poem, an oedipal world made up of a variety of fathers and sons in various oedipal attitudes. To analyze the world of the play as a whole is to give us certain expectations about the characters; to analyze the characters apart from their world is to tell us about the words and things in their world. Analysis of character—or analysis of text—is only a first step in criticism, and our six logical pigeonholes (two functions of the critic times three kinds of psychoanalytic criticism) do not form compartments at all, but simply different points of involvement in a net of interactions.

In this sense of continuum also lies the answer to the second question this chapter asked: How does the psychoanalytic critic affect the response of the audience? The orthodox critic suggests to his readers social, moral, aesthetic, religious, or intellectual themes in the work he is talking about and so affects what his readers bring to it. But the psychoanalytic critic, by the very nature of his discipline, deals in themes which are unconscious and which, in being brought to consciousness, encounter great resistance.

It is little wonder, then, that psychoanalytic criticism has languished in the antechambers of acceptability. The man who tells us the skulls in that Danish graveyard are testicles or that Desdemona suffers from penis envy meets, not unsurprisingly, a certain amount of puzzlement if not downright scoff. And yet *Othello* is very much a play of love and war, in which heterosexual love is replaced by a conflict between men; the Turkish navy or Iago's cynicism interrupts the marriage of the general and his "fair warrior." Is, then, a notion of penis envy or something like it so farfetched? *Hamlet,* we have seen, is a play about the ways in which an inner problem makes the outer world weary, stale, flat, and unprofitable. In that very graveyard Hamlet finds the outward visible signs of his inward resignation—is it so farfetched that he should also find there external symbols for those parts of his body so deeply involved in his disillusionment?

There is, in short, another continuum to be considered. So far we have been discussing the literary process as though it were, so to speak, horizontal: a transaction running from author to text to reader. The interactions among these three, complex as they are, run back and forth along this one line. There is, though, another dimension, a vertical continuum which gives that line "depth." And it is in revealing this continuum that the psychoanalytic critic can perform the traditional teaching function of the critic. He can help, as no other critic can, an audience to experience an essential function of works of art—the transmutation of grotesque unconscious fantasies into a meaningful social, moral, or intellectual wholeness.

THE PSYCHOLOGICAL CONTINUUM

Freud, in describing human personality, used the latest and richest version of the metaphor that Plato, Augustine, More, Bacon, Campanella, and many others before him had used: the city. Freud suggested that we think of the human mind as like the Rome he enjoyed so much. At the deepest level lies the primitive village of the Latin tribes. Erected on it are the cities of the republic and the empire. On their ruins, in turn, rose the city of medieval Christendom and from it the Rome of modern Italy. And yet the avenues clogged by the traffic jams of today follow the path worn down by the solitary herdsman of antiquity—indeed, his choice of route centuries before has much to do with the congestion and conflicts of today.

In the city, modern builds on ancient. Modern also brings much that is new, but it escapes only with considerable destruction and renewal the paths anciently laid down. So in the mind: the intellectual and moral concerns lately arrived at in the adult build on the primitive paths and communities of the child. We need to think of modern and ancient, adult and child, as coexisting, as if, by a kind of time-machine vision, we could see in the center of the magnificence of St. Peter's the dream shadow of the Circus Neronis dedicated to cruel and uncanny sports.

Adult and child coexist; but the orthodox critic sees only the adult mind, and the psychoanalytic critic, all too often, sees only the child. The truth lies rather in the continuum between them. The religious, aesthetic, social, moral, or intellectual themes the orthodox critic develops have their roots in the infantile fantasies and conflicts the psychoanalytic critic points out. Indeed, it is only because infantile basis and adult superstructure exist in us together that these intellectual concerns can have at all the emotional power they do in art. Both the psychoanalytic critic and his conventional counterpart need to recognize that each tells half the story. Not only are there complex two-way bonds back and forth between author, text, and reader—these bonds themselves have higher and lower sides, each of which informs the other. As in the joke we analyzed at the outset, the intellectual "point" acts as an adaptation and an opening for the infantile impulse, which, in turn, gives the intellectual point its charge of emotion and pleasure.

In short, the psychoanalytic critic has (by and large) been both too logical and not logical enough. That is, he has confined himself too rigidly (even if not too explicitly) to one or a combination of the three kinds of psychoanalytic criticism. He has thus failed to follow out the assumptions of his own discipline. As we saw in Chapter 1, the essence of psychoanalysis is that it deals objectively with the data of subjectivity. To do so, to think in a truly psychoanalytic way, one must move back and forth from one's own inner responses to what the objective, scientific descriptions of psychoanalysis have to say about those inner responses.

The psychoanalytic critic needs to recognize that he is himself part of the literary process he is describing. The character he analyzes does not exist "out there" in some never-never land; the realism of the character comes as one part—although only one part—of the critic's own responses. Conversely, the play itself is not an isolated reality, a text that can be analyzed separate from the analyzer. What criticism needs is a sense of the continuum and interaction between objective work of art and subjective response; or as this book has tried to act out by its own odd form, between the categories of actual psychoanalytic criticism (Part II) and the psychoanalytic concepts that show how these categories are really not categories but blend one into another (Part I). To understand a work of art, one must understand oneself.

That is clear enough for the critic's thinking, but how about his writing? How does he express this sense of continuum between work and self short of a most unseemly autobiographical baring? By careful language. Through a process of translating psychoanalytic insights into terms that can also describe the play in the moral and aesthetic terms of orthodox criticism. Incidentally, this same admonition applies to ordinary criticism as well, if the critic wishes to express this sense of continuum in the literary transaction. That is, a conventional critic who states simply that, at the outset of the tragedy, Macbeth is physically courageous gives us an isolated insight. If he were to rephrase it—at the outset, Macbeth has "animal courage"—he would bring his insight into meaningful relation with the rest of the tragedy: with a major series of images (animals) and a major theme, What is a man?

For the psychoanalytic critic, however, the difference in terminology spans a far greater range. He is involved in words like oedipus complex, sibling rivalry, repression, displacement, self-object differentiation, and the like. How can he translate these into words that describe the play as a whole? By showing how the intellectual "meaning" of the play grows from the emotional content.

SIX SHAKESPEAREAN INSTANCES

Macbeth is a useful example because psychoanalytic criticism, by and large, has not approached the play through the realistic analysis of character but rather through over-all patterns, thus removing one element from our problem.

From a conventional point of view, five recurring themes stand out for me in *Macbeth*: (1) uncertain perception (the vanishing witches and ghosts, the mysterious voices, such questions as, "Is this a dagger which I see before me?"). (2) The supernatural (witches, prophecies, apparitions, ghosts, and omens). (3) The natural world of eating, drinking, sleeping, having children, in short, domestic and political life. (4) The unnatural disease represented by the Macbeths who corrupt eating, drinking, sleeping, and having children, turning Scotland from "our mother" to "a grave." (5) Finally, the idea of breeding understood either as having children or as spreading evil: "Unnatural deeds do breed unnatural troubles." We could state the essential *Macbeth* quality as: uncertain perception of the way supernatural, natural, and unnatural mingle in a man's mind and breed outward.[4]

Psychoanalytic criticism, by contrast, sees *Macbeth* as the interaction of oedipal patterns. Macbeth, a bad "son," allies himself with a bad "mother" to kill a good "father," Duncan. Then, having become a bad "father" or king, Macbeth kills a mother and a son (the Macduffs). Then, a good son, Malcolm, and a not-so-good father, Macduff (both dissociated from women), slay the bad "father," and the good son becomes a good king (or "father").

We can see in these patterns the emotional roots of one of the five big intellectual themes of the tragedy: breeding. Good "fathers" and "sons" dissociate themselves from women: the sons show asexual filial piety, the fathers asexual authority. Bad "fathers" or "sons" get involved with women and concern themselves with breeding, understood either as the act of fathering children or as betraying and destroying family life.

Others of the five themes have the same sexual dualism as "breeding." For example, the concept of the supernatural seems to involve doing the will of another. Macbeth fights rebels for the Lord's anointed, King Duncan, whose virtues plead like angels. Malcolm and Macduff fight under the aegis of the "holy" English king "with Him above to ratify the work." Submission to a father justifies even murder (as of Macdonwald or Macbeth). But this submission is evil and unnatural when Macbeth acts under the auspices of the weird sisters or Lady Macbeth—women. The intellectual themes of the natural and unnatural involve a similar dualism. A noble wishes that

> we may again
> Give to our tables meat, sleep to our nights,

> Free from our feasts and banquets bloody knives,
> Do faithful homage and receive free honors—
> All which we pine for now,

(III. vi. 33–37)

all which, presumably, he had under Duncan (a man alone) but which Macbeth has now corrupted (a man acting in submission to a woman).

In short, beneath the intellectual dualisms seem to lie conflicting attitudes toward a father. Alone, he is a beneficent and justifying authority, but in relation to a woman, "He wants the natural touch." The witches themselves represent the deepest form of this ambiguity:

> You should be women,
> And yet your beards forbid me to interpret
> That you are so.

(I.iii.45–47)

Perhaps, too, this constant sense of uncertainty has a symbolic value: the ambiguities in gender, the blood, the darkness, the mysterious noises at night may represent a primal scene fantasy.

At any rate, this pervasive need to "interpret," this theme of ambiguity and uncertainty of perception functions defensively. Responding to a father as benevolent political authority works to reassure against or cancel out that other sense of the father as a frightening and dangerous sexual being. We see this dualism or ambiguity in all the episodes of uncertain perception. We see it, too, in the structure of the tragedy: two waves, one of crime, one of punishment. They act like the defense of doing and undoing (acting on an aggressive impulse, then trying magically to cancel the deed out). The antitheses in the language work the same way: "Fair is foul, and foul is fair." "Nothing is / But what is not."

This sense of uncertainty also functions as a projection: Is Macbeth responsible for his crimes? Or the witches? Or Lady Macbeth?

> Is this a dagger which I see before me,
> The handle toward my hand?

*   *   *   *

> Or art thou but
> A dagger of the mind, a false creation
> Proceeding from the heat-oppressèd brain?

(II.i.33–39)

If these impulses and attitudes are in me, I am guilty. If they are outside me, in destiny or, particularly, in a justifying father, I am innocent. But if I have taken them in, not from a father, but from a woman, I am even more guilty.

Thus, beneath the oedipal pattern of love and hate among fathers, mothers, and sons we come to a still deeper stratum, the problem of earliest infancy: taking things in from outside; what is me and what is not-me? Defensively, Macbeth uses the uncertainty to sustain himself, to justify and explain his actions:

> Upon my head *they* placed a fruitless crown,

and to supply himself with courage:

> Come, Fate, into the list,
> And champion me to th'utterance!

And yet this taking in from outside becomes also a fatal dependence. When the prophecies fail him, "I pull in resolution," "I 'gin to be aweary of the sun." "It hath cowed my better part of man."

At the deepest level, then, the "uncertain perception of the way supernatural, natural, and unnatural mingle in a man's mind and breed outward" (our intellectual statement of the essential *Macbeth* quality) translates into a wish to act aggressively justified by obedience to a parent poised against a fear of dependence and subsequent betrayal of a libidinal kind. In short, the psychoanalytic reading can tell us in a more or less scientific way how the unconscious conflicts and fears buried in us let us find in the fictitious events and intellectual issues of the tragedy emotional power.

Macbeth shows how psychoanalytic readings of over-all (nonrealistic) pattern lead us from intellectual response to its emotional roots in unconscious conflict. In *Coriolanus* the psychoanalytic readings of character lead us to our emotional response. The psychoanalytic critics of character see the hero as a phallic, authoritarian personality seeking to establish himself in terms of his aggression. Under the phallic pattern lies the deeper oral conflict from which it stems: the infant striving to prove his identity separate from a mother who encompasses him. To put it another way, Coriolanus behaves in adult life (in the contrived world of the tragedy) like a man who, through early frustrations, developed an extraordinary amount of unmastered aggression which his mother diverted from herself onto other objects. Farfetched as this statement about a nonexistent infancy may sound, the play provides more than ample evidence for it. But what has it to do with any ordinary reading of the play?

Conventional criticism might begin with a comment like Professor Harry Levin's, on a contrast in the imagery: between walls, buildings, gates, swords, shields, even the Tarpeian rock (hard things) to images of soft flesh or food or cloth. It is precisely Coriolanus' problem to move "from th' casque to th' cushion" and precisely this he cannot do, instead

> commanding peace
> Even with the same austerity and garb
> As he controlled the war.
>
> (IV.vii.43–45)

Similarly, the imagery contrasts deeds and words, Coriolanus failing at the latter even as he is successful at the former. We are seeing in a symbolic or intellectual form the infantile crisis of identity: Coriolanus forced from the soft and symbiotic unit of mother and son into trying to establish his identity by hard deeds in a harder context. Another group of images and episodes contrasts authority which is sole and authority which is divided. Coriolanus succeeds in battle where he is on his own, but fails when he must mingle himself with others, as in civil affairs—or in the primal mother-child unit.

The analysis of Coriolanus' character leads not only to the reason for his downfall but also to a handsome instance of the way realistic character traits blend into the nonrealistic poetic world of the play, each informing the other. We could say *Coriolanus* is, intellectually, a tragedy of contexts, but that rather late and adult tragedy reaches back to an earlier one, fighting oneself loose from the context of an overwhelming mother. What, though, of the nonrealistic psychoanalytic interpretations of the tragedy—that Coriolanus is a son confronted with helpful, aggressive, or treacherous fathers (Menenius, Aufidius, or the tribunes) and mothers (Volumnia, the citizens, Rome herself)? Here again Coriolanus can find his identity in aggressive actions either toward men or shared with men; he cannot stand being dependent on a mother figure. The total pattern of the play shades into the individual characterization and also into the tragedy's significance.

Perhaps, too, we have a clue to that feeling with which audiences always confront this play: the difficulty of identifying with Coriolanus. We have trouble identifying with him because his identity is, in fact, so precariously established, as shown by "thy stol'n name Coriolanus." The hero lacks the basic libidinal openness necessary before we can ourselves become libidinally involved in his fate: we cannot love a man who does not love himself. Coriolanus shares this disability with Shakespeare's other "Roman heroes," Brutus, Octavius, or even Hotspur, those men who cast aside libidinal ties to peace and family to pursue aggressive aims of war and murder. But these other plays take us into Shakespeare's own character and away from the process we are considering: the way psychoanalytic readings show the emotional roots of a play's theme and significance.

This process probably shows more clearly in *The Merchant of Venice* than in any other of the plays we have been considering in detail. The psychoanalytic readings are plentiful; the view of orthodox New Criticism is clear. We might begin with C. S. Lewis's statement that "The real play is not so much about men as about metals. The play, he goes on to say, sets off Shylock's efforts to take "a breed of barren metal" against Bassanio's marrying the almost-allegorical figure of The Princess, offering her all he has: "All the wealth I had ran in my veins." The play contrasts the cold, lifeless, mineral wealth worshiped by Shylock to the wealth of human relationships he tries to abuse: Jessica and Lorenzo, Bassanio and Portia, Bassanio and Antonio.

The psychoanalytic readings see the play also as contrasting two worlds. Both have oral and anal elements, but one, Venice, is harsh, aggressive, masculine, and niggardly; the other, Belmont, is bountiful, merciful, feminized, and libidinal. In other words, the psychoanalytic readings find the unconscious roots (in our minds or Shakespeare's) for these two different feelings about wealth, and about male and female. After all, it is woman who is the life-giver—man's role in the process is much more tenuous: "It's a wise child that knows its own father." In effect, we could say *The Merchant of Venice* deals with an early and ongoing human wish—to have. One way to "have" someone is aggressively, destructively, and such having leads to lifelessness, sterility, the "use" (usury) of people, to use the play's term. The other kind of having leads to mutual giving, to creating life, or riches of a nature quite unmonetary.

The notion of "having" leads to a second basic issue in the play, risk. An element of risk in making your money breed absolves you of the sin of usury. Shylock sins in that he seeks a certain return. Bassanio, Antonio, Portia, Jessica are all willing to take a chance: "Who chooseth me must give and hazard all he hath." [5] Again, the psychoanalytic readings contrasting libidinal and aggressive ways of "having" people tell us the roots of the feeling the play gives. To "have" aggressively is to destroy, to render lifeless. To "have" libidinally is to unite with the other, and to do that one must (quite literally) take a chance. To love another, I must risk myself, take the chance of being rebuffed. It is in this sense that Portia presents herself as a risky riddle. Life is a risky riddle, and Portia is life. At the deepest level *The Merchant of Venice* works with the feeling of trust a child needs to have toward his mother: I can depend on her, I can risk her displeasure without disastrous results. In the world of Venice, taking a chance

come means to supernatural power. From a conventional point of view, then, three contrasts inform the world of *Richard III:* love and hate; inside and outside; natural and supernatural.

In the play the retribution that sweeps Richard from the throne has something of a supernatural quality, symbolizing, from a psychoanalytic point of view, the unknown forces within the self. As Richard says, after his dreams before the final battle,

> Have mercy, Jesu! Soft! I did but dream.
> O coward conscience, how dost thou afflict me!
> The lights burn blue. It is now dead midnight.
> Cold fearful drops stand on my trembling flesh.
> What do I fear? Myself? There's none else by.
> Richard loves Richard; that is, I am I.
> Is there a murderer here? No. Yes, I am:
> Then fly. What, from myself? Great reason, why?
> Lest I revenge. What, myself upon myself?
> Alack, I love myself. Wherefore? For any good
> That I myself have done unto myself?
> O no! Alas, I rather hate myself
> For hateful deeds committed by myself.
> I am a villain. Yet I lie, I am not.
> Fool, of thyself speak well. Fool, do not flatter.
> My conscience hath a thousand several tongues,
> And every tongue brings in a several tale,
> And every tale condemns me for a villain.
> Perjury, perjury, in the highest degree,
> Murder, stern murder, in the direst degree,
> All several sins, all used in each degree,
> Throng to the bar, crying all, "Guilty! Guilty!"
>   (V.iii.179–199)

His self-dialogue shows the several dualisms of the play, between what is inside and what is outside, supernatural and natural, words as things and words as forces. The speech shows, too, Richard's ambivalence.

In effect, his trouble is that, despite his protestations, he does not love himself—enough. He lacks that basic substratum of self-esteem or narcissism that any human being (or literary character) must have in order to function: he can neither really love nor really be loved,

> And therefore, since I cannot prove a lover
> To entertain these fair well-spoken days,
> I am determined to prove a villain
> And hate the idle pleasures of these days.
>   (I.i.28–31)

Richard tries to make up this lack of self-love by making himself all, by making himself the kingdom which will then perforce respect Richard as its king:

> The wretched, bloody, and usurping boar,
> That spoiled your summer fields and fruitful vines,
> Swills your warm blood like wash, and makes his trough
> In your embowelled bosoms—this foul swine
> Is now even in the centre of this isle.
>
> (V.ii.7–11)

Richard devours his environment. He tries to make what is outside him part of himself; he tries to push the titantic forces within him onto the world around him. In technical terms, we are dealing with two opposed defenses: identification with the aggressor and projection, psychological forms of what the conventional critic would call the theme of inside and outside.

We can also guess at an oedipal motif: Richard behaves like a man who desperately needs to possess (devour) the nurturing mother. Measuring the retaliation he fears by his own brutality, he tries to make himself immune by becoming the thing he fears:

> I'll marry Warwick's youngest daughter.
> What though I killed her husband and her father?
> The readiest way to make the wench amends
> Is to become her husband and her father.
>
> (I.i.153–156)

Here we have a clue to the mythic pattern of the play. Good King Henry VI is murdered by a bad king in the image of a boar (as in the myths of Osiris or Adonis) and mourned by three queens. The boar-king, now his successor, lays the land waste, but he is finally killed by good King Henry VII who comes from across the sea to kill the boar-king and set the wasteland free. In effect, in the style of this play, the titanic forces within Richard become supernatural forces outside him. The catastrophe comes when the world outside Richard ceases to be a mere series of things he can manipulate, but takes on a libidinal and aggressive life of its own and revolts against its Frankenstein master.

Again we see the psychological (and mythic) pattern within the character giving rise to the dualistic themes of the tragedy: love and hate, inside and outside, natural and supernatural. Again we see the interaction of conscious theme and unconscious impulse and defense as giving rise to the distinctive style of the play. And, again, we see Shakespeare's concern with ambivalence and defenses against it. Here, Richard defends by attempting to make himself omnipotent, but he fails within and falls without.

Romeo and Juliet and *Richard III* are early plays—*The Tempest* comes at the very end of Shakespeare's career. Yet even in this late comedy we find the same attempt to master conflicting aggressive and libidinal impulses through isolating them and projecting them outward. The psychoanalytic insights into the play are two. From the realistic point of view of analyzing character, Prospero is giving over his oedipal attraction to his daughter. From a nonrealistic point of view (considering over-all patterns), the other characters in the comedy are projections of Prospero's own psyche.

Conventional criticism points to *The Tempest* as a play (like the also-late *Winter's Tale*) about art and nature: a play very much about plays, with its interest in acting, shows, masques, costume, music, and teaching. In effect, the play shows us a magus-king with godlike powers manipulating the other characters so as to lead them into the paths of justice and chastity. Prospero uses his island to teach the way to heaven, just as God (or destiny) "hath to instrument this lower world / And what is in't." As the myth critics have pointed out, the comedy is an initiation ritual, an imitation of death and rebirth (from the sea), with Prospero leading the conspirators through a maze, putting them to sleep, showing them supernatural visions, and finally welcoming them as adult members of the group:

> The charm dissolves apace;
> And as the morning steals upon the night,
> Melting the darkness, so their rising senses
> Begin to chase the ignorant fumes that mantle
> Their clearer reason.

(V.i.64–68)

Being controlled by outer force brings the conspirators against the "king" to a mature control of their impulses.[7] Conversely, by controlling the people around him (projections, according to the psychoanalytic critics), Prospero achieves control of his own inner impulses.

But what are those impulses? The psychoanalytic critics say that Prospero masters his oedipal, libidinal ties to his daughter. We can add that he plays with the death or subjugation of a son (of Alonso, parallel to Prospero). Thus, at the end of his life, we find Shakespeare dealing with the impulses of childhood in their latest development, the father's love for a daughter and his resentment of a son-in-law, one recapitulating the child's love for his mother, the other the last version of a child's aggression toward his father or older brother. And Prospero deals with these impulses very much as a writer-director of plays might, by putting them into dramatic characters and moving them through a plot toward catharsis.

SOME HYPOTHESES

By putting psychoanalytic insights and the readings of conventional criticism together to see the continuum of our response, we seem to have come a step closer to "the heart of the mystery," the creative gift itself. We found (in Chapter 6) that Shakespeare creates in his plays an oedipal world (rather than one primarily oral or anal, like Marlowe's or Jonson's). Further, in writing his plays, he uses an extraordinary range of defenses. Now we find that certain defenses stand out if we regard the plays as attempts to deal with love and hate toward the parents: splitting, isolation, and particularly projection. In *The Tempest* we see a play that shows us how projection may have led Shakespeare into becoming a playwright. In effect, we are dealing with an artist who combines an ability to regress to the inner sources of conflict (as any artist must) with the ability to project those sources into an outer world.

Perhaps we have come upon something essential to the nature of drama itself, for, after all, in a play (unlike a novel) the writer must project the character's psyche into episodes and events that an audience can see. By contrast, the novelist is free to lead us into the minds of his characters at will. This is nothing but Aristotle's time-worn distinction: that narrative imitates by language alone, while the dramatist presents "all his characters as living and moving before us." Psychoanalysis now adds that it is the inner life of the characters that lives and moves before us. As a result, the character, realistically considered as something visibly before us, shades into the nonrealistic invisible psychological and moral world of which he is a part.

There may be another new insight. We may have uncovered a basis for the notion of dramatic catharsis: the drama provides us with a ready-built defense which is different from those provided by the novel or the lyric. By projecting what is in the characters outward into externally visible events and actions, a play paves the way for the audience's own act of projection. We find in the external reality of a play what is hidden in ourselves. Drama shows virtue her own feature, scorn her own image, and the very age and body of the time his form and pressure. Watching a set of events in a play feels, for this reason, very different from reading them in a novel.

We may have also come upon a clue to another troublesome distinction, that between tragedy and comedy. In the tragedies (and the one "tragical-historical" play) we have considered so far, the defenses fail. Macbeth's external justifications betray him. Coriolanus' aggressions do not succeed in establishing an identity for him. The splittings and isolations of *Romeo and Juliet* collapse. Richard III does not manage to neutralize his impulses by mastering externals. Conversely, in the two comedies we have looked at, the defenses succeed. The love and hate isolated in *The Merchant of Venice* stay isolated, and the projection of impulses in *The Tempest* leads to their mastery. We can guess at a definition: it is a necessary condition for tragedy that the defense it embodies fail, leading to punishment for an impulse toward pleasure; it is a necessary condition for comedy that it build up a defense, leading to gratification without punishment of an impulse toward pleasure. Perhaps this is why tragedy "feels" deeper, more significant to us, comedy much less so: because in one, defense breaks down; in the other, a defense against unconscious material is set up.

FIVE FURTHER INSTANCES

It would be helpful in testing such a hypothesis if psychoanalytic criticism of Shakespeare had dealt at length with more plays, but we have only one more comedy at our disposal. At that, perhaps because the *Henry IV* and *V* plays deal so explicitly with the relation of father and son, perhaps because women are so peripherally involved in these histories, the readings of orthodox criticism and psychoanalytic blend to a point where it is difficult even to see them separately. Hal's action throughout the two parts of *Henry IV* is to choose between two ways of life, one represented by Falstaff, the other by Henry IV—in effect, he must choose between two fathers. From a psychoanalytic point of view, however, more than choice is involved. A son grows up by internalizing his father in the form of his superego. He must resolve his feelings of rivalry and aggression toward his father by making his father a part of his own character: his moral standards, his idea of what a man should be. He, to use the technical term, defends against his oedipal impulses by identifying with the aggressor.

At first, when we see Hal, he is rebelling against his father by his roistering. His rebellion parallels Hotspur's; both express essentially parricidal impulses. But by the end of *Part I* (and Hal does it again in *Part II*) he has managed to identify with his father and turn his own parricidal impulses outward against other would-be parricides, Hotspur or "they . . . That ever said I heark'ned for your death."

In a deeper sense, though, Henry IV, stained as he himself is with regicide, does not constitute a satisfactory source of moral ideals, and Hal uses other moral standards to replace him, as in his delinquency or his trying on the crown by his father's dying body. Falstaff becomes a father substitute on whom Hal can vent his contempt for a father. Falstaff behaves like a father at the same time that he gratifies Hal's parricidal impulses. Falstaff is the father-like-a-child; his bulk suggests the way he encompasses in one body impulses and attributes that are split off among the other characters. Hal's turning him away at the end of *Part II* represents a reversed version of the rightful outcome. Instead of incorporating this father-like-a-child, Hal turns him out. Falstaff is thus a kind of anti-hero who must be put aside for the hero-king, the child-like-a-father, to emerge. Hal's use of his own moral standards to abuse his father(s) turns out to be a magnificently successful defense.

There may not be enough psychoanalytic criticism of the comedies to test our hypothesis about the role of defenses in comedy. There are, however, tragedies aplenty. Even though the psychoanalytic readings of *Julius Caesar* are rather thin, they tend to confirm this concept of tragedy as "the defense that failed." Orthodox critics see this play as a tragedy of division or separation: the crime is to separate the spirit of Caesar from his body; Brutus and Cassius fail because they are two men with conflicting characters, not one man (like Caesar) bridging body and spirit, realism and idealism. The split at the end of the tragedy between Antony and Octavius presages future civil strife, even as the tragedy of Brutus and Cassius comes full circle. Important images are flawed love, parts of the body, and all kinds of fragmenting and splitting. The structure of the play involves two symmetrical waves: a crime against Caesar's body; the punishment from Caesar's spirit.[8]

From a psychoanalytic point of view, these terms, division or separation, suggest the defense of splitting or isolation. Brutus and Cassius murder a king-father to win the city-mother. In their different ways they each isolate the connotations of their act: Cassius by identifying with the aggressor and constantly threatening himself with death; Brutus, more interestingly, by treating the act as purely political:

> For my part,
> I know no personal cause to spurn at him,
> But for the general.
>
> (II.i.10–12)

"Not that I loved Caesar less, but that I loved Rome more."

> O that we then could come by Caesar's spirit
> And not dismember Caesar! But, alas,
> Caesar must bleed for it!
>
> (II.i.169–171)

The raw aggression behind the murder shows through when Brutus
cries,

> Stoop, Romans, stoop,
> And let us bathe our hands in Caesar's blood
> Up to the elbows and besmear our swords.
> (III.i.105–107)

The action of the tragedy as a whole undoes the defense, rejoining
that which has been separated. Cassius says,

> Time is come round,
> And where I did begin, there shall I end.
> My life is run his compass.
> (V.iii.23–25)

And he dies saying:

> Caesar, thou art revenged
> Even with the sword that killed thee.
> (V.iii.45–46)

The final suicides act out the murderous force of guilt from the superego turned by the guilty man upon himself:

> O Julius Caesar, thou art mighty yet!
> Thy spirit walks abroad and turns our swords
> In our own proper entrails.
> (V.iii.94–96)

> Caesar, now be still.
> I killed not thee with half so good a will,
> (V.v.50–51)

says Brutus as, running on his sword, he accepts the father's terrible
revenge for an act he thought he had robbed of emotion by disguising
it as reasons of state. The defense in the tragedy was to split or isolate
the aggressive impulses toward a father. The action of the tragedy is
to undo the isolation.

Something of the sort takes place in *Othello*. A conventional reading might begin with the fact that the opening line of the tragedy,
"Tush, never tell me!" and the closing couplet,

> Myself will straight aboard, and to the state
> This heavy act with heavy heart relate,

both deal with reports. In between there have been the report of
Othello's elopement, the report of the Turkish fleet or of Cassio's

drunken brawl, and, most terribly, Iago's report of Desdemona's adultery. Closely linked to this imagery of reporting or telling are images of seeing, hearing, reasoning, and, in general, trying to make rational decisions about value.[9]

The dominant position of the Venetian state throughout the play suggests another related theme: government. *Othello* is the tragedy of a man's failure to govern either love or war through rational perception of the true value of the people around him. In the words of Othello's remorse:

> O vain boast!
> Who can control his fate?
> (V.ii.265–266)

The psychoanalytic readings would seem to have little to do with this conscious, intellectual "meaning." There are realistic diagnoses of the characters: Othello doubts his own masculinity; Iago is motivated by a homosexual passion for Othello. And there are antirealistic analyses of the defensive pattern in the play: Iago projects aspects of Othello's personality, doubts and cynicism he has repressed, just as Othello projects a faith Iago lacks. Desdemona projects Othello's feminine side, he her masculine side.

These readings, however, are not irrelevant to a play about a man failing to make a rational choice among the people around him. The term "projection" is simply another way of stating the play's recurring interest in its characters' trying to find external causes or "ocular proof" of internal states of mind. Brabantio can find only in witchcraft a reason for his daughter's love for Othello; she herself finds the reason in Othello's soldierly stories (or "reports"). Iago's motive-hunting seeks in external events (or rumors of them) a reason for his more deeply rooted hatred of Othello, and Othello himself cries out in his anguish:

> O curse of marriage,
> That we can call these delicate creatures ours,
> And not their appetites!
> (III.iii.268–270)

As though it were marriage's fault!

In short, the psychoanalytic readings show how the intellectual "meaning" of the play has its roots in the unconscious, Shakespeare's, Othello's, and ours. What we repress biases our judgment so that we cannot "control [our] fate," but we foolishly look in external causes, projections of our true inner states, for answers. The fault is not in our stars but in ourselves. Perhaps it is this sense of misplaced trust or emphasis on external events instead of internal ones that gives rise to the strange double time scheme of the play: external time and inner, psychological time. In any case, the defense fails, the projection recoils upon the self, the isolation of love and war collapses, and Othello, killing himself, dies "upon a kiss."

Lear represents a particularly difficult problem in moving from the psychoanalytic insights to the very, very intellectual meanings assigned this play by conventional critical analysis. The central image is of a body twisted, racked, and tortured in every way, but in particular by loss of covering, as Lear loses kingdom, retainers, "all th'addition to a king," shelter, even his clothing. We are left with "unaccommodated man," and the question whether he is "good Athenian," "noble philosopher," or simply "a poor, bare, forked animal."

We are confronted with two conceptions of nature. One is Edmund's "goddess," red in tooth and claw, a nature of harsh facts; the other is the nature of traditional Christian or medieval values. Another series of images that points up the distinction are those of quantity and measure, the numbering of Lear's followers, for example, or his attempt to quantify the love of his daughters and see "Which of you . . . doth love us most." As against these numbers, rather meaningless in questions of value, is Cordelia's "nothing," the zero which seems to be in the center (like poor, "unaccommodated man") between measurable facts and unmeasurable values. We can say that this is the ultimate tension that racks man in *Lear,* the tension between facts and values, what is and what he wishes were so.[10]

The realistic psychoanalytic critics see Lear's actions as motivated by incestuous wishes for his daughters: in effect, as the Fool says, "thou mad'st thy daughters thy mothers," and Lear now seeks from them love and sustenance. In effect, he tries to disguise the "fact" (his incestuous impulses), as a "value" (filial piety), by regressing to the position of a child. Considered less realistically, Lear as child seeks to intrude (as Cordelia hints) in the relation between his mother (daughters) and father (sons-in-law):

> Why have my sisters husbands if they say
> They love you all? Haply, when I shall wed,
> That lord whose hand must take my plight shall carry
> Half my love with him, half my care and duty,
>
> (I.i.99–102)

and Lear flies into a rage.

Like a masochist, Lear "pays in advance" for his daughters' love by divesting himself of his kingdom. He then masochistically places himself in a dependent, submissive position toward them, expecting nourishment and love. They frustrate his wishes, and he responds by aggression (his rather childish curses), but (again, masochistically) pays for his aggression by turning it against himself, as he forces himself to suffer through the storm. In the last scenes he finds himself in a dependent position again, receiving love and care from a daughter-mother (her husband absent!)—this is a better love, one he did not "pay for." But (again masochistically) the price does not go long unpaid. First, Cordelia pays with her life; then Lear turns the aggression against himself and dies.

Gloucester shows the pattern in miniature. He, too, masochistically places himself in a dependent position to his son Edmund. In return, Edmund (*via* Cornwall) blinds (symbolically castrates) his father who, then, having paid for it, can receive the better, nominally undeserved love of Edgar. But then, like Lear, Gloucester pays for his dependency with his life, or, looked at another way, the son pays the price of his father's life.

Both plots seem to say, then, in a psychoanalytic sense, that love must be paid for at a terrible price (another version of Shakespeare's constant preoccupation with balancing off love and hate). Such a talionic view must stem from a feeling of guilt. The superego becomes projected outward as the harsh term "fact" of the conventional critic's thematic analysis. Conversely, the longing for trust and dependency as described by the psychoanalyst becomes the orthodox critic's theme of "value." More precisely, Lear is acting out a child's wish for omnipotence, that he can somehow, by "paying for it," by magical curses, make people adhere to values and give him love and nurture. In this tragedy the suffering is itself the defensive maneuver. The play tries to blackmail its audience into values, just as Lear, in effect, says to the other characters (except Kent), I am suffering, therefore you must love me. This maneuver, I think, accounts for the peculiarly ambiguous feeling we have at the end—much as we might wish it, one cannot win love by blackmail, whether by giving a kingdom away, or one's clothing, or one's life. Again, in a tragedy, the defense, here a kind of masochistic prepayment, fails.

At last we come to *Hamlet,* the first, both in time and number, of psychoanalytic readings. The plethora of readings, however, makes it hard to see *Hamlet* in terms of a continuum of conscious and unconscious response. Both conventional and psychoanalytic criticism might well take as a point of departure the play's preoccupation with splitting. We see good son and bad son, a variety of fathers, and two women who focus on themselves different attitudes toward women in general. The crucial splitting, though, is within Hamlet himself, who cannot bring together plan and deed or word and action. He can think, and he can act on impulse, but he cannot do them together—except in "play," that is, only if the deed has somehow been divested of any but magical efficacy.[11]

Related to the defense of splitting is that of projection. The tragedy puts different attitudes toward, say, a father into different characters: Hamlet's father, Fortinbras' father, Claudius, Polonius, the ghost; different attitudes of and toward a son into Hamlet, Laertes, or Fortinbras. The two defenses come together in the figures of Horatio and Fortinbras, who represent or project the two aspects of Hamlet, the splitting of which lies at the core of the tragedy: thought and action.

What, though, are these defenses (whether we regard them as Hamlet's, Shakespeare's, or our own) defending against? Psychoanalysis would say, the intolerable burden of the oedipal conflict. This conflict takes two forms. First, there is the task itself: the ghost's demand that Hamlet murder the man who killed his father and married his mother, who did, in short, what Hamlet himself wished unconsciously to do. Second, there is the ambivalence of Hamlet's feelings toward his father and his mother. As in *Macbeth*, we find these different feelings of love and hate split off onto different "fathers," but focused on only one mother figure (perhaps suggesting that the "father" is hated more than the "mother"). Some heavy burden gives rise to this need for splitting and projection. Whatever it is, it represents in psychoanalytic terms what conventional criticism of *Hamlet* would call the motif of the something that is somehow flawed and rotten.

That something becomes either so pervasive or so illusory as to remain quite indefinite (unconscious), and it is this indefiniteness that gives rise to the feeling of mystery and to the pervasive questioning that runs through the tragedy. As many critics have pointed out, *Hamlet* is a tragedy of questions: "Who hath relieved you?" "What, has this thing appeared again tonight?" "Murder?" "Lady, shall I lie in your lap?" Almost every question focuses attention on the external world and away from the questioner. They thus pave the way for the defenses we have seen, notably of projection.

This sense of a rotten world has another element of psychological truth, for in childhood our parents (oedipal as they and we are) are our world. In so far as we respond to adult life in the terms of our childhood, our parents are still our world. To Hamlet, perhaps, to some extent to all of us, that world failed us as we became disillusioned adults. It became "an unweeded garden" that only "things rank and gross in nature possess," as we realized that our parents were not gods but people, and sexual people at that. Hamlet's sense of despair speaks for our own sense of disillusion and also our own falling off. At some point in our growing up (often in the oedipal situation) we realized drastically and had to accept that we ourselves are not gods but merely people.

The sense of the rottenness of things leads us to another line of defense in the tragedy, regression. Confronted with an oedipal problem, Hamlet retreats to an earlier stage of development. He (and Shakespeare and we in the audience) see the world in terms of dust and filth, disease and rotting food. Hamlet adopts a child's technique of retaining his power over his body's productions—delay. He withholds from the demanding parent (the ghost) what he is supposed to give (the act of revenge) until the last moments of the play when he must do it then or never. A typical defense in anal concerns is doing and undoing, an expression of an aggressive impulse followed by an attempt to undo the supposedly magical effect of the expression. We see it here not only in Hamlet's obsessive ruminations ("To be or not to be"), his fondness for comparing or setting one thing off against another ("Look here upon this picture, and on this"), but also in his preoccupation with substituting words for deeds and vice versa. Still more sweepingly, we see doing and undoing in the two-wave structure of the tragedy, a first wave dominated by words and thoughts, a second by unplanned and impulsive action; the first in which Hamlet is the actor, the second in which he is acted upon.

Perhaps this conflict between active and passive is the deepest stratum of our response. In the language of conventional criticism, Hamlet is ultimately a tragedy of imperfection, the human condition, the necessity that dogs us to the end of our days of taking half or second best. In psychoanalytic language, like other Shakespearean tragedies we have seen, *Hamlet* (or *Lear* or *Richard III* or *Othello* or *Coriolanus*) represents the despairing abandonment of the belief that one is omnipotent ("They told me I was everything"), that one can be self-sufficient, the whole world, both parent and child, both active and passive, self and not-self. Conversely, then, we can think of Shakespearean comedy (or at least happy endings) as the achievement of self-sufficiency, becoming both parent and child, son and husband, active and passive, dependent and independent, even sometimes male and female—as Portia does or Rosalind or Viola or Antonio—or Prospero. But much remains to be done in the way of psychoanalytic studies of the Shakespearean canon before one could justify such a generalization in detail.

Much remains to be done, too, before we can accept our other hypotheses: that the central problem in Shakespeare's make-up was to sort out feelings of love and hate toward a single individual; that he adopted the defense of projection as a solution (at least in his playwriting); that comedy in general builds such a defense; tragedy in general breaks it down; that in Shakespearean comedy in particular the happy ending involves control, undoing projections, and bringing conflicting impulses back within the self without being overwhelmed by them; that in Shakespearean tragedy the unhappy ending consists in the failure of a defense followed by loss of control and being overwhelmed both by forces within and without.

AIMS FOR PSYCHOANALYTIC CRITICISM

Much, however, has been done, and some achievements and duties of psychoanalytic criticism have already, I hope, become clear. The insights of psychoanalysis complement and fulfill those of conventional criticism. Theoretically, psychoanalysis shows that literature is a continuum from author through text and imagined event to audience. The author's imagination shapes the text and is shaped by it—so also the audience's imagination. And the critic must see his analyses as directed, not toward a text in a vacuum, but as entering and participating in a complex interaction of text, imagined events, and audience.

Further, and most importantly, the unconscious conflicts in author's mind, audience's, or character's mature as they do in everyday life. Modern builds upon ancient, and the intellectual themes and devices of literature build on the childhood and unconscious foundations of our emotional life. The psychoanalytic critic needs to express this continuum by showing how the insights of his discipline translate the insights of ordinary critical analysis into the language of our inner lives. By such a translation, the psychoanalytic critic recapitulates his author's (and his audience's) original sublimation of the infantile material of the work into its moral and intellectual themes and into its aesthetic form.

If psychoanalytic critics will recognize this continuum and express it, then, to paraphrase Arnold, the future of psychoanalytic criticism is immense. For Shakespeare, there are immediate practical applications. Any criticism worth the ink to write it must have a place in the living theater. The psychoanalytic critic, no less than any other, speaks best when he speaks to that man in the Shakespearean process who most directly combines the roles of author and critic: the director. Quite clearly, the critic of "meaning" can contribute to staging Shakespeare's plays so that (as the author wished) they on our imaginary forces work. If the "meaning" of *Macbeth* involves a concept of supernatural intervention, then a director should so stage the play that his audience becomes aware of supernatural influences, perhaps the faint sound of religious music in the background of the scene involving the "miraculous work" of the English king, perhaps (as G. Wilson Knight suggests) an image of the "naked newborn babe," the Christ child, that becomes increasingly visible as the tragedy proceeds.

Similarly, a psychoanalytic understanding would enable a director so to stage a play as to increase its emotional effect. If the words of *Macbeth* make us fear again as we did when we were children what our parents do when they leave us at night, then the staging should supplement this effect. We should be acutely aware in a performance of *Macbeth* of darkness and mysterious sounds in the night. The witches should be frightening parental figures of doubtful sex and unknown power (not the customary biddies or beams of light). The star who acts Macbeth should convey to us beneath the adult warrior a child's perplexity about what is expected of him. Lady Macbeth should be so played as to hint at her psychological position with respect to her husband (and the audience) as a treacherous, frightening, seductive mother.

Awareness of the unconscious content of the play opens up possibilities in the staging, just as knowledge of meaning does. To achieve these possibilities, the director needs to respond to his own inner promptings and express them, not in the cookbook "Freudianism" of Robert Edmond Jones or Sir Laurence Olivier but in a deeper, more personal sense. After all, Shakespeare's plays ultimately take place, not on the traditional "boards," but "in the quick forge and workinghouse of thought."

But there are issues larger than staging that psychoanalytic criticism unfolds. Psychoanalysis represents a most important strategic bridge from the rigorous, external aims of the sciences and those internal aims of the humanities, less rigorous but more significant and, if you will, more practical. The traditional language of literature bristles with terms ostensibly literary but actually psychological: catharsis, sympathetic imagination, negative capability, stock response, irony, and so on. Such broader humanistic terms as love or virtue, will, courage, pity, these, too, psychoanalysis redefines, making them both specific and rich. So long as we use such humanistic terms without bringing to them all the comprehension our culture offers us, we are blinding ourselves to ourselves. The humanist who turns aside from what psychoanalysis or any other science has to say does both what he professes and himself a disservice, ostriching his wisdom when it is most needed.

We have begun an intellectual revolution every whit as farreaching as that of the seventeenth century, and we ignore it at our peril. The ineffables of art in our century, like the ineffables of religion in the last, have acquired the disconcerting habit of becoming quite rudely and suddenly effable. This is hardly the time to take the teen-age stance of Romeo and cry "Hang up philosophy! Unless philosophy can make a Juliet . . ." Rather, we are tied to the stake of knowledge and we must stand the course. Naturally, no criticism substitutes for the experience of art, psychoanalytic criticism least of all. But the psychoanalytic approach, properly understood and expressed, can perform one service and perform it better than any other approach to literature can. By expressing the continuum from infantile response to intellectual "significance," by translating the traditional terms of humane thought into their emotional roots, the psychoanalytic critic helps us find our alienated twentieth-century selves again by giving to those tired terms a new richness. Psychoanalytic criticism can help literature do what men have always thought it could do, namely, give to airy nothing a local habitation and a name.

Notes

In the notes, the following abbreviations are used:

CP   Sigmund Freud, *Collected Papers*, trans. and ed. Joan Rivière, 5 vols. (London: The Hogarth Press, 1924–1950).

GW   Sigmund Freud, *Gesammelte Werke,* 18 vols. (London: Imago Publishing Co., 1940–1942).

SE   *The Standard Edition of the Complete Psychological Works of Sigmund Freud,* trans. James Strachey, Anna Freud, Alix Strachey, and Alan Tyson, 24 vols. (London: Hogarth Press, 1953–   ).

Int. J. Psa.   *The International Journal of Psycho-Analysis and Bulletin of the International Psycho-Analytical Association* (London).

Jones   Ernest Jones, *The Life and Work of Sigmund Freud,* 3 vols. (New York: Basic Books, Inc., 1953–1957).

Minutes   *Minutes of the Vienna Psychoanalytic Society,* eds. Herman Nunberg and Ernst Federn, trans. M. Nunberg, 3 vols. (New York: International Universities Press, Inc., 1962–   ). At the time of writing, only Volume I was available.

Origins   Sigmund Freud, *The Origins of Psychoanalysis: Letters, Drafts and Notes to Wilhelm Fliess,* 1887–1902, ed. Marie Bonaparte, Anna Freud, Ernst Kris, trans. Eric Mosbacher and James Strachey (New York: Basic Books, Inc., 1954).

SL   *Letters of Sigmund Freud,* selected and edited by Ernst L. Freud, trans. Tania and James Stern (New York: Basic Books, Inc., 1960).

Chapter 1. Groundwork

1. Letter to C. G. Jung, 26 May 1907, *SL*, p. 254.
2. Letter to Heinrich Löwy, 30 March 1930, *SL*, p. 396.
3. Preface to *An Outline of Psychoanalysis* (1940 [1938]), trans. James

Strachey (New York: W. W. Norton, 1949). Freud repeated this idea many times: see, for example, "On the Sexual Theories of Children" (1908), *SE*, IX, 209; "On Psycho-Analysis" (1913 [1911]), *SE*, XII, 210–211; "The Resistances to Psycho-Analysis" (1925 [1924]), *SE*, XIX, 221–222; "The Question of Lay Analysis" (1926), *SE*, 198–199 and 248–249.

4. "Postscript" to *The Question of Lay Analysis* (1926), *SE*, XX, 254.
5. Freud, "On Narcissism: An Introduction," *SE*, XIV, 77. I have taken the five-level structure from Robert Waelder, "Psychoanalysis, Scientific Method and Philosophy," *Journal of the American Psychoanalytic Society*, X (1962), 617–637. Levels one and two, he says, "are entirely indispensable" to an understanding of psychoanalysis, level three follows "at close range." Level four "is necessary, too, though perhaps not in the same degree" and "Metapsychology is far less necessary."

Dr. Waelder is reviewing *Psychoanalysis, Scientific Method, and Philosophy*, ed. Sidney Hook (New York: New York University Press, 1959). This book, the proceedings of a symposium, constitutes virtually an index to all the possible ways of misunderstanding psychoanalysis.

6. See Edward Bibring, "The Development and Problems of the Theory of the Instincts," *Int. J. Psa.*, XXII (1941).
7. *New Introductory Lectures on Psycho-Analysis* (1932), *SE*, XXII, 95.
8. "The Moses of Michelangelo" (1914), *GW*, X, 172; *SE*, XIII, 211.
9. Ernst Kris, *Psychoanalytic Explorations in Art* (New York: International Universities Press, Inc., 1952), p. 14n.
10. "The Claims of Psycho-Analysis to Scientific Interest" (1913), II.f, *GW*, VIII, 416–417; *SE*, XIII, 187.

Chapter 2. Freud on the Artist

1. "Creative Writers and Day-Dreaming" (1908 [1907]); *SE*, IX, 147.
2. *Introductory Lectures on Psycho-Analysis* (1916–1917), Lecture V, *GW*, XI, 93; *SE*, XV, 98–99. *An Autobiographical Study* (1925 [1924]), *GW*, XIV, 90–91; *SE*, XX, 64–66. Preface to Marie Bonaparte, *The Life and Works of Edgar Allan Poe* (1933), *GW*, XVI, 276; *SE*, XXII, 254.
3. *Introductory Lectures* (n. 2), Lecture XXIII, *SE*, XVI, 375–377. *Three Essays on the Theory of Sexuality* (1905), *GW*, V, 140; *SE*, VII, 238–239.
4. *Introductory Lectures, ibid.*
5. *Leonardo da Vinci and a Memory of His Childhood* (1910), *GW*, VIII, 209; *SE*, XI, 136. *Introductory Lectures, ibid.*
6. *Three Essays* (n. 3), *GW*, V, 140; *SE*, VII, 238–239.
7. *Introductory Lectures* (n. 2), *SE*, XVI, 376.
8. "A Special Type of Choice of Object Made by Men" (1910), *GW*,

VIII, 66; *SE*, XI, 165. *Delusions and Dreams in Jensen's* "Gradiva" (1907), *GW*, VII, 33; *SE*, IX, 8.

9. "On the History of the Psycho-Analytic Movement" (1914), *GW*, X, 76–77; *SE*, XIV, 36 (italics mine). See "Gradiva" (n. 8), generally.
10. *Leonardo* (n. 5), *SE*, XI, 131.
11. Preface to Reik's *Ritual: Psycho-Analytic Studies* (1919), *GW*, XII, 327; *SE*, XVII, 261.
12. "Creative Writers" (n. 1), *GW*, VII, 219; *CP*, IV, 182; *SE*, IX, 152. *Totem and Taboo* (1912–1913), sec. IV–7, *GW*, IX, 187–188; *SE*, XIII, 156–158.
13. *Leonardo* (n. 5), *GW*, VIII, 204, 208; *SE*, XI, 132–136.
14. *Civilization and Its Discontents* (1930), *GW*, XIV, 437–438; *SE*, XXI, 79.
15. "Dostoevsky and Parricide" (1928), *SE*, XXI, 173–196, generally. See also Letter to Stefan Zweig, 19 October 1920, *SL*, pp. 331–333.
16. *Beyond the Pleasure Principle* (1920), *GW*, XIII, 15; *SE*, XVIII, 17.
17. *Autobiographical Study* (n. 2), *GW*, XIV, 90–91; *SE*, XX, 65.
18. "Gradiva" (n. 8), generally.
19. "Dostoevsky" (n. 15), generally.
20. *Totem and Taboo* (1912–1913), sec. IV–7, *SE*, XIII, 156–158.
21. *Origins*, Letter of 20 June 1898.
22. "The 'Uncanny'" (1919), *GW*, XII, 242n.; *SE*, XVII, 232n.
23. *Totem and Taboo* (n. 12), *loc. cit.*
24. "Gradiva" (n. 8), *SE*, IX, 85.
25. *Leonardo* (n. 5), *SE*, XI, 115.
26. "The 'Uncanny'" (n. 22), *SE*, XVII, 231.
27. "Medusa's Head" (1940 [1922]), *GW*, XVII, 47–48; *SE*, XVIII, 273–274. On the question of overdetermination, see *The Interpretation of Dreams* (1900), *GW*, II/III, 273; *SE*, IV, 266.
28. "Creative Writers" (n. 1), *SE*, IX, 144. "Formulations on the Two Principles of Mental Functioning" (1911), sec. 6, *GW*, VIII, 237; *SE*, XII, 224. "Five Lectures on Psycho-Analysis" (1910 [1909]), Fifth Lecture; *GW*, VIII, 52; *SE*, XI, 50.
29. "The 'Uncanny'" (n. 22), *SE*, XVII, 248–251. *Beyond the Pleasure Principle* (n. 16), *SE*, XVIII, 17.
30. "The 'Uncanny'" (n. 22), *SE*, XVII, 251. *Civilization* (n. 14), XXI, 80–81. "Psychopathic Characters on the Stage" (1942 [1905–1906]), *SE*, VII, 305.
31. See n. 10, Ch. 1.
32. "Creative Writers" (n. 1), *SE*, IX, 153. *Autobiographical Study* (n. 2), *loc. cit.*
33. *Three Essays* (n. 3), *GW*, V, 111–112; *SE*, VII, 211.
34. Preface to Marie Bonaparte's *Edgar Allan Poe* (1933); *GW*, XVI, 276; *SE*, XXII, 254.
35. "Psychopathic Stage Characters" (n. 30), *SE*, VII, 306.

36. Letter to Yvette Guilbert, 8 March 1931; to Max Schiller, 26 March 1931, *SL*, pp. 404–405.

Chapter 3. Freud on the Work

1. *Delusions and Dreams in Jensen's "Gradiva"* (1907), *GW*, VII, 33; *SE*, IX, 8.
2. "A Special Type of Choice of Object Made by Men" (1910), *GW*, VIII, 66; *SE*, IX, 8.
3. "Some Character-Types Met with in Psycho-Analytic Work" (1916), *GW*, X, 372ff.; *SE*, XIV, 318.
4. Letter to Richard Flatter, 30 March 1930, Jones, III, 451; *SL*, p. 395.
5. "Special Type" (n. 2), *loc. cit.*
6. "Fragment of an Analysis of a Case of Hysteria" (1905 [1901]), *SE*, VII, 60.
7. "The Claims of Psycho-Analysis to Scientific Interest" (1913), II.f., *GW*, VIII, 416–417; *SE*, XIII, 188.
8. Letter to Arnold Zweig, 11 May 1934; Jones, III, 459.
9. *Civilization and Its Discontents* (1930), *GW*, XIV, 441–442; *SE*, XXI, 82–83.
10. "The Moses of Michelangelo" (1914), *GW*, X, 173; *SE*, XIII, 212.

Chapter 4. Freud on the Response

1. "Undoing and Isolation," *Inhibitions, Symptoms, and Anxiety* (1926), Ch. VI, *SE*, XX, 119–123. See also Hugo Münsterberg, "Connection in Science and Isolation in Art," from *The Principles of Art Education* (New York, 1905) reprinted in *A Modern Book of Aesthetics*, ed. Melvin Rader (New York: Henry Holt and Co., 1952), pp. 387–405.
2. *Jokes and Their Relation to the Unconscious* (1905), secs. IV and V; *GW*, VI, 136–150, 174–176; *SE*, VIII, 119–139, 156–158. He extends the concept to literature in general in "Creative Writers and Day-Dreaming" (1908 [1907]), *GW*, VII, 223; *SE*, IX, 153.
3. "Psychopathic Characters on the Stage" (1942 [1905 or 1906]), *SE*, VII, 305.
4. *Ibid.*
5. "Creative Writers" (n. 2), *SE*, IX, 150–151.
6. "Psychopathic Stage Characters" (n. 3), *SE*, VII, 306.
7. "The 'Uncanny'" (1919), *SE*, XVII, 251–252.
8. "The Moses of Michelangelo" (1914), *SE*, XIII, 212.
9. *Jokes* (n. 2), *SE*, VIII, 150–151.
10. "Psychopathic Stage Characters" (n. 3), *SE*, VII, 306.
11. *Origins*, Letter of 15 October 1897.

12. Preface to Theodore Reik's *Ritual: Psycho-Analytic Studies* (1919), *GW*, XII, 327; *SE*, XVII, 261.
13. "Psychopathic Stage Characters" (n. 3), *SE*, VII, 306. "Creative Writers" (n. 2), *SE*, IX, 153.
14. *Introductory Lectures on Psycho-Analysis* (1916–1917), Lecture XIV, *SE*, XV, 224–225.
15. *Jokes* (n. 2), *SE*, VIII, 98–99.
16. "The 'Uncanny'" (1919), generally.
17. "Psychopathic Stage Characters" (n. 3), *SE*, VII, 305.
18. *Jokes* (n. 2), *SE*, VIII, 150–158.
19. "The 'Uncanny'" (1919), XVII, 251–252.
20. Monroe C. Beardsley, *Aesthetics* (New York: Harcourt, Brace and Co., 1958), Ch. 10, "Critical Evaluation" and Ch. 11, "Aesthetic Value." I am much indebted to my former student, Mr. Michael Padlipsky, for his perceptive comments on the problem of psycho-analysis and aesthetic value, particularly the suggestion that artistic unity may represent a general case of "sense in nonsense" or "dis-covery of the familiar."
21. *Civilization and Its Discontents* (1930 [1929]), *SE*, XXI, 145.
22. *Jokes* (n. 2), *SE*, VIII, 101.
23. Lodovico Castelvetro, *The Poetics of Aristotle* (1571), trans. Allan H. Gilbert, *Literary Criticism: Plato to Dryden* (New York: 1940), p. 314. Quoted in Alfred Harbage, *Shakespeare and the Rival Traditions* (New York: Macmillan, 1952), p. 219.
24. "Creative Writers" (n. 2), *SE*, IX, 149–151.
25. "The Theme of the Three Caskets" (1913), *GW*, X, 36; *SE*, XII, 300.
26. *Origins*, Letter of 21 October 1897.
27. *Civilization* (n. 21), *SE*, XXI, 75.
28. *The Future of an Illusion* (1927), *GW*, XIV, 334–335; *SE*, XXI, 14.
29. "On Transience" (1916); *GW*, X, 358–361; *SE*, XIV, 305–307.

Chapter 5. And Beside Freud

1. A number of writers have summarized Freud's views on art and literature, notably: Richard Sterba, "The Problem of Art in Freud's Writings," *Psychoanalytic Quarterly*, IX (1940), 256–268; Louis Fraiberg, "Freud's Writings on Art," *Int. J. Psa.*, XXXVII (1956), 82–96; amplified in *Literature and Psychology*, VI (No. 4, November, 1956), and in *Psychoanalysis & American Literary Criticism* (Detroit: Wayne State University Press, 1960), 1–46; Frederick J. Hoffman, "Psychology and Literature" in *Freudianism and the Literary Mind*, 2d edn. (Baton Rouge: Louisiana State University Press, 1957); Ludwig Marcuse, "Freuds Aesthetik," *PMLA* (1957), LXXII, 446–463. For a summary, like the present chapter, of the effect of ego psychology on psychoanalytic aesthetics, see Louis Fraiberg, "New Views on Art and the Creative Process in Psychoanalytic Ego Psychology," *Literature and Psychology*, XI (1961), 45–55.

2. Ernst Kris, "On Inspiration" in *Psychoanalytic Explorations in Art* (New York: International Universities Press, 1952), pp. 291–302. Martin Wangh, "The Scope of the Contribution of Psychoanalysis to the Biography of the Artist," *Journal of the American Psychoanalytic Association*, V (1957), 564–575 (a report of a colloquium). David Beres, "The Contribution of Psycho-Analysis to the Biography of the Artist," *Int. J. Psa.*, XL (1959), 26–35. Henry Lowenfeld, "Psychic Trauma and Productive Experience in the Artist," *Psychoanalytic Quarterly* (1941), reprinted in *Art and Psychoanalysis*, ed. William Phillips (New York: Criterion Books, 1957), pp. 293–305.

3. A. A. Brill, "Poetry as an Oral Outlet," *Psychoanalytic Review*, XVIII (1931), 357–378. Ludwig Jekels (with Edmund Bergler), "Instinct Dualism in Dreams" and "Transference and Love" in *Selected Essays* (New York: International Universities Press, 1952). Hanns Sachs, *The Creative Unconscious* (1942), 2d edn. (Cambridge, Mass.: Sci-Art Publishers, 1951), Chapters II, VI, VII, IX, and X. Edmund Bergler, *The Writer and Psychoanalysis* (New York: Doubleday, 1950). Hanns Sachs, "The Community of Daydreams," *The Creative Unconscious*. Harry B. Lee (Levey), "Poetry Production as a Supplemental Emergency Defense Against Anxiety," *Psychoanalytic Quarterly*, VII (1938), 232–242; "A Theory Concerning Free Creation in the Inventive Arts," *Psychiatry*, III (1940), 229–293; "On the Aesthetic States of the Mind," *Psychiatry*, X (1947), 281–306. The restitution theory is represented in such writings as: John Rickman, "On the Nature of Ugliness and Creative Impulse," *Int. J. Psa.*, XXI (1940), 294–313; Ella Freeman Sharpe, "Certain Aspects of Sublimation and Delusion" (1930), "Similar and Divergent Unconscious Determinants Underlying the Sublimations of Pure Art and Pure Science" (1935), "An Unfinished Paper on *Hamlet*" (1947), *Collected Papers on Psycho-Analysis*, ed. Marjorie Brierley, International Psycho-Analytic Library, No. 36 (London: The Hogarth Press, 1950), pp. 137–154 and 242–265; Hanna Segal, "A Psycho-Analytical Approach to Aesthetics," *Int. J. Psa.*, XXXIII (1952), 196–207.

4. On unity: Ludwig Jekels and Edmund Bergler, "Transference and Love" (1934), trans. Henry Alden Bunker, *Selected Papers* (New York: International Universities Press, 1952), pp. 178–201. On "pure form": Rudolf Arnheim, "Perceptual Abstraction and Art," *Psychological Review*, LIV (1947), 66–82; Franz Alexander, "The Psychoanalyst Looks at Contemporary Art," in *Art and Psychoanalysis*, ed. William Phillips (New York: Criterion Books, 1957), pp. 346–365; Anton Ehrenzweig, *The Psychoanalysis of Artistic Vision and Hearing* (New York: Julian Press, 1953). These works and others are reviewed by Mark Kanzer in "Contemporary Psychoanalytic Views of Aesthetics," *Journal of the American Psychoanalytic Association*, V (1957), 514–523. On plot splitting and doubling: the classic view appears in Theodore Reik, *Fragment of a Great Confession* (New York: Farrar, Straus, and Co., 1949), p. 336; Ernst Kris, "The

Psychology of Caricature," *Psychoanalytic Explorations in Art* (New York. International Universities Press, 1952), Ch. 6; a nonanalytic view is Harold Grier McCurdy's "A Mathematical Aspect of Fictional Literature Pertinent to McDougall's Theory of a Hierarchy of Sentiments," *Journal of Personality*, XVII (1948), 75–82; a Jungian view is Maud Bodkin's in *Archetypal Patterns in Poetry* (1934), 2d edn. (New York: Vintage Books, Inc., 1958), p. 22.

5. Melanie Klein, "The Importance of Symbol-Formation in the Development of the Ego," *Contributions to Psycho-Analysis 1921–1945*, The International Psycho-Analytic Library, No. 34 (London: The Hogarth Press, 1950), pp. 236–250. Emilio Rodrigué, "Notes on Symbolism," *Int. J. Psa.*, XXXVII (1956), 147–157. Charles Rycroft, "Symbolism and Its Relationship to the Primary and Secondary Processes," *Int. J. Psa.*, XXXVII (1956), 137–146. Hanna Segal, "Notes on Symbol Formation," *Int. J. Psa.*, XXXVIII (1957), 391–397. Lawrence S. Kubie, *Neurotic Distortion of the Creative Process*, Porter Lectures, Series 22 (Lawrence, Kansas: University of Kansas Press, 1958).

6. On language in general: Simon O. Lesser, *Fiction and the Unconscious* (Boston: Beacon Press, 1957), p. 175; Ernst Kris (with Abraham Kaplan), "Aesthetic Ambiguity," *Psychoanalytic Explorations in Art* (New York: International Universities Press, 1952). Victor H. Rosen, "The Relevance of 'Style,'" *Int. J. Psa.*, XLII (1961), 447–457. On ambiguity: Kris, *op. cit.* On obscene words: Ernest Jones, "A Linguistic Factor in English Characterology," *Int. J. Psa.*, I (1920), 265ff. reprinted in *Essays in Applied Psychoanalysis*, 2 vols. (London: Hogarth Press, 1951). On metaphor: Ella Freeman Sharpe, "An Examination of Metaphor" and "Cautionary Tales" in *Collected Papers*, ed. Marjorie Brierley (London: The Hogarth Press, 1950); Robert Fliess, "On Erogenic (Regressively Partial-Erotic) Language," *Erogeneity and Libido* (New York: International Universities Press, 1957); Mark Kanzer, "Autobiographical Aspects of the Writer's Imagery," *Int. J. Psa.*, XL (1959), 52–58. On clichés: Adrian Stokes, "Listening to Clichés and Individual Words," *Int. J. Psa.*, XXXVIII (1957), 412–418. On rhythm: Henri Flournoy, "Poetry and Memories of Childhood," *Int. J. Psa.*, XXXI (1950), 103–107; Ernst Kris, *Psychoanalytic Explorations in Art* (New York: International Universities Press, 1952), p. 90n.; B. F. Skinner, "A Quantitative Estimate of Certain Types of Sound-Patterning in Poetry," *American Journal of Psychology*, LIV (1941), 64–79.

7. Edward Bullough, " 'Psychical Distance' as a Factor in Art and an Aesthetic Principle," *British Journal of Psychology*, V (1913), 87–98, reprinted in *A Modern Book of Aesthetics*, ed. Melvin Rader (New York: Holt, 1952), pp. 401–428. Ernst Kris, *Psychoanalytic Explorations in Art* (New York: International Universities Press, 1952), pp. 44–47, 57–59. Ludwig Jekels, "The Psychology of Pity" (1930), *Selected Papers* (New York: International Universities Press, 1952).

pp. 88–96. Daniel E. Schneider, "One Psychoanalytic View of the Arts," *The Psychoanalyst and the Artist* (New York: Farrar, Straus, and Co., 1950), Ch. 12.

8. Roger Fry, *The Artist and Psycho-Analysis* (London: The Hogarth Press, 1924). Otto Fenichel, "Identification" (1926), in *Collected Papers,* ed. D. Rapaport (New York: Norton, 1953), I. Anna Freud, *The Ego and the Mechanisms of Defense* (London: The Hogarth Press, 1948), Ch. 9. Roy R. Grinker, "On Identification," *Int. J. Psa.,* XXXVIII (1957), 379–390 (summarizing the literature).

9. Walter Abell, *The Collective Dream in Art* (Cambridge: Harvard University Press, 1957). Ernst Kris (with E. H. Gombrich), "The Principles of Caricature," *Psychoanalytic Explorations in Art* (New York: International Universities Press, 1952), Ch. 7. Franz Alexander, "The Psychoanalyst Looks at Contemporary Art," in *Art and Psychoanalysis,* ed. William Phillips (New York: Criterion Books, 1957). Clyde Kluckhohn, "Myths and Rituals: A General Theory," *Harvard Theological Review,* XXXV (1942), 45–79.

10. Ernst Kris, *Psychoanalytic Explorations in Art* (New York: International Universities Press, 1952), Ch. 1, "Approaches to Art," pp. 13–63. Kris's book is, by all odds, the most important psychoanalytic book on aesthetics after Freud, indispensable reading for anyone who wishes to use psychoanalysis for literary criticism.

11. Simon O. Lesser, *Fiction and the Unconscious* (Boston: Beacon Press, 1957).

12. Fraiberg, "New Views" (n. 1), p. 55.

Chapter 6. Freud on Shakespeare

The notes to this chapter constitute *seriatim* a topical bibliography of Freud's references to Shakespeare in his published psychological works. In addition, I have included references to memoirs and biographies (particularly the late Ernest Jones's) which quote from otherwise unpublished materials and to the one volume of the *Minutes of the Vienna Psychoanalytic Society* available at the time of writing. The notes (and the chapter) are organized according to the following plan: first, Freud's remarks on Shakespeare generally; second, his views on authorship; third, the points he makes about particular plays and poems (arranged alphabetically). Within the last large division, references are arranged in order of generality, larger topics first. Topics of equal generality within a given play or poem are put in the order in which they appear in the work. Where Freud made more than one reference to a topic (e.g., a particular character or quotation) the references are arranged chronologically according to the time Freud made them (which may or may not coincide with the order of publication).

I have made reference in most notes to the best German text as well as the English *Standard Edition*.

GENERAL

1. "Some Character-Types Met with in Psycho-Analytic Work" (1916), Part I, *GW*, X, 368; *SE*, XIV, 313.
2. "Dostoevsky and Parricide" (1928), *GW*, XIV, 399; *SE*, XXI, 177.
3. *Civilization and Its Discontents* (1930), *GW*, XIV, 452; *SE*, XXI, 93.
4. *Moses and Monotheism* (1939 [1937–1939]), *GW*, XVI, 168; *SE*, XXIII, 65 and n.
5. Jones, I, 21, quoting a letter to Martha Bernays, 14 January 1884.
6. Joan Rivière, "An Intimate Impression," *The Lancet*, 20 September 1939, p. 765; quoted, Jones, II, 405.
7. Hanns Sachs, *Freud: Master and Friend* (Cambridge, Mass.: Harvard University Press, 1944), p. 105.
8. Letter to Martha Bernays, 14 July 1882, *SL*, p. 13.
9. Sachs (n. 7), p. 108.
10. *Minutes*, 24 October 1906, I, 21.
11. Ludwig Binswanger, *Sigmund Freud: Reminiscences of a Friendship* (New York and London: Grune and Stratton, 1947), p. 5.

AUTHORSHIP

A. Baconian Hypothesis
1. Jones, III, 428.
2. Jones, I, 21 and III, 428.

B. "Jacques Pierre" Hypothesis
3. Jones, I, 21, and III, 429.

C. Oxfordian Hypothesis
4. Jones, III, 429.
5. Letter to Theodore Reik, 23 March 1930, published in Theodore Reik, *The Search Within* (New York: Grove Press, 1956).
6. "Address Delivered in the Goethe House in Frankfort" (1930), *GW*, XIV, 549; *SE*, XXI, 211.
7. Footnote added in 1930 to *The Interpretation of Dreams* (1900), *GW*, II/III, 271–272; *SE*, IV, 266n.
8. Letter to Dr. Richard Flatter, 20 September 1932, quoted, Jones, III, 455; published in *Shakespeare Quarterly*, II (1951), 369.
9. Letter to James S. H. Bransom, 25 March 1934, quoted, Jones, III, 457–458.
10. *An Autobiographical Study* (1925 [1924], 1935), *GW*, 89, 96; *SE*, XX, 63–64.
11. Jones, II, 428.
12. Letter to J. Thomas Looney, June, 1938, quoted in A. Bronson Feldman, "The Confessions of William Shakespeare," *American Imago*, X (1953, No. 2), 165.
13. *An Outline of Psychoanalysis* (1940 [1938]), Ch. 7, *GW*, XVII, 119; *SE*, XXIII, 192n.

PARTICULAR PLAYS AND POEMS

Hamlet

a. General

1. Letter to Hugo Heller quoted, Jones, III, 452; published in *Int. J. Psa.*, XXXII (1951), 319; *SE*, IX, 245. The same letter is given as "To the Antiquary Hinterberger (Undated [1907])" in *SL*, pp. 268–269.

b. Supernatural Elements

2. "The 'Uncanny' " (1919), *GW*, XII, 242; *SE*, XVII, 230. See also *Delusion and Dream in Jensen's* "Gradiva" (1907 [1906]), *GW*, VII, 42; *SE*, IX, 17.

3. "The 'Uncanny' " (1919), *GW*, XII, 265; *SE*, XVII, 250.

c. Hamlet's Oedipus Complex

4. *Origins*, 15 October 1897.

5. *Origins*, 15 March 1898.

6. *The Interpretation of Dreams* (1900), *GW*, II/III, 271–273; *SE*, IV, 264–266.

7. "Psychopathic Characters on the Stage" (1942 [1905 or 1906]), *SE*, VII, 309–310.

8. *Minutes*, 27 November 1907, I, 250.

9. *Minutes*, 11 December 1907, I, 267.

10. Ludwig Binswanger, *Sigmund Freud: Reminiscences of a Friendship* (New York and London: Grune and Stratton, 1947), p. 5.

11. "Five Lectures on Psycho-Analysis" (1909–1910), Fourth Lecture, *GW*, VIII, 50; *SE*, XI, 47.

12. "The Moses of Michelangelo" (1914), *GW*, X, 174; *SE*, XIII, 212–213.

13. *Introductory Lectures on Psychoanalysis* (1916–1917), Lecture XXI, *GW*, XI, 348; *SE*, XVI, 335.

14. *An Autobiographical Study* (1925 [1924], 1935), *GW*, XIV, 89–90; *SE*, XX, 63–64.

15. "Dostoevsky and Parricide" (1928), *GW*, XIV, 412–413; *SE*, XXI, 188–189.

16. Letter to James S. H. Bransom, 25 March 1934, quoted, Jones, III, 457–458.

17. *An Outline of Psychoanalysis* (1940 [1938]), Ch. 7, *GW*, XVII, 119; *SE*, XXIII, 192.

d. Hamlet's Madness

18. *The Interpretation of Dreams* (1900), Ch. I, sec. E, *GW*, II/III, 63; *SE*, IV, 60.

19. *The Interpretation of Dreams* (1900), Ch. VI, sec. G, *GW*, II/III, 446; *SE*, V, 444.

e. Specific Details

20. (I.ii.180). *Jokes and Their Relation to the Unconscious* (1905), sec. II, *GW*, VI, 43; *SE*, VIII, 42.

21. (I.ii.180). *Jokes and Their Relation to the Unconscious* (1905), sec. II, *GW*, VI, 44; *SE*, VIII, 44.

22. (I.v.125). *The Interpretation of Dreams* (1900), Ch. V, sec. A, *GW*, II/III, 181; *SE*, IV, 175.

23. (I.v.165). Theodore Reik, *From Thirty Years with Freud*, trans. Richard Winston (New York: Farrar and Rinehart, Inc., 1940), pp. 12–13.

24. (I.v.166–167). Jones, III, 381.

25. (I.v.166–167). *Jokes and Their Relation to the Unconscious* (1905), sec. II, *GW*, VI, 77; *SE*, VIII, 72.

26. (I.v.166–167). *Delusion and Dream in Jensen's* "Gradiva" (1907 [1906]), *GW*, VII, 33; *SE*, IX, 8.

27. (I.v.166–167). *Leonardo da Vinci and a Memory of His Childhood* (1910), *GW*, VIII, 210–211; *SE*, XI, 137.

28. (I.v.166–167). "From the History of an Infantile Neurosis" (1918 [1914]), sec. I, *GW*, XII, 34–35; *SE*, XVII, 12.

29. (I.v.166–167). *New Introductory Lectures on Psycho-Analysis* (1933), Lecture XXX, *GW*, XV, 32; *SE*, XXII, 31.

30. (II.i.63). "Constructions in Analysis" (1937), *GW*, XVI, 48; *SE*, XXIII, 262.

31. (II.ii.90–92). *Jokes and Their Relation to the Unconscious* (1905), sec. I, *GW*, VI, 10; *SE*, VIII, 13.

32. (II.ii.116ff.) "Observations upon a Case of Obsessional Neurosis" (1909), Part II (c), *GW*, VII, 457; *SE*, X, 241.

33. (II.ii.194). *The Question of Lay Analysis* (1926), *GW*, XIV, 214; *SE*, XX, 187.

34. (II.ii.208). "Constructions in Analysis" (1937), *GW*, XVI, 55; *SE*, XXIII, 267.

35. (II.ii.208 and 397). See notes 18 and 19 (*Hamlet*).

36. (II.ii.457). *Interpretation of Dreams* (1900), Ch. VI, sec. G, *SE*, V, 442.

37. (II.ii.556). "Mourning and Melancholia" (1917 [1915]), *GW*, X, 432; *SE*, XIV, 246. See also note 15.

38. (II.ii.556). Letter to Arnold Zweig, 31 May 1936, quoted Jones, III, 208.

39. (II.ii.585). Letter to Martha Bernays, 23 July 1882, *SL*, p. 19.

40. (III.i.65). Hanns Sachs, *Freud: Master and Friend* (Cambridge, Mass.: Harvard University Press, 1944), p. 108.

41. (III.i.79). *Interpretation of Dreams* (1900), Ch. V, sec. D-β, *SE*, IV, 255.

42. (III.i.83). *Civilization and Its Discontents* (1930), Ch. VIII, *GW*, XIV, 494n.; *SE*, XXI, 134n.

43. (III.i.124). *Jokes and Their Relation to the Unconscious* (1905), sec. II, *GW*, VI, 36; *SE*, VIII, 36–37.

44. (III.ii.380ff.). "On Psychotherapy" (1905 [1904]), *GW*, V, 18–19; *SE*, VII, 261–262.
45. (III.iii.97–98). *Totem and Taboo* (1913), sec. III; *GW*, IX, 105n.; *SE*, XIII, 84n.
46. (V.ii.233). *Origins*, 21 September 1897. See Freud, *Aus den Anfängen der Psychoanalyse* (London: Imago Publishing Co., 1950).
47. (V.ii.369). Letter to Alexander Freud, 19 April 1938, *SL*, p. 442.

I and II Henry IV
   a. Falstaff
1. *Jokes and Their Relation to the Unconscious* (1905), sec. VII, *GW*, VI, 264n.; *SE*, VIII, 231n.

   b. Specific Details
2. (*1 H. IV*, II.iv.265). "The History of the Psycho-Analytic Movement" (1914), *GW*, X, 62; *SE*, XIV, 24.
3. (*1 H. IV*, II.iv.265). "Thoughts for the Times on War and Death" (1915), *GW*, X, 339; *SE*, XIV, 287.
4. (*1 H. IV*, V.i.127; see also *2 H. IV*, III.ii.251). *Origins*, 6 February 1899. See Jones, I, 16. The phrase also occurs in *Wilhelm Meisters Lehrjahre*, B.VI.
5. (*1 H. IV*, V.i.127). *The Interpretation of Dreams* (1900), Ch. V, sec. B, *GW*, II/III, 211; *SE*, IV, 205. See Jones, I, 16.
6. (*1 H. IV*, V.i.127). "Thoughts for the Times on War and Death" (1915), *GW*, X, 342; *SE*, XIV, 289.
7. (*2 H. IV*, II.iv.147). *Jokes and Their Relation to the Unconscious* (1905), sec. II, *GW*, VI, 36; *SE*, VIII, 36.
8. (*2 H. IV*, IV.v.43). *The Interpretation of Dreams* (1900), Ch. VI, sec. H, *GW*, II/III, 488; *SE*, V, 484.

I, II, and III Henry VI
1. (*1 H. VI*, II.iv). *The Interpretation of Dreams* (1900), Ch. V, sec. B, *GW*, II/III, 217; *SE*, IV, 212.

Julius Caesar
1. See note 3 (*Hamlet*).
2. (III.ii.13ff.) *The Interpretation of Dreams* (1900), Ch. VI, secs. F and H, *GW*, II/III, 427 and 487; *SE*, V, 424 and 484. See Jones I, 23.
3. (III.ii.13ff.) "Observations upon a Case of Obsessional Neurosis" (1909), *GW*, VII, 404; *SE*, X, 180.
4. (III.ii.87). *Jokes and Their Relation to the Unconscious* (1905), sec. II, *GW*, VI, 78; *SE*, VIII, 73.
5. (III.ii.111). *Origins*, 27 April 1895.
6. (III.iii). *The Psychopathology of Everyday Life* (1901), Ch. VI, sec. B, *GW*, IV, 130n.; *SE*, VI, 117n.

King Lear
1. (I.i.). *Delusion and Dream in Jensen's "Gradiva"* (1907), *GW*, VII, 69; *SE*, IX, 43.

2. (I.i). "The Theme of the Three Caskets" (1913), *GW*, X, 23–37; *SE*, XII, 290–301.
3. Letter to Martha Bernays, 13 July 1883, *SL*, pp. 40–41.
4. Letter to Ludwig Binswanger, 4 July 1912, in Binswanger's *Sigmund Freud: Reminiscences of a Friendship* (New York and London: Grune and Stratton, 1957), p. 45.
5. Letter to Sandor Ferenczi, 9 July 1913, *SL*, p. 301.
6. (III.iiff.) Letter to Richard Flatter, 30 March 1930, quoted, Jones, III, 452; published in *Shakespeare Quarterly*, II (1951), 368 and *SL*, p. 395.
7. (III.iiff.) Letter to James S. H. Bransom, 25 March 1934, quoted, Jones, III, 457–458.
8. (IV.vi.109). *Jokes and Their Relation to the Unconscious* (1905), sec. II, *GW*, VI, 82; *SE*, VIII, 76–77.

Love's Labour's Lost
1. (V.ii.871–873). *Jokes and Their Relation to the Unconscious* (1905), sec. V, *GW*, VI, 162; *SE*, VIII, 144.

Macbeth
   a. General
1. See note 6 (*Hamlet*).
2. *Minutes*, 11 December 1907, I, 267.
3. *Introductory Lectures on Psychoanalysis* (1916–1917), Lecture V, *GW*, XI, 93; *SE*, XV, 96.
4. See note 1 (*Hamlet*).
5. Letter to Arnold Zweig, 11 May 1934, quoted, Jones, III, 459.

   b. Supernatural Elements
6. *Totem and Taboo* (1913), sec. II-a, *GW*, IX, 49; *SE*, XIII, 38.
7. See note 2 (*Hamlet*).
8. See note 3 (*Hamlet*).

   c. Lady Macbeth
9. "Obsessions and Phobias" (1895), Case 11, *GW*, I, 350; *SE*, III, 79.
10. Freud and Josef Breuer, *Studies in Hysteria* (1893–1895), sec. III-6, *SE*, II, 245n.
11. *Minutes*, 27 March 1907, I, 156–157.
12. "The Fate of Two Women" (1912—unpublished), Jones, II, 350.
13. "Some Character-Types Met with in Psycho-Analytic Work" (1916), Part II; *GW*, X, 373–380 and 389; *SE*, XIV, 318–324 and 331.

   d. Specific Details (See note 13 for a number of quotations.)
14. (I.iii.67). "A Child Is Being Beaten" (1919), *GW*, XII, 207; *SE*, XVII, 187.
15. (IV.i.117). Letter to Wilhelm Knöpfmacher, 6 August 1878, *SL*, p. 6.

16. (IV.i.117). "Beitrag zur Kenntnis der Cocawirkung," *Wien. Medizinische Wochenschrift*, XXXV (No. 5, January, 1885), 129.
17. (V.v.52). Letter to Oskar Pfister, 6 March 1910, quoted, Jones, II, 396–397.
18. (V.viii.15–16). "A Special Type of Choice of Object Made by Men" (1910), *GW*, VIII, 76; *SE*, XI, 173.

The Merchant of Venice

1. "The Theme of the Three Caskets" (1913), *GW*, X, 23–37; *SE*, XII, 290–301. See notes 3, 4, 5 (*Lear*) above.
2. (III.ii.16–18). *The Psychopathology of Everyday Life* (1901), Ch. V, *GW*, IV, 108–109; *SE*, VI, 97–98. *Introductory Lectures on Psychoanalysis* (1916–1917), Lecture II, *GW*, XI, 31–32; *SE*, XV, 37–38.

Midsummer Night's Dream

1. See note 2 (*Hamlet*).
2. *Origins*, 31 May 1897.
3. Theodore Reik, *The Haunting Melody* (New York: Farrar, Straus, and Young, 1953), p. 49.
4. Theodore Reik, *From Thirty Years with Freud* (n. 23, *Ham.*), p. 29.
5. (V.i.12). *Origins*, 31 May, 1897.
6. (V.i.212). Freud and Josef Breuer, *Studies in Hysteria* (1893–1895), Ch. III (6), *SE*, II, 250–251.
7. (V.i.226). *The Interpretation of Dreams* (1900), Ch. VI, sec. H, *GW*, II/III, 465; *SE*, V, 462.

Much Ado About Nothing

1. (III.iii.55–56). "Analysis of a Phobia in a Five-Year-Old Boy" (1909), Conclusion, *GW*, VII, 374–375; *SE*, X, 144.

Othello

1. Letter to James S. H. Bransom, 25 March 1934, quoted, Jones, III, 457–458.
2. (III.iv.51ff.) *The Interpretation of Dreams* (1900), Ch. V, sec. A; *GW*, II/III, 183; *SE*, IV, 177.
3. (IV.iii.55–57). "Neurotic Mechanisms in Jealousy, Paranoia, and Homosexuality" (1922), *GW*, XIII, 197; *SE*, XVIII, 224n.

Pericles

1. *Civilization and Its Discontents* (1930 [1929]), *SE*, XXI, 91 and n. Letters to Theodore Reik, 18 November 1929, reprinted in Reik's *From Thirty Years with Freud* (n. 23, *Ham.*) and *The Search Within* (New York: Grove Press, 1956), p. 648.

Richard II

1. (II.ii.105). *The Psychopathology of Everyday Life* (1901), *SE*, VI, 100, footnote added in 1920.

Richard III

1. "Some Character-Types Met with in Psycho-Analytic Work" (1916), Part I, *GW*, X, 367–370; *SE*, XIV, 313–315.
2. (I.ii). "Some Character-Types Met with in Psycho-Analytic Work" (1916), Part II, *GW*, X, 379; *SE*, XIV, 323n.
3. See note 6 (*Macbeth*).

Romeo and Juliet

1. (III.i.111). Letter to Ernst Freud, 20 February 1934, *SL*, p. 420.
2. (III.v.2). *The Interpretation of Dreams* (1900), Ch. V, sec. C, *SE*, IV, 234.

Sonnets

1. Letter to Dr. Richard Flatter, 20 September 1932, quoted, Jones, III, 455; published in *Shakespeare Quarterly*, II (1951), 369.

The Tempest

1. See note 2 (*Hamlet*).
2. (I.ii.362–363). Letter from Max Eitingon to Charles Maylan, 22 March 1929, quoted, Jones, III, 145.
3. (I.ii.396–402). *Totem and Taboo* (1913), Chapter IV, sec. 7, *GW*, IX, 186; *SE*, XIII, 155n.

Timon of Athens

1. *The Interpretation of Dreams* (1900), *GW*, II/III, 271–273; *SE*, IV, 264–266.
2. *Minutes*, 11 December 1907, I, 267.

Twelfth Night

1. (II.iii.44ff.) Letter to Martha Bernays, 14 July 1882, quoted, Jones, I, 113; *SL*, p. 13.

Trivia

1. For the sake of bibliographical completeness I have included five further references in Freud's works, which do not represent any view of Freud's. For example,

A patient relearned the alphabet by copying it from Shakespeare. Freud and Josef Breuer, *Studies on Hysteria* (1893–1895), Ch. 11, Case 1, *SE*, II, 26.

Freud quotes James Sully, "The Dream as a Revelation," *Fortnightly Review*, LIII (1893), 354, who in turn says Shakespeare said dreams were "utter nonsense." *The Interpretation of Dreams* (1900), Ch. IV, *GW*, II/III, 140–141n.; *SE*, IV, 135n.

Freud quotes a hypocritical dream of Peter Rosegger, referring to "the incomparable Shakespeare." *The Interpretation of Dreams* (1900), Ch. VI, sec. H, *GW*, II/III, 478; *SE*, V, 474.

One of Alfred Adler's patients dreamed a number which turned out to be the library catalogue number of *Macbeth*. *The Psychopathology of Everyday Life* (1901), Ch. XII, *GW*, IV, 273; *SE*, VI, 244–246.

He quotes a joke from Heine: "Vile Macbeth does not rule here in Hamburg; the ruler here is *Banko* [bank-money]." *Jokes and Their Relation to the Unconscious* (1905), II[3], *SE*, VIII, 36.

A NOTE ON SCOPE

In the text I have described in general terms the problem of selecting materials for this and the two chapters following; naturally enough, the problem of selecting leads into the problem of finding. In this respect, I want to say again how exceedingly grateful I am to Professor Gordon Ross Smith who very kindly checked through these notes and helped me correct a number of omissions. I have also relied on the following bibliographies: from Shakespeareans, the annual bibliographies in *Shakespeare Survey*, *Shakespeare Quarterly*, and *Shakespeare Bulletin;* from the psychological side, John Rickman's *Index Psychoanalyticus (1893–1926);* Ilse Bry, Helen Bayne, and Myrl Ebert, "Bibliography of Early Psychoanalytic Monographs," *Journal of the American Psychoanalytic Association*, I (1953), 519–525 and 706–718; Alexander Grinstein, *Index of Psychoanalytic Writings*, 8 vols. (New York: International Universities Press, 1956–   ); and *Psychological Abstracts*. There are a few interdisciplinary bibliographies, notably that in *Literature and Psychology*, a partial survey by Kenneth Muir, "Some Freudian Interpretations of Shakespeare," *Proceedings of the Leeds Philosophical and Literary Society*, VII (1952), 43–52; and Norman Kiell, *Psychoanalysis, Psychology, and Literature* (Madison; University of Wisconsin Press, 1963).

Not all of these bibliographies proved equally reliable. Sometimes, to my surprise, I would find that an assiduous bibliographer of Shakespeare studies had caught an item his psychological counterpart had missed—and vice versa. Many of the references were fugitive. Who would guess, for example, that a book entitled *Erogeneity and Libido* would have much discussion of Shakespeare in it? And *per contra* many items that looked psychoanalytic turned out not to be. Who would think that a current article in the *Journal of Nervous and Mental Diseases* would be based on Elizabethan humours psychology? Obtaining the materials was a problem: references came from all over the globe, Buenos Aires, Johannesburg, Sydney, Leipzig, and Tokyo, to name a few. They represent a graphic if rather troublesome tribute to the ubiquity of Freud's contribution.

I am mentioning these miseries not so much to gain your sympathy as your forbearance if you do not find in the chapters hereafter all you seek. Perfection in matters bibliographical, I fear, is to be hoped for rather than achieved. The notes to these Chapters 7, 8, and 9, however, constitute what I believe is a complete list of "psychoanalytic" writings about Shakespeare other than those of Freud himself up to 1 January 1964. In addition, for the sake of anyone wishing to pursue this subject further, I have included in the supplementary notes a list of those items which turned up in bibliographies or whose titles looked relevant but which seemed to me to fall outside the scope of this survey as I have defined it in the text. I have also, alas, listed there a few items which proved unavailable or incomprehensible.

Chapter 7. Psychoanalysis and the Man

Authorship; External Data

1. A. Bronson Feldman, "The Confessions of William Shakespeare," *American Imago*, X (1953), 113–165.
2. A. Bronson Feldman, "Shakespeare Worship," *Psychoanalysis*, II (1955), 57–72.
3. Gordon Ross Smith, "Shakespeare and Freudian Interpretations," *American Imago*, XVI (1959), 226–229.
4. *Minutes*, 6 February 1907, I, 106. See also Rank (n. 11), p. 51n.

The Sonnets and Homosexuality

5. Otto Rank, *Art and Artist*, trans. C. F. Atkinson (New York: A. A. Knopf, 1932), p. 56.
6. H. McC. Young, *The Sonnets of Shakespeare: A Psycho-Sexual Analysis* (Columbia, Mo.: the author, 1937).
7. W. I. D. Scott, *Shakespeare's Melancholics* (London: Mills and Boon, Ltd., 1962), p. 171.
8. Conrad van Emde Boas, *Shakespeare's Sonnetten en hun Verband met de Travesti-Double Spelen* (Amsterdam: Wereld Bibliotheek, 1951); "The connection between Shakespeare's Sonnets and his 'travesti-double' Plays," *International Journal of Sexology*, IV (1950), 67–72.
9. Leslie A. Fiedler, "Some Contexts of Shakespeare's Sonnets," in *The Riddle of Shakespeare's Sonnets* (New York: Basic Books, 1962), pp. 55–90.

Attitudes toward the Father as Shown in Hamlet

10. Ernest Jones's essay first appeared as "The Oedipus Complex as an Explanation of Hamlet's Mystery: A Study in Motive," *American Journal of Psychology*, XXI (January, 1910), 72–113; then as "Das Problem des Hamlet und der Oedipus-Komplex," *Schriften zur Angewandten Seelenkunde*, Heft 10 (1911); then in Dr. Jones's collection of essays as "A Psycho-Analytic Study of Hamlet," *Essays in Applied Psycho-Analysis* (London: 1923, and several subsequent editions). The essay became an introduction to an edition of *Hamlet*: London: Vision Press, 1947; New York: Funk and Wagnalls, 1947. It reached its final form as *Hamlet and Oedipus* (New York: Norton, 1949), and I am working from the last revised reprint (Garden City, New York: Doubleday Anchor Books, 1955).
11. Otto Rank, *Das Inzest-Motiv in Dichtung und Sage*, 2d edn. (Leipzig

und Wien: Franz Deuticke, 1926), Kap. VI, "Shakespeares Vater-komplex."

12. Wulf Sachs, *Psychoanalysis: Its Meaning and Practical Applications* (London: Cassell, 1934), Part II. See also the appropriate references under *Hamlet* in Chapter 9 (*Hamlet*, nn. 7–9).

13. Otto Hinrichsen, "Der verständliche-unverstandene Hamlet," *Schweizer Archiv für Neurologie und Psychiatrie*, XXXI (1933), 261–283; XXXII (1934), 33–43. See also, by the same author, "Das Hamlet-Problem gelost?" *Psychiatrisch-Neurologische Wochenschrift*, XXXIX (1937), 36–40.

14. Ella Freeman Sharpe, "The Impatience of Hamlet" (1929), *Collected Papers on Psycho-Analysis*, ed. Marjorie Brierley, The International Psycho-Analytical Library, No. 36 (London: The Hogarth Press, 1950), pp. 203–213. "An Unfinished Paper on Hamlet" (1947), *ibid.*, pp. 242–265.

15. Ernest Jones, "The Death of Hamlet's Father," *Int. J. Psa.*, XXIX (1948), 174–176.

16. Harry Slochower, in *Complex*, III (Winter, 1951), 46–49.

17. K. R. Eissler, "On *Hamlet*," *Samiksa*, VII (1953), 85–132, 155–202.

18. A. André Glaz, "*Hamlet*, Or the Tragedy of Shakespeare," *American Imago*, XVIII (1961), 129–158.

Attitudes toward the Father as Shown in Other Plays

19. Rank (n. 11), *loc. cit.*

20. Isidor Sadger, *Über Nachtwandeln und Mondsucht; Eine medizinisch-literarische Studie* (Leipzig und Wien: Franz Deuticke, 1914), pp. 143–169; *Sleepwalking and Moonwalking*, trans. Louise Brink (New York and Washington: Nervous and Mental Disease Publishing Co., 1920), pp. 114–136.

21. Ludwig Jekels, "The Riddle of Shakespeare's *Macbeth*," *Imago*, V (1918), 170ff.; *Psychoanalytic Review*, XXX (1943), 361–385; *Selected Papers* (New York: International Universities Press, 1952), pp. 105–130.

Attitudes toward the Mother as Shown in Coriolanus

22. Rank (n. 11), *loc. cit.*

23. Charles K. Hofling, "An Interpretation of Shakespeare's *Coriolanus*," *American Imago*, XIV (1957), 407–435.

24. David B. Barron, "*Coriolanus*: Portrait of the Artist as Infant," *American Imago*, XIX (1962), 171–193.

25. Rufus Putney, "Coriolanus and His Mother," *Psychoanalytic Quarterly*, XXXI (1962), 364–381.

Attitudes toward Siblings Shown in Single Plays

26. Rank (n. 11), pp. 123, 209.

27. Weston A. Gui, "Bottom's Dream," *American Imago*, IX (1952–1953), 251–305.

Attitudes Shown in Miscellaneous Single Plays

28. Ernst Kris, "Prince Hal's Conflict," *Psychoanalytic Quarterly*, XVII (1948), 487–506; *Psychoanalytic Explorations in Art* (New York: International Universities Press, 1952), pp. 273–288.

29. T. A. Ross, "A Note on *The Merchant of Venice*," *British Journal of Medical Psychology*, XIV (1934), 303–311.

30. E. E. Krapf, "El judío de Shakespeare: una contribución a la psicología del anti-semitismo," *Revista de Psicoanálisis* (Buenos Aires), VIII (1951), 173–202; "Shylock and Antonio: A Psychoanalytic Study of Shakespeare and Antisemitism," *Psychoanalytic Review*, XLII (1955), 113–130.

31. Theodore Reik, *The Secret Self* (New York: Farrar, Straus, and Young, 1953), pp. 63–75.

32. L. A. G. Strong, "Shakespeare and the Psychologists," in *Talking of Shakespeare*, ed. John Garrett (London: Hodder and Stoughton, 1954), pp. 187–208.

33. A. Bronson Feldman, "Othello's Obsessions," *American Imago*, IX (1952–1953), 147–163.

34. A. Bronson Feldman, "Imaginary Incest," *American Imago*, XII (1955), 117–155.

35. A. Bronson Feldman, "Shakespeare's Early Errors," *Int. J. Psa.*, XXXVI (1955), 114–133.

36. A. Bronson Feldman, "Othello in Reality," *American Imago*, XI (1954), 147–179; "Portals of Discovery," *American Imago*, XVI (1959), 77–107.

37. Othar Mannoni, *Prospero and Caliban* (originally entitled *La Psychologie de la Colonisation*), trans. Pamela Powesland (New York: Frederick A. Praeger, 1956), pp. 12 and 97–109.

38. W. I. D. Scott, *Shakespeare's Melancholics* (London: Mills and Boon, Ltd., 1962), pp. 181–182.

Shakespeare the Man from Several Works

39. *Minutes*, 11 December 1907, I, 262–263 and 268.

40. Erich Wulffen [Wolf Hasso Erich], *Shakespeares grosse Verbrecher: Richard III, Macbeth, Othello* (Berlin: Langenscheidt, 1911).

41. Rank (n. 11), *loc. cit.*

42. F. Plewa, "Shakespeare und die Macht," *International Zeitschrift für Individual-Psychologie*, XIV (1936), 26–36.

43. Theodore Reik, "The Way of All Flesh," *From Thirty Years with Freud*, trans. Richard Winston (New York: Farrar and Rinehart, Inc., 1940), pp. 197–212.

44. Hanns Sachs, "The Unconscious in Shakespeare's 'Tempest,' Analytical Considerations," *The Creative Unconscious* (1942), 2d edn. (Cambridge, Mass.: Sci-Art Publishers, 1951), Chapter XI, pp. 289–323.

45. Hanns Sachs, "What Would Have Happened if . . . ?", *Creative Unconscious*, pp. 339–340.

46. K. M. Abenheimer, "Shakespeare's 'Tempest,' A Psychological Analysis," *Psychoanalytic Review*, XXXIII (1946), 399–415.
47. Jack Lindsay, "Shakespeare and Tom Thumb," *Life and Letters*, LVIII (1948), 119–127.
48. Daniel E. Schneider, *The Psychoanalyst and the Artist* (New York: Farrar, Straus, and Company, 1950), p. 266.
49. Joseph T. McCullen, Jr., "Brother Hate and Fratricide in Shakespeare," *Shakespeare Quarterly*, III (1952), 335–340.
50. Gilbert S. Moore, *The Theme of Family Disaster in the Tragedies of Euripides and Shakespeare, Dissertation Abstracts*, XX (1960), 3731.
51. David B. Barron, "The Babe That Milks: An Organic Study of Macbeth," *American Imago*, XVII (1960), 133–161.
52. David B. Barron, "*Coriolanus:* Portrait of the Artist as Infant," *American Imago*, XIX (1962), 171–193.
53. W. I. D. Scott, *Shakespeare's Melancholics* (London: Mills and Boon, Ltd., 1962), pp. 45–46, 60, and 175.

Shakespeare the Man from All the Works

54. Ella Freeman Sharpe, "The Cyclic Movement in Shakespeare's Plays," described in *Collected Papers on Psycho-Analysis* (n. 14), pp. 242–243.
55. *Loc. cit.* n. 14.
56. Ella Freeman Sharpe, "From *King Lear* to *The Tempest*," *Int. J. Psa.*, XXVII (1946), 19ff.; *Collected Papers* (n. 14), pp. 214–241.
57. Mark Kanzer, "The Central Theme in Shakespeare's Works," *Psychoanalytic Review*, XXXVIII (1951), 1–16.
58. Harold Grier McCurdy, *The Personality of Shakespeare: A Venture in Psychological Method* (New Haven: Yale University Press, 1953). See also his "A mathematical aspect of fictional literature pertinent to McDougall's theory of a hierarchy of sentiments," *Journal of Personality*, XVII (1948), 75–82.

Shakespeare the Man from Diction and Imagery

59. Caroline Spurgeon, *Shakespeare's Imagery and What It Tells Us* (Cambridge, Eng.: Cambridge University Press, 1935).
60. G. Wilson Knight, *The Shakespearean Tempest*, 3d edn. (London: Methuen and Co., 1953), pp. vii–xxiv.
61. Edward A. Armstrong, *Shakespeare's Imagination* (London: Lindsay Drummond, Ltd., 1946); revised edition (Lincoln: Nebraska University Press, 1963).
62. Mark Kanzer, "Autobiographical Aspects of the Writer's Imagery," *Int. J. Psa.*, XL (1959), 52–58.
63. Arthur Wormhoudt, "The Unconscious Bird Symbol in Literature," *American Imago*, VII (1950), 173–181.
64. Sidney J. Baker, "Shakespeare and Sex," *International Journal of Sexology*, IV (1950), 35–39.
65. Robert Fliess, *Erogeneity and Libido* (New York: International Universities Press, 1957), pp. 129, 133, and generally.

Conclusions and Speculations

66. *Loc. cit.*, n. 17.
67. Kris (n. 28), p. 288.
68. Charles R. Osgood, George J. Suci, Percy H. Tannenbaum, *The Measurement of Meaning* (Urbana: University of Illinois Press, 1957), particularly Ch. 6, "Semantic Measurement in Personality and Psychotherapy Research."
69. Noam Chomsky, *Syntactic Structures* (The Hague: Mouton and Co., 1957).
70. Robert Boies Sharpe, *Irony in the Drama* (Chapel Hill: University of North Carolina Press, 1959), pp. 96–97.
71. C. L. Barber, "The form of Faustus' fortunes good or bad," *Tulane Drama Review*, VIII (1964), 92–119.
72. Edmund Wilson, "Morose Ben Jonson," *The Triple Thinkers*, rev. edn. (New York: Charles Scribner's Sons, 1948); reprinted in *Ben Jonson: A Collection of Critical Essays*, ed. Jonas A. Barish (Englewood Cliffs, N.J.: Prentice-Hall, Inc., 1963), pp. 60–74.

Chapter 8. Psychoanalysis and the Artist

1. Otto Rank, *Art and Artist*, trans. C. F. Atkinson (New York: A. A. Knopf, 1932), pp. 382–383 and generally.
2. Rank (n. 1), p. 56.
3. Rank (n. 1), pp. 222–223.
4. Rank (n. 1), p. 285. See also, Otto Rank, *Psychology and the Soul* (*Seelenglaube und Psychologie*, 1932), trans. William D. Turner (Philadelphia: University of Pennsylvania Press, 1950), pp. 61–70.
5. J. I. M. Stewart [Michael Innes], *Character and Motive in Shakespeare* (London: Longmans, Green, 1949).
6. Stewart (n. 5), p. 29.
7. Stewart (n. 5), p. 136.
8. F. L. Lucas, *Literature and Psychology* (1951), (Ann Arbor: University of Michigan Press, 1957).
9. Edmund Bergler, *The Writer and Psychoanalysis* (New York: Doubleday, 1950).
10. Arthur Wormhoudt, *The Demon Lover* (New York: Exposition Press, 1949), pp. 7–8.
11. Arthur Wormhoudt, *Hamlet's Mouse Trap* (New York: Philosophical Library, 1956). For a review of this book, see *Literature and Psychology*, VIII (1958), 12–13 (Glenn H. Blayney, Jr.).
12. Edmund Bergler, "The Seven Paradoxes in Shakespeare's 'Hamlet,'" *American Imago*, XVI (1959), 379–405.
13. Weston A. Gui, "Bottom's Dream," *American Imago*, IX (1952–1953), 251–305.
14. David B. Barron, "The Babe That Milks: An Organic Study of Macbeth," *American Imago*, XVII (1960), 133–161.

15. Wolfgang J. Weilgart, *Shakespeare Psychognostic: Character Evolution and Transformation* (Tokyo: Hokuseido Press, 1952).
16. D. Müller-Hegemann, "Über die Beziehungen der Psychopathologie zur Literatur," *Psychiatrie, Neurologie und medizinische Psychologie* (Leipzig), V (1953), 341–346.

Chapter 9. Psychoanalysis and the Works

All's Well That Ends Well

1. Barbara Hannah, "All's Well That Ends Well," *Studien zur analytische Psychologie C. G. Jungs*, Festschrift zum 80. Geburtstag von C. G. Jung, 2 B. (Zurich: Rascher Verlag, 1955), II, 344–363.
2. P. R. Vessie, "Interpretation of Shakespeare's Sex Play, 'All's Well That Ends Well,' " *Medical Record*, CXLVI (July 7, 1937), 14–16.
3. John F. Adams, "*All's Well That Ends Well*: The Paradox of Procreation," *Shakespeare Quarterly*, XII (1960), 261–270.
4. Otto Rank, *Das Inzest-Motiv in Dichtung und Sage* (1912), 2d edn. (Leipzig: Franz Deuticke, 1926), p. 394n.
5. (I.i.1–7). Rank (n. 4), p. 215n.
6. (I.iii.143ff.) Rank (n. 4), p. 394n.
7. (IV.iii.183). Samuel A. Tannenbaum, "Slips of the Tongue," *Shakespere Studies, No. 1* (New York: the author, 1930).

Antony and Cleopatra

1. Herbert Weisinger, "The Myth and Ritual Approach to Shakespearean Tragedy," *Centennial Review of Arts and Science*, I (1957), 142–166.
2. K. R. Eissler, "On Hamlet," *Samiksa*, VII (1953), 183.
3. Cynthia Kolb Whitney, "The War in 'Antony and Cleopatra,' " *Literature and Psychology*, XIII (1963), 63–66.
4. (I.i.28 and V.i.60). Tannenbaum (*All's W.*, n. 7).

As You Like It

1. Conrad van Emde Boas, *Shakespeare's Sonnetten en hun Verband met de Travesti-Double Spelen* (Amsterdam: Wereld-Bibliotheek, 1951); "The Connection between Shakespeare's Sonnets and his 'travesti-double' Plays," *International Journal of Sexology*, IV (1950), 67–72. (See Ch. 7, n. 8.)
2. William Inglis Dunn Scott, *Shakespeare's Melancholics* (London: Mills and Boon, Ltd., 1962), pp. 61–72.
3. (I.iii.10; IV.iii.133; and IV.iii.160). Samuel A. Tannenbaum, "Psychanalytic Gleanings from Shakespeare," *Psyche and Eros*, I (1920), 29–39; "Slips of the Tongue," *Shakespere Studies, No. 1* (New York: the author, 1930), a revision of "Slips of the Tongue in Shakespeare," *Shakespeare Association Bulletin*, V (1930), 63–71. See also his "Slips of the Tongue in Shakespeare," *The Dial*, LXI (August 15, 1916), 89–91.

The Comedy of Errors

1. A. Bronson Feldman, "Shakespeare's Early Errors," *Int. J. Psa.,* XXXVI (1955), 114–133; "Portals of Discovery," *American Imago,* XVI (1959), 77–107.
2. Rank, *Inzest-Motiv* (*All's W.,* n. 4), p. 353n.

Coriolanus

1. Rank, *Inzest-Motiv* (*All's W.,* n. 4), Ch. 6.
2. Jackson Edmund Towne, "A Psychoanalytic Study of Shakespeare's *Coriolanus,*" *Psychoanalytic Review,* VIII (1921), 84–91.
3. Charles K. Hofling, "An Interpretation of Shakespeare's *Coriolanus,*" *American Imago,* XIV (1957), 407–435.
4. Gordon Ross Smith, "Authoritarian Patterns in Shakespeare's *Coriolanus,*" *Literature and Psychology,* IX (1959), 45–51.
5. Robert Seidenberg and Evangelos Papathomopoulos, "Sophocles' *Ajax*—A Morality for Madness," *Psychoanalytic Quarterly,* XXX (1961), 410n.
6. Rufus Putney, "Coriolanus and His Mother," *Psychoanalytic Quarterly,* XXXI (1962), 364–381.
7. David B. Barron, "*Coriolanus:* Portrait of the Artist as Infant," *American Imago,* XIX (1962), 171–193.
8. (I.i.99–164). Otto Rank, *Art and Artist,* trans. C. F. Atkinson (New York: A. A. Knopf, 1932), pp. 225–226.
9. (I.ix.90). Samuel A. Tannenbaum, "Shakespeare and the New Psychology," *The Dial,* LIX (December 23, 1915), 601–603; "Coriolanus's Slip of Memory," *The Dial,* LX (February 17, 1916), 153–155. See also the same author's "Psychoanalytic Gleanings from Shakespeare," *Psyche and Eros,* I (1920), 29–39.
10. Towne (n. 2).
11. (IV.v.232–250). Robert Fliess, *Erogeneity and Libido* (New York: International Universities Press, 1957), pp. 6–7.

Cymbeline

1. Hanns Sachs, "The Unconscious in Shakespeare's 'Tempest,' Analytic Considerations," *The Creative Unconscious,* 2d edn. (Cambridge, Mass.: Sci-Art Publishers, 1951), pp. 289–323.
2. K. M. Abenheimer, "Shakespeare's 'Tempest,' A Psychological Analysis," *Psychoanalytic Review,* XXXIII (1946), 399–415.
3. Fliess (*Cor.,* n. 11), p. 98.

Hamlet

A. General

1. Surveys: Marshall W. Stearns, "Hamlet and Freud," *College English,* X (1949), 265–272. Clifford Leech, "The Freudians," *Shakespeare Survey,* IX (1956), 12–13—Professor Leech is surveying twentieth-century *Hamlet* criticism. Francis G. Schoff, "Hamlet and His Critics:

A Series. I. The Problem and One Approach," *Discourse*, IV (1961), 125–137; "II. Elizabethan Psychology," *Discourse*, IV (1962), 248–260. Jack Norman Renfrow, "Psychologists' Criticism of *Hamlet*," unpub. dis., Louisiana State University, 1961, *Dissertation Abstracts*, XXII (1962), 3671–3672; "Hamlet and the Psychologists," *Shakespeare Newsletter*, XIII (No. 2, April, 1963), 20.

2. Wulf Sachs, *Black Hamlet: The Mind of an African Negro Revealed by Psychoanalysis* (London: G. Bles, 1937).

3. Frederic Wertham, *Dark Legend: A Study in Murder* (New York: Duell, Sloan and Pearce, 1941).

4. Alberta E. Feynman, "The Infernal Machine, Hamlet, and Ernest Jones," *Modern Drama*, VI (1963), 72–83.

B. The Character of Hamlet; Why Does Hamlet Delay?

a. The Freud-Jones View

5. See Chapter 6, *Hamlet*, nn. 4–17.

6. See Chapter 7, n. 10.

b. Restatements of the Freud-Jones View.

7. Favorable: Otto Juliusberger, "Shakespeares Hamlet ein Sexualproblem," *Die neue generation*, IX (1913). Lucile Dooley, "Psychoanalytic Studies of Genius," *American Journal of Psychology*, XXVII (1916), 363–416. Honorio F. Delgado, "El enigma psicológico de Hamlet," *La Crónica Médica*, XXXVII (1920), 158–162. Christin, "Hamlet," *Semaine littéraire*, Genève, 7 Mai 1921. Ernest Jones, review of Alan Clutton-Brock, *Shakespeare's Hamlet* (London: 1922), *Int. J. Psa.*, III (1922), 495–497. Fritz Wittels, "Psycho-Analysis and Literature," *Psycho-Analysis Today*, ed. Sandor Lorand (New York: Covici-Friede, 1933), pp. 345–346. Wulf Sachs, *Psychoanalysis: Its Meaning and Practical Applications* (London: Cassell, 1934), Ch. XI. J. F. C. Gutteling, "Modern Hamlet-Criticism," *Neophilologus*, XXV (1941), 276–286. Ives Hendrick, *Facts and Theories of Psychoanalysis*, 2d edn. (New York: Alfred A. Knopf, 1941), pp. 298–299, and in subsequent editions—this is a particularly clear statement of the oedipal view of the tragedy. Mario Carlisky, *De Hamlet a Fausto* (Buenos Aires: Editorial Ayacucho, 1947). Joseph Katz, "Faith, Reason and Art," *American Scholar*, XXI (1952), 151–160 (with an objecting letter at 363). Mabel Collins Donnelly, "Freud and Literary Criticism," *College English*, XV (1953), 155–158. Simon O. Lesser, "Freud and *Hamlet* Again," *American Imago*, XII (1955), 207–220. N. N. Dracoulides, "Tracé Psychoanalytique sur 'Hamlet' de Shakespeare," *Psyché* (Paris), XI (1957), 129–155. Martin Grotjahn, *Beyond Laughter* (New York: McGraw-Hill, 1957), pp. 83–85. Simon O. Lesser, *Fiction and the Unconscious* (Boston: Beacon Press, 1957), p. 102. Harry Slochower, "Incest in *The Brothers Karamazov*," *American Imago*, XVI (1959), 127–145. No doubt there are many more restatements of this most

oft-repeated of psychoanalytic literary insights that I have not run across in my bibliographic travels.

8. Hostile but witty: Harvey Wickham, "Did Shakespeare Murder His Father," *Catholic World*, CXXXIV (1932), 538–546. H. K., "Hamlet Psycho-Analysed," *Punch*, CCXIV (1948), 128–129. William Frost, "Shakespeare His Own Granpaw," *College English*, XVII (1956), 219–222.

9. Hostile but not witty: Harley Granville-Barker, *The Study of Drama* (Cambridge: Cambridge University Press, 1934), pp. 53–56. James Hendrie Lloyd, "The So-Called Oedipus-Complex in *Hamlet*," *Journal of the American Medical Association*, LVI (1911), 1377–1379. Emil Ludwig, *Doctor Freud: An Analysis and a Warning* (New York: Hellman, Williams, & Co., 1947), pp. 237–242. Robert Withington, "Why Put Freud into *Hamlet*," *College English*, X (1949), 475–476. Again there are no doubt many more such attacks on the Freud-Jones view.

c. Stagings of the Freud-Jones View

10. Samuel A. Tannenbaum, "The Hearts of Hamlet's Mystery," *Journal of Sexology and Psychoanalysis*, I (1923), 316–323.

11. Patrick Kearney, "Symbolism and the New 'Hamlet,' " *Vanity Fair*, XIX (January, 1923), pp. 41, 98.

12. Henriette Brunot, Review of the *Hamlet* of Jean-Louis Barrault, *Psyché*, I (1946), 230–231.

13. Sir Laurence Olivier, Foreword, *Hamlet: The Film and the Play*, ed. Alan Dent (London: World Film Publications, Ltd., 1948).

14. Theodore Reik, "In My Mind's Eye, Horatio," *Complex*, VII (1952), 15–31, reprinted in various works by this author. See also Claude Dominique, Review of Laurence Olivier's *Hamlet*, *Psyché*, III (1948), 1179–1182. There are, of course, a great many reviews of Olivier's *Hamlet* besides these, mostly of a merely journalistic kind.

d. Amplifications of the Freud-Jones View Within Orthodox Psychoanalysis

15. Otto Rank, *Das Inzest-Motiv in Dichtung und Sage* (1912), 2d edn. (Leipzig: Franz Deuticke, 1926), Kapitel 2, "Typen des Inzestdramas," and pp. 90, 110, 112, 135n., 147 and 154.

16. Rank (n. 15), Kapitel 6, "Shakespeares Vaterkomplex."

17. Ella Freeman Sharpe, "The Impatience of Hamlet" (1929) and "An Unfinished Paper on Hamlet" (1947), *Collected Papers on Psycho-Analysis*, ed. Marjorie Brierley, International Psycho-Analytical Library, No. 36 (London: The Hogarth Press, 1950), pp. 203–213 and 242–265.

18. Erland Lindbäck, "Hamlet i psykoanalytisk belysning," *Studier Tillägnade Anton Blanck den 29 December 1946*, Skrifter Utgivna av Svenska Litteratursällskapet 30 (Uppsala: Almqvist & Wiksells, 1946), pp. 61–79.

19. Theodore Reik, *Fragment of a Great Confession* (New York: Farrar, Straus and Co., 1949), pp. 269–270.
20. Theodore Reik, *The Secret Self* (New York: Farrar, Straus and Young, 1953), pp. 17–32. See also Reik, n. 14.
21. Theodore Reik, *The Haunting Melody* (New York: Farrar, Straus and Young, 1953), p. 137.
22. Jack Meltzer, "Some Psycho-Analytical Angles on Aspects of Shakespearean Drama," *Discussion* (South Africa), I (No. 6, December, 1952), 47–50.
23. K. R. Eissler, "On *Hamlet*," *Samiksa*, VII (1953), 85–132 and 155–202.
24. Lora and Abraham Heller, "Hamlet's Parents: The Dynamic Formulation of a Tragedy," *American Imago*, XVII (1960), 413–421.
25. Frank W. Wadsworth, "Hamlet and the Methods of Literary Analysis; A Note," *American Imago*, XIX (1962), 85–90.
26. Erik H. Erikson, "Youth: Fidelity and Diversity," *Daedalus*, XCI (1962), 5–27.
27. Neil Friedman and Richard M. Jones, "On the Mutuality of the Oedipus Complex: Notes on the Hamlet Case," *American Imago*, XX (1963), 107–131.

e. Variations on the Freud-Jones View:

i. Doubting and Delaying
28. Alan Clutton-Brock, *Shakespeare's Hamlet* (London: Methuen, 1922). Dr. Jones's review appears in *Int. J. Psa.*, III (1922) at 495–497.
29. Wilhelm Stekel, *Compulsion and Doubt*, 2 vols. (New York: Liveright, 1949), II, 606.
30. Theodor Hartwig, *Hamlets Hemmungen: Psychologische Studie* (Vienna: R. Cerny, 1952).
31. A. André Glaz, "Hamlet, Or the Tragedy of Shakespeare," *American Imago*, XVIII (1961), 129–158.
32. Morton Kaplan, "*The American Imago* in Retrospect: An Article-Review," *Literature and Psychology*, XIII (1963), 112–116.
33. Karl Menninger with Martin Mayman and Paul Pruyser, *The Vital Balance* (New York: Viking Press, 1963), p. 191.

ii. The Theme of Matricide
34. Erich Wulffen, *Shakespeares Hamlet ein Sexualproblem* (Berlin: Carl Duncker, 1913). Wulffen's book is amusingly reviewed and the whole psychoanalytic approach attacked by Eugen Kalkschmidt, "Hamlet, ein Mutterproblem," *März*, VII (1913), iv, 573–575.
35. Wertham, n. 3.
36. Frederic Wertham, "The Matricidal Impulse; Critique of Freud's Interpretation of *Hamlet*," *Journal of Criminal Psychopathology*, II, (1941), 455–464.
37. Ernst Kris, *Psychoanalytic Explorations in Art* (New York: Inter-

national Universities Press, 1952), pp. 17–18. L. A. G. Strong also endorses Wertham's position in "Shakespeare and the Psychologists," *Talking of Shakespeare*, ed. John Garrett (London: Hodder and Stoughton, 1954).

38. Henry Alden Bunker, "Mother-Murder in Myth and Legend," *Psychoanalytic Quarterly*, XIII (1944), 198–207.
39. Arthur Wormhoudt, Ch. 8, nn. 10 and 11. Edmund Bergler, Ch. 8, n. 12.
40. James Clark Moloney and Laurence Rockelein, "A New Interpretation of *Hamlet*," *Int. J. Psa.*, XXX (1949), 94–107.
41. E. E. Krapf, "Shylock and Antonio: A Psychoanalytic Study of Shakespeare and Antisemitism," *Psychoanalytic Review*, XLII (1955), 113–130. "El judío de Shakespeare: una contribución a la psicología del antisemitismo," *Revista de Psicoanálisis* (Buenos Aires), VIII (1951), 173–202.
42. Marcel Pagnol, "Le plus grand rôle de tous les temps: Hamlet," *Shakespeare*, Marcel Pagnol et al., Collection Génies et Réalitiés (Paris: Hachette, 1962), pp. 275–280.
43. Ralph J. Hallman, *Psychology of Literature: A Study of Alienation and Tragedy* (New York: Philosophical Library, 1961), pp. 140–142.

f. Literary Critiques of the Freud-Jones View

44. Oscar J. Campbell, "What's the Matter with Hamlet," *Yale Review*, XXXII (1942), 309–322.
45. F. W. Dupee, "Adjusting Hamlet," *Partisan Review*, XV (1948), 1136–1139.
46. F. L. Lucas, *Literature and Psychology* (1951) (Ann Arbor: University of Michigan Press, 1957), pp. 32–51.
47. Lionel Trilling, "Freud and Literature," *The Liberal Imagination* (Garden City, N.Y.: Doubleday and Co., 1953), pp. 44–64. Hiag Akmakjian, "Psychoanalysis and the Future of Literary Criticism," *Psychoanalysis and the Psychoanalytic Review*, LI (Spring, 1962), 3–28.
48. Leo Kirschbaum, "Hamlet and Ophelia," *Philological Quarterly*, XXXV (1956), 376–393. Reprinted in the author's *Character and Characterization in Shakespeare* (Detroit: Wayne State University Press, 1962), Ch. 4.
49. John E. Hankins, "Hamlet and Oedipus Reconsidered," *Shakespeare Newsletter*, VI (1956), 11.
50. Robert R. Reed, Jr., "Hamlet, the Pseudo-Procrastinator," *Shakespeare Quarterly*, IX (1958), 177–186.

g. Semi- or Anti-Psychoanalytic Views:
i. Existential Psychoanalysis

51. Annemarie Dührssen, "Lebensproblem und Daseinskrise bei Hamlet und Ophelia," *Zeitschrift für Psychosomatische Medizin*, II (1956),

220–235, 295–311. Compare Wylie Sypher, *"Hamlet: The Existential Madness," The Nation,* 21 June 1946.

ii. Adlerian

52. Alfred Adler, *Social Interest* (London: Faber and Faber, 1938), p. 106.
53. Philippe Mairet, "Hamlet, der Neurotiker," *Internationale Zeitschrift für Individual-psychologie,* VI (1931), 424–437.

iii. Myth and Ritual

54. Gilbert Murray, *Hamlet and Orestes: A Study in Traditional Types,* The Annual Shakespeare Lecture of the British Academy (New York: Oxford University Press, 1914).
55. John T. MacCurdy, "Concerning Hamlet and Orestes," *Journal of Abnormal Psychology,* XIII (1918–1919), 250–260.
56. William Montgomerie, "More an Antique Roman Than a Dane," *Hibbert Journal,* LIX (1960–1961), 67–77.

iv. Later Rank

57. Otto Rank, *Art and Artist,* trans. C. F. Atkinson (New York: A. A. Knopf, 1932), pp. 284–285 and 296.
58. Otto Rank, *Psychology and the Soul (Seelenglaube und Psychologie,* 1932), trans. William D. Turner (Philadelphia: University of Pennsylvania Press, 1950), pp. 61–70.

v. Jungian

59. Maud Bodkin, *Archetypal Patterns in Poetry* (1934), 2d edn. (New York: Vintage Books, Inc., 1958), pp. 10–22.
60. Peter Dow Webster, "Arrested Individuation, or the Problem of Joseph K. and Hamlet," *American Imago,* V (1948), 225–245.
61. Harry Slochower, review of Jones's *Hamlet and Oedipus, Complex,* III (1951), 46–49.
62. Harry Slochower, "Hamlet: The Myth of Modern Sensibility," *American Imago,* VII (1950), 197–238.
63. Weisinger (*Antony,* n. 1).
64. W. I. D. Scott, *Shakespeare's Melancholics* (London: Mills and Boon, Ltd., 1962), pp. 105–107.

C. Particular Topics

a. Poison in the Ear

65. Otto Rank, "Das 'Schauspiel' in 'Hamlet,' " *Imago,* IV (1915), 41–51.
66. Sharpe (n. 17).
67. Ernest Jones, "The Death of Hamlet's Father," *Int. J. Psa.,* XXIX (1948), 174–176. See Kris (n. 37).

b. Hamlet's Madness

68. MacCurdy (n. 55).
69. Nils Antoni, "Hamlet. En psykologisk studie," *Bonniers litterära magasin* (Stockholm), XXIX (May–June, 1960), 405–408.

70. E. S. Stern and W. H. Whiles, "Three Ganser States and *Hamlet,*" *Journal of Mental Science,* LXXXVIII (1942), 134–141. T. M. Davie, "Hamlet's 'Madness,'" *ibid.,* 449–450. A number of other discussions of Hamlet's madness from a medical point of view will be found in the Supplementary Notes.

71. Eissler (n. 23).

c. The Play Within the Play

72. Rank (n. 65)

73. See notes 6, 17, and 23.

74. Alexander Grinstein, "The Dramatic Device: A Play Within a Play," *Journal of the American Psychoanalytic Association,* IV (1956), 49–52.

d. Ophelia's Madness

75. Ira S. Wile, "Some Shakespearean Characters in the Light of Present Day Psychologies," *Psychiatric Quarterly,* XVI (1942), 62–90, particularly 68–71.

76. Elizabeth Foulds, "Enter Ophelia, Distracted," *Life and Letters Today,* XXXVI (1943), 36–41.

77. Jean B. Jofen, "Two Mad Heroines: A Study of the Mental Disorders of Ophelia in *Hamlet* and Margarete in *Faust,*" *Literature and Psychology,* XI (1961), 70–77.

78. Carroll Camden, "On Ophelia's Madness," *Shakespeare Quarterly,* XV (1964), 247–255.

e. The Graveyard Scene

79. Norman J. Symons, "The Graveyard Scene in *Hamlet,*" *Int. J. Psa.,* IX (1928), 96–119.

f. Osric

80. Anton Ehrenzweig, *The Psycho-Analysis of Artistic Vision and Hearing* (London: Routledge and Kegan Paul, Ltd., 1953), p. 129.

g. Particular Speeches (See also note 69.)

81. (I.ii.129). Robert Fliess, *Erogeneity and Libido* (New York: International Universities Press, 1957), p. 198.

82. (I.v.30). Simon O. Lesser, *Fiction and the Unconscious* (Boston: Beacon Press, 1957), p. 141.

83. (I.v.107). Fliess (n. 81), pp. 136–137.

84. (II.ii.472). Samuel A. Tannenbaum, "Psychanalytic Gleanings from Shakespeare," *Psyche and Eros,* I (1920), 29–39.

85. (III.i.56ff.) Wile (n. 75), pp. 68–71.

86. (III.ii.135). Theodore Reik, "Shakespeare Visits a Psychoanalyst," *Complex,* VI (1951), 34–39.

87. (III.ii.124ff., 157). Fliess (n. 81), pp. 174–175.

88. (III.ii.184). L. A. G. Strong, "Shakespeare and the Psychologists," in

Talking of Shakespeare, ed. John Garrett (London: Hodder and Stoughton, 1954), pp. 187–208.
89. (III.ii.226ff.) R. S. Miller, "Contributions to the Psychopathology of Everyday Life," *Psychoanalytic Review*, II (1915), 121–151, particularly 133–134 and 148.
90. (III.ii.226ff., 240). Karl Menninger, *The Human Mind* (Garden City, N.Y.: Garden City Publishing Co., 1930), p. 271.
91. (IV.v.187). Harry Morris, "Ophelia's 'Bonny Sweet Robin,'" *PMLA*, LXXIII (1958), 601–603.

I and II Henry IV
   a. *General*
1. Theodore Reik, *Fragment of a Great Confession* (New York: Farrar, Straus and Co., 1949), p. 336.
2. Ernst Kris, "Prince Hal's Conflict" (1948), *Psychoanalytic Explorations in Art* (New York: International Universities Press, 1952), pp. 273–288.

   b. *Myth-and-Ritual Approaches*
3. J. I. M. Stewart, *Character and Motive in Shakespeare: Some Recent Appraisals Examined* (London: Longmans, Green, 1949), pp. 132–139.
4. Philip Williams, "The Birth and Death of Falstaff Reconsidered," *Shakespeare Quarterly*, VIII (1957), 359–365.
5. C. L. Barber, "From Ritual to Comedy: An Examination of *Henry IV*," *English Stage Comedy*, ed. W. K. Wimsatt, Jr., English Institute Essays, 1954 (New York: Columbia University Press, 1955), pp. 22–51.
6. Norman N. Holland, "Literature, the Irrational, and Professor Shumaker," *Literature and Psychology*, XII (1962), 51–54.

   c. *The Character of Falstaff*
7. Franz Alexander, "A Note on Falstaff," *Psychoanalytic Quarterly*, II (1933), 592–606.
8. Theodore Reik, *The Haunting Melody* (New York: Farrar, Straus and Young, 1953), pp. 137–145.
9. Diego García Reinoso, "Notas Sobre la Obesidad a través del Estudio de Falstaff," *Revista de Psicoanálisis* (Buenos Aires), XIII (1956), 170–177.
10. W. H. Auden, "The Fallen City: Some Reflections on Shakespeare's 'Henry IV,'" *Encounter*, November, 1959, pp. 21–31; reprinted as "The Prince's Dog" in *The Dyer's Hand* (New York: Random House, 1962), pp. 182–208.

Henry V
1. Fliess (*Cor.*, n. 11), p. 133
2. (II.iv.103–105). Bertram D. Lewin, *The Psychoanalysis of Elation* (New York: W. W. Norton, 1950), p. 111.

I, and II, and III Henry VI (See also *Richard III.*)

1. Rank (*All's W.*, n. 4), pp. 208–209.
2. Theodore Reik, *The Search Within* (New York: Grove Press, 1956), p. 610.

Henry VIII

1. (IV.i.92–99 and V.i.161–166). Samuel A. Tannenbaum, "Slips of the Tongue," *Shakespere Studies, No. 1* (New York: the author, 1930), a revision of "Slips of the Tongue in Shakespere," *Shakespeare Association Bulletin,* V (1930), 63–71.

Julius Caesar

1. Rank (*All's W.*, n. 4), pp. 69n., 234, and Ch. 6.
2. Ernest Jones, *Hamlet and Oedipus* (Garden City, N.Y.: Doubleday Anchor Books, 1955), pp. 137–142.
3. Harold Feldman, "Unconscious Envy in Brutus," *American Imago,* IX (1952–1953), 307–335.
4. Gordon Ross Smith, "Brutus, Virtue, and Will," *Shakespeare Quarterly,* X (1959), 367–379.
5. (II.i.10ff.) Samuel A. Tannenbaum, "Psychanalytic Gleanings from Shakespeare," *Psyche and Eros,* I (1920), 29–39.
6. (III.ii.78ff.) Bernard C. Ewer, *Social Psychology* (New York: The Macmillan Co., 1929), pp. 255–256.
7. (III.ii.78ff.) H. Lundholm, "Mark Antony's Speech and the Psychology of Persuasion," *Character and Personality,* VI (1938), 293–305.

King Lear

   a. Lear as Child

1. Ella Freeman Sharpe, "From *King Lear* to *The Tempest*" (1947), *Collected Papers on Psycho-Analysis,* ed. Marjorie Brierley, The International Psycho-Analytical Library, No. 36 (London: The Hogarth Press, 1950), pp. 214–241, particularly p. 219.

   b. Lear as Father

2. James S. H. Bransom, *The Tragedy of King Lear* (Oxford: B. Blackwell, 1934).
3. Arpad Pauncz, "Der Learkomplex, die Kehrseite des Ödipuskomplexes," *Zeitschrift für Neurologie und Psychiatrie,* CXLIII (1933), 294–332; "The Concept of Adult Libido and the Lear Complex," *American Journal of Psychotherapy,* V (1951), 187–195; "Psychopathology of Shakespeare's 'King Lear,'" *American Imago,* IX (1952–1953), 57–77; "The Lear Complex in World Literature," *American Imago,* XI (1954), 51–83.
4. F. L. Lucas, *Literature and Psychology* (1951), (Ann Arbor: University of Michigan Press, 1957), pp. 62–71.
5. Jack Meltzer, "Some Psycho-Analytical Angles on Aspects of Shakespearean Drama," *Discussion* (South Africa), I (No. 6, December, 1952), 47–50.

6. L. A. G. Strong, "Shakespeare and the Psychologists," in *Talking of Shakespeare*, ed. John Garrett (London: Hodder and Stoughton, 1954), pp. 187–208, particularly p. 201.

c. Myth-and-Ritual Approaches

7. Theodore Reik, "Zu Freuds Deutung der Cordeliagestalt," *Die Psychoanalytische Bewegung*, I (1929), 211. Victor Hugo, *William Shakespeare*, 4th edn. (Paris, 1869), pp. 208ff.
8. Stewart (*H. IV*, n. 3), Chapter V-c and II.
9. Weisinger (*Antony*, n. 1).
10. William Frost, "Shakespeare's Rituals and the Opening of *King Lear*," *Hudson Review*, X (1957–1958), 577–585.

d. Jungian Readings

11. Maud Bodkin, *Archetypal Patterns in Poetry* (1934), (New York: Vintage Books, Inc., 1958), pp. 14–17 and 273–276.
12. Maud Bodkin, *Studies of Type-Images in Poetry, Religion, and Philosophy* (New York: Oxford University Press, 1951), p. 138.
13. K. M. Abenheimer, "On Narcissism—Including an Analysis of Shakespeare's *King Lear*," *British Journal of Medical Psychology*, XX (1945), 322–329.

e. Lear's Insanity

14. Henry Somerville, *Madness in Shakespearean Tragedy* (London: Richards Press, 1929).
15. John Donnelly, "Incest, Ingratitude, and Insanity: Aspects of the Psychopathology of King Lear," *Psychoanalytic Review*, XL (1953), 149–155.

f. Gloucester Plot

16. Rank (*All's W.*, n. 4), pp. 123, 209.
17. Lucas (n. 4), pp. 66–71.

Macbeth

a. General

1. Rank (*All's W.*, n. 4), pp. 69n. and 209–211.
2. Isadore Henry Coriat, *The Hysteria of Lady Macbeth* (1912), 2d edn. (Boston: Four Seas Company, 1920). See also *Die Psychoanalyse der Lady Macbeth* (Wiesbaden: Bergmann, 1914).
3. Patrick Kearney, "Symbolism and the New 'Hamlet,' " *Vanity Fair*, XIX (January, 1923), 41, 98.
4. Ludwig Jekels, "The Riddle of Shakespeare's *Macbeth*," *Imago*, V (1917); *Psychoanalytic Review*, XXX (1943), 361–385; "The Problem of the Duplicated Expression of Psychic Themes," *Imago*, XIX (1933); *Int. J. Psa.*, XIV (1933), 300–309. Both papers also appear in his *Selected Papers* (New York: International Universities Press, 1952), pp. 105–130 and 131–141.
5. Stewart (*H. IV*, n. 3), Ch. V.

6. S. Jankélévitch, "Le délire onirique dans les drames de Shakespeare," *Psyché* (Paris), V (1950), No. 42, 305–324.
7. Daniel E. Schneider, *The Psychoanalyst and the Artist* (New York: Farrar, Straus and Co., 1950), Ch. XI.
8. Meltzer (*Lear*, n. 5).
9. L. A. G. Strong, "Shakespeare and the Psychologists," in *Talking of Shakespeare*, ed. John Garrett (London: Hodder and Stoughton, 1954), pp. 187–208.
10. David B. Barron, "The Babe That Milks: An Organic Study of Macbeth," *American Imago*, XVII (1960), 133–161.

b. Non-Freudian Interpretations
11. Lucas (*Lear*, n. 4), pp. 22–24 and 76–79.
12. Rank (*Cor.*, n. 8), p. 285.
13. Weisinger (*Antony*, n. 1).

c. Lady Macbeth
14. Frieda Mallinckrodt, "Zur Psychoanalyse der Lady Macbeth," *Zentralblatt für Psychoanalyse und Psychotherapie*, IV (1914), 612–613.
15. Isador Sadger, *Über Nachtwandeln und Mondsucht; Eine medizinisch-literarische Studie* (Leipzig und Wien: Franz Deuticke, 1914); *Sleepwalking and Moonwalking*, trans. Louise Brink (New York and Washington: Nervous and Mental Disease Publishing Co., 1920), pp. 114–136.
16. R. S. Miller, "Contributions to the Psychopathology of Everyday Life," *Psychoanalytic Review*, II (1915), 121–151, 148.
17. *Psychology through Literature*, eds. Caroline Shrodes, Justine van Gundy, and Richard W. Husband (New York: Oxford University Press, 1943), p. 305.
18. Fliess (*Cor.*, n. 11), p. 31.

d. The Knocking at the Gate
19. Henry Wexler, "Fate Knocks," *Int. J. Psa.*, XL (1959), 232–237.

e. Particular Speeches
20. (I.v.32) Samuel A. Tannenbaum, "Slips of the Tongue," *Shakespere Studies, No. 1* (New York: the author, 1930), a revision of "Slips of the Tongue in Shakespere," *Shakespeare Association Bulletin*, V (1930), 63–71. See also "Slips of the Tongue in Shakespeare," *The Dial*, LXI (August 15, 1916), 89–91 and "Psychanalytic Gleanings from Shakespeare," *Psyche and Eros*, I (1920), 29–39.

Measure for Measure
1. Rank (*All's W.*, n. 4), p. 394n.
2. Hanns Sachs, "The Measure in *Measure for Measure*" (1942), (*Cym.*, n. 1), Ch. 3.
3. Fliess (*Cor.*, n. 11), pp. 109–110.

The Merchant of Venice
  a. Readings of the Play as a Whole
1. Rank (*All's W.*, n. 4), pp. 258 and 355.
2. Ludwig Jekels, "On the Psychology of Comedy," *Imago*, XII (1926); trans. I. Jarosy in *Selected Papers* (New York: International Universities Press, 1952), pp. 97–104.
3. Otto Rank, *Psychology and the Soul* (*Seelenglaube und Psychologie*, 1932), trans. William D. Turner (Philadelphia: University of Pennsylvania Press, 1950), pp. 61–70.
4. Theodore Reik, *The Haunting Melody* (New York: Farrar, Straus and Young, 1953), p. 136.
5. Theodore Reik, *The Secret Self* (New York: Farrar, Straus and Young, 1953), pp. 77–96.
6. Theodore Reik, *Masochism in Modern Man* (New York: Farrar and Rinehart, Inc., 1941), pp. 234–235.
7. Reik (n. 4), p. 144.
8. Theodore Reik, *Fragment of a Great Confession* (New York: Farrar, Straus and Co., 1949), p. 336.
9. Reik (n. 5), pp. 33–56.
10. E. Eduardo Krapf, "El judío de Shakespeare: una contribución a la psicología del anti-semitismo," *Revista de Psicoanálisis* (Buenos Aires), VIII (1951), 173–202; "Shylock and Antonio: A Psychoanalytic Study of Shakespeare and Antisemitism," *Psychoanalytic Review*, XLII (1955), 113–130.
11. Robert Fliess, *Erogeneity and Libido* (New York: International Universities Press, 1957), pp. 80–85, 89, 121, 125 and 163–168.
12. A. Fodor, "Shakespeare's Portia," *American Imago*, XVI (1959), 49–64.

  b. Realistic Readings of Shylock and Antonio
13. Isadore H. Coriat, "Anal-Erotic Character Traits in Shylock," *Int. J. Psa.*, II (1921), 354–360.
14. Reik (n. 4).
15. Thomas Arthur Ross, "A Note on *The Merchant of Venice*," *British Journal of Medical Psychology*, XIV (1934), 303–311.
16. Krapf (n. 10).
17. L. A. G. Strong, "Shakespeare and the Psychologists," in *Talking of Shakespeare*, ed. John Garrett (London: Hodder and Stoughton, 1954), p. 206.
18. Graham Midgley, "*The Merchant of Venice*: A Reconsideration," *Essays in Criticism*, X (1960), 119–133.
19. W. I. D. Scott, *Shakespeare's Melancholics* (London: Mills and Boon, Ltd., 1962), Ch. 3.

  c. Particular Speeches
20. (II.v.20). Samuel A. Tannenbaum, "Slips of the Tongue," *Shakespere Studies*, No. *1* (New York: the author, 1930), a revision of

"Slips of the Tongue in Shakespere," *Shakespeare Association Bulletin*, V (1930), 63–71. See also "Slips of the Tongue in Shakespeare," *The Dial*, LXI (August 15, 1916), 89–91. Also "Ueber das Versprechen im *Kaufman von Venedig*," H. Josef Gas, 1912, April (*sic;* reference as given in Grinstein's *Index of Psychoanalytic Writings*). See also "Psychoanalytic Gleanings from Shakespeare," *Psyche and Eros*, I (1920), 29–39.

21. (III.ii.17). See Ch. VI, *Merchant of Venice*, text and n. 2. R. S. Miller, "Contributions to the Psychopathology of Everyday Life," *Psychoanalytic Review*, II (1915), 121–151, p. 131.

22. (III.ii.17). See note 20.

23. (IV.i.40–62). Fliess (n. 11), pp. 163–168.

The Merry Wives of Windsor (See *Henry IV* for comments on Falstaff.)

1. Theodore Reik, *The Secret Self* (New York: Farrar, Straus and Young, 1953), pp. 63–75.

A Midsummer Night's Dream

1. Abenheimer (*Cym.*, n. 2), p. 402n.

2. Weston A. Gui, "Bottom's Dream," *American Imago*, IX (1952–1953), 251–305.

3. Donald F. Jacobson, "A Note on Shakespeare's *Midsummer Night's Dream*," *American Imago*, XIX (1962), 21–26.

4. Morton Kaplan, "*The American Imago* in Retrospect: An Article-Review," *Literature and Psychology*, XIII (1963), 112–116.

5. (II.i.128–132). Ernest Jones, "The Madonna's Conception through the Ear," *Selected Essays in Applied Psycho-Analysis*, International Psycho-Analytical Library, No. 5 (London: International Psycho-Analytical Press, 1923), pp. 261–359.

6. (V.i.4–22). Harry B. Lee, "A Theory Concerning Free Creation in the Inventive Arts," *Psychiatry*, III (1940), 292.

Much Ado About Nothing

1. W. I. D. Scott, *Shakespeare's Melancholics* (London: Mills and Boon, Ltd., 1962), pp. 47–49.

Othello

a. *The Anti-Realist View*

1. Otto Rank, "Die Don Juan-Gestalt," *Imago*, VIII (1922), 142–196, 150.

2. Maud Bodkin, *Archetypal Patterns in Poetry* (1934), 2d edn. (New York: Vintage Books, Inc., 1958), pp. 211–218.

3. J. I. M. Stewart, *Character and Motive in Shakespeare: Some Recent Appraisals Examined* (London: Longmans, Green, 1949), Ch. V.

4. Herbert Weisinger, "The Myth and Ritual Approach to Shakespearean Tragedy," *The Centennial Review of Arts and Science*, I (1957), 142–166.

b. The Realist View: Iago

5. Coriat (*Macb.*, n. 2), p. xiii.
6. Lucas (*Lear*, n. 4), pp. 74–76.
7. L. A. G. Strong, "Shakespeare and the Psychologists," in *Talking of Shakespeare*, ed. John Garrett (London: Hodder and Stoughton, 1954), pp. 187–208, 203.
8. Marvin Rosenberg, *The Masks of Othello: The Search for the Identity of Othello, Iago, and Desdemona by Three Centuries of Actors and Critics* (Berkeley and Los Angeles: University of California Press, 1961), pp. 175–184. The particular point referred to here appeared earlier as "In Defense of Iago," *Shakespeare Quarterly*, VI (1955), 145–158.
9. Martin Wangh, "*Othello:* The Tragedy of Iago," *Psychoanalytic Quarterly*, XIX (1950), 202–212. Reprinted in *The Yearbook of Psychoanalysis*, VII.
10. Gordon Ross Smith, "Iago the Paranoiac," *American Imago*, XVI (1959), 155–167.
11. Rosenberg (n. 8), p. 184.
12. James Bridie, Letter to *New Statesman and Nation* (12 March 1938), p. 405.

c. The Realist View: Othello

13. *Psychology through Literature*, eds. Caroline Shrodes, Justine van Gundy, and Richard W. Husband (New York: Oxford University Press, 1943), p. 142.
14. Theodore Reik, *Psychology of Sex Relations* (New York: Farrar and Rinehart, 1945), pp. 178–180.
15. Enrique Racker, "Sobre los celos de Otelo," *Revista de Psicoanálists* (Buenos Aires), III (1945–1946), 1–18.
16. Abraham Bronson Feldman, "Othello's Obsessions," *American Imago*, IX (1952–1953), 147–163.
17. Strong (n. 7), p. 203.
18. A. Bronson Feldman, "The Yellow Tragedy: Short Studies of Five Tragedies of Jealousy," *Literature and Psychology*, VI (1956), 38–52.
19. John V. Hagopian, "Psychology and the Coherent Form of Shakespeare's *Othello*," "*Papers of the Michigan Academy of Science, Arts, and Letters*, XLV (1960), 373–380. Leo F. McNamara, "Dramatic Convention and the Psychological Study of Character in *Othello*," *ibid.*, XLVII (1962), 649–658.

d. The Realist View: Desdemona

20. Theodore Reik, *A Psychologist Looks at Love* (New York: Farrar and Rinehart, 1944), p. 84.
21. Theodore Reik, *The Secret Self* (New York: Farrar, Straus and Young, 1953), "A Note on Desdemona," pp. 57–62.
22. Strong (n. 7), p. 203.

e. Bridging Realism and Antirealism

23. Jack Meltzer, "Some Psycho-Analytical Angles on Aspects of Shake-spearean Drama," *Discussion* (South Africa), I (No. 6, December, 1952), 47–50.

24. W. H. Auden, "The Alienated City: Reflections on 'Othello,' " *Encounter*, August, 1961, pp. 3–14; reprinted as "The Joker in the Pack" in *The Dyer's Hand* (New York: Random House, 1962), pp. 246–272.

25. A. André Glaz, "Iago or Moral Sadism," *American Imago*, XIX (1962), 323–348.

f. Particular Speeches and Details

26. (I.i.112). Robert Fliess, *Erogeneity and Libido* (New York: International Universities Press, 1957), p. 272.

27. (III.iii.287). Samuel A. Tannenbaum, " 'Your Napkin Is Too Little, Let It Alone,' A Freudian Commentary," *Studies in Philology*, XV (1918), 73–81. For more on this point by this author, see the references cited in this chapter, *Merchant of Venice*, n. 20.

28. (III.iii.413–429). Fliess (n. 26), pp. 66–69.

29. (III.iv.51). Kenneth Burke, *"Othello:* An Essay to Illustrate a Method," *Hudson Review*, IV (1951–1952), 186–198.

30. (IV.i.45). John P. Emery, "Othello's Epilepsy," *Psychoanalysis and the Psychoanalytic Review*, XLIV (1959), 30–32.

Pericles

1. *Minutes*, 10 October 1906, I, 12.

2. Rank (*All's W.*, n. 4), p. 350.

3. Sachs (*Cym.*, n. 1).

4. A. Bronson Feldman, "Imaginary Incest," *American Imago*, XII (1955), 117–155.

5. W. I. D. Scott, *Shakespeare's Melancholics* (London: Mills and Boon, Ltd., 1962), pp. 131–144.

Richard II

1. *Psychology through Literature*, eds. Caroline Shrodes, Justine van Gundy, and Richard W. Husband (New York: Oxford University Press, 1943), p. 307.

2. L. A. G. Strong, "Shakespeare and the Psychologists," in *Talking of Shakespeare*, ed. John Garrett (London: Hodder and Stoughton, 1954), pp. 187–208.

3. James A. S. McPeek, "Richard and His Shadow World," *American Imago*, XV (1958), 195–212.

4. (II.ii.105). Samuel A. Tannenbaum, "Slips of the Tongue," *Shakspere Studies, No. 1* (New York: the author, 1920); a revision of "Slips of the Tongue in Shakspere," *Shakespeare Association Bulletin*, V (1930), 63–71.

5. (V.iii). M. P. Taylor, "A Father Pleads for the Death of his Son," *Int. J. Psa.*, VIII (1921), 53–55.

Richard III

1. Rank (*All's W.*, n. 4), pp. 69n., 123n., 208, and 211–212.
2. Charles A. Adler, "Richard III—His Significance as a Study in Criminal Life-Style," *International Journal of Individual Psychology*, II (1936), 55–60.
3. Ira S. Wile, "Some Shakespearean Characters in the Light of Present Day Psychologies," *Psychiatric Quarterly*, XVI (1942), 62–90, 72–74.
4. Murray Krieger, "The Dark Generations of Richard III," *Criticism*, I (1959), 32–48.
5. (I.iv.4–7, 61–63). Ernest Jones, *On the Nightmare*, The International Psycho-Analytical Library, No. 20 (London: The Hogarth Press, 1931), p. 20.
6. (I.iv.48–57). Robert Fliess, *The Revival of Interest in the Dream* (New York: International Universities Press, 1953), pp. 134 and 152.
7. (IV.i.13–19). Tannenbaum (*R. II*, n. 4).
8. (V.iii.117–177). Gerald H. Zuk, "A Note on Richard's Anxiety Dreams," *American Imago*, XIV (1957), 37–39.

Romeo and Juliet

1. Karl A. Menninger, *Man Against Himself* (New York: Harcourt, Brace and Co., 1938), pp. 320–321.
2. Strong (*R. III*, n. 2).
3. Theodore Reik, *Psychology of Sex Relations* (New York: Farrar and Rinehart, 1945), pp. 88–89 and *A Psychologist Looks at Love* (New York: Farrar and Rinehart, 1944), p. 69.
4. Joseph L. Vredenburgh, "The Character of the Incest Object: A Study of Alternation between Narcissism and Object Choice," *American Imago*, XIV (1957), 45–52, and "Further Contributions to a Study of the Incest Object," *American Imago*, XVI (1959), 263–268.
5. (II.v. and II.i.15–20). Robert Fliess, *Erogeneity and Libido* (New York: International Universities Press, 1957), pp. 263–264 and 274.
6. (V.i.6–9). Norman N. Holland, "Romeo's Dream and the Paradox of Literary Realism," *Literature and Psychology*, XIII (1963), 97–103.

The Sonnets

1. Clarissa Rinaker, "Some Unconscious Factors in the Sonnet as a Poetic Form," *Int. J. Psa.*, XII (1931), 167–187.
2. Gordon Ross Smith, "A Note on Shakespeare's Sonnet 143," *American Imago*, XIV (1957), 33–36.
3. B. F. Skinner, "The Alliteration in Shakespeare's Sonnets: A Study in Literary Behavior," *Psychological Record*, III (1939), 186–192.

The Taming of the Shrew
1. Lucas (*Lear*, n. 4), p. 73.
2. Reik (*Merch.*, n. 5), p. 237.

The Tempest
   a. General
1. Rank (*All's W.*, n. 4), p. 352n.
2. Sachs (*Cym.*, n. 1). See also "Der Sturm," *Imago*, V (1919), 203–242.
3. Abenheimer (*Cym.*, n. 2).
4. Harry Slochower, "Hamlet: The Myth of Modern Sensibility," *American Imago*, VII (1950), 197–238.
5. Theodore Reik, *Fragment of a Great Confession* (New York: Farrar, Straus and Co., 1949), p. 336.
6. Othar Mannoni, *Prospero and Caliban* (*La Psychologie de la Colonisation*), trans. Pamela Powesland (New York: Frederick A. Praeger, 1956), pp. 12 and 97–109.
7. Leo Lowenthal, *Literature and the Image of Man: Sociological Studies of the European Drama and Novel, 1600–1900* (Boston: Beacon Press, 1957), pp. 63–65.
8. W. I. D. Scott, *Shakespeare's Melancholics* (London: Mills and Boon, Ltd., 1962), p. 181.

   b. Particular Details
9. Alfred Freiherr von Winterstein, "Zur Psychoanalyse des Reisens," *Imago*, I (1912), 497.
10. Robert Eisler, "Der Fisch als Sexualsymbol," *Imago*, III (1914), 165–196.
11. (I.ii.186, *et al.*) L. H. Allen, "The Hypnosis Scene in 'The Tempest,' " *Australasian Journal of Psychology and Philosophy*, IV (1926), 110–118.
12. (I.ii.421). Ira S. Wile, "Love at First Sight as Manifest in 'The Tempest,' " *American Journal of Orthopsychiatry*, VIII (1938), 341–356. See also Wile (*R. III*, n. 3), pp. 86–90.
13. (III.i.36–37). Samuel A. Tannenbaum, "Slips of the Tongue," *Shakspere Studies, No. 1* (New York: the author, 1930), a revision of "Slips of the Tongue in Shakspere," *Shakespeare Association Bulletin*, V (1930), 63–71. See also "Slips of the Tongue in Shakespeare," *The Dial*, LXI (15 August 1916), 89–91.

Timon of Athens
1. F. Plewa, "Shakespeare und die Macht," *International Zeitschrift für Individual Psychologie*, XIV (1936), 26–36.
2. A. H. Woods, "Syphilis in Shakespeare's Tragedy of *Timon of Athens*," *American Journal of Psychiatry*, XCI (1934), 95–107.

3. W. I. D. Scott, *Shakespeare's Melancholics* (London: Mills and Boon, Ltd., 1962), pp. 124–125.
4. (I.i.206–211). Robert Fliess, *Erogeneity and Libido* (New York: International Universities Press, 1957), p. 238.

Titus Andronicus

1. Rank (*All's W.*, n. 4), pp. 209 and 367n.
2. J. C. Flügel, "A Note on the Phallic Significance of the Tongue and of Speech," *Int. J. Psa.*, VI (1925), 209–215.
3. William H. Desmonde, "The Ritual Origin of Shakespeare's 'Titus Andronicus,' " *Int. J. Psa.*, XXXVI (1955), 61–65.
4. Gordon Ross Smith, "The Credibility of Shakespeare's Aaron," *Literature and Psychology*, X (1960), 11–13.
5. (V.iii.67–91). J. C. Flügel, "Some Unconscious Factors in the International Language Movement with Especial Reference to Esperanto," *Int. J. Psa.*, VI (1925), 171–208, 192–193.

Troilus and Cressida

1. Fritz Wittels, "Psycho-Analysis and Literature," *Psycho-Analysis Today*, ed. Sandor Lorand (New York: Covici-Friede, 1933), pp. 342 and 375.

Twelfth Night

1. Wile (*R. III.*, n. 3), p. 75.
2. Melvin Seiden, "Malvolio Reconsidered," *University of Kansas City Review*, XXVIII (1961), 105–114.
3. L. A. G. Strong, "Shakespeare and the Psychologists," in *Talking of Shakespeare*, ed. John Garrett (London: Hodder and Stoughton, 1954), pp. 187–208.
4. W. I. D. Scott, *Shakespeare's Melancholics* (London: Mills and Boon, Ltd., 1962), pp. 57–60.
5. (II.v.67). Samuel A. Tannenbaum, "Slips of the Tongue," *Shakspere Studies, No. 1* (New York: the author, 1930), a revision of "Slips of the Tongue in Shakspere," *Shakespeare Association Bulletin*, V (1930), 63–71. See also "Slips of the Tongue in Shakespeare," *The Dial*, LXI (15 August 1916), 89–91. By the same author, "Psychanalytic Gleanings from Shakespeare," *Psyche and Eros*, I (1920), 29–39.
6. (III.i.1–25 and 49–59). Fliess (*Tim.*, n. 4), pp. 137 and 120–121.

Venus and Adonis

1. Peter Dow Webster, "A Critical Fantasy or Fugue," *American Imago*, VI (1949), 297–309.

The Winter's Tale

1. Rank (*All's W.*, n. 4), pp. 350 and 352.
2. Abenheimer (*Cym.*, n. 2), p. 413.

3. L. A. G. Strong, "Shakespeare and the Psychologists," *Talking of Shakespeare*, ed. John Garrett (London: Hodder and Stoughton, 1954), pp. 202–203.

4. J. I. M. Stewart, *Character and Motive in Shakespeare: Some Recent Appraisals Examined* (London: Longmans, Green, 1949), pp. 30–37.

5. W. H. Auden, "The Alienated City: Reflections on 'Othello,'" *Encounter*, August, 1961, pp. 3–14, p. 11; reprinted as "The Joker in the Pack," in *The Dyer's Hand* (New York: Random House, 1962), p. 264.

6. (I.ii.138–146). W. I. D. Scott, *Shakespeare's Melancholics* (London: Mills and Boon, Ltd., 1962), pp. 145–162.

Chapter 10. Conclusions Logical

1. Ernst Kris, "Prince Hal's Conflict," in *Psychoanalytic Explorations in Art* (New York: International Universities Press, 1952), p. 287.

2. Ernest Jones, *Hamlet and Oedipus* (1949), (Garden City, New York: Doubleday and Company, Inc., 1955), p. 20 (Ch. 1).

3. Louis Fraiberg, *Psychoanalysis & American Literary Criticism* (Detroit: Wayne State University Press, 1960), pp. 178–179.

4. L. C. Knights, "How Many Children Had Lady Macbeth?" (1933), in *Explorations* (London: Chatto & Windus, 1951), pp. 16–17 and 4.

5. Norman N. Holland, "Realism and the Psychological Critic; or, How Many Complexes Had Lady Macbeth?" *Literature and Psychology*, X (1960), 5–8.

6. Kenneth Muir, "The Jealousy of Iago," *English Miscellany*, II (Rome, 1951), 65–83, 67.

7. Kenneth Burke, "Othello: An Essay to Illustrate a Method," *Hudson Review*, IV (1951–1952), 187–188.

8. Edmund Wilson, "J. Dover Wilson on Falstaff," *Classics and Commercials* (New York: Farrar, Straus and Company, 1951), pp. 162–163.

9. Elmer Edgar Stoll, *Shakespeare Studies, Historical and Comparative in Method* (New York: Macmillan, 1927), pp. 119–127; *Art and Artifice in Shakespeare* (Cambridge: Cambridge University Press, 1933), pp. 120, 165–170. For a more recent statement, see Bernard Beckerman, *Shakespeare at the Globe, 1599–1609* (New York: Macmillan, 1962), Ch. 4

10. C. S. Lewis, "Hamlet, the Prince or the Poem?" Annual Shakespeare Lecture of the British Academy, in *Proceedings of the British Academy*, XXXVIII (1942), 7–9.

11. Laurence Lerner, "The Machiavel and the Moor," *Essays in Criticism*, IX (1959), 339–360, 339.

12. F. R. Leavis, "Diabolic Intellect and the Noble Hero: A Note on *Othello*," *Scrutiny*, VI (1937), 259–283, 266.

13. G. Wilson Knight, *The Wheel of Fire* (London: Oxford University Press, 1930), p. 16.

14. Leo Kirschbaum, *Character and Characterization in Shakespeare* (Detroit: Wayne State University Press, 1962), pp. 1, 6, and 151–152.
15. F. R. Leavis, Introduction to *Towards Standards of Criticism,* reprinted in *The Importance of Scrutiny,* ed. Eric Bentley (New York: Grove Press, 1948), p. 401.
16. C. H. Rickword, "A Note on Fiction," *Towards Standards of Criticism,* ed. F. R. Leavis, reprinted in *Forms of Modern Fiction,* ed. William Van O'Connor (1948).
17. Mark Schorer, "Fiction and the 'Matrix of Analogy,'" *Kenyon Review,* XI (1949), 539–560, 539.
18. Georg Lukács, *Studies in European Realism,* trans. Edith Bone (London: Hillway Publishing Co., 1950), pp. 8 and 123.
19. See, for example, Harry Levin, "The Example of Cervantes" (1955) in *Society and Self in the Novel,* ed. Mark Schorer (New York: Columbia University Press, 1956). Erich Auerbach, *Mimesis: The Representation of Reality in Western Literature,* trans. Willard Trask (Princeton: Princeton University Press, 1953).
20. E. H. Gombrich, *Art and Illusion: A Study in the Psychology of Pictorial Representation,* The A. W. Mellon Lectures in the Fine Arts, 1956, National Gallery of Art, Washington, Bollingen Series, XXXV. 5 (New York: Pantheon Books, 1960), pp. 90 and 299.
21. Edgar Allan Poe, Review of William Hazlitt, *The Characters of Shakespeare* (Wiley and Putnam's Library of Choice Reading, No. XVII), in *Broadway Journal* (August 16, 1845), in *The Complete Works of Edgar Allan Poe,* ed. James A. Harrison, 17 vols. (New York: George D. Sproul, 1902), XII, 225.
22. Virginia Woolf, *Jacob's Room* (1923), Ch. 5, in *Jacob's Room and the Waves* (New York: Harcourt, Brace and Company, n.d.), pp. 71–72.
23. T. S. Eliot, "Four Elizabethan Dramatists," *Selected Essays,* 2d edn. (New York: Harcourt, Brace and Company, 1950), p. 93.
24. Marcel Proust, "Combray," in *Swann's Way, Remembrance of Things Past,* trans. C. K. Scott Moncrieff, 2 vols. (New York: Random House, 1934), I, 64–65.
25. E. M. Forster, *Aspects of the Novel* (New York: Harcourt, Brace and Company, 1927), pp. 75–87 and 98.
26. Henri Matisse, "Notes d'un peintre sur son dessin," *Le Point IV,* XXI (1939), 14; quoted in Gombrich (n. 20), p. 115.
27. *SE,* IX, 41–44; XIV, 329–330; VII, 59–60.
28. Maurice Morgann, "An Essay on the Dramatic Character of Sir John Falstaff," reprinted in *Shakespeare Criticism; A Selection,* ed. D. Nichol Smith (London: Oxford University Press, 1954), pp. 171–172.
29. Jones (n. 2), pp. 91 and 20–21.
30. Jones (n. 2), p. 103.
31. F. W. Dupee, "Adjusting Hamlet," *Partisan Review,* XV (1948), 1136–1139.

32. Harry Levin, "Symbolism and Fiction" (1956) in *Contexts of Criticism*, Harvard Studies in Comparative Literature, No. 22 (Cambridge, Mass.: Harvard University Press, 1957), p. 197.

33. Samuel Johnson, "Preface to Shakespeare" (1765), reprinted in *Samuel Johnson on Shakespeare*, ed. W. K. Wimsatt, Jr., (New York: Hill and Wang, 1960), p. 39. To sharpen the argument I have taken Johnson's remarks out of context, and a number of Johnson's other statements in this paragraph suggest a less naïve view of realism. He seems to be saying (1) if a drama moves us, it strikes us "as a just picture of a real original"; (2) it represents to the spectator how "he would himself feel if he were to do or suffer what is there feigned"; (3) "The delight of tragedy proceeds from our consciousness of fiction; if we thought murders and treasons real, they would please no more." In other words, the "moving" comes from the justness of the representation, the possibility of being moved from the knowledge it is a representation. If so, then Johnson, like Coleridge, makes a quite remarkable anticipation of the psychoanalytic solution of the problem, at least in his second point.

34. Samuel T. Coleridge, *Biographia Literaria* (1817), ed. J. Shawcross (Oxford: Clarendon Press, 1907), II, 6.

35. C. L. Barber, "From Ritual to Comedy: An Examination of *Henry IV*," *English Stage Comedy*, ed. W. K. Wimsatt, Jr., English Institute Essays, 1954 (New York: Columbia University Press, 1955), p. 50.

Chapter 11. *Conclusions Not So Logical*

1. T. S. Eliot, "The Function of Criticism," *Selected Essays*, 2nd edn. (New York: Harcourt, Brace and Company, 1950), p. 20.

2. Harry Levin, "Art as Knowledge" (1954) in *Contexts of Criticism*, Harvard Studies in Comparative Literature, No. 22 (Cambridge, Mass., Harvard University Press, 1957), p. 33.

3. Matthew Arnold, *On Translating Homer* (1861), Lecture II; "The Function of Criticism at the Present Time" (1865).

4. Norman N. Holland, *The Shakespearean Imagination* (New York: Macmillan, 1964), pp. 50–71 and 323.

5. Holland (n. 4), pp. 91–108.

6. Holland (n. 4), pp. 72–90.

7. Holland (n. 4), pp. 304–322.

8. Holland (n. 4), pp. 130–149.

9. Holland (n. 4), pp. 197–215.

10. Holland (n. 4), pp. 233–260.

11. Holland (n. 4), pp. 150–179.

SUPPLEMENTARY NOTES

In addition to the works referred to in Chapters 7, 8, and 9, I have examined a number of books and articles that might appear to contain psychoanalytic comments on Shakespeare, either from their titles or their being listed as such in bibliographies. While some of these works have considerable merit in their own right, they are either not "psychoanalytic" as I have defined that term on pp. 76–77, or they do not deal with Shakespeare. I list them here in the hope of saving time for anyone wishing to do further work on psychoanalysis and Shakespeare.

Adnès, André. *Shakespeare et la folie.* Paris: Libraire Maloine, 1936.

Babb, Lawrence. *Elizabethan Malady: A Study of Melancholia in English Literature from 1580 to 1640.* East Lansing, Michigan: Michigan State University Press, 1951.

Bacon, Leonard. "Analytical Psychology and Poetry" in *Die Kulturellebedeutung der Komplexen Psychologie,* Festschrift zum 60. Geburtstag von C. G. Jung. Berlin: Julius Springer, 1935.

Brock, J. H. *The Dramatic Purpose of Hamlet.* Cambridge: W. Heffer and Sons, 1935.

———. *Iago and Some Shakespearean Villains.* Cambridge: W. Heffer and Sons, 1937.

Bryant, Margaret M. and Janet R. Aiken. *Psychology of English.* New York: Columbia University Press, 1940.

Bucknill, J. C. *The Psychology of Shakespeare.* London: Macmillan and Co., 1860.

———. *The Mad Folk of Shakespeare.* London: Macmillan and Co., 1867.

Burke, Kenneth. "Trial Translation (from *Twelfth Night*)," *The Philosophy of Literary Form: Studies in Symbolic Action.* Baton Rouge: Louisiana State University Press, 1941.

Camden, Carroll. "Shakespeare on Sleep and Dreams," *Rice Institute Pamphlets,* XXIII (1936), 106–133.

Campbell, Joseph. *The Hero with a Thousand Faces.* New York: Meridian Books, 1956.

Cazamian, Louis. *Études de psychologie littéraire.* Paris: Payot et cie., 1913.

———. "La psychanalyse et la critique littéraire" in *Essais en deux langues.* Paris: H. Didier, 1938.

Chapelan, Maurice. "Bientôt Molière et Shakespeare délivrés sur ordonnance," *Le Figaro Littéraire*, no. 828 (3 Mars 1962), p. 3.

Clark, Cumberland. *Shakespeare and Psychology*. London: Williams and Northgate, 1936.

Cohn, E. J. "Shakespeare, the Psychiatrist," *Welfare Magazine*, XIX (1928), 1124–1127.

Cunningham, James V. *Woe or Wonder: The Emotional Effect of Shakespearean Tragedy*. Denver: University of Denver Press, 1951.

Darwin, L. "Nature and Nurture in Shakespeare's Plays and Elsewhere," *Eugenics Review*, XIX (1927), 181–191.

Dees. "Timon von Athen, Drama von Shakespeare, nach psychopathologischen Gesichtspunken erklärt," *Zeitschrift für die gesamte Neurologie und Psychiatrie*, XXVIII (1915), 50–64.

Draper, John W. "Kate the Curst," *Journal of Nervous and Mental Disease*, LXXXIX (1939), 757–764. (There are a great many articles by this author dealing with Shakespearean characters from the point of view of Elizabethan psychology.)

Edgar, Irving I. "Shakespeare's Medical Knowledge with Particular Reference to His Delineation of Madness; Preliminary Survey of Critical Opinion," *Annals of Medical History*, VI, n.s. (1934), 150–168.

————. "Shakespeare's Psychopathological Knowledge: A Study in Criticism and Interpretation," *Journal of Abnormal and Social Psychology*, XXX (1935), 70–83.

————. "Amariah Brigham, Isaac Ray and Shakespeare," *Psychiatric Quarterly*, XXXV (1961), 666–674.

Ehrl, Charlotte. *Sprachstil und Charakter bei Shakespeare*. Heidelberg: Quelle und Meyer, 1957.

Ewing, Fayette C. *Hamlet: an analytic and psychologic study*. Boston: Stratford Co., 1934.

Farnell, Frederick J. *Erotism as Portrayed in Literature, International Journal of Psycho-Analysis*, I (1920), 396–413.

Frye, Northrop. "The Argument of Comedy," *English Institute Essays*. New York: Columbia University Press, 1948.

Gerber, Richard. "Elizabethan Convention and Psychological Realism in the Dream and Last Soliloquy of Richard III," *English Studies*, XL (1959), 294–300.

Geyer, Horst. *Dichter des Wahnsinns; eine Untersuchung über die dichterische Darstellbarkeit seelischer Ausnahmezustände*. Göttingen: Musterschmidt, 1955.

Glicksberg, Charles I. "Literature and Freudianism," *Prairie Schooner*, XXIII (1949), 359–372.

Goll, Augustus. "Criminal Types in Shakespeare," *Journal of Criminal Law and Criminology*, XXX (1939), 22–51.

Goode, Bill. "How Little the Lady Knew Her Lord: A Note on *Macbeth*," *American Imago*, XX (1963), 349–356.

Hirschfeld, J. "Shakespeare as a Psychologist of Crime," *Ethological Journal*, XIV (1929), 8–10.

Hoche, Alfred E. "Shakespeare und die Psychiatrie," in *Aus der Werkstatt*. Munich: 1935.

——. *Jahresringe: Innenansicht eines Menschenlebens*. München: J. F. Lehmann, 1937.

Howarth, Herbert. "An old man looking at life: *Henry VIII* and the late plays," *Stratford Papers on Shakespeare 1961*, ed. B. W. Jackson. Toronto: W. J. Gage, Ltd., 1962.

Huhner, Max. *Shakespeare's Hamlet*. New York: Farrar, Straus and Company, 1950.

——. *Shakespearean Studies and Other Essays*. New York: Farrar, Straus and Young, 1952.

Jelliffe, Smith Ely. Review of Otto Rank, *Das Inzest-motiv in Dichtung und Sage*, *Psychoanalytic Review*, I (1913), 353–355.

Kirschbaum, Leo. "The Modern Othello," *English Literary History*, II (1944), 283–296.

Kocher, Paul H. "Lady Macbeth and the Doctor," *Shakespeare Quarterly*, V (1954), 341–349.

Lähr, H. *Die Darstellung krankhafter Geisteszustände in Shakespeares Dramen. Mit ausfürlichen Verzeichnis der einschlägigen Literatur*. Stuttgart: Paul Neff, 1898.

Legouis, P. "Presentation de La Tempête de Shakespeare," *Études Anglaises*, XIII (1960), 260–263.

Levin, A. J. "Maine, McLennan and Freud," *Psychiatry*, XI (1948), 177–191.

Lewis, C. S. "Psycho-Analysis and Literary Criticism," *Essays and Studies by Members of the English Association*, XXVII (1941), 7–21.

Libby, Walter. "Shakespeare as a Psychologist," *Archeion: Archivio di storia della scienza*, XII (Roma, 1930), 282–295.

Lindner, Robert M. "The Equivalents of Matricide," *Psychoanalytic Quarterly*, XVII (1948), 453–470.

Loewenstein, Rudolph M. *Christians and Jews: A Psychoanalytic Explanation*. New York: International Universities Press, 1951.

Lynd, Helen Merrell. *On Shame and the Search for Identity*. New York: Harcourt, Brace and Co., 1958.

McDonald, Charles O. "*Decorum, Ethos*, and *Pathos* in the Heroes of Elizabethan Tragedy with Particular Reference to *Hamlet*," *Journal of English and Germanic Philology*, LXI (1962), 330–348.

MacIntyre, Jean. "Shakespeare's *King Lear*, III.vi.8," *The Explicator*, XXI, 3, No. 24.

Mackenzie, Agnes M. *The Women in Shakespeare's Plays*. New York: Doubleday, 1924.

March, Richard. "Psychology and Criticism," *Scrutiny*, V (1936), 32–43.

Maurois, André. "Un Psychiatre pour Hamlet," *Nouvelles Littéraires*, no. 1838 (22 Nov. 1962), pp. 1, 10.

Mendel, Sydney. "Hamletian Man," *Arizona Quarterly*, XVI (1960), 223–236.

Menninger, C. F. "The Insanity of Hamlet," *Journal of the Kansas Medical Society,* XXXV (1934), 334–338.

Menon, C. Narayana. *Shakespeare Criticism: An Essay in Synthesis.* London: Oxford University Press, 1938.

Mordell, Albert. *The Erotic Motive in Literature* (1919). Rev. edn., New York: Collier Books, 1962.

Morrell, Roy. "The Psychology of Tragic Pleasure," *Essays in Criticism,* VI (1956), 22–37.

Muir, Kenneth. "The Jealousy of Iago" in *English Miscellany,* II (Rome, 1951), 65–83.

Nietsch, Erich. "Das Menschenbild bei William Shakespeare," *Psychologische Hefte der Siemens-Studien-Gesellschaft für praktische Psychologie,* no. 12 (Hanover, 1957), 351–354.

Overholser, Winfred. "Shakespeare's Psychiatry—And After," *Shakespeare Quarterly,* X (1959), 335–392.

Pastor, José Francisco. "Zur Problematik der Anwendung der Psychoanalytischen Methode auf literarhistorischen Gebiet," *Neophilologus,* XXII (1937), 205–209.

Phillips, Daniel E. *The Human Element in Literature.* New York: Fortuny, 1940.

Rahner, Richard. *Ophelia in Shakespeares "Hamlet"; eine psychologisch-psychiatrische studie.* Leipzig: Xenien-Verlag, 1910.

Rohrmoser, Günter. ". . . Denn er hat sein Ideal verloren," *Schauspielhaus Bochum, Shakespeare-Tage 1961,* pp. 1–3.

Roscelli, William John. "Isabella, Sin, and Civil Law," *University of Kansas City Review,* XXVIII (1962), 215–227.

Ruggiero, A. "William Shakespeare, M.D.," *International Record of Medicine,* CLXXIII (1960), 524–536.

Schücking, Levin L. *Character Problems in Shakespeare's Plays.* New York: Holt, 1922.

Schultz, Julius. "Psychologie des Wortspiels," *Zeitschrift für Aesthetik und allgemeine Kunstwissenschaft,* XXI (1927), 16–37.

Siegel, Paul N. "Christianity and the Religion of Love in *Romeo and Juliet,*" *Shakespeare Quarterly,* XII (1960), 371–392.

Simpson, R. R. *Shakespeare and Medicine.* London: Livingstone, 1959.

Stafford, William T. "James Examines Shakespeare: Notes on the Nature of Genius," *PMLA,* LXXIII (1958), 123–128.

Stevenson, G. H. "Social Psychiatry and Hamlet," *Proceedings of the Royal Society of Canada,* XLIII (1949), Section Two, 143–151.

Stocker, Arnold. "La Prière du Grand Will—Étude psychologique de quelques sonnets de Shakespeare," in *Des Hommes Qui Racontent Leur Ame.* St. Maurice, Suisse: Editions St. Augustin, 1943.

Tannenbaum, Samuel. "Freudism and Shakespeare," *Shakespeare Association Bulletin,* XII (1937), 260.

Tissi, Silvio. *Al Microscopio Psicanalitico.* 4th edn. Milan: Ulrico Hoepli, 1946.

Traversi, Derek. *"Othello," The Wind and the Rain,* VI (1950), 248–269.

Vessie, P. R. "Psychiatry Catches Up with Shakespeare," *Medical Record,* CXLIV (1936), 141–145.

Wagner, Richard. "Zum Hamletproblem," *Zentralblatt für Psychoanalyse,* I (1911), 525–527.

Walker, Albert L. "Convention in Shakespeare's Description of Emotion," *Philological Quarterly,* XVII (1938), 26–66.

Wasserstrom, William. "In Gertrude's Closet," *Yale Review,* XLVIII (1958), 245–265.

Weigandt, W. *Abnorme Charaktere in der dramatischen Literatur: Shakespeare, Goethe, Ibsen, G. Hauptmann.* Hamburg und Leipzig: Voss, 1910.

Weisinger, Herbert. "Iago's Iago," *University of Kansas City Review,* XX (1953), 83–90.

West, Robert H. "Sex and Pessimism in *King Lear,*" *Shakespeare Quarterly,* XI (1960), 55–60.

White, David M. "Shakespeare and Psychological Warfare," *Public Opinion Quarterly,* XII (1948), 68–72.

Wolff, Gustav. *Der Fall Hamlet.* Munich: Reinhardt, 1914.

Wollenberg, Robert. "Die Stellung der Psychiatrie in der Universitas Litterarum," *Breslauer Universitätsreden,* H. 3. Breslau: Ferdinand Hirt, 1928.

————. *Shakespeare Personliches aus Welt und Werk: Eine psychologische studie.* Berlin, 1939.

Alas I must also confess to eight references I could not obtain or which I felt would not be sufficiently useful to this study to repay the effort that would be involved in obtaining them.

Holzhausen, Paul. "Dichter und Psychopathen," *Kölnische Zeitung,* Nr. 406a, 415a vom 13 u. 16 Juni 1923.

Iwakura, Tomohide. "Psychosexuale Analyse von Shakespeare's 'Sonnetten,'" *Tokyo Zeitschrift für Psychoanalyse,* VI (Januar–Februar, Mai–Juni, Juli–August, 1938).

Nakano, Yoshio. "Shakespeare's Psychological Techniques," *Eigo Seinen* (Rising Generation, Japan), XCIII (1947).

Oczeret, Herbert. "Das Hamlet-Problem und die Psychoanalyse," *Frankfurter Zeitung,* Nr. 65 vom 6 März 1914.

Ohtski, Kenji, "Analytische Würdigung von Shakespeares 'Hamlet,'" *Tokyo Zeitschrift für Psychoanalyse* (1938).

Schwerer, Margarethe. *Shakespeares tragische Helden im Lichte der Kretschmerschen Lehre.* Dissertation, Vienna, 1950.

Semotán, Jiří and Milada. "Shakespeare psychiatr," *Vesmír,* XLII (Praha, 1962), 323–324.

Silva, Casemiro da. "Hamlet e o Complexo de Édipo," *Jornal do Comércio* (Rio de Janeiro), 7 May 1961.

Subject Index

Author Index

Index only of authorities cited for substantive points, not, for example, recipients of letters or other persons named in the text. Page references to notes are given only when the author is not referred to in the text.